QUEEN MARGARET COLLEGE

D1149906

Withdrawn from
Queen Margaret University Library

Se...
of D... Boucicault

Irish Drama Selections

General Editors
Joseph Ronsley
Ann Saddlemyer

QUEEN MARGARET COLLEGE LIBRARY

IRISH DRAMA SELECTIONS

Already Published

1. SELECTED PLAYS OF LENNOX ROBINSON
   Chosen and introduced by Christopher Murray.
   Contains *Patriots, The Whiteheaded Boy, Crabbed Youth and Age, The Big House, Drama at Inish, Church Street*, Bibliographical Checklist.

2. SELECTED PLAYS OF DENIS JOHNSTON
   Chosen and introduced by Joseph Ronsley.
   Contains *The Old Lady Says 'No!', The Moon in the Yellow River, The Golden Cuckoo, The Dreaming Dust, The Scythe and the Sunset*, Bibliographical Checklist.

3. SELECTED PLAYS OF LADY GREGORY
   Chosen and introduced by Mary FitzGerald.
   Foreword by Sean O'Casey.
   Contains *The Travelling Man, Spreading the News, Kincora, Hyacinth Halvey, The Doctor in Spite of Himself, The Gaol Gate, The Rising of the Moon, Dervorgilla, The Workhouse Ward, Grania, The Golden Apple, The Story Brought by Brigit, Dave*, Lady Gregory on Playwriting and her Plays, Bibliographical Checklist.

SELECTED PLAYS

OF DION BOUCICAULT

chosen and with an introduction by
Andrew Parkin

Irish Drama Selections 4

1987
COLIN SMYTHE
Gerrards Cross, Bucks.

THE CATHOLIC UNIVERSITY
OF AMERICA PRESS
Washington, D.C.

Introduction copyright © 1987 by Andrew Parkin

This selection first published in 1987 by
Colin Smythe Limited, Gerrards Cross, Buckinghamshire
Reprinted in 1988

British Library Cataloguing in Publication Data

Boucicault, Dion
   Selected plays of Dion Boucicault.—(Irish Drama
   selections, ISSN 0260-7962; 4)
   I. Title   II. Parkin, Andrew   III. Series

   ISBN 0-86140-150-6
   ISBN 0-86140-151-4 Pbk

First published in North America in 1987 by
The Catholic University of America Press, Washington, D.C.

Library of Congress Cataloging in Publication Data

Boucicault, Dion, 1820-1890.
   Selected plays of Dion Boucicault.

   (Irish Drama selections; 4)
   Bibliography: p.
   Partial contents: London assurance — The Corsican brothers
   — The Octoroon — [etc.]
   I. Parkin, Andrew, 1937-0000. II. Title. III. Series.
   PR4161.B2A6 1986   822'.8   85-31345
   ISBN 0-8132-0616-2
   ISBN 0-8132-0617-0 (pbk.)

Produced in Great Britain
Printed and bound by The Guernsey Press Co. Ltd.,
Guernsey, Channel Islands

CONTENTS

Acknowledgements   6

Introduction by Andrew Parkin   7

Glossary of Irish Expressions as Anglicized in *The Colleen Bawn* and *The Shaughraun*.   23

A Note on the Texts   24

London Assurance   25
     Author's Preface to the First Edition (1841)   27
     The Play   31

The Corsican Brothers   97

The Octoroon   135
     The English Happy Ending   184

The Colleen Bawn   191

The Shaughraun   257

Robert Emmet   331

Bibliographical Checklist by Frances-Jane French   399

ACKNOWLEDGEMENTS

I am indebted to Professor Joel Kaplan for the use of his material on Boucicault and for his encouraging conversation about the project. It was a fascinating evening of genial talk with George Rowell that first awakened my interest in nineteenth-century theatre, and to him I shall always be grateful. Mary O'Malley very generously sent me her material on her productions of Boucicault plays.

INTRODUCTION

Dion Boucicault, the most prolific of Irish playwrights, had two alleged fathers, several supposed birthdates, and three wives. The first bride died in mysterious circumstances; the second, after thirty-three years of marriage, five children and the death of their eldest son, he abandoned; the third, a young actress on tour with him in Australia, he married bigamously. His private life was a target for the sometimes vicious gossip of his Victorian contemporaries. Yet they rushed in hordes to see his plays. They accused him of plagiarism. They relished his smart dialogue. They revelled in his sensation scenes. They condemned him for creating vulgar theatricality and pandering to the contemporary taste for it. They exalted him as an Irish Shakespeare, and at the end turned from his plays to applaud new types of social comedy and drama. Less than forty years after his death, few theatregoers had heard of Boucicault. Intellectuals and critics hungered for the new drama bred in the little theatre movement across Europe. Only aging theatre people and professional historians of nineteenth-century theatre would remember this Irish demiurge, except, that is, for a few dramatists canny enough to realize he was a master from whom they could learn: writers such as Wilde, Shaw, Synge and O'Casey.

At the outset, it is worth remembering Robert Hamilton Ball's warning, 'All statements regarding the early life of Boucicault must be highly tentative'. This account relies on comparison of contemporary accounts, including Boucicault's highly coloured autobiographical writings, and modern authorities, such as the indispensable biographies by Townsend Walsh and Richard Fawkes, the concise critical book by Robert Hogan, and that entertaining collection of key documents, *Dion Boucicault, the Shaughraun: A Documentary Life, Letters and Selected Works*, compiled by Sven Eric Molin and Robin Goodefellowe.

It is probable that Dionysius Lardner Boursiquot was born

7

either late on 26 December, or early on the 27th of that month, in 1820 in Dublin. He was the fourth child of Anne Maria Darley of the well-known Darley family from the Scalp in County Wicklow. She had married Samuel Smith Boursiquot, a Dublin wine merchant of French Huguenot stock, on 29 July 1813 in St. Thomas's Protestant Church, Dublin. In the next six years they had three sons, William, Arthur and George. According to Arthur Darley, the musician who worked for a while at the Abbey Theatre, Samuel and Anne separated in 1819. By the summer of 1820 it seems certain that Anne, pregnant with Dion, had become the mistress of Dr. Dionysius Lardner. Samuel remained in Dublin until 1829, and it seems that he took his family to London in 1828 or 1829. When his business failed, he returned to Dublin, leaving his sons in the care of the family friend, Dr. Lardner. Meanwhile, Anne gave birth to a daughter who died in 1831. By the end of that year, Samuel was in Florence, and by August 1839 was back in Ireland, living in Athlone. Christopher Calthrop, Boucicault's great-grandson, has established that Samuel died in 1853, leaving a will in which Dion appears as a legitimate son. Indeed, there is no real proof that he was the son of Lardner, though biographers find it curious that Lardner should have supported the boy after his affair with Anne. But since Lardner was a family friend and godfather to the boy, it is natural that Dion should have been named after him. Nor is Lardner's support unusual considering his friend's business difficulties. Boucicault himself always referred to Samuel as his father and Lardner as his guardian. But Lardner's divorce and his affair with Anne at least throw the shadow of the bend sinister over Dion. Be that as it may, the boy, moved restlessly from school to school, seems to have had a somewhat unpleasant childhood.

According to the actor Frank Dalton, Dion attended a Dr. Geoghegan's Academy in Dublin, where he was a courageous fighter. Later, in 1833, he was attending Mr. Hessey's private school in Hampstead, where he hated Latin and arithmetic, preferring to daydream and read *Seven Champions of Christendom*. He next attended London University school and met there his lifelong friend, Charles Lamb Kenney. He and Kenney were frequent victims of the school's system of solitary confinement for its scholastic offenders. But in 1838 Dion went to Dr. Jamieson's at Brentford and there discovered his métier. He played Rolla in a school production of *Pizarro*. For an afterpiece he wrote a 'little sketch', later reworked as *Napoleon's Old Guard* and played at the Princess's Theatre in London.

Before he could become an actor, however, Dion was apprenticed to Lardner as a civil engineer. But he very soon ran away, for the 1838-39 season saw him, under the stage name of Lee Moreton, playing Irish and broad comedy parts at Bristol. His first professional part was probably Norfolk in *Richard III*, but on 24 April 1838 in Cheltenham he played of all things Sir Giles Overreach. While acting in Cheltenham, Hull and Brighton, he wrote short plays: *A Legend of the Devil's Dyke* was staged in Brighton on 1 October 1838, and *Lodgings to Let* was done at the Theatre Royal, Bristol, on 23 February 1839. Barton Hill wrote an engaging account of how his father, Charles Hill, gave Lee Moreton his first chance as an actor, of how Dion was 'a handsome youth, and generous to a fault', and how Dion left Brighton with a new play (probably *A Lover by Proxy*) and 'letters of introduction' to the London managers.

Boucicault recalled later that, on arrival in London, he took a garret in Villiers Street and submitted *A Lover by Proxy* to Charles Mathews, manager at Covent Garden. Supposing it to be by Madison Morton, Mathews read the play and allowed Lee Moreton up to the office to discuss the work. The error being explained, Mathews rejected the play, but impressed by its author's youth kept it to show Mme. Vestris, gave Boucicault free ticket privileges and mentioned that he really wanted a five-act comedy. This Boucicault supplied four weeks later on a Thursday. Mathews promised to read the script, then called *Out of Town*, and invited his new author to a party the following Sunday. Mathews and Vestris decided to stage the play, Vestris supplying the new title, *London Assurance*. During rehearsals Boucicault rewrote it extensively, and his first great success opened at Covent Garden on 4 March 1841.

The success owed much to the brilliance of the cast, as Boucicault's Preface readily admits, and also to the novelty of the 'boxed-in scenery' with real carpet and furniture in the drawing room. *The Times* reviewer noted the settings as 'equal to anything yet known in the way of theatrical embellishment.' Soon after his triumph, Boucicault sent fifteen pounds to his mother, asking 'that you will come over to me immediately. I have now five pieces in Covent Garden, all accepted ... I am now looked upon as the great rising dramatic poet of the age.' As he noted later, his mother and brother came for six months and stayed forty years. It seemed as if he might be able to live by writing and develop his literary aspirations. But he was like Goldsmith, extravagant and generous. He soon found that he needed to sell translations of proven French plays in order to live, for these were quicker to do than original work, of course, and paid well. Authors were not given a percentage of the box office take. By 1 February 1842, we find the case of Bourcicault versus Hart in the Court of Exchequer. Using his real name but with a spelling different from that of his father, he got off on the grounds that he was not yet of age when the debts to Hart were incurred. His mother's evidence about his birthdate confirmed the argument. She is reported to have said he was born 7 December (instead of 27th) 1820. She may have been misheard by the reporter, for she had no motive for making her son twenty days older than he was, especially under oath in a court.

Boucicault continued writing. *The Irish Heiress* ran only two nights at the Garden, but was later successful at the Park Theatre in New York. His short farce, *A Lover by Proxy*, opened on 21 April 1842 at the Haymarket, his *Alma Mater: or, A Cure for Coquettes* opened on 19 September, gleefully accepted by the public and severely condemned by *The Times* for a chilling want of heart. Three months later, *The Bastile* (sic) was used as a Haymarket afterpiece. Boucicault was irretrievably involved in the rapid hackwork of the theatre; his early promise as a new force in the native tradition of comedy was fading. But *Old Heads and Young Hearts*, staged at the Haymarket on 18 November 1844, though not as popular in its own time as *London Assurance*, was another substantial comedy of which its author could feel proud. It deserves revival. Boucicault was learning his craft as a dramatist from translations and adaptations, and becoming already a knowledgeable man of the theatre. Eighteen plays produced within four years was a remarkable, perhaps unique, apprenticeship. His association with Benjamin Webster, the theatre manager, and the awkward necessity of raising cash, however, steered him from the art of drama toward the siren box office; but this had the advantage of making him keenly aware of the possibilities of theatricality, for nineteenth-century theatre was alive with experiments and novel effects. He was sent to Paris by Webster in December 1844 to see the latest plays and send translations of them back to England for production. Boucicault was soon back in London for the opening of his *The Soldier of Fortune, or the Irish Settler* on 6 February 1845. After the opening of his *Peg Woffington, or The State Secret* the following June, Boucicault turned briefly from theatre to courtship, for on 9 July 1845 in St. Mary's Lambeth, he married a French gentlewoman, Anne Guiot, the widowed daughter of Etienne St. Pierre. Gossip had it that the first Mrs. Boucicault was a Quaker. She apparently had a modicum of land in France and an income. Stephen Fiske repeated the rumour that Anne died mysteriously while on honeymoon in the Alps. It is more probably that she died at some time between May 1847 and May the following year, a period when Boucicault was abroad. Agnes Robertson, the second wife, believed that Anne had died in March 1848 at Aix-la-Chapelle after an illness. Despite access to his wife's money, Vicomte Dion de Bourcicault, as he now styled himself, appeared in Insolvent Debtors' Court in 1848. On this occasion he was saved by Ben Webster.

Having learned from his time in Paris that French playwrights reaped ten percent of the receipts from their works' performances, Boucicault waxed indignant about the way English playwrights had to sell a work for a modest lump sum, without further fee or profit. He tried without success to persuade the Dramatic Authors' Society to strive for the introduction of the French system into England. The managers were now reluctant to stage his plays. But in August 1850 Charles Kean leased the Princess's with the aim of producing all Shakespeare's plays. To swell the box office take he hired Boucicault as resident hack to turn out popular pot-boilers. Boucicault obliged. In 1851 there were five, perhaps six, new Boucicault plays put on in London, including another full-length comedy, *Love in a Maze*, notable for its brisk dialogue but little else. On 24 February 1852 Kean opened in *The Corsican Brothers*. It was a triumph. Boucicault had at once given Kean one of his (and later Irving's) best vehicles and himself a new place as a master of theatrical as opposed to literary theatre. He even scored success as an actor in *The Vampire* (1852) with Agnes Robertson, who recalled that he wrote his version in six days, working without sleep. Agnes, who had learned her craft in the stock company system, taking elocution from the stage manager, fencing, opera dancing, and playing every sort of role, had joined Kean's company for her London debut. She remarked, 'It was at the Princess's I met my fate.' In 1852 she and Boucicault began living together, and may even have married. Agnes was nineteen.

The affair caused the break with her guardian, Kean. In August 1853 Agnes sailed for America. Having arranged a season for Agnes at Burton's, New York, and borrowed their fares from the tolerant Webster, Boucicault followed her three weeks later. Thus began the most successful and lucrative part of their careers.

Agnes acted and had children. Her husband acted, wrote and

11

became a manager. This first sojourn in America saw the birth of their ill-fated eldest child, Dion William, who was to be killed in a railway accident a few months before his twentieth birthday. In America, Boucicault found others willing to push for authors' rights. His efforts, together with those of Robert Montgomery Bird and George Henry Boker, helped a copyright law through Congress on 18 August 1856. This meant that henceforth Boucicault would derive considerable revenue from the profits of his successful plays. It also heralded far-reaching changes in the economics of the theatre and eventually a better deal for all dramatists.

In *The Poor of New York* (1857) Boucicault exploited the taste for spectacular melodrama he had found to be successful in *The Corsican Brothers*. He was also responding to his new environment. He used the topical material of New York financial crashes together with the climactic spectacle of a tenement block on fire. His writing of the role of the honest sea captain was dismally sentimental, but his topicality and amazingly realistic spectacle earned him the applause of the public and the dollars that accompanied it. In 1857, Agnes had a daughter, Eve, in New York. Another son, Darley George (Dot) came along in 1859, the year in which *The Octoroon* played amid considerable controversy and with great success at the Winter Garden, New York. This was capped on 29 March 1860 when *The Colleen Bawn* opened at Keene's in New York. It was the first real triumph among his Irish plays. That summer the Boucicaults left for London, where Agnes opened in the title role on 10 September at the Adelphi for a record (at that time) run of 278 performances. After conquering Dublin with the play the following spring, Boucicault completed his London campaign by becoming lessee of Drury Lane on 23 June 1862. A wealthy man with a star for a wife and a fourth child, Patrice, born the following August, Boucicault now spent his fortune on refurbishing Astley's Amphitheatre in Westminster Bridge Road as the Theatre Royal, which was to be the centre of an entertainment complex. The project was neither finished nor successful, and Boucicault lost his money as surely as if he had thrown it into the Thames.

Quick thinking resourcefulness came to his aid: he revised *The Poor of New York* for a run in Liverpool as *The Poor of Liverpool*, and realized he could do the same in London and in Dublin. The sensation melodrama was as protean as it was profitable. Bouncing confidently back, he added to his repertoire and fortunes *Arrah-na-Pogue* (1864; revised 1865), his version of *Rip Van Winkle* (1865) that made Joseph Jefferson a star on both sides of the Atlantic, *The Flying Scud* (1866) that exploited the sensations of horse racing more profitably than if its author had gambled at the track, and *Hunted Down* (1866), in which Irving made his London debut. With two more children, Nina born in February 1867, and Aubrey Robertson, a June baby of 1869, and wealthy again, Boucicault seemed the epitome of Victorian success. In partnership with the Earl of Londesborough, he leased Covent Garden for the opening on 29 August 1872 of a sumptuous spectacular full of opulent pageantry, costuming, and scenic effects. It gloried in the alliterative title, *Babil and Bijou*. The combined talents of Boucicault and J. R. Planché secured for it a long run at the end of which it had still lost about £50,000.

The Boucicaults were meanwhile back in America, Dion on tour without Agnes. But on 14 November 1874 he opened at Wallack's in New York as Conn in *The Shaughraun*. This play gave him his most effective role and his third fortune. It was a smash hit when it opened the following September in London. But the success was made bitter by the untimely death of the eldest son, Dion William, in January 1876.

After two brilliant decades, Boucicault had now written most of his significant work and established himself as the leading playwright of his age. He had done much also for the art of stage management, not only in the exploitation of sensational illusion, but also in the pains he took at rehearsal and his concern for ensemble playing. Taste in the late 1870s was changing, however, and Boucicault did not produce the profound kind of social analysis or intricacies of feeling that could have made him a master of a greater kind of drama. In 1885 he left America for Australia, taking in his company the young actress Louise Thorndyke whom he married there. He denied that he was legally married already to Agnes, but she divorced him in London in 1888. Once back in America he found little interest aroused by any new work of his, and contented himself with teaching acting and writing articles. He died of a heart attack complicated by pneumonia in New York on 18 September 1890. It is said that Boucicault once remarked that his epitaph should read, 'Dion Boucicault; his first holiday'.

II

Boucicault was the cleverest, most theatrically inventive English-speaking playwright of his age. His Irish plays alone are good

13

enough to make him the most rewarding playwright for study and sheer amusement in Victorian theatre. *Robert Emmet* (1884) is considerably better than its neglect suggests, for it has suspense, genuine political feeling, high sentiment balanced by earthy humour and common sense, rascally, vivid characters in the sub-plot, aphoristic dialogue, and mordant wit. He is further distinguished by having written the two best comedies of the period between Goldsmith and Gilbert: *London Assurance* and *Old Heads and Young Hearts*. If these plays looked back to *She Stoops to Conquer*, his *Forbidden Fruit* anticipated Pinero. But that seems to state some of the problem with Boucicault; his career spans the decline before the modern resurgence of British drama. At his worst he is sentimental, merely derivative, and lacks literary energy; at his best, character, dialogue and action are integrated in such a way as to produce high energy theatre of a most absorbing kind.

Modern detractors of *London Assurance*, taking their cue from Shaw, who made it clear he would not want it revived, stress its lightweight, thoughtless fun. This is less than fair. It has great dash and spirit. The dialogue retains the flair and pace noticed by contemporary reviewers. It contains four vivid and individual comic roles of great scope: Sir Harcourt Courtly, the very mirror of the *beau monde* but showing an aging figure and face and contriving to be at once the heavy father and the *roué*; Grace Harkaway, more than a mere romantic heroine by virtue of her streak of poetic blarney, intelligence, and the will that enables her to instruct Young Courtly in how to make love to her (the blend of bookishness and sexuality in her was evident in Boucicault's earlier version, *Out of Town*, from which the Royal Shakespeare Company took the hint for its 1970 revival of the play); the egregious Dazzle — an opportunist, but a genial one, this Autolycus of the dawn of the great age of credit claims to be a gentleman yet lacks origins, having only the 'bare-faced assurance' of a man-about-London, 'the vulgar substitute for gentlemanly ease' as Sir Harcourt puts it in 'the tag' or last speech of the play that Mathews, playing Dazzle, insisted on speaking; and finally but, in my view, most brilliantly, there is Boucicault's exuberant comic observation of Lady Gay Spanker, hail-fellow-well-met rider to hounds who thinks that foxes are 'the most blessed dispensations of a benign Providence' and with hearty briskness has married Dolly to preserve her freedom. Her infectious high spirits, crisp as a breath of Boxing Day air, enliven the comic mania expressed in her remark, 'one might as well live without laughing as without hunting'. Her first entry and glorious steeplechase aria are rich in comedy. When she interrupts Young Courtly's wooing of Grace, she announces 'I always like to be in at the death' and coaches him as she would advise a jockey. On the point of an adulterous elopement with Sir Harcourt, she suddenly remembers 'I have left Max — a pet stag-hound, in his basket — without whom life would be unendurable — I could not exist!' Her beau hastily suggests the beast should be sent after them in a hamper, provoking her magnificent scorn: 'In a hamper! Remorseless man! Go — you love me not.' That an elopement should hang on a hound in a hamper is a brilliant farcical invention, and Wilde must be eternally grateful to Boucicault for having shown him the way to the infant in a handbag.

From rehearsals of the play with a brilliant cast, and especially from the ideas of Madame Vestris, Boucicault, as he acknowledged in the Preface (see page 27 below), learned how to rewrite for specifiic actors, specific demands of stage dialogue and the stage effects anticipated by wonderful, seasoned West End actors. There seems little sense, though, in John Coleman's notion that when submitted, the play was an inchoate maladroit thing; Mathews and Vestris would hardly have bothered to work with it. They saw Boucicault's great talent, and were not mistaken. Augustin Filon in *The English Stage* berated Boucicault as 'plagiarism incarnate' working 'crazy-quilt-like plays' and undervalued *London Assurance* partly because he misunderstood it (he thought Lady Gay called her husband a doll, when in fact she was using the nickname for Adolphus, quite popular in Victorian England). But he responded to the poetry of the theatre in *The Colleen Bawn* and clarified the achievement of the Irish plays: 'Until Boucicault's time it had been the fashion to laugh over Ireland, never to weep over her.'

In the best of his early comedies, *Old Heads and Young Hearts*, Boucicault juggled the complex plot elements very dextrously. In Jesse Rural he provided us with a benignly comic old clergyman. Careful attention to sets and furniture earned this production the description 'the upholstery school of comedy'. Boucicault remarked that the play added more, however, to his literary than his pecuniary credit. Some recent critics rank it higher than *London Assurance,* yet it failed to hold the stage as well and has not been revived. Both plays have a Regency setting, perhaps because of the author's early reading or temperament, perhaps because of the very structure and manners of the dramatic models for English comedy. But the comic design is derived from the Restoration:

15

there are two love triangles intertwined in the pleasingly absurd plot with its use of disguise, misunderstandings, and dialogue at cross-purposes, that completely bewilder old Jesse Rural. As in *London Assurance* town and country meet, but here the setting is London, and the theme is complicated by the addition of the North versus South aspect, for although Littleton Coke hails from Yorkshire, he is a 'southernized' barrister, trying not particularly hard to practise in London, while his brother Tom has remained a true Yorkshireman, rude of speech yet good-hearted, direct not subtle, and having a surplus of 'brass', though lacking the polish to make it glitter. Where Tom is solid, virtuous and rich, Littleton is dashing and light-hearted. The collision of this pair and their rivalry in love add depth to a comedy in which Boucicault sparkles with racy dialogue and scenes that beg for enactment: the love letter scene when Littleton teases Lady Alice, and its reversal when she gets her revenge; the manservant Bob, posing as a solicitor and audaciously introducing the legitimate Charles as if he were illegitimate to his own father, the Earl of Pompion. Pompion and Tom Coke explore the political theme in the play, but from the outset Littleton muses on class distinctions, the snobbery he dislikes in his mother, and the paradox that the Eton and Oxford education that prepared him for his profession has also stimulated in him the tastes of a landed gentleman, which is indeed a misfortune for one whose inheritance has been all mortgaged away. Boucicault's satirical humour, if raising social issues, is genial rather than bitter and his taste is for the debonair *mot* rather than the mordant snarl. When Roebuck confesses to his friend that he is in love, Littleton's reply catches the tone Wilde picked up: 'How? vulgarly, with a woman — or fashionably, with yourself?'

Boucicault's most characteristic method was adaptation, sometimes brilliant restructuring of sources, arriving at sharper dialogue, increased tension and extravagance of stage effect. He took full advantage of the ingenuities of spectacle possible in the Victorian theatre. His exciting *The Corsican Brothers* has brilliant symmetry of structure matching the use of twins in the play. Charles Kean, impressed by Grangé and de Montépin's stage version of Dumas *père's* novel, *Les Frères Corses,* decided to have it 'Boucicaulted'. *The Corsican Brothers* opened to great acclaim on 24 February 1852 at the Princess's. Its clever structure deploys a ghost scene at the end of Act I such that its stage picture is repeated exactly in the duel scene at the end of Act II. This confirms the uncanny operations of telepathic powers and increases the impact of the simultaneity of action featured in the play. For the ghost Boucicault employed the novel sliding ghost trap very effectively. And scenic splendour gave added lustre in the ballroom scene. The emotional range of the play lifts it above many another melodrama: tension and suspense, villainy and seemly devotion to duty are enriched by the revenge theme complicated by its supernatural elements, the realistic dialogue of the young revellers about the town, the manners of the age, and the comic scene of feudal justice aimed at *ending* vendetta. The high sense of honour in the aristocratic revenger contrasts with the trivial dispute of the rustics. Furthermore, the demise of Louis, dying beautifully, encourages acceptance of his elevated moral sense, and neatly removes any possibility of a new conflict between this high code and his love for Émilie. Time also adds depth to the play. Simultaneity of events is theatrically interesting, but timing is at the root of disaster in the action: Émilie is married to the wrong man really because of the way events have unfolded in the workings of time, and the hour strikes fatefully, as in the Montgiron party scene. The unscrupulous duellist, Chateau-Renaud, is trapped by a time-space effect that demands his death in the very place his victim perished. This villain, moreover, is not merely conventional. He dies more honourably than we might have expected. Boucicault gives him a brilliantly cool piece of business when, after slyly regaining Émilie's trust, he sends her to the rendezvous and casually consults his watch: 'Ten minutes to four. I shall win my wager, and preserve my reputation.' The ironies are manifold. Boucicault's emphasis of course falls not so much on character as on swift changes of mood achieved through dialogue and the scenic transformations. A cleverly economical effect arises from the swift change from the challenge at Montgiron's party to the death by duel in the forest to give the splendid second act curtain. It has been argued that whatever theatrical excellence is in *The Corsican Brothers* was in the original French play. Yet Fawkes maintains that before the end of 1852 there were seven other versions staged, Boucicault's running sixty-six nights and remaining the most effective. Kean excelled as the twins. Stage effects were superbly managed. To G. H. Lewes it was 'the most daring, ingenious and exciting melodrama I remember to have seen'. Queen Victoria saw it no less than five times and made a unique sketch of the duel scene for her Journal. It played in London over a period of fifty years and its Corsican trap was adopted by many British theatres. 'The Ghost Melody' sold thousands of copies as sheet music. The age of chivalrous, gentlemanly melodrama had arrived.

So also had the age of staging the sensational illusion. Boucicault, the most inventive and daring of those who experimented in that way, anticipated the kind of spectacle in the film business that later helped to banish such effects from the playhouses.

In the United States, Boucicault rapidly acclimatized himself to the audiences and the speech patterns. He soon had an intelligent grasp of American issues and wrote about them to the extent that his work is important in the history of drama and theatre in America. We have already mentioned *The Poor of New York,* easily adapted to other environments. More indigenous was *The Octoroon.* This is a better written, even more inflammatory study of American issues. It opened on 6 December 1859, only four days after the hanging of John Brown for his Abolitionist rebellion at Harper's Ferry. Boucicault had travelled in the South, meeting many slave-owners and slaves. He managed to depict slavery in its best light through life on the Louisiana plantation of his play, yet show also its demeaning, immoral essence in the pathos of the slave auction scene. He crafted an exciting and humane action, finding things to blame in both Americas; his villain is a Yankee, yet the dice are also loaded against a southern mentality which could see no way for Zoe, the octoroon slave, to marry a white gentleman. The unhappy American ending is supplied here together with the alternative demanded by London's audience, who preferred the picture of gentleman hero, octoroon sweetheart in his arms, backed by the exploding steamboat — an orgasmic sensation scene. The subtlety that made some of his work superior to that of other writers of melodrama may be seen in Boucicault's letter to *The Times:* '... there are features in slavery far more objectionable than any hitherto held up to human execration, by the side of which physical suffering appears as a vulgar detail.' Around the bright and beautiful Zoe, illegitimate daughter of a Judge, Boucicault builds an aura of gaiety and vulnerability. Already this challenges orthodox moral values. When the English heir to the estate realizes his genuine love for her, and we recognize the rightness of the match, the melodrama does not as in so many cases enforce standard Victorian morals; it undermines them totally, finding its norms in the warmth and decencies of truth to the heart and humane feeling. As usual with Boucicault, he attacks grasping materialism, violence against the weak, and the conventional morality its agents use as their mask. *Uncle Tom's Cabin* had treated slavery before on the stage, and Mayne Reid's novel *The Quadroon* gave Boucicault most of his story, but the pace, tone and emotional impact are his own. The

18

lynch mob scene is developed to a brilliant reversal, using the device of a camera which records the murder of a child and thus incriminates the villain. Boucicault explored his theme of class and race barriers with more complexity than he has been credited with, and was attacked by some contemporary reviewers for his efforts.

The theme of subject race or nation was next pursued by Boucicault in his Irish plays. Although he cannot be properly considered a systematic thinker, it would be wrong to overlook this deep and genuine concern in his work, for all his commercialism. The Home Rule movement made Ireland a subject of popular interest. Yet he had an abiding interest in Robert Emmet and did what he could for the Irish cause. His plays kept the transatlantic Irish mindful of problems in the home land, helped to promote a sympathetic view of Ireland to English audiences, as well as giving the writer and his wife incredibly lucrative runs in the theatres. He remodelled the stage Irishman to portray a more realistic gallery of types. What had once been a foolish, drunken butt of English wits, he transformed into a clever, courageous and resourceful descendant of the tricky slave of ancient comedy. David Krause's introduction to the Dolmen Boucicault puts the case well: 'It is in his creation of this distinctly Irish yet universal character — as Myles-na-Coppaleen, Shaun the Post, or Conn the Shaughraun — that Boucicault finally transcends the Victorian world. And it is part of this triumph that Irish drama as we know it today had its origins in Boucicault.' His Irishness and his sojourns in America gave him the necessary distance from English life to prevent his remaining merely a creature of its attitudes and a technician of its theatre.

The Colleen Bawn, the last play Queen Victoria saw in a theatre, was partly inspired when its author bought a set of steel engravings of the lakes of Killarney, as Booth has noted. Percy Fitzgerald, writing in *Principles of Comedy* (1870), praised the tone and flavour of the play as 'infinitely characteristic, touching, and national' and praised the sensation scene of the watery cave because it was integral, the action *required* it. The play was first staged in New York on 27 March 1860 at Laura Keene's Theatre. Agnes Robertson was Eily O'Connor, the fair-haired girl of the title, and Boucicault Myles-na-Coppaleen (Myles of the ponies). He had dramatized the climactic events of Gerald Griffin's ponderous three volume novel, *The Collegians,* to great effect. Boucicault enlivened his sententious source, giving it his characteristic pace, liveliness of dialogue, and tension. Over it all presided the spirit of a new kind of comedy expressing real affection for Ireland and those Irish untainted by Victorian materialism and snobbery. The spirit of Irish popular ballads can also be discerned; another source was Samuel Lover's treatment of Rory O'More in ballad and the novel. Boucicault used Rory, perhaps remembered as Tyrone Power had played him, and possibly Samuel Lever's Tipperary Joe from the novel *Jack Hinton* to transform Myles from a minor character in Griffin's work to the richly comic rogue who became a favourite with audiences. Above all, Boucicault had learned how to stage Irish life in a way that was more sensitive to the country and its people than were the previous treatments. And he used the conventions of popular commercial theatre with drive, pace and excitement, mixing elements of melodrama, farce and politics in a fertile new combination. Over all was a love for the landscape itself. It was a vein rich enough for further development.

Rory O'More, indeed, was also a source for his next Irish play, *Arrah-na-Pogue* (1864). The play, more political than *The Colleen Bawn*, recalls the rising of 1798 and features a version of the popular ballad 'The Wearing of the Green' openly attacking British rule of Ireland. The play was a success, but the song was considered so subversive that the government banned its singing from performances in the British Isles. Krause rightly points out that Boucicault had some trouble in getting the play just as he wanted it, and rewrote during performance. It lacks much of the humour and charm of *The Colleen Bawn*, and offers too sentimental a treatment of love and patriotism. But in the prison scenes Shaun the Post comes forcefully to life. The trial at the end of Act II is masterly and was used as a model by Shaw for the trial in *The Devil's Disciple*. Shaw wrote the better play, but Boucicault's scene remains superior.

After a decade of routine theatre work, Boucicault returned to his Irish material with *The Shaughraun* (The Vagabond) first performed at Wallack's Theatre, New York on 14 November 1874. He had been working on *Boyne Water*, a play about the conflict in a young English officer between his duty as a soldier and his love for an Irish lady. Augustin Daly, the theatre manager, advised Boucicault to change the period from the reign of James II and rewrite the script as a comedy. Theatrically, it was good advice, and Boucicault took it. His new comic rascal, Conn, the Shaughraun, quickly became a firm favourite with audiences and Boucicault's perfect role, 'the soul of every fair, the life of every funeral, the first fiddle at all weddings and patterns'. A development of Myles and Shaun, he is the definitive Irish clown and free-spirit, a masterly

20

and permanent creation in the comic repertoire; he is also the
very spirit of comedy in the play, resurrecting at his own wake,
and insomuch as he directs the action like a 'clown-ex-machina' as
Krause has it, he becomes a haunting image of Boucicault himself,
alert to the limitations of his art, but asking the indulgence of an
audience he knows he can charm more often than not. At the end
of the play he turns to the audience as he begs Moya to go bail for
him, saying: 'Many a time have you looked over my faults — will
you be blind to them now, and hould out your hands once more
to a poor Shaughraun?' Tough but good-hearted, craftier than the
villains who surround him, he is totally different from the blustering
buffoon of a stage Irishman rightly despised by the best Irish
artists and audiences. For his acting of Conn, Boucicault was
praised by contemporaries for mastery of detail in the character-
ization, the timing and adroitness of his comedy, and his charming
air of spontaneity. In the rescue scene, the gag in which Conn
pops up from a hogshead and shoots the villainous Kinchela is
akin to some of the best moments of the Marx Brothers: 'A shot
is fired from the hogshead. Kinchela throws up his hands, staggers,
falls. Moya utters a cry and falls on her knees, covering her face
with her hands. The hogshead rises a little — advances to Moya,
and covers her like an extinguisher. The legs of Conn have been
seen under the barrel as it moves.' But in this, his Irish masterpiece,
Boucicault works his comedy and political theme simultaneously
through his language more than through stage business. The inter-
play of English and Irish character and speech in the dialogue
creates a significant counterpoint throughout the action. It is stage
speech that can render the feeling for Ireland of one who returns
from political exile, and the anguish of one who is 'obliged to
arrest the brother of the woman I love'. Even when chords of
music invade the scene in which Kinchela convinces Robert that
he is no villain but a patriotic friend, the ironies and tensions in
the dialogue make its melodrama work very powerfully. The moral
values of faith, hope, Christian and romantic love, honour and love
of country set against greed, betrayal, cruelty, deception, abuse of
power are not as simple as they sound, for they are the fuel of the
necessary involvement of the audience that occurs in good melodrama and are here complicated by the fact that they cut across
the national and class boundaries, as Boucicault deployed them, to
give depth and colour to his picture of humanity.

Boucicault also achieves a true poetry of the theatre in the
richly comic scene of Conn's wake. It is here that we see so clearly
how he anticipates Synge and the Abbey peasant drama.

When Conn faces Reilly and Sullivan, the criminal associates of the villains, he becomes a true stage symbol, both of comic regeneration and of 'murdher alive' in the land. Even the suicidal leap of Harvey Duff at the end is not mere sensation, but integral to the emotional dynamics of the action: we need his death, though we would not want to see him bludgeoned and slashed with peasant scythes.

Boucicault's enormous output as dramatist, translator, and play doctor gave him an extraordinary range of dramatic and theatrical conventions. Consider this together with his fluent energy and personal talent and one has gone a long way towards accounting for the ease, versatility and authority of his best work. M. R. Booth's *Victorian Spectacular Theatre 1850-1910* gives a detailed idea of the sheer technical skill Boucicault and his contemporaries developed, often to the detriment of literary merit in their scripts. Lamenting the lack of such merit in Boucicault and others, George Rowell, in his astute and elegant *The Victorian Theatre 1792-1914,* notes that *London Assurance* in its Royal Shakespeare Company revival 'proved a great deal more entertaining in performance'. That production, together with the Lyric Belfast's revival of *The Colleen Bawn* and the Abbey Dublin's of *The Shaughraun* confirm that Boucicault is above all a playwright for performance. His ingenuity, nimbleness and deft sureness of touch are unmistakeable. The plays here collected show that he was no literary giant; yet he was a master of stagecraft. We should not forget that a man as refined as Henry James realized, along with Shaw and the others, that Boucicault's best qualities had much to teach anyone genuinely interested in theatre. The reason is simple. Boucicault was an intelligent and highly talented artist. But he worked for audiences he at times merely exploited, and whose taste certainly restricted him. He was a practical writer, undeceived about his strengths and limitations, who usually improved what he copied. His dialogue is often fresh, even modern in tone and attitude. He has thus dated less than many of his colleagues in the Victorian theatre. Given the conditions of that theatre and the genres available to him, he even bequeathed us some masterpieces for performance. And single-handedly Boucicault gave Ireland a theatre in the nineteenth century on which others could draw. If his successors outgrew him intellectually and reacted against him, he still has much to teach, because art, after all, has to respond to life with more than the intellect.

Andrew Parkin
University of British Columbia
December, 1983.

22

GLOSSARY OF IRISH EXPRESSIONS
As Anglicized in *The Colleen Bawn* and *The Shaughraun*

acushla: my pulse
agrah: my love
alaina, alanna: my dear
ardhiol: oh devil
aroon: my darling
arrah: oh, ah! Used as girl's name in *Arrah-na-Pogue* (Arrah of the kiss)
asthore: my treasure
avick: my son
bawn: fair-haired
bocanns: billy goats
bouchal: boy
colleen: girl
coppleens: ponies
cruiskeen lawn: little full jug
Gramachree, mavourneen, slanta gal avourneen: Love of my heart, my darling, bright health of my darling
gore doutha: without a doubt
hogoola: a wail for lamentation
keen: lament or wail
lawn: full
machree: my heart

mavourneen: my darling
och hone, ochone: oh alas!
och oolaghaun: a refrain for lamenting
och murra: oh Mary!
omadhaun: fool
pogue: kiss
polthogue: slap or punch
shaughraun: vagabond
shule: walk
spalpeen: wandering labourer, hence tramp or vagrant and scoundrel
sthreel: anything clumsy or untidy
sthrippens: the last, rich milk from the cow at milking
suilish, sweelish: light
suilish machree: light of my heart
thurra mon dhiol: your soul to the devil
weir asthru, weerasthru: oh Mary, what sorrow!
whist: hush, quiet!

NOTE: Boucicault's spellings of the Irish words are rough attempts, sometimes plainly wrong, to give a phonetic rendering of these expressions for the benefit of actors and readers. The conventional spelling of the Irish words on which this list is based can be found in the fuller Glossary in *The Dolmen Boucicault*.

A NOTE ON THE TEXTS

London Assurance is reprinted from *English and American Drama of the Nineteenth Century* edited by George Freedley and Allardyce Nicoll (Readex Microprint Collection). The text of *The Corsican Brothers* derives from the manuscript submitted to the Lord Chamberlain by Kean's management in September 1851 and reprinted with silent corrections of minor errors and amplified stage directions by James L. Smith in *Victorian Melodramas*. This text is used here because of its readability and dramatic force. *The Octoroon* (American version) is the text that appears in John Gassner's *Best Plays of the Early American Theatre From the Beginning to 1916*. The happy ending, printed directly following the American text, is contained in Act IV of the Dicks' Standard Plays penny edition. *The Colleen Bawn* and *The Shaughraun* follow the texts in *The Dolmen Boucicault*, derived from the Acting Editions of Lacy, French and Dicks in the case of the former play, and of French and Dicks in the case of the latter. *Robert Emmet* is reprinted from *Forbidden Fruit and Other Plays*, edited by Allardyce Nicoll and F. Theodore Cloak.

LONDON ASSURANCE

To

CHARLES KEMBLE

this comedy

(*with his kind permission*)

is dedicated

by

his fervent admirer and humble servant

DION L. BOUCICAULT

AUTHOR'S PREFACE TO FIRST EDITION (1841)

There is a species of literary modesty observed by authors of the present day — I mean, that of prefacing their works with an apology for taking the liberty of inflicting them upon the patient public. Many require no such plea; but the following pages are too full of flagrant faults to pass from me without some few words of extenuation.

The Management of Covent Garden Theatre requested me to write a comedy — a modern comedy; I feared that I was unequal to the task; but, by the encouragement and kindness of Mr CHARLES MATHEWS, I was induced to attempt it. Once begun, the necessity of excessive rapidity became evident; and, on the spur of the moment, I completed this work in thirty days. I had no time to revise or correct — the ink was scarcely dry before it was in the theatre and accepted. I am aware that it possesses all the many faults, incongruities and excrescences of a hastily-written performance. It will not bear analysis as a literary production. In fact, my sole object was to throw together a few scenes of a dramatic nature; and, therefore, I studied the stage rather than the moral effect. I attempted to instil a pungency into the dialogue, and to procure vivid tones by a strong antithesis of character. The moral which I intended to convey is expressed in the last speech of the comedy; but as I wrote 'currente calamo' I have doubtless through the play strayed far wide of my original intent.

Let me take this opportunity of stating the facts attending my reception at Covent Garden Theatre — as it may also hold out encouragement to the faint hearts of many entering the perilous shoals of dramatic literature.

In the beginning of last November I entered this establishment under the assumed name of LEE MORETON. I was wholly unknown to any person therein. I received every mark of kindness and attention on the part of the Management and was cordially

27

welcomed on all sides; my productions were read without loss of time; and the rapidity with which this play was produced — together with the unsparing liberality of its appointments — give ample proof that the field is open to all comers.

London Assurance was made to order, on the shortest possible notice. I could have wished that my first appearance before the public had not been in this out-of-breath style; but I saw my opportunity at hand — I knew how important it was not to neglect the chance of production; the door was open — I had a run for it — and here I am.

How shall I return thanks adequate to the general sympathy and hearty good-will I have received at the hands of the mass of talent congregated in this piece.

MR W. FARREN'S personation of *Sir Harcourt,* made me regret that I had not the part to rewrite; the *ci-devant jeune homme* — the veteran *roué* — consummate vanity — blunt, lively perception, redolent with the very essence of etiquette — the exquisite — the vane of the *beau monde,* — were consummated in his appearance; before a word was uttered, he more than shared the creation of the character.

MR HARLEY in *Meddle,* was, as Mr Harley is universally acknowledged to be — irresistible.

Who could view the quiet, deliberate impertinence — the bare-faced impudence of *Dazzle*, reflected in MATHEWS, without the reiterated roars of laughter which attended nearly every word he uttered — passages which I never intended as hits, were loaded, primed and pointed, with an effect as unexpected to me as it was pleasing.

MR BARTLEY as *Max,* gave a tone and feeling to the country squire, both fresh and natural. To this gentleman I am under the greatest obligation for the numerous and valuable suggestions which he tendered; and to him I must attribute to a great extent, the success of the piece.

I have to offer my most sincere thanks to MR ANDERSON, for the kind manner in which he accepted the part of *Courtly*; the prominence which it held in the representation, was wholly attributable to his excellent impersonation.

What can I say to MR KEELEY; praise would be superfluous; his part had one fault in his hands: it was not long enough. [*Mem.* To correct that another time.]

Out of the trivial character of *Cool,* MR BRINDAL produced effects wholly unexpected. Let him not imagine, that by mentioning him last, I prize him least.

MRS NISBETT did not enact — she was *Lady Gay Spanker* — the substance of my thoughts; she wore the character with grace and ease, divesting it of any coarseness, yet enjoying all its freedom. She dashed in like a flash of lightning, and was greeted with a thunder of appluase. What can I say of this laughing, frolic creature? — Has Momus a wife? If he has not, let him make haste.

MRS HUMBY, with her usual good-nature, undertook a very paltry page or two, grinding blunt humour into the keenest edge, with a power which she alone possesses.

To those who have witnessed this play, I need not describe my gratitude to MRS C. MATHEWS; to those who have not seen it, I must express my inability of expression. I am well aware, that to her judgement, taste, and valuable suggestions, with regard to the alterations of character, situation, dialogue, expunging passages, and dilating others — to her indefatigable zeal, I owe my position. All this, being independent of her participation in the performance would it not be vanity in me to add a mite of praise to that which has been showered round her throughout her life. Details were vain. No one could guess my countless obligations, had they not witnessed the conferring of them.

For the success of this play, I have to thank a most indulgent audience, an ultra-liberal management, an unrivalled cast; but little, very little is due to

The Public's
Humble Servant,
D.L.B.

The original full version of the play was first performed on Thursday, 4 March 1841, at the Theatre Royal, Covent Garden, with the following cast:

Sir Harcourt Courtly	MR W. FARREN
Max Harkaway	MR BARTLEY
Charles Courtly	MR ANDERSON
Mr Spanker	MR KEELEY
Dazzle	MR C. MATHEWS
Mark Meddle	MR HARLEY
Cool (*Valet*)	MR BRINDAL
James [Simpson] (*Butler*)	MR HONNER
Martin	MR AYLIFFE
Solomon Isaacs	
Lady Gay Spanker	MRS NISBETT
Grace Harkaway	MADAME VESTRIS
Pert	MRS HUMBY

The Scene lies in London and Gloucestershire in 1841. Time — Three days.

ACT ONE

An Ante-room in SIR HARCOURT COURTLY's *House in Belgrave Square. Enter* COOL *C.*

COOL. Half-past nine, and Mr Charles has not yet returned, I am in a fever of dread. If his father happens to rise earlier than usual on any morning, he is sure to ask first for Mr Charles. Poor deluded old gentleman — he little thinks how he is deceived.
(*Enter* MARTIN, *lazily L.2.E.*)
Well, Martin, he has not come home yet!
MARTIN. No; and I have not had a wink of sleep all night. I cannot stand this any longer; I shall give warning. This is the fifth night Mr Courtly has remained out, and I'm obliged to stand at the hall window to watch for him.
COOL. You know, if Sir Harcourt was aware that we connived at his son's irregularities, we should all be discharged.
MARTIN. I have used up all my common excuses on his duns. 'Call again,' 'Not at home,' and 'Send it down to you,' won't serve any more; and Mr Crust, the wine merchant swears he will be paid.
COOL. So they all say. Why, he has arrests out against him already. I've seen the fellows watching the door —
(*Loud knock and ring heard.*)
There he is, just in time — quick, Martin, for I expect Sir Harcourt's bell every moment —
(*Bell rings.*)
And there it is.
(*Exit* MARTIN *slowly L.2.E.*)
Thank heaven! He will return to College tomorrow, and this heavy responsibility will be taken off my shoulders. A valet is as difficult a post to fill properly as that of prime minister.
(*Exit R.C.*)
YOUNG COURTLY (*without*). Hello!

DAZZLE (*without*). Steady!
    (*Enter* YOUNG COURTLY *and* DAZZLE *L.3.E.*)
YOUNG COURTLY. Hollo-o-o!
DAZZLE. Hush! What are you about, howling like a Hotentot. Sit down there, and thank heaven you are in Belgrave square, instead of Bow street.
YOUNG COURTLY. D--n — damn Bow street.
DAZZLE. Oh, with all my heart! You have not seen as much of it as I have.
YOUNG COURTLY. I say, let me see — what was I going to say, oh, look here —
    (*Pulls out a large assortment of bell-pulls, knockers, etc, from his pocket.*)
There! dam'me! I'll puzzle the twopenny postman, I'll deprive them of their right of disturbing the neighbourhood. That black lion's head did belong to old Vampire, the money-lender; this bell-pull to Miss Stitch, the milliner.
DAZZLE. And this brass griffin —
YOUNG COURTLY. That! Oh let me see — I think I twisted that off our own hall-door as I came in, while you were paying the cab.
DAZZLE. What shall I do with them?
YOUNG COURTLY. Pack 'em in a small hamper, and send 'em to the nearest sitting magistrate with my father's compliments; in the meantime, come into my room, and I'll astonish you with some Burgundy. (*Re-enter* COOL *R.C.*)
COOL (*R*). Mr Charles —
YOUNG COURTLY. Out! out! Not at home to anyone.
COOL. And drunk —
YOUNG COURTLY. As a lord.
DAZZLE. As a whole house of Lords.
COOL. If Sir Harcourt knew this, he would go mad, he would discharge me.
YOUNG COURTLY. You flatter yourself; that would be no proof of his insanity.
    (*To* DAZZLE)
This is Cool, — this is Mr Cool, he keeps the keys of the wine cellar.
DAZZLE (*crosses to* COOL). I am always happy to shake hands with the man that keeps the keys of the wine cellar.
    (*Crosses back to L.*)
YOUNG COURTLY. He is the best liar in London — there is a pungency about his invention, and an originality in his equivocation, that is perfectly refreshing.

COOL (*aside*). Why, Mr Charles, where did you pick him up?

YOUNG COURTLY. You mistake, he picked me up.
 (*Bell rings.*)

COOL. Here comes Sir Harcourt — pray do not let him see you in this state.

YOUNG COURTLY. State! What do you mean? I am in a beautiful state.

COOL. I should lose my character.

YOUNG COURTLY. That would be a fortunate epoch in your life, Cool.

COOL. Your father would discharge me.

YOUNG COURTLY. Cool, what right have —

COOL. Retire to your own room, for heaven's sake, Mr Charles.

YOUNG COURTLY. I'll do so for my own sake. Here, Cool, take these and lock them up with the rest of the family plate.
 (*Gives* COOL *the bell-pulls.*)
 (*To* DAZZLE)
 I say, old fellow, (*staggering*) just hold the door steady while I go in.

DAZZLE. This way. Now then — take care!
 (*Helps him into the room R.3.E.*)
 (*Enter* SIR HARCOURT COURTLY *R.C. in an elegant dressing-gown, and Greek scull-cup and tassels, &c.*)

SIR HARCOURT. Cool, is breakfast ready?

COOL. Quite ready, Sir Harcourt.

SIR HARCOURT. Apropos. I omitted to mention that I expect Squire Harkaway to join us this morning, and you must prepare for my departure to Oak Hall immediately.

COOL. Leave town in the middle of the season, Sir Harcourt? So unprecedented a proceeding!

SIR HARCOURT. It is! I confess it; there is but one power could effect such a miracle — that is divinity.

COOL. How!

SIR HARCOURT. In female form, of course. Cool, I am about to present society with a second Lady Courtly; young — blushing eighteen; lovely! I have her portrait; rich! I have her banker's account; an heiress, and a Venus!

COOL. Lady Courtly could be none other.

SIR HARCOURT. Ha! ha! Cool, your manners are above your station — Apropos, I shall find no further use for my brocade dressing-gown.

COOL. I thank you, Sir Harcourt; might I ask who the fortunate lady is?

SIR HARCOURT. Certainly: Miss Grace Harkaway, the niece of my old friend, Max.

COOL. Have you never seen the lady, Sir?

SIR HARCOURT. Never — that is, yes — eight years ago. Having been as you know, on the continent for the last seven years, I have not had the opportunity of paying my devoirs. Our connection and betrothal was a very extraordinary one. Her father's estates were contiguous to mine; — being a penurious, miserly, ugly old scoundrel, he made a market of my indiscretion, and supplied my extravagance with large sums of money on mortgages, his great desire being to unite the two properties. About seven years ago, he died — leaving Grace, a girl, to the guardianship of her uncle, with this will; — if, on attaining the age of nineteen, she would consent to marry me, I should receive those deeds, and all his property, as her dowry. If she refused to comply with this condition, they should revert to my heir-presumptive or apparent. She consents.

COOL. Who would not?

SIR HARCOURT. I consent to receive her £15,000 a year.

COOL. Who would not?

SIR HARCOURT. So prepare, Cool, prepare; but where is my boy, where is Charles?

COOL. Why — oh, he is gone out, Sir Harcourt; yes, gone out to take a walk.

SIR HARCOURT. Poor child! A perfect child in heart — a sober, placid mind — the simplicity and verdure of boyhood, kept fresh and unsullied by any contact with society. Tell me, Cool, at what time was he in bed last night?

COOL. Half-past nine, Sir Harcourt.

SIR HARCOURT. Half-past nine! Beautiful! Whan an original idea! Reposing in cherub slumbers, while all around him teems with drinking and debauchery! Primitive sweetness of nature! No pilot-coated bear-skinned brawling!

COOL. Oh, Sir Harcourt!

SIR HARCOURT. No cigar-smoking —

COOL. Faints at the smell of one.

SIR HARCOURT. No brandy and water bibbing.

COOL. Doesn't know the taste of anything stronger than barley-water.

SIR HARCOURT. No night parading —

COOL. Never heard the clock strike twelve, except at noon.

SIR HARCOURT. In fact, he is my son, and became a gentleman by right of paternity — he inherited my manners.

(*Enter* MARTIN *L.3.E.*)

34

MARTIN. Mr Harkaway.

> (*Enter* MAX HARKAWAY *L.3.E. and gives* MARTIN *his hat and cane which* MARTIN *places on table L.U. and exits.*)

MAX. Squire Harkaway, fellow, or Max Harkaway, another time.

> (MARTIN *bows and exits.*)

Ah! Ha! Sir Harcourt, I'm devilish glad to see you. Dang it, but I'm glad to see you. Let me see; six — seven years, or more since we have met. How quickly they have flown!

SIR HARCOURT (*throwing off his studied manner*). Max, Max give me your hand, old boy.

> (*Aside*)

Ah, he is glad to see me; there is no fawning pretence about that squeeze. Cool, you may retire.

> (*Exit* COOL *R.C.*)

MAX. Why, you are looking quite rosy.

SIR HARCOURT. Ah! ah! rosy! Am I too florid!

MAX. Not a bit; not a bit.

SIR HARCOURT. I thought so —

> (*Aside*)

Cool said I had put too much on.

MAX. How comes it, Courtly, you manage to retain your youth? See, I'm as grey as an old badger, or a wild rabbit; while you are — are as black as a young rook. I say, whose head grew your hair, eh?

SIR HARCOURT. Permit me to remark, that all the beauties of my person are of home manufacture. Why should you be surprised at my youth? I have scarcely thrown off the giddiness of a very boy — elasticity of limb — buoyancy of soul! Remark this position —

> (*Throws himself into an attitude.*)

I held that attitude for ten minutes at Lady Acid's last reunion, at the express desire of one of our first sculptors, while he was making a sketch of me for the Apollo.

MAX (*aside*). Making a butt of thee for their gibes.

SIR HARCOURT. Lady Sarah Sarcasm started up, and pointing to my face, ejaculated. 'Good gracious! does not Sir Harcourt remind you of the countenance of Ajax, in the Pompeian portrait?'

MAX. Ajax! — humbug!

SIR HARCOURT. You are complimentary.

> (*Sits L. of R. table.*)

MAX. I'm a plain man, and always speak my mind. What's in a face or figure? Does a Grecian nose entail a good temper? Does a waspish waist indicate a good heart? Or, do oily perfumed locks necessarily thatch a well-furnished brain?

> (*Sits R. of L. table.*)

SIR HARCOURT. It is an undeniable fact, plain people always praise the beauties of the mind.

MAX. Excuse the insinuation; I had thought the first Lady Courtly had surfeited you with beauty.

SIR HARCOURT. No; she lived fourteen months with me, and then eloped with an intimate friend. Etiquette compelled me to challenge the seducer; so I received satisfaction and a bullet in my shoulder at the same time. However, I had the consolation of knowing that he was the handsomest man of the age. She did not insult me, by running away with a damned ill-looking scoundrel.

MAX. That, certainly, was flattering.

SIR HARCOURT. I felt so, as I pocketed the ten thousand pounds damages.

MAX. That must have been a great balm to your sore honour.

SIR HARCOURT. It was — Max, my honour would have died without it; for on that year the wrong horse won the Derby by some mistake. It was one of the luckiest chances — a thing that does not happen twice in a man's life — the opportunity of getting rid of his wife and his debts at the same time.

MAX. Tell the truth, Courtly — did you not feel a little frayed in your delicacy — your honour, now? Eh?

SIR HARCOURT. Not a whit. Why should I? I married money, and I received it — a virgin gold! My delicacy and honour had nothing to do with it. The world pities the bereaved husband, when it should congratulate. No, the affair made a sensation, and I was the object. Besides, it is vulgar to make a parade of one's feelings, however acute they may be; impenetrability of countenance is the sure sign of your highly bred man of fashion.

MAX. So a man must, therefore, lose his wife and his money with a smile — in fact, everything he possesses but his temper.

SIR HARCOURT. Exactly; and greet ruin with vive la bagatelle! For example; your modish beauty never discomposes the shape of her features with convulsive laughter. A smile rewards the bon mot, and also shows the whiteness of her teeth. She never weeps impromptu — tears might destroy the economy of her cheek. Scenes are vulgar, hysterics obsolete; she exhibits a calm, placid, impenetrable lake —

(*Both rise*)

whose surface is reflection, but of unfathomable depth — a statue, whose life is hypothetical, and not a prima facie fact —

(SIR HARCOURT *crosses to L.*)

MAX. Well, give me the girl that will fly at your eyes in an argument, and stick to her point like a fox to his own tail.

SIR HARCOURT. But etiquette, Max! Remember etiquette!

MAX. Damn etiquette! I have seen a man who thought it sacrilege to eat fish with a knife, that would not scruple to rise up and rob his brother of his birth-right in a gambling-house. Your thorough-bred, well-blooded heart, will seldom kick over the traces of good feeling. That's my opinion, and I don't care who knows it.

SIR HARCOURT. Pardon me — etiquette is the pulse of society, by regulating which the body politic is retained in health. I consider myself one of the faculty in the art.

MAX. Well, well; you are a living libel upon common sense, for you are old enough to know better.

SIR HARCOURT. Old enough! What do you mean? Old! I still retain all my little juvenile indiscretions, which your niece's beauties must teach me to discard. I have not sown my old oats yet.

MAX. Time you did, at sixty-three.

SIR HARCOURT. Sixty-three! Good God! — forty, 'pon my life! Forty, next March!

MAX. Why, you are older than I am.

SIR HARCOURT. Oh, you are old enough to be my father.

MAX. Well, if I am, that's etiquette, I suppose. Poor Grace! How often I have pitied her fate! That a young and beautiful creature should be driven into wretched splendour, or miserable poverty!

SIR HARCOURT. Wretched! Lady Courtly wretched! Impossible! Wherefore?

MAX. Will she not be compelled to marry you, whether she likes you or not? — a choice between you and poverty.

(*Aside*)

And hang me if it isn't a tie! But why do you not introduce your son Charles to me? I have not seen him since he was a child. You would never permit him to accept any of my invitations to spend his vacation at Oak Hall, — of course, we shall have the pleasure of his company now.

SIR HARCOURT. He is not fit to enter society yet. He is a studious, sober boy.

MAX. Boy! Why, he's five-and-twenty.

SIR HARCOURT. Good gracious! Max — you will permit me to know my own son's age, — he is not twenty.

MAX. I'm dumb.

SIR HARCOURT. Cool!

(*Enter* COOL *R.C.*)

Prepare my toilet.

(*Exit* COOL *L.C.*)

You will excuse me while I indulge in the process of dressing. That is a ceremony which, with me, supersedes all others. I consider it a duty which every gentleman owes to society, to render himself as agreeable an object as possible; and the least compliment a mortal can pay to nature, when she honours him by bestowing extra care in the manufacture of his person, is to display her taste to the best possible advantage, and so au revoir.

(*Exit R.C.*)

MAX (*crosses to L.U.*). That's a good soul — he has his faults, and who has not? Forty years of age! Oh, monstrous — but he does look uncommonly young for sixty, spite of his foreign looks and complexion.

(*Enter* DAZZLE *R.S.E.*)

DAZZLE. Who's my friend with the stick and gaiters, I wonder — one of the family — the governor, maybe?

MAX. Who's this? Oh, Charles — is that you, my boy? How are you?

DAZZLE. How are you?

MAX. Your father has just left me.

DAZZLE. The honour you would confer upon me, I must unwillingly disclaim — I am not Mr Courtly.

MAX. I beg pardon — a friend, I suppose?

DAZZLE. Oh, a most intimate friend — a friend of years — distantly related to the family — one of my ancestors married one of his.

(*Aside*)

Adam and Eve, long way back.

MAX. Are you on a visit here?

DAZZLE. Yes. Oh! yes.

MAX. Sir, if you are not otherwise engaged, I shall feel honoured by your company at my house, Oak Hall, Gloucestershire.

DAZZLE. Your name is —

MAX. Harkaway — Max Harkaway.

DAZZLE. Harkaway — let me see — I ought to be related to the Harkaways, somehow.

MAX. A wedding is about to come off — will you take a part on the occasion?

DAZZLE. With pleasure! Any part but that of the husband.

MAX. Have you any previous engagement?

DAZZLE. I was thinking — eh! Why, let me see.

(*Aside.*)

Promised to meet my tailor and his account tomorrow; however, I'll postpone that.

(*Aloud.*)

Have you good shooting?

MAX. Shooting! Why, there's no shooting at this time of the year.

DAZZLE. Oh! I'm in no hurry — I can wait till the season, of course. I was only speaking precautionally — you have good shooting?

MAX. The best in the country.

DAZZLE. Make yourself comfortable! Say no more — I'm your man — wait till you see how I'll murder your preserves.

MAX. Do you hunt?

DAZZLE. Pardon me — but will you repeat that?

MAX. Do you hunt?

DAZZLE (*aside*). Delicious and expensive idea!

MAX. You ride?

DAZZLE. Anything. Everything. From a blood to a broomstick. Only catch me a flash of lightning, and let me get on the back of it, and dam'me if I wouldn't astonish the elements.

MAX. Ha! ha!

DAZZLE. I'd put a girdle round about the earth in very considerably less than forty minutes.

MAX. Ah! ha! We'll show old Fiddlestrings how to spend the day. He imagines that Nature, at the earnest request of Fashion, made summer days long for him to saunter in the Park, and winter nights, that he might have good time to get cleared out at hazard or at whist. Give me the yelping of a pack of hounds, before the shuffling of a pack of cards. What state can match the chase in full cry, each vying with his fellow which shall be the most happy? A thousand deaths fly by unheeded in that one hour's life of ecstasy. Time is outrun, and Nature seems to grudge our bliss by making the day so short.

DAZZLE. No, for then rises up the idol of my great adoration.

MAX. Who's that?

DAZZLE. The bottle — that lends a lustre to the soul! When the world puts on its night-cap, and extinguishes the sun — then comes the bottle! Oh, mighty wine! Don't ask me to apostrophise. Wine and love are the only two indescribable things in nature; but I prefer the wine, because its consequences are not entailed and are more easily got rid of.

MAX. How so?

DAZZLE. Love ends in matrimony, wine in soda water.

MAX. Well, I can promise you as fine a bottle as ever was cracked.

DAZZLE. Never mind the bottle, give me the wine. Say no more; but, when I arrive, just shake one of my hands, and put the key of the cellar into the other, and if I don't make myself intimately acquainted with its internal organisation — well, I say nothing — time will show.

MAX. I foresee some happy days.

DAZZLE. And I some glorious nights.

MAX. It mustn't be a flying visit.

DAZZLE. I despise the word — I'll stop a month with you.

MAX. Or a year or two.

DAZZLE. I'll live and die with you!

MAX. Ha! ha! Remember Max —

DAZZLE. Harkaway!

MAX. Oak Hall —

DAZZLE. Gloucestershire!

(MAX *is going.*)

Tallyho-o-o-o!

MAX. Yoicks! Tallyhoa-o-o-o!

(*Exit L.3.E.*)

DAZZLE. There I am — quartered for a couple of years, at the least. The old boy wants somebody to ride his horses, shoot his game, and keep a restraint on the morals of the parish; I'm eligible. What a lucky accident to meet Young Courtly last night! Who could have thought it! Yesterday I could not make certain of a dinner, except at my own proper peril; today, I would flirt with a banquet.

(*Enter* YOUNG COURTLY *R.3.E.*)

YOUNG COURTLY. What infernal row was that? Why, —

(*Seeing* DAZZLE)

— are you here still?

DAZZLE. Yes. Ain't you delighted? I'll ring, and send the servant for my luggage.

YOUNG COURTLY. The devil you will! Why, you don't mean to say you seriously intend to take up a permanent residence here?

(*Rings the bell.*)

DAZZLE. Now, that's a most inhospitable insinuation.

YOUNG COURTLY. Might I ask your name?

DAZZLE. With a great deal of pleasure — Richard Dazzle, late of the Unattached Volunteers, vulgarly entitled the Dirty Buffs.

(*Enter* MARTIN *L.3.E.*)

YOUNG COURTLY. Then, Mr Richard Dazzle, I have the honour of wishing you a very good morning. Martin, show this gentleman the door.

DAZZLE. If he does, I'll kick Martin out of it. No offence.

(*Exit* MARTIN *L.*)

Now, sir, permit me to place a dioramic view of your conduct before you. After bringing you safely home this morning — after indulgently waiting, whenever you took a passing fancy to a knocker or bell-pull — after conducting a retreat that would have reflected honour on Napoleon — you would kick me into the street, like a mangy cur; and that's what you call gratitude. Now, to show you how superior I am to petty malice, I give you an unlimited invitation to my house — my country house to remain as long as you please.

(COOL *enters R.U.C. and exits L.3.E.*)

YOUNG COURTLY. Your house!

DAZZLE. Oak Hall, Gloucestershire, fine old place! For further particulars see road book — that is, it nominally belongs to my old friend and relation, Max Harkaway; but I'm privileged. Capital old fellow — say, shall we be honoured?

YOUNG COURTLY. Sir, permit me to hesitate a moment.

(*Aside.*)

Let me see, I go back to College tomorrow, so I shall not be missing; tradesmen begin to dun.

(*Enter* COOL *L.C. drops down L.*)

I hear thunder, here is shelter ready for me.

COOL. Oh, Mr Charles, Mr Solomon Isaacs is in the hall, and swears he will remain till he has arrested you!

YOUNG COURTLY. Does he — sorry he is so obstinate — take him my compliments, and I will bet him five to one he will not.

DAZZLE. Double or quits, with kind regards.

COOL. But, sir, he has discovered the house in Curzon street; he says he is aware the furniture, at least belongs to you, and he will put a man in immediately.

YOUNG COURTLY. That's awkward — what's to be done?

DAZZLE. Ask him whether he couldn't make it a woman.

YOUNG COURTLY. I must trust that to fate.

DAZZLE. I will give you my acceptance, if it will be of any use to you — it is of none to me.

YOUNG COURTLY. No, sir; but in reply to your most generous and kind invitation if you be in earnest, I shall feel delighted to accept it.

DAZZLE. Certainly.

YOUNG COURTLY. Then off we go — through the stables — down the Mews, and so slip through my friend's fingers.

DAZZLE. But, stay, you must do the polite... say farewell to him before you part. Damn it, don't cut him!

41

YOUNG COURTLY. You jest!

DAZZLE. Here, lend me a card.

(COURTLY *gives him one.*)

Loan me your pencil.

(*He borrows* YOUNG COURTLY's *pencil and uses* COOL's *back for a desk, after having written the card, he is about to put the pencil in his own pocket.*)

YOUNG COURTLY. I beg your pardon, but [that] is my pencil.

DAZZLE. Excuse me.

(*Gives* YOUNG COURTLY *his pencil.*)

'Our respects to Mr Isaacs — sorry to have been prevented from seeing him.' Ha! Ha!

YOUNG COURTLY. Ha! ha!

DAZZLE. We'll send him up some game.

YOUNG COURTLY. Yes, we'll send him a couple of rabbits.

DAZZLE. Yes, we'll send him a brace of rats.

YOUNG COURTLY (*to* COOL). Don't let my father see him.

(*Exeunt* YOUNG COURTLY *and* DAZZLE *R.3.E.*)

COOL. What's this? 'Mr Charles Courtly, P.P.C., returns thanks for obliging inquiries.'

(*Exit L.3.E.*)

END OF ACT ONE

ACT TWO

The lawn before Oak Hall, a fine Elizabethan mansion; a drawing-room is seen through large French windows at the back. Statues, urns, and garden chairs about the stage. Enter PERT *and* JAMES *L. from house.*

PERT. James, Miss Grace desires me to request that you will watch at the avenue and let her know when the squire's carriage is seen on the London road.

JAMES. I will go to the lodge.

(*Exit L.1.E.*)

PERT. How I do long to see what kind of a man Sir Harcourt Courtly is. They say he is sixty; so he must be old, and consequently ugly. If I was Miss Grace, I would rather give up all my fortune and marry the man I liked, than go to church with a stuffed eel-skin. But taste is everything, — she doesn't seem to care whether he is sixty or sixteen; jokes at love; prepares for matrimony as she would for dinner; says it is a necessary evil, and what can't be cured must be endured. Now, I say this is against all nature; and she is either no woman, or a deeper one than I am, if she prefers an old man to a young one. Here she comes, looking as cheerfully as if she was going to marry Mr Jenks! my Mr Jenks! whom nobody won't lead to the halter till I have that honour.

(*Enter* GRACE *from the house L.U.*)

GRACE. Well, Pert? Any signs of the squire yet?

PERT. No, Miss Grace; but James has gone to watch the road.

GRACE. In my uncle's letter, he mentions a Mr Dazzle, whom he has invited; so you must prepare a room for him. He is some friend of my husband that is to be, and my uncle seems to have taken an extraordinary predilection for him. Apropos! I must not forget to have a bouquet for the dear old man when he arrives.

43

PERT.   The dear old man! Do you mean Sir Harcourt?

GRACE.   La, no! My uncle, of course.

(*Plucking flowers*)

What do I care for Sir Harcourt Courtly?

PERT.   Isn't it odd, Miss, you have never seen your intended, though it has been so long since you were betrothed?

GRACE.   Not at all; marriage matters are conducted now-a-days in a most mercantile manner; consequently, a previous acquaintance is by no means indispensable. Besides, my prescribed husband has been upon the continent for the benefit of his — property. They say a southern climate is a great restorer of consumptive estates.

PERT.   Well, Miss, for my own part, I should like to have a good look at my bargain before I paid for it; 'specially when one's life is the price of the article. But why, ma'am, do you consent to marry in this blind-man's-buff sort of manner? What would you think if he were not quite old?

GRACE.   I should think he was a little younger.

PERT.   I should like him all the better.

GRACE.   That wouldn't I? A young husband might expect affection and nonsense, which 'twould be deceit in me to render; nor would he permit me to remain with my uncle. Sir Harcourt takes me with the incumbrances of his estate, and I shall beg to be left among the rest of the live stock.

PERT.   Ah, Miss! but some day you might chance to stumble over the man, what could you do then?

GRACE.   Do! Beg the man's pardon, and request the man to pick me up again.

PERT.   Ah! you were never in love, Miss.

GRACE.   I never was, nor will be, till I am tired of myself and common sense. Love is a pleasant scape-goat for a little epidemic madness. I must have been inoculated in my infancy, for the infection passes over poor me in contempt.

(*Enter* JAMES *L.1.E.*)

JAMES.   Two gentlemen, Miss Grace, have just alighted.

GRACE.   Very well, James.

(*Exit* JAMES *L.*)

Love is pictured as a boy; in another century they will be wiser and paint him as a fool, with cap and bells, without a thought above the jingling of his own folly. Now, Pert, remember this as a maxim — a woman is always in love with one of two things.

PERT.   What are they, Miss?

GRACE. A man, or herself – and I know which is the most profitable.
(*Exit L.1.E.*)

PERT. I wonder what my Jenks would say, if I was to ask him. La! here comes Mr Meddle, his rival, contemporary solicitor, as he calls him, – a nasty, prying ugly wretch, – what brings him here? He comes puffed with some news.
(*Retires up R.*)
(*Enter* MEDDLE, *with a newspaper L.1.E.*)

MEDDLE. I have no hesitation in saying and I say it boldly, I have secured the only newspaper in the village – my character, as an attorney-at-law, depended on the monopoly of its information. I took it up by chance, when this paragraph met my astonished view.

(*Reads*)

'We understand that the contract of marriage so long in abeyance on account of the lady's minority, is about to be celebrated, at Oak Hall, Gloucestershire, the well-known and magnificent mansion of Maximilian Harkaway, Esq., between Sir Harcourt Courtly, Baronet, of fashionable celebrity, and Miss Grace Harkaway, niece to the said Mr Harkaway. The preparations are proceeding in the good old English style.' Is it possible! I seldom swear, except in a witness box, but, damme, had it been known in the village, my reputation would have been lost; my voice in the parlour of the Red Lion mute, and Jenks, a fellow who calls himself a lawyer, without more capability than a broomstick, and as much impudence as a young barrister after getting a verdict by mistake; why, he would actually have taken the Reverend Mr Spout by the button, which is now my sole privilege. Ah! here is Mrs Pert; couldn't have hit upon a better person. I'll cross-examine her – lady's maid to Miss Grace, – a confidential purloiner of second-hand silk – a nisi prius of her mistress – ah! sits on the wool-sack in the pantry, and dictates the laws of kitchen etiquette. Ah! Mrs Pert –
(PERT *coming down L.*)
good morning; permit me to say, and my word as a legal character is not unduly considered – I venture to affirm, that you look a – quite like the – a –

PERT. Law! Mr Meddle.

MEDDLE. Exactly like the law.

PERT. Ha! indeed; complimentary, I confess; like the law; tedious, prosy, made up of musty paper. You shan't have a long suit of me. Good morning.

(*Going*)

MEDDLE. Stay, Mrs Pert; don't calumniate my calling, or disseminate vulgar prejudices.

PERT. Vulgar! you talk of vulgarity to me! You, whose sole employment is to sneak about like a pig, snouting out the dusthole of society, and feeding upon the bad ends of vice! You, who live upon the world's iniquity; you miserable specimen of a bad six-and-eightpence!

MEDDLE. But, Mrs Pert —

PERT. Don't but me, sir; I won't be butted by any such low fellow.

MEDDLE. This is slander; an action will lie.

PERT. Let it lie, lying is your trade. I'll tell you what Mr Meddle; if I had my will, I would soon put a check on your prying propensities. I'd treat you as the farmers do inquisitive hogs.

MEDDLE. How?

PERT. I would ring your nose.

(*Exit into house L.U.*)

MEDDLE. I know you would. Not much information elicited from that witness. Jenks is at the bottom of this. I have very little hesitation in saying, Jenks is a libellous rascal; I heard reports that he was undermining my character here, through Mrs Pert. Now I'm certain of it. Assault is expensive; but I certainly will put by a small weekly stipendium, until I can afford to kick Jenks.

DAZZLE (*outside*). Come along; this way!

MEDDLE. Ah! whom have we here? Visitors; I'll address them.

(*Enter* DAZZLE *L.1.E.*)

DAZZLE. Who's this, I wonder; one of the family? I must know him.

(*To* MEDDLE)

Ah! how are ye?

MEDDLE. Quite well. Just arrived? — ah! — um! Might I request the honour of knowing whom I address?

DAZZLE. Richard Dazzle, Esquire: and you —

MEDDLE. Mark Meddle, attorney-at-law.

(*Enter* YOUNG COURTLY *L.1.E.*)

DAZZLE. What detained you?

YOUNG COURTLY. My dear fellow, I have just seen such a woman!

DAZZLE (*aside*). Hush!

(*Aloud*)

Permit me to introduce you to my very old friend, Meddle. He's a capital fellow, know him.

MEDDLE. I feel honoured. Who is your friend?

DAZZLE. Oh, he? What, my friend? Oh! Augustus Hamilton.

YOUNG COURTLY. How d'ye do?
   (*Looking off*)
   There she is again!

MEDDLE (*looking off L*). What, that is Miss Grace.

DAZZLE. Of course, Grace.

YOUNG COURTLY. Grace? Do you know her?

DAZZLE. Why I used to pick daisies with her when I was a little boy.

YOUNG COURTLY. I'll go and introduce myself.
   (DAZZLE *stops him.*)

DAZZLE (*aside*). What are you about? Would you insult my old friend, Puddle, by running away?
   (*Aloud*)
   I say, Puddle, just show my friend the lions, while I say how d'ye do to my young friend, Grace.
   (*Aside*)
   Cultivate his acquaintance.
   (*Exit L.* YOUNG COURTLY *looks after him.*)

MEDDLE. Mr Hamilton, might I take the liberty?

YOUNG COURTLY (*looking off*). Confound the fellow.

MEDDLE. Sir, what did you remark?

YOUNG COURTLY. She's gone! Oh, are you here still, Mr Thingo-merry Puddle?

MEDDLE. Meddle, sir, Meddle, in the list of attorneys.

YOUNG COURTLY. Well, Muddle, or Puddle, or whoever you are, you are a bore!

MEDDLE (*aside*). How excessively odd! Mrs Pert said I was a pig, now I'm a boar! There goes the whole hog.

YOUNG COURTLY. Mr Thingamy, will you take a word of advice?

MEDDLE. Fell honoured.

YOUNG COURTLY. Get out.

MEDDLE. Do you mean to — I don't understand.

YOUNG COURTLY. Delighted to quicken your apprehension. You are an ass, Puddle.

MEDDLE. Ha! ha! another quadruped! I shall be a walking menagerie next. Yes; beautiful.
   (*Aside*)
   I wish he'd call me something libellous; but that would be too much to expect.
   (*Aloud*)
   Anything else?

47

YOUNG COURTLY. Some miserable, pettifogging scoundrel!

MEDDLE. Good! ha! ha!

YOUNG COURTLY. What do you mean by laughing at me?

MEDDLE. Ha! ha! ha! excellent delicious!

YOUNG COURTLY. Mr — are you ambitious of a kicking?

MEDDLE. Very, very — go on — kick — go on.

YOUNG COURTLY (*looking off*). Here she comes! I'll speak to her.

MEDDLE. But, sir — sir —

YOUNG COURTLY. Oh, go to the devil!

(*Runs off L.*)

MEDDLE. There, there's a chance lost — gone! I have no hesitation in saying, that, in another minute, I should have been kicked, literally kicked — a legal luxury. Costs, damages, and actions rose up like sky-rockets in my aspiring soul, with golden tails reaching to the infinity of my hopes.

(*Looking*)

They are coming this way; Mr Hamilton in close conversation with Lady Courtly that is to be. Crim. Con. — Courtly versus Hamilton — damages problematical — Meddle, chief witness for plaintiff — guinea a day — professional man! I'll take down their conversation verbatim.

(*Retires behind a bush R.*)

(*Enter* GRACE *followed by* YOUNG COURTLY *L.*)

GRACE. Perhaps you would follow your friend into the dining-room; refreshment, after your long journey, must be requisite.

YOUNG COURTLY. Pardon me, madam! but the lovely garden and the loveliness before me, is better refreshment than I could procure in any dining-room.

GRACE. Ha! Your company and compliments arrived together.

YOUNG COURTLY. I trust that a passing remark will not spoil so welcome an introduction as this by offending you.

GRACE. I am not certain that anything you could say would offend me.

YOUNG COURTLY. I never meant —

GRACE. I thought not. In turn, pardon me, when I request you will commence your visit with this piece of information; I consider compliments impertinent, and sweet meat language fulsome.

YOUNG COURTLY. I would condemn my tongue to a Pythagorean silence, if I thought it could attempt to flatter.

GRACE. It strikes me, sir, that you are a stray bee from the hive of fashion; if so, reserve your honey for its proper cell. A truce to compliments — You have just arrived from town, I apprehend.

(*Sitting R. on bench.*)

YOUNG COURTLY. This moment I left mighty London, under the fever of a full season, groaning with the noisy pulse. of wealth and the giddy whirling brain of fashion. Enchanting, busy London! how have I prevailed on myself to desert you. Next week the new ballet comes out — the week after comes Ascot. Oh!

GRACE. How agonising must be the reflection.

YOUNG COURTLY. Torture! Can you inform me how you manage to avoid suicide here? If there was but an opera even, within twenty miles! We wouldn't get up a rustic ballet among the village girls? No — ah!

GRACE. I am afraid you would find that difficult. How I contrive to support life I don't know — it is wonderful — but I have not precisely contemplated suicide yet, nor do I miss the opera.

YOUNG COURTLY. How can you manage to kill time?

GRACE. I can't. Men talk of killing time, while time quietly kills them. I have many employments — this week I devote to study and various amusements — next week to being married — the following week to repentance, perhaps.

YOUNG COURTLY. Married!

GRACE. You seem surprised; I believe it is of frequent occurrence in the metroplis — is it not?

YOUNG COURTLY. Yes, I believe we do it sometimes. Might I ask to whom?

GRACE. A gentleman who has been strongly recommended to me for the situation of husband.

YOUNG COURTLY. What an extraordinary match. You seem to laugh at love.

GRACE (*rising*). Love! Why, the very word is a breathing satire upon man's reason — a mania, indigenous to humanity — nature's jester, who plays off tricks upon the world, and trips up common sense. When I'm in love, I'll write an almanac, for very lack of wit — prognosticate the sighing season — when to beware of tears — about this time, expect matrimony to be prevalent! Ha! Ha! Why should I lay out my life in love's bonds upon the bare security of a man's word?

(*Enter* JAMES *L.1.E.*)

JAMES. The Squire, Madam, has just arrived, and another gentleman with him.

GRACE (*aside*). My intended, I suppose.

(*Crosses to L.*)

(*Exit* JAMES *L.*)

YOUNG COURTLY. I perceive you are one of the railers against what is termed the follies of high life.

GRACE. No, not particularly; I deprecate all folly. By what prerogative can the west-end mint issue absurdities which, if coined in the east, would be voted vulgar?

YOUNG COURTLY. By a sovereign right — because it has Fashion's head upon its side, and that stamps it current.

GRACE. Poor Fashion, for how many sins hast thou to answer! The gambler pawns his birth-right for fashion — the roué steals his friend's wife for fashion — each abandons himself to the storm of impulse, calling it the breeze of fashion.

YOUNG COURTLY. Pardon me, madam, you wrong yourself to rail against your own inheritance — the kingdom to which loveliness and wit attest your title.

GRACE. A mighty realm, forsooth, with milliners for ministers, a cabinet of coxcombs, envy for my homage, ruin for my revenue — my right of rule depending on the shape of a bonnet or the set of a pelisse, with the next grand noodel as my heir-apparent. Mr Hamilton, when I am crowned, I shall feel happy to abdicate in your favour. (*Curtseys and exits L. into house.*)

YOUNG COURTLY. What did she mean by that? Hang me if I can understand her — she is evidently not used to society. Ha! — takes every word I say for infallible truth — requires the solution of a compliment, as if it were a problem in Euclid. She said she was about to marry, but I rather imagine that she was in jest. 'Pon my life, I feel very queer at the contemplation of such an idea — I'll follow her.

    (MEDDLE *comes down.*)

Oh! perhaps this booby can inform me something about her.

    (MEDDLE *makes signs at him.*)

What the devil is he at?

MEDDLE. It won't do — no — ah! um — it's not to be done.

YOUNG COURTLY. What do you mean?

MEDDLE (*points after* GRACE). Counsel retained — cause to come off.

YOUNG COURTLY. Cause to come off!

MEDDLE. Miss Grace is about to be married.

YOUNG COURTLY. Is it possible?

MEDDLE. Certainly. If I have the drawing out of the deeds —

YOUNG COURTLY. To whom?

MEDDLE. Ha! hem! Oh, yes! I dare say — information being scarce in the market, I hope to make mine valuable.

YOUNG COURTLY. Married! Married!

MEDDLE. Now I shall have another chance. (*Turns his back on* YOUNG COURTLY *to have him kick him.*)

YOUNG COURTLY. I'll run and ascertain the truth of this from Dazzle. (*Exit L. into house.*)

MEDDLE. It's of no use; he either dare not kick me, or he can't afford it — in either case, he is beneath my notice. Ah! who comes here? — can it be Sir Harcourt Courtly himself? It can be no other.

    (*Enter* COOL *L.1.E.*)

Sir, I have the honour to bid you welcome to Oak Hall and the village of Oldborough.

COOL (*aside*). Excessively polite — sir, thank you.

MEDDLE. The township contains two thousand inhabitants.

COOL. Does it! I am delighted to hear it.

MEDDLE (*aside*). I can charge him for that — ahem — six and eightpence is not much — but it is a beginning. (*Aloud*) If you will permit me, I can inform you of the different commodities for which it is famous.

COOL. Much obliged — but here comes Sir Harcourt Courtly, my master, and Mr Harkaway — any other time I shall feel delighted.

MEDDLE. Oh! (*aside*) Mistook the man for the master. (*Retires up R.*)

    (*Enter* MAX *and* SIR HARCOURT *L.1.E.*)

MAX. Here we are at last. Now give ye welcome to Oak Hall, Sir Harcourt, heartily.

SIR HARCOURT (*languidly*). Cool, assist me.

    (COOL *takes off his cloak and gloves; gives him white gloves and handkerchief.*)

MAX. Why, you require unpacking as carefully as my best bin of port. Well, now you are decanted, tell me what did you think of my park as we came along.

SIR HARCOURT. That it would never come to an end. You said it was only a stone's throw from your infernal lodge to the house; why, it's ten miles, at least.

MAX. I'll do it in ten minutes any day.

SIR HARCOURT. Yes, in a steam carriage. Cool, perfume my handkerchief.

MAX. Don't do it. Don't! perfume in the country! Why, it's high treason in the very face of Nature; 'tis introducing the robbed to the robber. Here are the sweets from which your fulsome essences are pilfered, and libelled with their names; — don't insult them too.

    (MEDDLE *comes down C.*)

QUEEN MARGARET COLLEGE LIBRARY

SIR HARCOURT (*to* MEDDLE). Oh! cull me a bouquet, my man.

MAX (*turning*). Ah, Meddle! how are you? This is Lawyer Meddle.

SIR HARCOURT. Oh! I took him for one of your people.

MEDDLE. Ah! naturally — um — Sir Harcourt Courtly, I have the honour to congratulate — happy occasion approaches. Ahem! I have no hesitation in saying this very happy occasion approaches.

SIR HARCOURT. Cool, is the conversation addressed towards me?

COOL. I believe so, Sir Harcourt. (COOL *exits into house and returns immediately, having left* SIR HARCOURT'*s coat.*)

MEDDLE. Oh, certainly! I was complimenting you.

SIR HARCOURT. Sir, you are very good; the honour is undeserved; but I am only in the habit of receiving compliments from the fair sex. Men's admiration is so damnably insipid.

MEDDLE. I had hoped to make a unit on that occasion.

SIR HARCOURT. Yes, and you hoped to put an infernal number of cyphers after your unit on that and any other occasion.

MEDDLE. Ha! ha! very good. Why, I did hope to have the honour of drawing out the deed; for, whatever Jenks may say to the contrary, I have no hesitation in saying —

SIR HARCOURT (*putting him aside, crosses to* MAX). If the future Lady Courtly be visible at so unfashionable an hour as this, I shall beg to be introduced.

MAX. Visible! Ever since six this morning, I'll warrant ye. Two to one she is at dinner.

SIR HARCOURT. Dinner! Is it possible? Lady Courtly dines at half past one p.m.

MEDDLE. I rather prefer that hour to peck a little my —

SIR HARCOURT. Dear me! Who was addressing you?

MEDDLE. Oh, I beg pardon.

MAX. Here, James! (*Calling.*)

(*Enter* JAMES L. *from house.*)

Tell Miss Grace to come here directly.

(*Exit* JAMES L. *into house.*)

Now prepare, Courtly, for, though I say it, she is — with the exception of my bay mare, Kitty — the handsomest thing in the country. Considering she is a biped, she is a wonder! Full of blood, sound wind and limb, plenty of bone, sweet coat, in fine condition, with a thoroughbred step, as dainty as a pet greyhound.

SIR HARCOURT. Damme, don't compare her to a horse!

MAX. Well, I wouldn't, but she's almost as fine a creature — close similarities.

52

MEDDLE. Oh, very fine creature! Close similarity, amounting to identity.

SIR HARCOURT. Good gracious, sir! What can a lawyer know about a woman!

MEDDLE. Everything. The consistorial court is a fine study of the character, and I have no hesitation in saying that I have examined more women than Jenks, or —

SIR HARCOURT. Oh, damn Jenks. (*Crosses L.*)

MEDDLE. Sir, thank you. Damn him again, sir damn him again!
(*Enter* GRACE *L. from house.*)

GRACE. My dear uncle!

MAX. Ah, Grace, you little jade come here.

SIR HARCOURT (*eyeing her through his glass*). Oh, dear! she is a rural Venus! I'm astonished and delighted.

MAX. Won't you kiss your old uncle? (*Kisses her.*)

SIR HARCOURT (*draws an agonising face*). Oh! — ah — um! N'importe! — my privilege in embryo — hem! It's very tantalising, though.

MAX. You are not glad to see me, you are not.

SIR HARCOURT. Oh; no, no!
(*Aside*)
That is too much. I shall do something horrible presently, if this goes on.
(*Aloud*)
I should be sorry to curtail any little ebullition of affection but — ahem! May I be permitted?

MAX. Of course you may. There, Grace, is Sir Harcourt, your husband that will be. Go to him, girl.

SIR HARCOURT. Permit me to do homage to the charms, the presence of which have placed me in sight of Paradise.
(SIR HARCOURT *and* GRACE *retire.*)
(*Enter* DAZZLE *L. Crosses to* MAX *L.U.*)

DAZZLE. Ah! old fellow, how are you?
(MEDDLE *thinks that* DAZZLE *is speaking to him, steps between* DAZZLE *and* MAX *to shake hands — but* DAZZLE *pays no attention to him, and crosses and shakes* MAX *by the hand.*)

MAX. I'm glad to see you. Are you comfortably quartered yet, eh?

DAZZLE. Splendidly quartered! What a place you've got here! Here Hamilton.
(*Crosses to* YOUNG COURTLY, *and brings him down to* MAX *R.U.*)

(*Enter* YOUNG COURTLY *L. from house.*)

DAZZLE. Permit me to introduce my friend, Augustus Hamilton. Capital fellow! drinks like a sieve, and rides like a thunderstorm.

MAX. Sir, I'm devilish glad to see you — (*Up to him.*) Here, Sir Harcourt, permit me to introduce to you —

YOUNG COURTLY. The devil!

DAZZLE (*aside*). What's the matter?

YOUNG COURTLY (*aside*). Why, that is my governor, by Jupiter!

DAZZLE (*aside*). What, old Whiskers, you don't say that?

YOUNG COURTLY (*aside*). It is; what's to be done now?

MAX. Mr Augustus Hamilton, Sir Harcourt Courtly — Sir Harcourt Courtly, Mr Augustus Hamilton.

SIR HARCOURT. Hamilton! Good gracious! God bless me! Why, Charles, is it possible? — why, Max, that's my son.

YOUNG COURTLY (*aside*). What shall I do?

MAX. Your son?

GRACE. Your son, Sir Harcourt! have you a son as old as that gentleman?

SIR HARCOURT. No — that is — a yes, — not by twenty years — a — Charles, why don't you answer me, sir?

YOUNG COURTLY (*aside to* DAZZLE). What shall I say?

DAZZLE (*aside*). Deny your identity.

YOUNG COURTLY (*aside*). Capital! (*Aloud.*) What's the matter, sir?

SIR HARCOURT. How came you down here, sir?

YOUNG COURTLY. By one of Newman's best fours — in twelve hours and a quarter.

SIR HARCOURT. Isn't your name Charles Courtly?

YOUNG COURTLY. Not to my knowledge.

SIR HARCOURT. Do you mean to say that you are usually called Augustus Hamilton?

YOUNG COURTLY. Lamentable fact — and quite correct.

DAZZLE. How very sad.

SIR HARCOURT. Cool, is that my son?

(COOL *drops down L.*) (*Puts on a pair of eye glasses; looks at* YOUNG COURTLY *who makes a threatening gesture.* COOL *is undecided whether it is best to tell the truth or not, but a moment's pause concludes to keep* SIR HARCOURT *in the falsehood and says 'No, sir,' very boldly.*)

COOL. No, sir — it is not Mr Charles — but it is very like him. (*Retires up again.*)

DAZZLE. Cool is the best liar in London.

YOUNG COURTLY (YOUNG COURTLY *and* DAZZLE *cross to* SIR HARCOURT). Allow me to say, Sir what d'ye-call-'em Hartly —

SIR HARCOURT. Hartly, sir! Courtly, sir. Courtly!

YOUNG COURTLY. Well, Hartly, or Court-heart, or whatever your name may be, I say your conduct is a — a —, and were it not for the presence of this lady, I should feel inclined — to — to —
   (DAZZLE *and* YOUNG COURTLY *retire up R.*)

SIR HARCOURT. No, no, that can't be my son, — he never would address me in that way.

MAX (*coming down*). What is all this?

SIR HARCOURT. Sir —
   (YOUNG COURTLY *drops down R.*)
— your likeness to my son Charles is so astonishing, that it, for a moment — God bless me — the equilibrium of my etiquette — 'pon my life, I — permit me to request your pardon.

MEDDLE. Sir Harcourt, don't apologise, don't — bring an action. I'm witness.

SIR HARCOURT. Someone take this man away.
   (*Enter* JAMES *L. from house.*)

JAMES. Luncheon is on the table, sir.

SIR HARCOURT. Miss Harkaway, I never swore before a lady in my life — except when I promised to love and cherish the late Lady Courtly, which I took care to preface with an apology, I was compelled to the ceremony, and consequently not answerable for the language — but to that gentleman's identity I would have pledged — my hair.

GRACE (*aside*). If that security were called for, I suspect the answer would be — no effects.
   (*Exeunt* SIR HARCOURT *and* GRACE *L. into house.*)

MEDDLE (*to* MAX). I have something very particular to communicate.

MAX. Can't listen at present. (*Crosses to L.*)
   (*Exit L. into house.*)

MEDDLE (*to* DAZZLE *and* YOUNG COURTLY). I can afford you information, which I —

DAZZLE. Oh, don't bother! (*Crosses to L.*)   ⎫
YOUNG COURTLY. Go to the devil! (*Crosses to L.*) ⎬ (*Together.*)
   (*Exeunt L. into house.*)

MEDDLE. Now, I have no hesitation in saying that is the height of ingratitude. Oh — Mr Cool — can you oblige me? (*Presents his account.*)

COOL. Why, what is all this?

MEDDLE. Small account versus you — to giving information concerning the last census of the population of Oldborough and vicinity, six and eightpence.

COOL. Oh, you mean to make me pay for this, do you?

MEDDLE. Unconditionally.

COOL. Well, I have no objection — the charge is fair — but remember, I am a servant on board wages, will you throw in a little advice gratis — if I give you the money?

MEDDLE. Ahem! — I will.

COOL. A fellow has insulted me. I want to abuse him — what terms are actionable?

MEDDLE. You may call him anything you please, providing there are no witnesses.

COOL. Oh, may I? (*Looks round crosses to L.*) — then you rascally, pettifogging scoundrel!

MEDDLE. Hallo!

COOL. You mean — dirty — disgrace to your profession.

MEDDLE. Libel — slander —

COOL. Ay, but where are you witnesses?

MEDDLE. Give me the costs — six and eightpence.

COOL. I deny that you gave me information at all.

MEDDLE. You do!

COOL. Yes, where are you witnesses?

(*Exit L. into house.*)

MEDDLE. Ah — Jenks is at the bottom of this. I have no hesitation in saying and I say it boldly — Damn Jenks.

(*Exit L.*)

END OF ACT TWO

ACT THREE

A morning-room in Oak Hall, French windows, opening to the lawn. MAX *and* SIR HARCOURT *seated on one side,* DAZZLE *on the other;* GRACE *and* YOUNG COURTLY *playing chess at back. All dressed for dinner.*

MAX (*aside to* SIR HARCOURT). What can I do?

SIR HARCOURT. Get rid of them civilly.

MAX. What, turn them out, after I particularly invited them to stay a month or two?

SIR HARCOURT. Why, they are disreputable characters; as for that young fellow, in whom my Lady Courtly appears so particularly absorbed, — I am bewildered — I have written to town for my Charles, my boy — it certainly is the most extraordinary likeless —

DAZZLE. Sir Harcourt, I have an idea —

SIR HARCOURT. Sir, I am delighted to hear it. (*Aside to* MAX.) That fellow is a swindler.

MAX. I met him at your house. (*Goes up stage.*)

DAZZLE (*coming down* L. *of* SIR HARCOURT; *crossing to him*). I will bet you five to one that I can beat you three out of four games at billiards, with one hand.

SIR HARCOURT. No, sir.

DAZZLE. I don't mind giving you ten points in fifty.

SIR HARCOURT. Sir, I never gamble.

DAZZLE. You don't! Well, I'll teach you — easiest thing in life — you have every requisite — good temper.

SIR HARCOURT. I have not, sir.

DAZZLE. A long headed, knowing old buck.

SIR HARCOURT. Sir!

(*They go up conversing with* MAX C.)

GRACE. Really, Mr Hamilton, you improve. A young man pays us a visit as you half intimate, to escape inconvenient friends — that is complimentary to us, his hosts.

57

YOUNG COURTLY. Nay, that is too severe.

GRACE. After an acquaintanceship of two days, you sit down to teach me chess and domestic economy at the same time. Might I ask where you graduated in that science — where you learned all that store of matrimonial advice which you have obliged me with?

YOUNG COURTLY. I imbibed it, madam, from the moment I beheld you, and having studied my subject con amore, took my degrees from your eyes.

GRACE. Oh, I see you are a Master of Arts already.

YOUNG COURTLY. Unfortunately, no — I shall remain a bachelor — till you can assist me to that honour.

(SIR HARCOURT *comes down — aside to* DAZZLE.)

Keep the old boy away.

DAZZLE (*aside*). How do you get on?

(*Drops down on* YOUNG COURTLY *R.U.*)

YOUNG COURTLY (*aside*). Splendidly!

SIR HARCOURT. Is the conversation strictly confidential — or might I join you?

(SIR HARCOURT *dropping down on* YOUNG COURTLY's *R.* DAZZLE *steps between him and* YOUNG COURTLY *and takes him down stage.*)

DAZZLE (*taking his arm*). Oh, not in the least, my dear sir — we were remarking that rifle shooting was an excellent diversion during the summer months.

SIR HARCOURT (*drawing himself up*). Sir, I was addressing —

DAZZLE. And I was saying what a pity it was I couldn't find anyone reasonable enough to back his opinion with long odds — come out on the lawn, and pitch up your hat, and I will hold you ten to one I put a bullet into it every time, at forty paces.

SIR HARCOURT. No, sir, I consider you —

MAX. Here, all of you — look, here is Lady Gay Spanker coming across the lawn at a hand gallop.

(*Up centre looking off R.U.E.*)

SIR HARCOURT (*running to the window*). Bless me, the horse is running away!

MAX. Look how she takes that fence! There's a seat.

SIR HARCOURT. Lady Gay Spanker — who may she be?

GRACE. Gay Spanker, Sir Harcourt? My cousin and dearest friend — you must like her.

SIR HARCOURT. It will be my devoir, since it is your wish — though it will be a hard task in your presence.

GRACE. I am sure she will like you.

SIR HARCOURT. Ha! ha! I flatter myself.

YOUNG COURTLY. Who, and what is she?
(All coming down.)

GRACE. Glee, glee, made a living thing — Nature, in some frolic mood, shut up a merry devil in her eye, and spiting Art, stole joy's brightest harmony to thrill her laugh, which peals out sorrow's knell. Her cry rings loudest in the field — the very echo loves it best, and as each hill attempts to ape her voice, Earth seems to laugh that it made a thing so glad.

MAX. Ay, the merriest minx I ever kissed.
(LADY GAY laughs without R.U.E.)

LADY GAY *(without)*. Max!

MAX. Come in, you mischievous puss.
(Enter JAMES R.U.E.)

JAMES. Mr Adolphus and Lady Gay Spanker. *(Exit R.U.E.)*
(Enter LADY GAY R.U.E. fully equipped in riding habit, &c.)

LADY GAY. Ha! ha! Well, governor, how are ye? I have been down five times, climbing up your stairs in my long clothes. How are you, Grace, dear? *(Kisses her.)* There, don't fidget, Max. And there — *(Kisses him.)* — there's one for you.

SIR HARCOURT. Ahem!

LADY GAY. Oh, gracious, I didn't see you had visitors.

MAX. Permit me to introduce — Sir Harcourt Courtly, Lady Gay Spanker. Mr Dazzle, Mr Hamilton — Lady Gay Spanker.

SIR HARCOURT *(aside)*. A devilish fine woman!

DAZZLE *(aside to SIR HARCOURT)*. She's a devilish fine woman.

LADY GAY. You mustn't think anything of the liberties I take with my old papa here — bless him!

SIR HARCOURT. Oh, no!
(Aside.) I only thought I should like to be in his place.

DAZZLE *(aside to SIR HARCOURT)*. Would you, — would you, would you?

LADY GAY. I am so glad you have come, Sir Harcourt. Now we shall be able to make a decent figure at the heels of a hunt.

SIR HARCOURT. Does your Ladyship hunt?

LADY GAY. Ha! I say, Governor, does my Ladyship hunt? I rather flatter myself that I do hunt! Why, Sir Harcourt, one might as well live without laughing as without hunting. Man was fashioned expressly to fit a horse. Are not hedges and ditches created for leaps? Of course! And I look upon foxes to be one of the most blessed dispensations of a benign Providence.

SIR HARCOURT. Yes, it is all very well in the abstract; I tried it once.

LADY GAY. Once! Only once?

SIR HARCOURT. Once, only once. And then the animal ran away with me.

LADY GAY. Why, you would not have him walk?

SIR HARCOURT. Finding my society disagreeable, he instituted a series of kicks, with a view to removing the annoyance; but aided by the united stays of the mane and tail, I frustrated his intentions.

(*All laugh.*)

His next resource, however, was more effectual, for he succeeded in rubbing me off against a tree.

MAX & LADY GAY. Ha! ha! ha!

DAZZLE. How absurd you must have looked with your legs and arms in the air, like a shipwrecked tea-table.

SIR HARCOURT. Sir, I never looked absurd in my life.

(*Omnes laugh.*)

Ah, it may be very amusing in relation, I dare say, but very unpleasant in effect.

LADY GAY. I pity you, Sir Harcourt; it was criminal in your parents to neglect your education so shamefully.

SIR HARCOURT. Possibly; but be assured, I shall never break my neck awkwardly from a horse, when it might be accomplished with less trouble from a bedroom window.

YOUNG COURTLY (*aside*). My dad will be caught by this she Bucephalus-tamer.

MAX (*to* SIR HARCOURT). You must leave your town habits in the smoke of London; here we rise with the lark.

SIR HARCOURT. Haven't the remotest conception when that period is.

GRACE. The man that misses sunrise loses the sweetest part of his existence.

SIR HARCOURT. Oh, pardon me; I have seen sunrise frequently after a ball, or from the windows of my travelling carriage, and I always considered it disagreeable.

GRACE. I love to watch the first tear that glistens in the opening eye of morning, the silent song the flowers breathe, the thrilling choir of the woodland minstrels, to which the modest brook trickles applause; these swelling out the sweetest chord of sweet creation's matins, seem to pour some soft and merry tale into the daylight's ear, as if the waking world had dreamed a happy thing, and now smiled o'er the telling of it.

SIR HARCOURT. The effect of a rustic education! Who could ever discover music in a damp foggy morning, except those

confounded waits, who never play in tune, and a miserable
wretch who makes a point of crying coffee under my window
just as I am persuading myself to sleep; in fact, I never heard
any music worth listening to, except in Italy.

LADY GAY. No? then you never heard a well-trained English
pack in full cry?

SIR HARCOURT. Full cry!

LADY GAY. Ah! there is harmony, if you will. Give me the
trumpet-neigh; the spotted pack just catching scent. What a
chorus is their yelp! The view-hallo, blent with a peal of free
and fearless mirth! That's our old English music, — match it
where you can.

SIR HARCOURT (*aside*). I must see about Lady Gay Spanker.

DAZZLE (*aside to* SIR HARCOURT). Ah, would you —

LADY GAY. Time then appears as young as love, and plumes as
swift as a wing. Away we go! The earth flies back to aid our
course! Horse, man, hound, earth, heaven! — all — all — one
piece of glowing ecstasy! Then I love the world, myself, and
every living thing, my jocund soul cries out for very glee, as it
could wish that all creation had but one mouth, that I might
kiss it!

SIR HARCOURT (*aside*). I wish I were the mouth!

MAX. Ah! Sir Harcourt, had you been here a month ago, you
would have witnessed the most glorious run that ever swept
over merry England's green cheek — a steeplechase, sir, which
I intended to win, but my horse broke down the day before. I
had a chance, notwithstanding, and but for Gay here, I should
have won. How I regretted my abscence from it! How did my
filly behave herself, Gay?

LADY GAY. Gloriously, Max! gloriously! There were sixteen horses
in the field, all mettle to the bone; the start was a picture — away
we went in a cloud — pell-mell — helter-skelter — the fools first,
as usual, using themselves up — we soon passed them — first,
your Kitty, then my Blueskin, and Craven's colt last. Then came
the tug — Kitty skimmed the walls — Blueskin flew over the
fences — the colt neck-and-neck, and half a mile to run — at
last the colt baulked a leap and went wild. Kitty and I had it all
to ourselves — she was three lengths ahead as we breasted the
last wall, six feet, if an inch, and a ditch on the other side. Now,
for the first time, I gave Blueskin his head — ha! ha! Away he
flew like a thunderbolt — over went the filly — I over the same
spot, leaving Kitty in the ditch — walked the steeple, eight miles
in thirty minutes, and scarcely turned a hair.

ALL. Bravo! Bravo!

LADY GAY. Do you hun.?

DAZZLE. Hunt! I belong to a hunting family. I was born on horse-back.

MAX. Why, we will regenerate you, Baronet!

DAZZLE. Yes, we will regenerate you Baronet.
(*Slapping* SIR HARCOURT *on the shoulder, which makes him very much annoyed*.)

MAX. But Gay, where is your husband? Where is Adolphus?

LADY GAY. Bless me, where is my Dolly?

SIR HARCOURT. You are married, then?

LADY GAY. I have a husband somewhere, though I can't find him just now. Dolly, dear!
(*Aside to* MAX.) Governor, at home I always whistle when I want him.
(*Enter* SPANKER *R.U.E.*)

SPANKER. Here I am — did you call me, Gay?

SIR HARCOURT (*eyeing him*). Is that your husband?

LADY GAY (*aside*). Yes, bless his stupid face, that's my Dolly.

MAX. Permit me to introduce you to Sir Harcourt Courtly.
(SPANKER *appears frightened. Repeats speech after* GAY, *sentence by sentence as she does*.)

LADY GAY. Delighted to have the honour of making the ac-quaintance of a gentleman so highly celebrated in the world of fashion. That will do stupid.
(SPANKER *gets quite confused, draws on his glove, and tears it.*)

LADY GAY. Where have you been, Dolly?

SPANKER. Sitting on the dog house outside.

MAX. Why did you not come in?

SPANKER. I'm sure I didn't — I don't exactly know, but I thought as — perhaps — I can't remember.

DAZZLE. Shall we have the pleasure of your company to dinner?

SPANKER. I always dine at dinner — that is, unless Gay remains —

LADY GAY. Stay dinner, of course; we came on purpose to stop three or four days with you.

GRACE. Will you excuse my absence, Gay? (*Crosses to L.*)

MAX. What! What! Where are you going? What takes you away?

GRACE. We must postpone the dinner till Gay is dressed.

MAX. Oh, never mind, — stay where you are.

GRACE. No, I must go.

MAX. I say you shan't! I will be king in my own house.

GRACE. Do, my dear uncle; — you shall be king, and I'll be your

62

prime minister, — that is, I'll rule, and you shall have the honour of taking the consequences.

(SIR HARCOURT *is about to offer his arm to* GRACE, *when* DAZZLE *intercepts and hands her off, then returns and makes* SIR HARCOURT *a very polite bow.*)

(*Exit* GRACE *L.I.E.*)

MAX. Come Gay, dress for dinner.

SIR HARCOURT. Permit me, Lady Gay Spanker.

LADY GAY. With pleasure — what do you want? (*Crosses L. and turns round.*)

SIR HARCOURT. To escort you.

LADY GAY. Oh, never mind, I can escort myself, thank you, and Dolly too; come, dear! (*Exit L.I.E.*)

SIR HARCOURT. Au revoir!

SPANKER. Eh?

SIR HARCOURT. Au revoir!

SPANKER. Thank you, I never do before dinner. (*Exit awkwardly L.I.E.*)

SIR HARCOURT. What an ill-assorted pair!

MAX. Not a bit! She married him for freedom, and she has it; he married her for protection, and he has it.

SIR HARCOURT. How he ever summoned courage to propose to her, I can't guess.

MAX. Bless you, he never did. She proposed to him. She says he would if he could; but as he couldn't, she did it for him.

(*Exeunt laughing L.U.E.*)

(*Enter* COOL *with a letter R.U.E.*)

COOL. Mr Charles, I have been watching to find you alone. Sir Harcourt has written to town for you.

YOUNG COURTLY. The devil he has!

COOL. He expects you down tomorrow evening.

DAZZLE. Oh! He'll be punctual. A thought strikes me.

YOUNG COURTLY. Pooh! Confound your thoughts! I can think of nothing but the idea of leaving Grace, at the very moment when I had established the most —

DAZZLE. What if I can prevent her marriage with your Governor?

YOUNG COURTLY. Impossible!

DAZZLE. He's pluming himself for the conquest of Lady Gay Spanker. It will not be difficult to make him believe she accedes to his suit. And if she would but join in the plan —

YOUNG COURTLY. I see it all. And do you think she would?

DAZZLE. I mistake my game, if she would not.

COOL. Here comes Sir Harcourt.

DAZZLE. I'll begin with him. Retire, and watch how I'll open the campaign for you.

(YOUNG COURTLY *and* COOL *retire*.)

(*Enter* SIR HARCOURT *L.U.E.*)

SIR HARCOURT. Here is that cursed fellow again.

DAZZLE. Ah, my dear old friend! (*About to take his hand*.)

SIR HARCOURT. Mr Dazzle!

DAZZLE. I have a secret of importance to disclose to you. Are you a man of honour? Hush! don't speak; you are. It is with the greatest pain I am compelled to request you as a gentleman, that you will shun studiously the society of Lady Gay Spanker.

SIR HARCOURT. Good gracious! Wherefore, and by what right do you make such a demand?

DAZZLE. Why, I am distantly related to the Spankers.

SIR HARCOURT. Why, damme, sir, if you don't appear to be related to every family in Great Britain!

DAZZLE. A good many of the nobility claim me as a connection. But, to return — she is much struck with your address; evidently, she laid herself out for display —

SIR HARCOURT. Ha! you surprise me!

DAZZLE. To entangle you.

SIR HARCOURT. Ha! ha! why, it did appear like it.

DAZZLE. You will spare her for my sake; give her no encouragement; if disgrace come upon my relatives, the Spankers, I should never hold up my head again.

SIR HARCOURT (*aside*). I shall achieve an easy conquest, and a glorious. Ha! ha! I never remarked it before, but this is a gentleman.

DAZZLE. May I rely on your generosity?

SIR HARCOURT. Faithfully. (*Shakes his hand*.) Sir, I honour and esteem you; but, might I ask, how came you to meet our friend, Max Harkaway, in my house in Belgrave Square?

(*Re-enter* YOUNG COURTLY *R.U.E. sits on chair R.U.*)

DAZZLE. Certainly. I had an acceptance of your son's for one hundred pounds.

SIR HARCOURT (*astonished*). Of my son's? Impossible!

DAZZLE. Ah, sir, fact! he paid a debt for a poor unfortunate man — fifteen children — half a dozen wives — the devil knows what all.

SIR HARCOURT. Simple boy!

DAZZLE. Innocent youth, I have no doubt; when you have the hundred convenient, I shall feel delighted.

SIR HARCOURT. Oh! Follow me to my room, and if you have the

document, it will be happiness to me to pay it. Poor Charles! good heart!

DAZZLE. Oh, a splendid heart. Fine liver, I dare say.

(*Exit* SIR HARCOURT *L.U.E.*)

Come here; splendid heart, write me the bill.

YOUNG COURTLY. What for?

DAZZLE. What for? why, to release the unfortunate man and his family, to be sure, from jail.

YOUNG COURTLY. Who is he?

DAZZLE. Yourself.

YOUNG COURTLY. But I haven't fifteen children?

DAZZLE. Will you take your oath of that?

YOUNG COURTLY. Nor four wives.

DAZZLE. More shame for you, with all that family. Come, don't be obstinate; write and date it back.

YOUNG COURTLY. Ay, but where is the stamp?

DAZZLE. Here they are, of all patterns. (*Pulls out a pocket-book.*) I keep them ready drawn in case of necessity, all but the date and acceptance. Now, if you are in an autographic humour, you can try how your signature will look across half a dozen of them; there — write — exactly — you know the place — across good — and thank your lucky stars that you have found a friend at last, that gives you money and advice. (*Takes paper and exits L.U.E.*)

YOUNG COURTLY. Things are approaching to a climax; I must appear in propria persona — and immediately — but I must first ascertain what are the real sentiments of this riddle of a woman. Does she love me? I flatter myself — by Jove — here she comes — I shall never have such an opportunity again!

(*Retires up stage and comes down L.U. after* GRACE *enters.*)

(*Enter* GRACE *L. sits on ottoman.*)

GRACE. I wish I had never seen Mr Hamilton. Why does every object appear robbed of the charm it once presented to me? Why do I shudder at the contemplation of this marriage, which, till now, was to me a subject of indifference? Am I in love? In love! if I am, my past life has been the word of raising up a pedestal to place my own folly on — I — the infidel — the railer!

YOUNG COURTLY. Meditating upon matrimony, madam?

GRACE (*aside*). He little thinks he was the subject of my meditations! (*Aloud.*) No.

(*Rising.*)

YOUNG COURTLY (*aside*). I must unmask my battery now.

65

GRACE (*aside*). How foolish I am — he will perceive that I tremble — I must appear at ease.
  (*A pause.*)
YOUNG COURTLY. Eh? ah! um!
GRACE. Ah!
  (*They sink into silence again. Aside.*)
  How very awkward!
YOUNG COURTLY (*aside*). It is a very difficult subject to begin.
  (*Aloud.*) Madam — ahem — there was — is I mean I was about to remark — a —
  (*Aside.*) Hang me if it is not a very slippery subject. I must brush up my faculties; attack her in her own way.
  (*Aloud.*) Sing! oh, muse!
  (*Aside.*) Why, I have made love before to a hundred women!
GRACE (*aside*). I wish I had something to do, for I have nothing to say.
YOUNG COURTLY. Madam — there is — a subject — frate with fraught, no, no, no, so fraught — fraught with fate to my future life, that you must pardon my lack of delicacy should a too hasty expression mar the fervent courtesy of its intent. To you, I feel aware, I must appear in the light of a comparative stranger.
GRACE (*aside*). I know what's coming.
YOUNG COURTLY. Of you — I know perhaps too much —
  (*Pause.*)
GRACE. Eh!
YOUNG COURTLY. For my own peace.
GRACE (*aside*). He is in love.
YOUNG COURTLY. I forget all that befell before I saw your beauteous self; I seem born — born — born —
  (GRACE *turns toward him.*)
  Well Madam, I was born into another world — my nature changed — the beams of that bright face falling on my soul, have, from its chaos, warmed into life the flowrets of affection, whose maiden odours now float toward the clouds — the clouds — damme I am in the clouds myself, the sun, pouring forth on their pure tongue a mite of adoration, midst the voices of a universe. (*Aside.*) That's something in her own style.
GRACE. Mr Hamilton!
YOUNG COURTLY. You cannot feel surprised —
GRACE. I am more than surprised.
  (*Aside.*) I am delighted.
YOUNG COURTLY. Do not speak so coldly.

GRACE. You have offended me.

YOUNG COURTLY. Say, when a man throws his feet at your head, I mean when he throws his head at your feet, no I mean when he throws his heart at your feet. No, madam, no woman, whatever her state, can be offended by the adoration even of the meanest; it is myself whom I have offended and deceived — but still I ask your pardon.

GRACE (*aside*). Oh! he thinks I am refusing him.

(*Aloud.*) I am not exactly offended, but —

YOUNG COURTLY. Consider my position — a few days — and an insurmountable barrier would have placed you beyond my wildest hopes — I would have been your mother, no, no, no, I would have been your father, no, no, no, you would have been my mother — you would have been my mother.

GRACE. I should have been your mother!

(*Aside.*) I thought so.

YOUNG COURTLY. No — that is, I meant Sir Harcourt Courtly's bride.

GRACE (*with great emphasis*). Never!

YOUNG COURTLY. How! never! may I then hope? — you turn away — you would not lacerate me by a refusal?

GRACE (*aside*). How stupid he is!

(*Turns her back on him and puts her hand behind her for him to take it.* YOUNG COURTLY *is bewildered and does not seem to comprehend until she says 'Unhand me sir!'*)

YOUNG COURTLY. Still silent! I thank you, Miss Grace — I ought to have expected this — fool that I have been — one course alone remains — farewell!

GRACE (*aside*). Now he's going.

YOUNG COURTLY. Farewell forever! (*Sits.*) Will you not speak one word? I shall leave this house immediately — I shall not see you again. I am going — going — gone!

GRACE. Unhand me, sir, I insist.

YOUNG COURTLY (*aside*). Oh! what an ass I've been! (*Rushes up to her and seizes her hand.*) Release this hand! Never! never! (*Kissing it.*) Never will I quit this hand! it shall be my companion in misery — in solitude — when you are far away.

GRACE. Oh! should anyone come!

(*Drops her handkerchief, he stoops to pick it up, and puts it in his breast for business next scene.*)

For heaven's sake do not kneel.

YOUNG COURTLY (*kneels*). Forever thus prostrate before my soul's saint, I will lead a pious life of eternal adoration.

GRACE. Should we be discovered thus — pray, Mr Hamilton — pray — pray.

YOUNG COURTLY. Pray! I am praying; what more can I do?

GRACE. Your conduct is shameful.

YOUNG COURTLY. It is. (*Rises.*)

GRACE. And if I do not scream; it is not for your sake — that — but it might alarm the family.

YOUNG COURTLY. It might — it would. Say, am I wholly indifferent to you? I entreat one word — I implore you — do not withdraw your hand — (*She snatches it away — he puts his around her waist.*) You smile.

GRACE. Leave me, dear Mr Hamilton!

YOUNG COURTLY. Dear! Then I am dear to you; that word once more; say — say you love me!

GRACE. Is that fair?

(*He catches her in his arms and kisses her. He turns for the moment to the left as* LADY GAY *enters.* GRACE *on seeing* LADY GAY *enter runs off R.* YOUNG COURTLY *turns as if to speak to* GRACE, *and discovers his mistake, and is embarrassed for the moment.*)

(*Enter* LADY GAY *L.U.E.*)

LADY GAY. Ha! oh!

GRACE. Gay! destruction! (*Exits R.I.E.*)

YOUNG COURTLY. Fisgig! The devil!

LADY GAY. Don't mind me — pray, don't let me be any interruption!

YOUNG COURTLY. I was just —

LADY GAY. Yes, I see you were.

YOUNG COURTLY. Oh! madam, how could you mar my bliss in the very ecstasy of its fulfilment?

LADY GAY. I always like to be in at the death. Never drop your ears; bless you, she is only a little fresh — give her her head, and she will outrun herself.

YOUNG COURTLY. Possibly, but what am I to do?

LADY GAY. Keep your seat.

YOUNG COURTLY. But in a few days she will take a leap that must throw me — she marries Sir Harcourt Courtly.

LADY GAY. Why, that is awkward, certainly; but you can challenge him, and shoot him.

YOUNG COURTLY. Unfortunately, that is out of the question.

LADY GAY. How so?

YOUNG COURTLY. You will not betray a secret, if I inform you?

LADY GAY. All right — what is it?

68

YOUNG COURTLY. I am his son.

LADY GAY. What — his son? But he does not know you?

YOUNG COURTLY. No. I met him here by chance, and faced it out, I never saw him before in my life.

LADY GAY. Beautiful! — I see it all — you're in love with your mother, that should be — your wife, that will be.

YOUNG COURTLY. Now, I think I could distance the old gentleman, if you will but lend us your assistance.

LADY GAY. I will in anything.

YOUNG COURTLY. You must know then, that my father, Sir Harcourt, has fallen desperately in love with you.

LADY GAY. With me! — (*Utters a scream of delight.*) That is delicious!

YOUNG COURTLY. Now, if you only could —

LADY GAY. Could! — I will. Ha! ha! I see my cue, I'll cross his scent, I'll draw him after me. Ho! ho! won't I make love to him? Ha!

YOUNG COURTLY. The only objection might be Mr Spanker who might —

LADY GAY. No, he mightn't, he 'as no objection. Bless him, he's an inestimable little character — you don't know him as well as I do, I dare say — ha! ha! (*Dinner bell rings.*) Here they come to dinner. I'll commence my operations on your governor immediately. Ha! ha! how I shall enjoy it!

YOUNG COURTLY. Be guarded!

(*Enter* MAX HARKAWAY, SIR HARCOURT, DAZZLE, GRACE. GRACE *comes from R.I.E. where she went off, and* SPANKER *L.U.E.*)

MAX. Now gentlemen — Sir Harcourt, do you lead Grace.

LADY GAY. I believe Sir Harcourt is engaged to me. (*Takes his arm.*)

MAX. Well, please yourselves.

(*They file out,* MAX *first,* YOUNG COURTLY *and* GRACE, SIR HARCOURT *coquetting with* LADY GAY, *leaving* DAZZLE *who offers his arm to* SPANKER, *which he does not succeed in getting, but endeavours to, till he gets off L.U.E.*)

END OF ACT THREE

ACT FOUR

A handsome drawing-room in Oak Hall, chandeliers, tables with books, drawings, &c. GRACE *and* LADY GAY *discovered.*

GRACE. If there be one habit more abominable than another, it is that of the gentlemen sitting over their wine; it is a selfish, unfeeling fashion, and a gross insult to our sex.

LADY GAY. We are turned out just when the fun begins. How happy the poor wretches look at the contemplation of being rid of us.

GRACE. The conventional signal for the ladies to withdraw, is anxiously and deliberately waited for.

LADY GAY. Then I begin to wish I were a man.

GRACE. The instant the door is closed upon us, there rises a roar!

LADY GAY. In celebration of their short-lived liberty, my love; rejoicing over their emancipation.

GRACE. I think it very insulting, whatever it may be.

LADY GAY. Ah! my dear; philosophers say that man is the creature of an hour — it is the dinner hour, I suppose.
　　(*Loud noise. Cries of 'A song, a song'.*)

GRACE. I am afraid they are getting too pleasant to be agreeable.

LADY GAY. I hope the squire will restrict himself; after his third bottle he becomes rather voluminous. (*Cries of 'Silence'.*) Someone is going to sing. (*Jumps up.*) Let us hear!
　　(SPANKER *is heard to sing.*)

GRACE. Oh, no, Gay, for heaven's sake!

LADY GAY. Oho! ha! ha! why, that is my Dolly.
　　(*At the conclusion of the verse.*) Well, I never heard my Dolly sing before! I hope I never shall again. Happy wretches, how I envy them!
　　(*Enter* JAMES *L.I.E. with a note.*)

JAMES. Mr Hamilton has just left the house for London.

GRACE. Impossible! — that is, without seeing — that is —

LADY GAY. Ha! ha!

GRACE. He never — speak, sir!

JAMES. He left, Miss Grace, in a desperate hurry, and this note, I believe for you. (*Presenting a note on a salver.*)

GRACE. For me! (*About to snatch it but restraining herself, takes it coolly. Exit* JAMES.)

(*Reads.*) 'Your manner during dinner has left me no alternative but instant departure; my absence will release you from the oppression which my society must necessarily inflict on your sensitive mind. It may tend also to smother, though it can never extinguish, that indomitable passion, of which I am the passive victim. Dare I supplicate pardon and oblivion for the past? It is the last request of the self-deceived, but still loving.

'Augustus Hamilton.'

    (*Puts her hand to her forehead and appears giddy.*)

LADY GAY. Hallo, Grace! what's the matter?

GRACE (*recovering herself*). Nothing — the heat of the room.

LADY GAY. Oh! what excuse does he make? particular unforeseen business, I suppose?

GRACE. Why, yes — a mere formula — a — a — you may put it in the fire. (*Puts it in her bosom.*)

LADY GAY (*aside*). It is near enough to the fire where it is.

GRACE. I'm glad he's gone.

LADY GAY. So am I.

GRACE. He was a disagreeable, ignorant person.

LADY GAY. Yes; and so vulgar!

GRACE. No, he was not at all vulgar.

LADY GAY. I mean in appearance.

GRACE. Oh! how can you say so; he was very distingué.

LADY GAY. Well, I might have been mistaken, but I took him for a forward intrusive —

GRACE. Good gracious, Gay! he was very retiring — even shy.

LADY GAY (*aside*). It's all right. She is in love, blows hot and cold in the same breath.

GRACE. How can you be a competent judge? Why, you have not known him more than a few hours, — while I — I —

LADY GAY. Have known him two days and a quarter? I yield — I confess, I never was, or will be so intimate with him as you appeared to be! Ha! ha!

    (*Loud noise of argument. The folding doors are thrown open. Enter L.U.E. the whole party of gentlemen, apparently engaged in warm discussion.* MAX, SIR HARCOURT, DAZZLE *and* SPANKER, *together.*)

DAZZLE. But, my dear sir, consider the position of the two countries, under such a constitution.

SIR HARCOURT. The two countries! What have they to do with the subject?

MAX. Everything. Look at their two legislative bodies.

SPANKER. Ay, look at their two legs and bodies.

SIR HARCOURT. Why, it would inevitably establish universal anarchy and confusion.

GRACE. I think they are pretty well established already.

SPANKER. Well, suppose it did, what has anarchy and contusion to do with it?

LADY GAY. Do look at my Dolly; he is arguing — talking politics 'pon my fate he is. (*Calling.*) Mr Spanker, my dear!

SPANKER. Excuse me, love, I am discussing a point of importance.

LADY GAY. Oh, that is delicious; he must discuss that to me. (*She goes up and leads him down, he appears to have shaken off his gaucherie, she shakes her head.*) Dolly! Dolly!

SPANKER. Pardon me, Lady Gay Spanker, I conceive your mutilation of my sponsorial appellation derogatory to my amour propre.

LADY GAY. Your what? Ho! ho!

SPANKER. And I particularly request that, for the future, I may not be treated with that cavalier spirit which does not become your sex nor your station, your ladyship.

LADY GAY. You have been indulging till you have lost the little wit nature dribbled into your unfortunate little head — your brains want the whipper-in — you are not yourself.

SPANKER. Madam, I am doubly myself; and permit me to inform you, that unless you voluntarily pay obedience to my commands, I shall enforce them.

LADY GAY. Your commands!

SPANKER. Yes, madam; I mean to put a full stop to your hunting.

LADY GAY. You do! ah!

(*Aside.*) I can scarcely speak from delight. (*Aloud.*) Who put such an idea into your head, for I am sure it is not an original emanation of your genius?

SPANKER. Sir Harcourt Courtly, my friend, and now, mark me! I request, for your own sake, that I may not be compelled to assert my a — my authority, as your husband. I shall say no more than this — if you persist in your absurd rebellion —

LADY GAY. Well!

SPANKER. Contemplate a separation. (*Looks at her haughtily and retires.*)

LADY GAY. Now, I'm happy! My own little darling, inestimable Dolly, has tumbled into a spirit, somehow. Sir Harcourt, too! Ha! ha! he's trying to make him ill-treat me, so that his own suit may thrive.

SIR HARCOURT (*advances*). Lady Gay?

LADY GAY. Now for it.

SIR HARCOURT. What hours of misery were those I passed, when, by your secession, the room suffered a total eclipse.

LADY GAY. Ah! you flatter.

SIR HARCOURT. No, pardon me, that were impossible. No, believe me, I tried to join in the boisterous mirth, but my thoughts would desert to the drawing-room. Ah! how I envied the careless levity and cool indifference with which Mr Spanker enjoyed your absence.

DAZZLE (*who is lounging in a chair*). Max, that Madeira is worth its weight in gold; I hope you have more of it.

MAX. A pipe, I think.

DAZZLE. I consider a magnum of that nectar, and a meerschaum of Canaster to consummate the ultimatum of all mundane bliss. To drown myself in liquid ecstasy, and then blow a cloud on which the enfranchised soul could soar above Olympus. Oh!
    (*Enter* JAMES *R.U.E.*)

JAMES. Mr Charles Courtly! (*Exit L.I.E.*)

SIR HARCOURT. Ah, now, Max, you must see a living apology for my conduct.
    (*Enter* YOUNG COURTLY *dressed very plain R.U.E.*)
Well, Charles, how are you? Don't be afraid. Here, Max, what do you say now?

MAX. Well, this is the most extraordinary likeness.

GRACE (*aside*). Yes — considering it is the original. I am not so easily deceived!

MAX. Sir, I am delighted to see you. (*Crosses to* YOUNG COURTLY *and goes up stage.*)

YOUNG COURTLY. Thank you, sir.

DAZZLE. Will you be kind enough to introduce me, Sir Harcourt?

SIR HARCOURT. This is Mr Dazzle, Charles.

YOUNG COURTLY. Which —
    (DAZZLE *crosses from R. corner and gives* YOUNG COURTLY *a knowing dig in the side, and then* DOLLY *repeats the business in an exaggerated manner.*)
    (YOUNG COURTLY *looking from* SPANKER *to* DAZZLE.)

SIR HARCOURT (*to* LADY GAY). Is not that refreshing? Miss Harkaway — Charles, this is your mother, or rather will be.

(LADY GAY *steps down unintentionally between* YOUNG COURTLY *and* GRACE *at the introduction.*)

YOUNG COURTLY. Madam, I shall love, honour, and obey you punctually. (*Discovers that he is speaking to* LADY GAY, *is embarrassed for the moment, then crosses to* GRACE.) Madam, I shall love, honour and obey you punctually. (*Takes out a book, sighs, and goes up reading.*)

(GRACE *gets round to L. after introduction.*)

(*Enter* JAMES *L.I.E.*)

SIR HARCOURT. You perceive? Quite unused to society — perfectly ignorant of every conventional rule of life.

JAMES. The Doctor and the young ladies have arrived.

(DAZZLE *takes* SPANKER *by the arm and exits him off L.I.E. crossing the stage from R. to L.*)

MAX. The young ladies — now we must to the ball — I make it a rule always to commence the festivities with a good old country dance — a rattling Sir Roger de Coverly; come, Sir Harcourt.

SIR HARCOURT. Does this antiquity require a war-whoop in it?

MAX. Nothing but a nimble foot and a light heart.

SIR HARCOURT. Very antediluvian indispensables! Lady Gay Spanker, will you honour me by becoming my preceptor?

LADY GAY. Why, I am engaged — but — (*Aloud.*) on such a plea as Sir Harcourt's, I must waive all obstacles.

MAX. Now, Grace, girl — give your hand to Mr Courtly.

GRACE. Pray, excuse me, uncle — I have a headache.

SIR HARCOURT (*aside*). Jealousy! by the gods — Jealous of my devotions at another's fane! (*Aloud.*) Charles my boy! amuse Miss Grace during our absence.

(*Exit with* LADY GAY *L.I.E.*)

MAX. But don't you dance, Mr Courtly?

YOUNG COURTLY. Dance, sir! — I never dance — I can procure exercise in a much more rational manner — and music disturbs my meditations.

MAX. Well, do the gallant.

YOUNG COURTLY. I never studied that Art — but I have a Prize Essay on a Hydrostatic subject, which would delight her — for it enchanted the Reverend Doctor Pump, of Corpus Christi.

MAX. Oh, Pump! (*Exit* MAX *L.U.E.*)

GRACE (*aside*). What on earth could have induced him to disguise himself in that frightful way — I rather suspect some plot to entrap me into a confession.

YOUNG COURTLY (*aside*). Dare I confess this trick to her? No! Not until I have proved her affection indisputably. Let me see — I must concoct. (*Takes a chair, and forgetting his assumed character, is about to take his natural free manner.* GRACE *looks surprised. He turns abashed.*) Madam, I have been desired to amuse you.

GRACE. Thank you.

YOUNG COURTLY. The labour we delight in, physics pain. I will draw you a moral, ahem! Subject, the effects of inebriety! — which, according to Ben Jonson — means perplexion of the intellects, caused by imbibing spirituous liquors. About an hour before my arrival, I passed an appalling evidence of the effects of this state — a carriage was overthrown — horses killed — gentleman in a hopeless state, with his neck broken — in several places — all occasioned by the intoxication of the post-boy.

(*Business of pocket handkerchief.* YOUNG COURTLY *takes handkerchief out of his pocket, which he picked up from off stage in the previous act in which he had a scene with* GRACE, *and wipes his eyes, in so doing* GRACE *discovers that it is her handkerchief, he sees the discovery immediately and puts it under him quick as possible.*)

GRACE. That is very amusing.

YOUNG COURTLY. I found it edifying — nutritious food for reflection — the expiring man desired his best compliments to you.

GRACE. To me?

YOUNG COURTLY. Yes.

GRACE. His name was —

YOUNG COURTLY. Mr Augustus Hamilton.

GRACE. Augustus! Oh! (*Affects to faint.*)

YOUNG COURTLY (*aside*). Hurra!

GRACE. But where, sir, did this happen?

YOUNG COURTLY. About four miles down the road.

GRACE. He must be conveyed here.

(*Enter* SERVANT *R.U.E.*)

SERVANT. Mr Meddle, madam. (*Exit R.U.E.*)

(*Enter* MEDDLE *R.U.E.*)

MEDDLE. On very particular business.

GRACE. This very person. My dear sir!

MEDDLE. My dear madam!

(YOUNG COURTLY *crosses to R.U.*)

GRACE. You must execute a very particular commission for me immediately. Mr Hamilton has met with a frightful accident on the London road, and is in a dying state.

MEDDLE (YOUNG COURTLY *crosses to R. corner*). He takes up a good deal of territory for a dying state. Well! I have no hesitation in saying, he takes it uncommonly easy — he looks as if he was used to it.

GRACE. You mistake; that is not Mr Hamilton, but Mr Courtly, who will explain everything, and conduct you to the spot.

YOUNG COURTLY (*aside*). Oh! I must put a stop to all this, or I shall be found out — (*Aloud*.) Madam, that were useless for I omitted to mention a small fact — which occurred before I left Mr Hamilton — he died.

GRACE. He died?

YOUNG COURTLY. He did.

GRACE. He did?

YOUNG COURTLY. Dead.

GRACE. Dead.

YOUNG COURTLY. Painfully dead and very much defunct.

GRACE. Dear me! Oh, then we needn't trouble you, Mr Meddle. (*Music heard*.) Hark! I hear they are commencing a waltz — if you will ask me — perhaps your society and conversation may tend to dispel the dreadful sensations you have aroused.

YOUNG COURTLY (*aside*). Hears of my death — screams out — and then asks me to waltz! I am bewildered! Can she suspect me? I wonder which she likes best — me or my double? Confound this disguise — I must retain it — I have gone too far with my dad to pull up now. At your service madam.

GRACE (*aside*). I will pay him well for this trick!
     (*Exeunt L. all but* MEDDLE.)

MEDDLE. Well, if that is not Mr Hamilton, scratch me out with a big blade, for I am a blot — a mistake upon the rolls. There is an error in the pleadings somewhere, and I will discover it. I would swear to his identity before the most discriminating jury. By the bye, this accident will form a capital excuse for my presence here. I just stepped in to see how matters worked, and — stay — here comes the bridegroom elect — and, oh! in his very arms, Lady Gay Spanker! (*Looks round*.) Where are my witnesses? Oh, that someone else were here! However, I can retire and get some information, oh — Spanker versus Courtly — damages — witness. (*Gets into an armchair, which he turns round*.)

(*Enter* SIR HARCOURT COURTLY, *supporting* LADY GAY *L.*)

SIR HARCOURT. This cool room will recover you.

LADY GAY. Excuse my trusting to you for support.

SIR HARCOURT. I am transported! Allow me thus ever to support this lovely burden, and I shall conceive that Paradise is regained. (*They sit.*)

LADY GAY. Oh! Sir Harcourt, I feel very faint.

SIR HARCOURT. The waltz made you giddy.

LADY GAY. And I have left my salts in the other room.

SIR HARCOURT. I always carry a flacon, for the express accommodation of the fair sex. (*Producing a smelling bottle.*)

LADY GAY. Thank you — ah! (*She sighs.*)

SIR HARCOURT. What a sigh was there!

LADY GAY. The vapour of consuming grief.

SIR HARCOURT. Grief? Is it possible? Have you grief? Are you unhappy? Dear me!

LADY GAY. Am I not married?

SIR HARCOURT. What a horrible state of existence!

LADY GAY. I am never contradicted, so, there are none of those enlivening, interesting little differences, which so pleasingly diversify the monotony of conjugal life, like spots of verdure — no quarrels, like oases in the desert of matrimony — no rows.

SIR HARCOURT. How vulgar! what a brute!

LADY GAY. I never have anything but my own way; and he won't permit me to spend more than I like.

SIR HARCOURT. Mean-spirited wretch!

LADY GAY. How can I help being miserable?

SIR HARCOURT. Miserable? I wonder you are not in a lunatic asylum, with such unheard-of barbarity!

LADY GAY. But worse than all that!

SIR HARCOURT. Can I be out-heroded?

LADY GAY. Yes, I could forgive that — I do — it is my duty. But only imagine — picture to yourself, my dear Sir Harcourt, though I, the third daughter of an Earl, married him out of pity for his destitute and helpless situation as a bachelor with ten thousand a year — conceive, if you can — he actually permits me, with the most placid indifference, to flirt with any old fool I may meet.

SIR HARCOURT. Good gracious! miserable idiot!

LADY GAY. I fear there is an incompatibility of temper, which renders a separation inevitable.

SIR HARCOURT. Indispensable, my dear madam! Ah! had I been

77

the happy possessor of such a realm of bliss — what a beatific eternity unfolds itself to my extending imagination! Had another man but looked at you, I should have annihilated him at once; and if he had the temerity to speak, his life alone could have expiated his crime.

LADY GAY. Oh, an existence of such a nature is too bright for the eye of thought — too sweet to bear reflection.

SIR HARCOURT. My devotion, eternal, deep —

LADY GAY. Oh, Sir Harcourt!

SIR HARCOURT (*more fervently*). Your every thought should be a separate study, — each wish forestalled by the quick apprehension of a kindred soul.

LADY GAY. Alas! how can I avoid my fate?

SIR HARCOURT. If life — a heart — were offered to your astonished view by one who is considered the index of fashion — the vane of the beau monde — if you saw him at your feet, begging, beseeching your acceptance of all, and more than this, what would your answer —

LADY GAY. Ah! I know of none so devoted!

SIR HARCOURT. You do! (*Throwing himself upon his knees.*) Behold Sir Harcourt Courtly!

(MEDDLE *jumps up in the chair.*)

LADY GAY (*aside*). Ha! ha! Yoicks! Puss has broken cover.

SIR HARCOURT. Speak, adored, dearest Lady Gay! — speak — will you fly from the tyranny, the wretched misery of such a monster's roof, and accept the soul which lives but in your presence!

LADY GAY. Do not press me. Oh, spare a weak, yielding woman, — be contented to know that you are, alas! too dear to me. But the world — the world would say —

SIR HARCOURT. Let us be a precedent, to open a more extended and liberal view of matrimonial advantages to society.

LADY GAY. How irresistible is your argument! Oh! pause!

SIR HARCOURT. I have ascertained for a fact, that every tradesman of mine lives with his wife, and thus you see it has become a vulgar and plebeian custom.

LADY GAY. Leave me; I feel I cannot withstand your powers of persuasion. Swear that you will never forsake me.

SIR HARCOURT. Dictate the oath. May I grow wrinkled, may two inches be added to the circumference of my waist — may I lose the fall in my back — may I be old and ugly the instant I forego one tithe of adoration.

LADY GAY. I must believe you.

SIR HARCOURT. Shall we leave this destestable spot — this horrible vicinity? (*He rises with the assistance of* LADY GAY.)

LADY GAY. The sooner the better; tomorrow evening let it be. Now let me return; my absence will be remarked. (*He kisses her hand.*) Do I appear confused? Has my agitation rendered me unfit to enter the room?

SIR HARCOURT. More angelic by a lovely tinge of heightened colour.

LADY GAY. Tomorrow, in this room, which opens on the lawn.

SIR HARCOURT. At eleven o'clock.

LADY GAY. Have your carriage waiting, and four horses. Remember, please be particular to have four; don't let the affair come off shabbily. Adieu, dear Sir Harcourt.
(*Exit L.U.E.*)

SIR HARCOURT. Veni, vidi, vici! Hannibal, Caesar, Napoleon, Alexander never completed so fair a conquest in so short a time. She dropped fascinated. This is an unprecedented example of the irresistible force of personal appearance combined with polished address. Poor creature! how she loves me! I pity so prostrating a passion, and ought to return it. I will; it is a duty I owe to society and fashion. (*Exit L.U.E.*)

MEDDLE (*Turns the chair round*). 'There is a tide in the affairs of men, which, taken at the flood', leads to a fortune. This is my tide — I am the only witness. 'Virtue is sure to find its own reward.' But I've no time to contemplate what I shall be — something huge. Let me see — Spanker versus Courtly — Crim. Con. — Damages placed at £150,000 at least, for juries always decimate your hopes.
(*Enter* SPANKER *R.U.E.*)

SPANKER. I cannot find Gay anywhere.

MEDDLE. The plaintiff himself — I must commence the action. Mr Spanker, as I have information of deep vital importance to impart, will you take a seat? (*They sit solemnly.* MEDDLE *takes out a notebook and pencil.*) Ahem! You have a wife!
(*Re-enter* LADY GAY *behind L.U.E.*)

SPANKER. Yes, I believe I —

MEDDLE. Will you be kind enough, without any prevarication, to answer my questions?

SPANKER. You alarm me, I —

MEDDLE. Compose yourself and reserve your feelings; take time to consider. You have a wife?

SPANKER. Yes —

MEDDLE. He has a wife — (*Appealing to an imaginary jury with his arm extended.*) good — a bona fide wife — bound morally and legally to be your wife, and nobody else's in effect, except on your written permission —

SPANKER. But what has this —

MEDDLE. Hush! allow me, my dear sir, to congratulate you. (*Shakes his hand.*)

SPANKER. Thank you — what for?

MEDDLE. Lady Gay Spanker is about to dishonour the bond of wedlock by eloping from you.

SPANKER (*starting*). What?

MEDDLE. Be patient — I thought you would be overjoyed. Place the affair in my hands, and I will venture to promise the largest damages on record.

SPANKER. Damn the damages! — I want my wife. Oh, I'll go and ask her not to run away. She may run away with me — she may hunt — she may ride — anything she likes. Oh, sir, let us put a stop to this affair.

MEDDLE. Put a stop to it! do not alarm me, sir. Sir, you will spoil the most exquisite brief that was ever penned. It must proceed — it shall proceed. It is illegal to prevent it, and I will bring an action against you for wilful intent to injure the profession.

SPANKER. Oh, what an ass I am! Oh, I have driven her to this. It was all that damned brandy punch on top of Burgundy. What a fool I was!

MEDDLE. It was the happiest moment of your life.

SPANKER. So I thought at the time; but we live to grow wiser. Tell me, who is the vile seducer?

MEDDLE. Sir Harcourt Courtly.

SPANKER. Ha! he is my best friend.

MEDDLE. Them's the fellows. (*Rises croses to L.*) If you will accompany me — here is a verbatim copy of the whole transaction in shorthand — sworn to by me.

SPANKER. Only let me have Gay back again.

MEDDLE. Even that may be arranged; this way.

SPANKER. That ever I should live to see my wife run away. Oh, I will do anything — keep two packs of hounds — buy up every horse and ass in England — myself included — oh!

(*Exit* SPANKER *and* MEDDLE *L.I.E.*)

LADY GAY. Ha! ha! ha! Poor Dolly! I'm sorry I must continue to deceive him. If he would kindle up a little — So, that fellow overheard all — well, so much the better.

(*Enter* YOUNG COURTLY *L.U.E.*)

YOUNG COURTLY. My dear madam, how fares the plot? Does my governor nibble?

LADY GAY. Nibble! He is caught and in the basket. I have just left him with a hook in his gills, panting for very lack of element. But how goes on your encounter?

YOUNG COURTLY. Bravely. By a simple ruse, I have discovered that she loves me. I see but one chance against the best termination I could hope.

LADY GAY. What is that?

YOUNG COURTLY. My father has told me that I return to town again tomorrow afternoon.

LADY GAY. Well, I insist you stop and dine — keep out of the way.

YOUNG COURTLY. Oh, but what excuse shall I offer for disobedience? What can I say, when he sees me before dinner?

LADY GAY. Say — say Grace.

(*Enter* GRACE *L.U.E. and gets behind the window curtains.*)

YOUNG COURTLY. Ha! ha!

LADY GAY. I have arranged to elope with Sir Harcourt myself tomorrow night.

YOUNG COURTLY. The deuce you have!

LADY GAY. Now if you could persuade Grace to follow that example — his carriage will be waiting at the park — be there a little before eleven, and it will just prevent our escape. Can you make her agree to that?

YOUNG COURTLY. Oh, without the slightest difficulty, if Mr Augustus Hamilton supplicates.

LADY GAY. Success attend you. (*Going R.I.E.*)

YOUNG COURTLY. I will bend the haughty Grace. (*Going L.I.E.*)

LADY GAY. Do.

YOUNG COURTLY. I will.

(*Exeunt severally.*)

GRACE. Will you?

END OF ACT FOUR

ACT FIVE

A drawing-room in Oak Hall. Enter COOL *R.U.E.*

COOL. This is the most serious affair Sir Harcourt has ever been engaged in. I took the liberty of considering him a fool when he told me he was going to marry; but voluntarily to incur another man's incumbrance is very little short of madness. If he continues to conduct himself in this absurd manner, I shall be compelled to dismiss him.

    (*Enter* SIR HARCOURT *L.U.E. equipped for travelling.*)

SIR HARCOURT. Cool!

COOL. Sir Harcourt.

SIR HARCOURT. Is my chariot in waiting?

COOL. For the last half hour at the park wicket. But, pardon the insinuation, sir; would it not be more advisable, to hesitate a little for a short reflection before you undertake the heavy responsibility of a woman?

SIR HARCOURT. No; hesitation destroys the romance of a faux pas, and reduces it to the level of mere mercantile calculation.

COOL. What is to be done with Mr Charles?

SIR HARCOURT. Ay, much against my will, Lady Gay prevailed on me to permit him to remain. You, Cool, must return him to college. Pass through London, and deliver these papers; here is a small notice of the coming elopement for the Morning Post; this, by an eyewitness; for the Herald; this, with all the particulars, for the Chronicle; and the full and circumstantial account for the evening journals — after which, meet us at Boulogne.

COOL. Very good, Sir Harcourt. (*Going L.*)

SIR HARCOURT. Lose no time, remember — Hotel Anglais, Boulogne-sur-Mer. And, Cool, bring a few copies with you, and don't forget to distribute some amongst very particular friends.

82

COOL. It shall be done. (*Exit L.I.E.*)

SIR HARCOURT. With what indifference does a man of the world view the approach of the most perilous catastrophe! My position, hazardous as it is, entails none of that nervous excitement which a neophyte in the school of fashion would feel. I am as cool and steady as possible. Habit, habit! oh! how many roses will fade upon the cheek of beauty, when the defalcation of Sir Harcourt Courtly is whispered — then hinted — at last, confirmed and bruited. I think I see them. Then, on my return, they will not dare to eject me — I am their sovereign! Whoever attempts to think of treason, I'll banish him from the West End — I'll out him — I'll put him out of fashion!

   (*Enter* LADY GAY *R.I.E.*)

LADY GAY. Sir Harcourt!

SIR HARCOURT. At your feet.

LADY GAY. I had hoped you would have repented.

SIR HARCOURT. Repented!

LADY GAY. Have you not come to say it was a jest? — say you have!

SIR HARCOURT. Love is too sacred a subject to be trifled with. Come, let us fly! I have procured disguises —

LADY GAY. My courage begins to fail me. Let me return.

SIR HARCOURT. Impossible!

LADY GAY. Where do you intend to take me?

SIR HARCOURT. You shall be my guide. The carriage waits.

LADY GAY. You will never desert me?

SIR HARCOURT. Desert! Oh, Heavens! Nay, do not hesitate — flight, now, alone is left to your desperate situation! Come, every moment is laden with danger.

   (*They are going.*)

LADY GAY. Oh! gracious!

SIR HARCOURT. Hush! what is it?

LADY GAY. I have forgotten — I must return.

SIR HARCOURT. Impossible!

LADY GAY. I must! I must! I have left Max — a pet staghound, in his basket — without whom, life would be unendurable — I could not exist!

SIR HARCOURT. No, no. Let him be sent after us in a hamper.

LADY GAY. In a hamper! Remorseless man! Go — you love me not. How would you like to be sent after me — in a hamper? Let me fetch him! Hark! I hear him squeal! Oh! Max — Max!

SIR HARCOURT. Hush! for Heaven's sake. They'll imagine you're calling the Squire. I hear footsteps; where can I retire?

(*Exit L.I.E.*)

(*Enter* MEDDLE, SPANKER, DAZZLE, *and* MAX *L.U.E.* LADY GAY *screams.*)

MEDDLE. Spanker versus Courtly! — I subpoena every one of you as witnesses! I have 'em ready — here they are — shilling a piece. (*Giving them round.*)

LADY GAY. Where is Sir Harcourt?

MEDDLE. There! — bear witness! call on the vile delinquent for protection!

SPANKER. Oh! his protection!

LADY GAY. What? ha!

MEDDLE. I'll swear I overheard the whole elopement planned — before any jury! — where's the book?

SPANKER. Do you hear, you profligate?

LADY GAY. Ha! ha! ha! ha!

DAZZLE. But where is this wretched Lothario? (*Coming down to R.*)

MEDDLE. Ay, where is the defendant?

SPANKER. Where lies the hoary headed villain?

LADY GAY. What villain?

SPANKER. That will not serve you! — I'll not be blinded that way!

MEDDLE. We won't be blinded any way!

MAX. I must seek Sir Harcourt, and demand an explanation! Such a thing never occurred in Oak Hall before — it must be cleared up! (*Exit R.U.E.*)

MEDDLE (*aside to* SPANKER). Now take my advice; remember your gender. Mind the notes I have given you.

SPANKER (*aside*). All right! Here they are! Now, madam, I have procured the highest legal opinion on this point.

MEDDLE. Hear! hear!

SPANKER. And the question resolves itself into a — into — What's this? (*Looks at notes.*)

MEDDLE. A nutshell!

SPANKER. Yes, we are in a nutshell. Will you, in every respect, subscribe to my requests — desires — commands — (*Looks at notes.*) — orders — imperative — indicative — injunctive — or otherwise? With particular stress on the otherwise.

LADY GAY (*aside*). 'Pon my life, he's actually going to assume the ribbons, and take the box-seat. I must put a stop to this. I will! It will end in smoke. I know Sir Harcourt would rather run than fight! (*Retiring up.*)

DAZZLE. Oh, I smell powder! — command my services. My dear madam, can I be of any use?

SPANKER. Oh! a challenge! I must consult my legal adviser.

MEDDLE. No! impossible!

DAZZLE. Pooh! the easiest thing in life! Leave it to me: what has an attorney to do with affairs of honour? — they are out of his element.

MEDDLE Compromise the question? Pull his nose! — we have no objection to that.

DAZZLE (*turning to* LADY GAY). Well, we have no objection either — have we?

LADY GAY. No! — pull his nose — that will be something.

SPANKER. Who's to do it?

DAZZLE. Why you.

SPANKER. Oh no.

MEDDLE. And moreover, it is not exactly actionable!

DAZZLE. Isn't it! — thank you — I'll note down that piece of information — it may be useful.

MEDDLE. How! cheated out of my legal knowledge?

LADY GAY (*coming down*). Mr Spanker, I am determined — I insist upon a challenge being sent to Sir Harcourt Courtly! — and mark me — if you refuse to — I'll fight him.

MEDDLE. Don't. Take my advice — you'll incapacit —

LADY GAY. Look you, Mr Meddle, unless you wish me to horse-whip you, hold your tongue.

MEDDLE (*option of* MEDDLE *whether he will speak this speech or the one from book*). I have no hesitation in saying, and I say it boldly — (LADY GAY *turns on him suddenly*.) That I am wanted in the next room. What a she-tiger — I shall retire and collect my costs. (*Exit L.*)

LADY GAY. Mr Spanker, oblige me by writing as I dictate.

SPANKER. He's gone — and now I am defenceless! Is this the fate of husbands! — a duel! — Is this the result of becoming master of my own family?

LADY GAY. 'Sir —

DAZZLE. Sir.

SPANKER. Two Sirs —

DAZZLE. Don't write two sirs.

LADY GAY. The situation in which you were discovered with my wife —

DAZZLE (*repeating after* LADY GAY). With my wife.

SPANKER. Your wife.

DAZZLE. No, no, your wife.

LADY GAY. Admits neither of explanation nor apology.

DAZZLE. Dot your wife's eyes.

SPANKER. Oh, yes! but it does — I don't believe you really intended to run quite away.

LADY GAY. You do not; but I know better, I say I did! and if it had not been for your unfortunate interruptions, I do not know where I might have been by this time. Go on.

SPANKER (*whispers to* DAZZLE). Apology? Oh one 'p'. Not apology. I'm writing my own death-warrant — committing suicide on compulsion.

LADY GAY. 'The bearer will arrange all preliminary —

SPANKER. Preliminary —

DAZZLE. One limb amputate the other limb.

LADY GAY. — matters; for another day —

(SPANKER *makes a full stop and throwing down pen.*)

LADY GAY. — must see this sacrilege —

SPANKER. Sacrilege, do you spell it with an 'R'?

LADY GAY. — expiated by your life, or that of —

SPANKER. Or that of the bearer.

DAZZLE. Oh no, I am the bearer. Scratch out the bearer.

LADY GAY. No! Yours very sincerely. 'Dolly Spanker.'

SPANKER. Adolphus Spanker.

LADY GAY. Now, Mr Dazzle. (*Gives it over his head.*)

DAZZLE. The document is as sacred as if it were a hundred pound note.

LADY GAY. We trust to your discretion.

SPANKER. His discretion! Oh, put your head in a tiger's mouth, and trust to his discretion!

DAZZLE (*sealing letter, &c. with* SPANKER's *seal*). My dear Lady Gay, matters of this kind are indigenous to my nature, independently of their pervading fascination to all humanity; but this is the more especially delightful, as you may perceive I shall be the intimate and bosom friend of both parties. (*Crosses to L.*)

LADY GAY. Is it not the only alternative in such a case?

DAZZLE. It is a beautiful panacea in any, in every case — (*Crosses to L.*)

(*Going, returns.*) By the way, where would you like this party of pleasure to come off?

SPANKER. As far off as possible.

DAZZLE. Open air shooting is pleasant enough, but if I might venture to advise, we could order half a dozen of that Madeira and a box of cigars into the billiard-room —

SPANKER. I don't smoke.

DAZZLE. So make a night of it; take up the irons every now and then, strong for first shot, and blaze away at one another in an amicable and gentlemanlike way; so conclude the matter before the potency of the liquor could disturb the individuality of the object, or the smoke of the cigars render the outlines dubious. Does such an arrangement coincide with your views?

LADY GAY. Perfectly. (*Sitting on sofa L.*)

DAZZLE. I trust shortly to be the harbinger of happy tidings. (*Exit L.I.E.*)

SPANKER (*crosses up to L.D.*). Lady Gay Spanker, are you ambitious of becoming a widow?

LADY GAY (*seated on ottoman C.*). Why, Dolly, woman is at best but weak, and weeds become me.

SPANKER. Female! am I to be immolated on the altar of your vanity.

LADY GAY. If you become pathetic, I shall laugh.

SPANKER. Farewell — base, heartless, unfeeling woman! (*Exit L.U.E.*)

LADY GAY. Ha! well, so I am. I am heartless for he is a dear, good little fellow, and I ought not to play upon his feelings; but 'pon my life he sounds so well up at concert pitch, that I feel disinclined to untune him. Poor Doll, I didn't think he cared so much about me. I will put him out of pain. (*Exit L.U.E.*)

(SIR HARCOURT *enters L.S.E.*)

SIR HARCOURT. I have been a fool! a dupe to my own vanity. I shall be pointed at as a ridiculous old coxcomb — and so I am. The hour of conviction has arrived. Have I deceived myself? Have I turned all my senses inwards — looking towards self — always self? — and has the world been ever laughing at me? Well, if they have, I will revert the joke; — they may say I am an old ass; but I will prove that I am neither too old to repent my folly, nor such an ass as to flinch from confessing it. A blow half met is but half felt.

(*Enter* DAZZLE *L.I.E.*)

DAZZLE. Sir Harcourt, may I be permitted the honour of a few minutes conversation with you?

SIR HARCOURT. With pleasure.

DAZZLE. Have the kindness to throw your eye over that. (*Gives letter.*)

SIR HARCOURT (*reads*). 'Situation — my wife — apology — expiate — my life.' Why, this is intended for a challenge.

DAZZLE. Why, indeed, I am perfectly aware that it is not quite en règle in the couching, for with that I had nothing to do;

but I trust that the irregularity of the composition will be confounded in the beauty of the subject.

SIR HARCOURT. Mr Dazzle, are you in earnest?

DAZZLE. Sir Harcourt Courtly, upon my honour, I am, and I hope that no previous engagement will interfere with an immediate reply in propria persona. We have fixed upon the billiard-room as the scene of action, which I have just seen properly illuminated in honour of the occasion; and, by the bye, if your implements are not handy, I can oblige you with a pair of the sweetest things you ever handled — hair-triggered — saw grip, heirlooms in my family. I regard them almost in the light of relations.

SIR HARCOURT. Sir, I shall avail myself of one of your relatives. (*Aside.*) One of the hereditaments of my folly — I must accept it. (*Aloud.*) Sir, I shall be happy to meet Mr Spanker at any time or place he may appoint.

DAZZLE. The sooner the better, sir. Allow me to offer you my arm. (SIR HARCOURT *refuses to take his arm.*) I see you understand these matters; — my friend Spanker is wholly ignorant — miserably uneducated. (*Exeunt L.U.E.*)
  (*Re-enter* MAX, *with* GRACE *R.U.E.*)

MAX. Give ye joy, girl, give ye joy. Sir Harcourt Courtly must consent to waive all title to your hand in favour of his son Charles.

GRACE. Oh, indeed! Is that the pith of your congratulation — humph! the exchange of an old fool for a young one? Pardon me if I am not able to distinguish the advantage.

MAX. Advantage!

GRACE. Moreover, by what right am I a transferable cipher in the family of Courtly? So, then, my fate is reduced to this, to sacrifice my fortune, or unite myself with a wormeaten edition of the Classics?

MAX. Why, he certainly is not such a fellow, as I could have chosen for my little Grace; but consider, to retain fifteen thousand a year! Now, tell me honestly — but why should I say honestly? Speak, girl, would you rather not have the lad?

GRACE. Why do you ask me?

MAX. Why, look ye, I'm an old fellow; another hunting season or two, and I shall be in at my own death — I can't leave you this house and land, because they are entailed, nor can I say I'm sorry for it, for it is a good law; but I have a little box with my Grace's name upon it, where, since your father's death and miserly will, I have yearly placed a certain sum to be yours, should you refuse to fulfil the conditions prescribed!

GRACE. My own dear uncle! (*Clasping him round the neck.*)

MAX. Pooh! pooh! what's to do now? Why, it was only a trifle — why, you little rogue, what are you crying about?

GRACE. Nothing, but —

MAX. But what? Come, out with it; will you have young Courtly?
(*Re-enter* LADY GAY *L.U.E.*)

LADY GAY. Oh! Max, Max!

MAX. Why, what's amiss with you?

LADY GAY. I'm a wicked woman?

MAX. What have you done?

LADY GAY. Everything — oh, I thought Sir Harcourt was a coward, but now I find a man may be a coxcomb without being a poltroon. Just to show my husband how inconvenient it is to hold the ribands sometimes, I made him send a challenge to the old fellow, and he, to my surprise, accepted it, and is going to blow my Dolly's brains out in the billiard-room.

MAX. The devil!

LADY GAY. Just when I imagined I had got my whip hand of him again, out comes my linchpin — and over I go — oh!

MAX. I will soon put a stop to that — a duel under my roof! Murder in Oak Hall! I'll shoot them both! (*Exit L.U.E.*)

GRACE. Are you really in earnest?

LADY GAY. Do you think it looks like a joke? Oh! Dolly, if you allow yourself to be shot, I will never forgive you — never! Ah, he is a great fool, Grace! but I can't tell you why, I would sooner lose my bridle hand than he should be hurt on my account. (*Enter* SIR HARCOURT *L.U.E.*) Tell me — tell me — have you shot him — is he dead — my dear Sir Harcourt? You horrid old brute — have you killed him? I shall never forgive myself. (*Exit L.U.E.*)

GRACE. Oh! Sir Harcourt, what has happened?

SIR HARCOURT. Don't be alarmed, I beg — your uncle interrupted us — discharged the weapons — locked the challenger up in the billiard-room to cool his rage.

GRACE. Thank Heaven!

SIR HARCOURT. Miss Grace, to apologise for my conduct were useless, more especially as I am confident that no feelings of indignation or sorrow for my late acts are cherished by you; but still, reparation is in my power, and I not only waive all title, right, or claim to your person or your fortune, but freely admit your power to bestow them on a more worthy object.

GRACE.   This generosity, Sir Harcourt, is most unexpected.

SIR HARCOURT.   No, not generosity, but simply, justice, justice!

GRACE.   May I still beg a favour?

SIR HARCOURT.   Claim anything that is mine to grant.

GRACE.   You have been duped by Lady Gay Spanker.

SIR HARCOURT.   Hem!

GRACE.   I have also been cheated and played upon by her and Mr Hamilton — may I beg that the contract between us, may to all appearances, be still held good?

SIR HARCOURT.   Certainly, although I confess I cannot see the point of your purpose. (*Crosses to R.*)

(*Enter* MAX *with* YOUNG COURTLY *L.U.E.*)

MAX.   Now, Grace, I have brought the lad.

GRACE.   Thank you, uncle, but the trouble was quite unnecessary — Sir Harcourt holds to his original contract.

MAX.   The deuce he does!

GRACE.   And I am willing — nay, eager to become Lady Courtly.

YOUNG COURTLY   (*aside*). The deuce you are!

MAX.   But, Sir Harcourt —

SIR HARCOURT.   One word, Max, for an instant. (*They exit L.U.E.*)

YOUNG COURTLY   (*aside*). What can this mean? Can it be possible that I have been mistaken — that she is not in love with Augustus Hamilton?

GRACE.   Now we shall find out how he intends to bend the haughty Grace.

YOUNG COURTLY.   Madam — Miss, I mean, — are you really in earnest, are you in love with my father?

GRACE.   No, indeed I am not.

YOUNG COURTLY.   Are you in love with anyone else?

GRACE.   No, or I should not marry him.

YOUNG COURTLY.   Then you actually accept him as your real husband?

GRACE.   In the common acceptance of the word.

YOUNG COURTLY   (*aside*). Hang me if I have not been a pretty fool! (*Aloud.*) Why do you marry him, if you don't care about him?

GRACE.   To save my fortune.

YOUNG COURTLY   (*aside*). Mercenary, cold-hearted girl! (*Aloud.*) But if there be anyone you love in the least — marry him, — were you never in love?

GRACE.   Never!

YOUNG COURTLY   (*aside*). Oh! What an ass I've been! (*Aloud.*) I heard Lady Gay mention something about Mr Hamilton.

GRACE. Ah, yes, a person who, after an acquaintance of two days, had the assurance to make love to me, and I —

YOUNG COURTLY. Yes, — you — well?

GRACE. I pretended to receive his attentions.

YOUNG COURTLY (*aside*). It was the best pretence I ever saw.

GRACE. An absurd, vain conceited coxcomb, who appeared to imagine that I was so struck with his fulsome speech, that he could turn me round his finger.

YOUNG COURTLY (*aside*). My very thoughts!

GRACE. But he was mistaken.

YOUNG COURTLY (*aside*). Confoundedly! (*Aloud.*) Yet you seemed rather concerned about the news of his accident.

GRACE. His death?

YOUNG COURTLY. Oh, I forgot I was dead.

GRACE. His neck broken in several places — yes that is — no but —

YOUNG COURTLY. But what?

GRACE (*aside*). What can I say? (*Aloud.*) Ah! but my maid Pert's brother is a post-boy, and I thought he might have sustained an injury, poor post-boy.

YOUNG COURTLY (*aside*). Damn the post-boy! (*Aloud.*) Madam, if the retention of your fortune be the plea on which you are about to bestow your hand on one you do not love, and whose very actions speak his carelessness for what inestimable jewel he is incapable of appreciating — know that I am devotedly madly attached to you.

GRACE. You, sir? Impossible!

YOUNG COURTLY. Not at all, — but inevitable, — I have been so for a long time.

GRACE. Why, you never saw me till last night.

YOUNG COURTLY. I have seen you in imagination — you are the ideal I have worshipped.

GRACE. Since you press me into a confession, — which nothing but this could bring me to speak, — know, I did love poor Augustus Hamilton.

YOUNG COURTLY. He died.

GRACE. He did.

YOUNG COURTLY. He did.

GRACE. He died, he did, painfully and very much defiant. (*Re-enter* MAX *and* SIR HARCOURT *L.U.E.*) But he — he is — no — more! Pray, spare me, sir. (*Crosses to R.*)

YOUNG COURTLY (*aside*). She loves me! And oh! what a situation I am in! — If I own I am the man, my governor will overhear, and

91

ruin me; if I do not, she'll marry him. What is to be done? (*Crosses to* GRACE.)

(*Enter* LADY GAY *L.I.E.*)

LADY GAY. Where have you put my Dolly? I have been racing all round the house — tell me, is he quite dead!

MAX. I'll have his body brought in. (*Exit L.U.E.*)

SIR HARCOURT. My dear madam, you must perceive this unfortunate occurrence was no fault of mine. I was compelled to act as I have done — I was willing to offer any apology, but that resource was excluded, as unacceptable.

LADY GAY. I know — I know — 'twas I made him write that letter — there was no apology required — 'twas I that apparently seduced you from the paths of propriety; 'twas all a joke, and here is the end of it. (*Enter* MAX, SPANKER *and* DAZZLE *L.U.E*) Oh! if he had but lived to say, 'I forgive you Gay!'

SPANKER. So I do!

LADY GAY (*seeing him*). Ah! he is alive. (*She catches* DOLLY *and swings him round with joy.*)

SPANKER. Of course I am!

LADY GAY. Ha! ha! ha! (*Embraces him.*) I will never hunt again — unless you wish it. Sell your stable —

SPANKER. No, no — do what you like — say what you like for the future! I find the head of a family has less ease and more responsibility than I, as a member, could have anticipated. I abdicate! (*They skip together up stage.*)

(*Enter* COOL *L.I.E.*)

SIR HARCOURT. Ah! Cool, here! (*Aside to* COOL.) You may destroy those papers — I have altered my mind, and I do not intend to elope at present. Where are they?

COOL. As you seemed particular, Sir Harcourt, I sent them off to London by mail.

SIR HARCOURT. Why, then, a full description of the whole affair will be published tomorrow.

COOL. Most irretrievably!

SIR HARCOURT. You must post to town immediately, and stop the press.

COOL. Beg pardon — but they would see me hanged first. Sir Harcourt, they don't frequently meet with such a profitable lie.

SERVANT (*without R.U.E.*). No, sir! No, sir!

(*Enter* SIMPSON *R.U.E.*)

SIMPSON. Sir, there's a gentleman, who calls himself Mr Solomon Isaacs insists upon following me up. (*Exit R.U.E.*)

(*Enter* MR SOLOMON ISAACS, *R.U.E. cross and go down on the L.*)

ISAACS. Mr Courtly, you will excuse my performance of a most disagreeable duty at any time, but more expecially in such a manner. I must beg the honour of your company to town.

SIR HARCOURT. What! how! what for?

ISAACS. For debt, Sir Harcourt.

SIR HARCOURT. Arrested? Impossible! There must be some mistake.

ISAACS. Not the slightest, sir. Judgment has been given in five cases, for the last three months; but Mr Courtly is an eel rather too nimble for my men. We have been on his track, and traced him down to this village, with Mr Dazzle.

DAZZLE. Ah! Isaacs! how are you? How is Mrs Isaacs and all the little Isaacs?

ISAACS. Thank you, sir, very well. (*Speaks to* SIR HARCOURT.)

MAX. Do you know him?

DAZZLE. Oh, intimately! Distantly related to his family — same arms on our escutcheon — empty purse falling thro' a hole in a — pocket; motto. 'Requiescat in pace' — which means 'Let virtue be its own reward.'

SIR HARCOURT (*to* ISAACS). Oh, I thought there was a mistake. Know, to your misfortune, that Mr Hamilton was the person you dogged to Oak Hall, between whom and my son a most remarkable likeness exists.

ISAACS. Ha! ha! Know, to your misfortune, Sir Harcourt, that Mr Hamilton and Mr Courtly are one and the same person!

SIR HARCOURT. Charles!

YOUNG COURTLY. Concealment is in vain — I am Augustus Hamilton.

SIR HARCOURT. Hang me if I didn't think it all along! Oh, you infernal cozening dog! (*Crosses to him.*)

ISAACS. Now, then, Mr Hamilton —

GRACE. Stay, sir — Mr Charles Courtly is under age — ask his father. (*Dropping down R.*)

SIR HARCOURT. Ahem! I won't — I won't pay a shilling of the rascal's debts — not a sixpence!

GRACE. Then I will — you may retire.
    (*Exit* ISAACS *R.*)

YOUNG COURTLY. I can now perceive the generous point of your conduct towards me; and believe me, I appreciate, and will endeavour to deserve it.

MAX (*coming down*). Ha! ha! Come, Sir Harcourt, you have

93

been fairly beaten — you must forgive him — say you will.
(*Goes up.*)

SIR HARCOURT. So, sir, it appears you have been leading, covertly,
an infernally town life?

YOUNG COURTLY. Yes, please, father.
    (*Imitating* MASTER CHARLES.)

SIR HARCOURT. None of your humbug, sir! (*Aside.*) He is my own
son — how could I expect him to keep out of the fire? (*Aloud.*)
And you, Mr Cool! — have you been deceiving me?

COOL. Oh! Sir Harcourt, if your perception was played upon,
how could I be expected to see? (*Exit L.I.E.*)

SIR HARCOURT. Well, it would be useless to withhold my hand.
There, boy! (*He gives his hand to* YOUNG COURTLY. GRACE
comes down on the other side and offers her hand; he takes it.)
What is all this? What do you want?

YOUNG COURTLY. Your blessing, father. (*Kneels.*)

GRACE. If you please, father. (*Kneels.*)

SIR HARCOURT. Oho! the mystery is being solved. So, so, you
young scoundrel, you have been making love — under the rose.

LADY GAY. He learnt that from you, Sir Harcourt.

SIR HARCOURT. Ahem! What would you do now, if I were to
withhold my consent?

GRACE. Do without it. (*Rising.*)

MAX (*coming down*). The Will says, if Grace marries any one
but you, her property reverts to your heir apparent — and there
he stands.

LADY GAY. Make a virtue of necessity. (*L.C.*)

SPANKER. I married from inclination, and see how happy I am.
And if ever I have a son —

LADY GAY. Hush! Dolly, dear! (*Drawing* SPANKER *up stage and
putting him in a corner with his back to audience.*)

SIR HARCOURT. Well! take her, boy! Although you are too young
to marry. (*They retire with* MAX.)

LADY GAY. Am I forgiven, Sir Harcourt? (*Coming down.*)

SIR HARCOURT. Ahem! Why — a — (*Aside.*) Have you really
deceived me?

LADY GAY. Can you not see through this?

SIR HARCOURT. And you still love me?

LADY GAY. As much as I ever did.

SIR HARCOURT (*is about to kiss her hand, when* SPANKER *inter-
poses between*). A very handsome ring, indeed.

SPANKER. Very. And my money paid for it. (*Puts her arm in his,
and they go up.*)

94

SIR HARCOURT. Poor little Spanker!

MAX (*coming down, aside to* SIR HARCOURT). One point I wish to have settled. Who is Mr Dazzle?

SIR HARCOURT. A relative of the Spankers, he told me.

MAX. Oh, no, a near connection of yours.

SIR HARCOURT. Never saw him before I came down here, in all my life. (*To* YOUNG COURTLY.) Charles, who is Mr Dazzle?

YOUNG COURTLY. Dazzle, Dazzle — hang me, if I know — will you excuse an impertinent question?

DAZZLE. Certainly —

YOUNG COURTLY. But who the deuce are you?

DAZZLE. I have not the remotest idea.

ALL. How sir?

DAZZLE. Simple question as you may think it, it would puzzle half the world to answer. One thing I can vouch — Nature made me a gentleman — that is, I live on the best that can be procured for credit. I never spend my own money when I can oblige a friend. I'm always thick on the winning horse. I'm an epidemic on the trade of tailor. For further particulars, inquire of any sitting magistrate.

SIR HARCOURT. And these are the deeds which attest your title to the name of gentleman? I perceive you have caught the infection of the present age. Charles, permit me, as your father, and you, sir, as his friend, to correct you on one point. Barefaced assurance is the vulgar substitute for gentlemanly ease; and there are many, who, by aping the vices of the great, imagine that they elevate themselves to the rank of those, whose faults alone they copy. No, sir. The title of gentleman is the only one out of any monarch's gift, yet within the reach of every peasant. It should be engrossed by Truth — stamped with Honour — sealed with good-feeling — signed Man — and enrolled in every true and honest heart.

CURTAIN

THE CORSICAN BROTHERS

First performed at the Princess's Theatre, London, 24 February 1852.

CAST

Fabien Dei Franchi Louis Dei Franchi	(twin brothers)	MR CHARLES KEAN
Alfred De Meynard Baron Giordano Martelli	(friends to Louis)	MR G. EVERETT MR C. WHEATLEIGH
Château-Renaud		MR ALFRED WIGAN
Baron De Montgiron (his friend)		MR JAMES VINING
Beauchamp Verner	(fashionable gentlemen)	MR STACEY MR ROLLESTON
Orlando Colonna	(heads of two Corsican families)	MR RYDER MR MEADOWS
Antonio Sanola (judge of the district)		MR F. COOKE
Griffo (a domestic)		MR PAULO
Guido (a guide)		MR STOAKES
Boissec (a woodcutter)		MR J. CHESTER
Surgeon		MR DALY
Servants		MR HAINES MR WILSON
Madame Savilia Dei Franchi		MISS PHILLIPS
Madame Émilie De l'Esparre		MISS MURRAY
Maria (servant to Madame Savilia)		MISS ROBERTSON
Coralie		MISS CARLOTTA LECLERCQ
Estelle (ladies of the ballet)		MISS VIVASH
Celestina		MISS DALY

Ladies, gentlemen, masks, dominoes, officers, male and female Corsican peasants, servants, &c.

The incidents of the First Act in Corsica, and of the Second Act in Paris, are supposed to occur at the same time. The Third Act takes place five days later, in the Forest of Fontainebleau. Period: 1841.

ACT ONE

Principal saloon in the château of MADAME LA CONTESSA
SAVILIA DEI FRANCHI *at Sullacaro in Corsica; a large chimney-
piece, R, surmounted by a trophy of carbines suspended from the
horns of a moufflon; at the back, C, the door of entrance; at the
two sides, lateral doors.*

MARIA (*discovered, singing at her spinning wheel*).
   The sun shines bright across the plain,
   From Aleria to Sartène,
   But at the end there's gloom!
   For there the murm'ring rivulet flows,
   And sadly bends the laurel rose
   O'er poor Peppino's tomb.
   (*A knocking is heard at the door.*)
   Some one knocks. (*Knocking again.*) Yes, I am not deceived!
   Griffo! Griffo!
   (GRIFFO *enters.*)
GRIFFO. What's the matter? Is the house on fire?
MARIA. No, but there's somebody knocking at the gate.
GRIFFO. Well, go and open it.
MARIA. At this late hour, by myself? No thank you.
GRIFFO. Timid individual. (*Goes out.*)
MARIA (*putting her spinning wheel away*). Go and open it! Yes,
   to be agreeably saluted by a pistol or a stiletto.
   (*Re-enter* GRIFFO.)
   Well, what is it?
GRIFFO. A French gentleman — a traveller — who requests our
   hospitality.
MARIA (*joyfully*). A French traveller! I hope you haven't refused
   him?
GRIFFO. Refused! Refuse hospitality in Corsica! Go and announce
   his arrival to the Countess.

99

MARIA. I should like to have a peep at him first.

GRIFFO. Go, I tell you.

MARIA. Just one glimpse. Is he young and handsome?

GRIFFO. That's nothing to you. He stays all night.

MARIA. Oh, then I can wait a little. I fly to tell Madame. (*Exit.*)
(*Enter* ALFRED DE MEYNARD *and* GUIDO *with a valise.*)

GRIFFO (*at the door*). This way, your excellency. I have sent to inform the Signora Savilia of your arrival.

ALFRED. My good friend, I fear this unseasonable intrusion —

GRIFFO (*smiling*). Intrusion! we have no such word in Corsica. Here a stranger honours the house he stops at. (*To* GUIDO.) Ah! honest Guido, is that you?

ALFRED. I can dismiss you now. Here are two piastres.

GUIDO. Thank you sir. (*Exit.*)

GRIFFO. Is your excellency acquainted with the Countess?

ALFRED. I have not yet that honour, but I bring a letter from her son.

GRIFFO. From Monsieur Louis?

ALFRED. Yes; he is my intimate friend.
(*Enter* MADAME DEI FRANCHI *and* MARIA.)

MADAME. From my son Louis, did you say, sir?

ALFRED (*bowing*). Madame, I ought to apologise for my intrusion, but the well-known hospitality of your country, and this letter, will, I trust, plead my excuse.

MADAME (*taking the letter*). I thank you, sir. You can understand a mother's joy when she sees the handwriting of an absent son. (*Reads.*) Ah, my dear Louis! He recommends you to us, as one of his most valued friends. There needed not this to ensure your welcome. In Corsica, every traveller may throw his bridle on his horse's neck, and stop where he conducts him. His stay is limited by his own pleasure, and the only regret he occasions is when he announces his departure. Maria, tell them to prepare the chamber Louis occupied before he left us. Griffo, carry there the luggage of our guest; while he stays with us, you will devote yourself entirely to him. (SERVANTS *exeunt.*)

ALFRED. I know not how to thank you, Madame.

MADAME. On my son's part as well as my own, I repeat your hearty welcome.

ALFRED. Oh, I recollect — your second son, Monsieur Fabien.

MADAME. I have two sons, twins.

ALFRED. I have heard of the extraordinary resemblance which exists between them.

MADAME. You shall judge for yourself when you have seen Fabien.

He went this morning early to the mountains; I expect
return every instant.

ALFRED. I long to shake him by the hand.

(GRIFFO *enters*.)

GRIFFO (*as he enters*). Madame, Monsieur Fabien has arrived.

MADAME. Where is he?

GRIFFO. Just entering the gate; he stopped to speak with the
Judge. (*To* ALFRED.) Your excellency's apartment is ready.

ALFRED. I thank you, my worthy friend, but I am not tired;
my reception here has driven away fatigue. (*He continues
talking in a low voice with* GRIFFO, *to whom he gives his hat
and cane*.)

(*Enter* FABIEN, *carrying a carbine, which he lays down on
entering*.)

MADAME (*going to meet him*). My son, you have been expected
home.

FABIEN. By you, dear mother?

MADAME. Yes, and by some one else; how late you are this evening.

FABIEN. Yes, that devil Orlando is a true Corsican; I could hardly
persuade him. At last however I succeeded and all is settled.
This unhappy feud will now be terminated. He and Colonna
have promised to meet here this evening with their kinsmen
and friends, and having once promised they are sure to come.

MADAME. And now let me introduce to you Monsieur Alfred de
Meynard, a friend of your brother.

FABIEN (*going towards* ALFRED, *and offering him his hand*). A
friend of Louis! Sir, you are most welcome.

ALFRED. Good heavens! It is identity! I could swear that I held
by the hand my old friend.

FABIEN. Believe it, sir. Louis and myself are one.

ALFRED. The voice, too, is tone for tone the same.

MADAME. Monsieur is the bearer of a letter.

FABIEN (*in an agitated tone*). A letter from Louis? Dear mother,
allow me to look at it. (*She gives it, and he reads*.) By the date you
have not seen Louis for three weeks — then you know nothing.

MADAME. What say you, Fabien?

FABIEN. Nothing, mother, nothing. How did you leave my brother,
when you last saw him?

ALFRED. His health was excellent.

FABIEN. So much for the body; but his mind? Did he appear
thoughtful, harassed, in low spirits?

ALFRED. Far from it. He seemed wholly occupied in preparing
for his degree, which he felt confident of obtaining.

time, then, you observed in him no trace of
n?

whatever. Have you any reason to think otherwise?
eived more recently any evil tidings?
ed? No — that is, not in the sense in which *you* use

MADAME. on!

ALFRED. I scarcely comprehend you.

MADAME. Fabien, I trust nothing of consequence has happened to your brother.

FABIEN (*going towards her*). No, mother, I hope not; still —

MADAME. The fears you entertained yesterday on account of Louis —

FABIEN. I have them still; they never leave me.

MADAME. But you have had no further warning?

FABIEN (*after a moment's hesitation*). No — none.

MADAME. But if your brother's life was threatened —

FABIEN. Mother!

MADAME. If he was dead, you would have known it?

FABIEN. Yes, for I should have seen him.

ALFRED (*aside, and astonished*). He would have seen him!

MADAME. And you would have told me?

FABIEN. Assuredly, dearest mother.

MADAME. Fabien, I thank you. The absent are in the hands of Providence — you know that Louis lives. Let us endeavour to dismiss this anxiety for the moment, and think of nothing but to do honour to our guest.

(*She salutes* ALFRED, *who bows to her —* FABIEN *accompanies her to the door on the left, and she goes out.*)

ALFRED (*looking at them, as she is going*). All this is very strange. But I am in the land of adventures, and this old château appears the head quarters of romance.

FABIEN (*returning towards* ALFRED). You will excuse us, sir, of speaking before you of family affairs, but we cannot treat you with reserve, having come from our dear Louis. The last few words exchanged between me and my mother appear to you a little unintelligible?

ALFRED. I confess it. You have received no recent news of your brother. Why, then, do you suppose him restless, melancholy and in pain?

FABIEN. Because for the last three days I have been restless, melancholy and in pain myself.

ALFRED. Excuse me, but I cannot follow the coincidence.

FABIEN. You know, probably, that Louis and I are twins?

ALFRED. He has often told me so, and the Countess also mentioned it when I arrived.

FABIEN. There is a strange, mysterious sympathy between us — no matter what space divides us we are still one in body, in feeling, in soul. Any powerful impression which the one experiences is instantly conveyed, by some invisible agency, to the senses of the other.

ALFRED. This is most singular.

FABIEN. Within these last few days, in spite of myself, my temperament has changed. I have become sad, uneasy, gloomy, with a depression of the heart I cannot conquer. I am convinced my brother is unhappy.

ALFRED. And you attribute this feeling of causeless fear to some danger impending over your brother?

FABIEN. I am sure of it.

ALFRED. And the nature of this unhappiness — cannot you divine it?

FABIEN. No. I feel the effect but the cause is hid from me.

ALFRED. Perhaps some trifling professional annoyance.

FABIEN. Not so. It implicates the heart.

ALFRED. I thought him too much engaged with his studies to care for the attractions of the sex.

FABIEN. For the sex generally, yes; but he is deeply in love with one.

ALFRED. And that one — (*Rising.*) But I am indiscreet, pray pardon me.

FABIEN. You shall know all. From my brother's friend I will have no secrets. About a year since, the daughter of the general commanding in Corsica came on a visit of two months, with her father, to Ajaccio. She was young, amiable, beautiful. Louis and I had frequent opportunities of meeting her, and as all our feelings are in unison, need I tell you we both saw — and loved her. Each of us perceived the passion of the other, and tried to extinguish his own. I know not whether I succeeded, but Louis thought I had, and his increased affection for me proved his gratitude. The general was recalled to France, his daughter accompanied him, and the lovely vision was dissolved. Some time after, my brother asked me whether I intended to go to Paris, to study law or medicine. We had always promised never to leave our mother solitary. I told him I had no desire to travel. His countenance beamed with joy. He left us, and I remained. Most probably I shall never quit my native village.

103

ALFRED. What! at your age, in the springtime of life — bury yourself from the active world!

FABIEN. You wonder, naturally, that anyone should choose to live in such a wild and ignorant land. But I am native to the soil, like the green oak, or laurel rose. I love to explore the forest and to rove over chasm and torrent with my rifle for a companion, to sit upon the mountain ledge with the theatre of nature at my feet, and revel in the sense of liberty and boundless space. In the city I should be stifled as in a prison. No; let Louis obey his destiny. He will become great and noble —

ALFRED. While you?

FABIEN. Am free, and Corsican.

ALFRED (*laughing*). A characteristic reply. And this lady, you think, is the cause of your brother's uneasiness?

FABIEN. Yes. Although he never names her in his letters, his love increases — the wound is a deep one.

ALFRED (*gaily*). Such wounds are seldom mortal, and if you have no other subject of inquietude —

FABIEN. Something else has happened to my brother.

ALFRED. Do you imagine he is in any danger?

FABIEN. I do, certainly.

ALFRED. Or dead?

FABIEN. No — not dead; had it been so, as I told my mother, I should have seen him since.

ALFRED (*smiling*). You would have seen him.

FABIEN. Look you, sir, you are what is called a man of the world. I saw by the incredulous smile with which you listened to me but now —

ALFRED. Oh, believe me —

FABIEN. No, do not apologise. You dwellers in cities — what you gain in art you lose in nature. You are more prone to believe the miracles of a science which you have invented, than to believe the wonders of that creation which a divinity has made.

ALFRED. Nay, do not mistake surprise for misbelief. I accuse nothing of being impossible.

FABIEN. All this appears to you childish and absurd. As a man of the world you scoff at idle tales of superstition. Yet I could relate a tale existing in our family three hundred years ago which might shake your scepticism. Do you believe in apparitions?

ALFRED. Why no, I can't say I believe, but nothing proves their non-existence.

FABIEN. Give me then your attention, while I recount briefly a story well attested in the annals of the Dei Franchi. (*They both sit down near the table*.) Three hundred years ago, our immediate ancestor, the Count Bartolomeo dei Franchi, died, leaving two orphan sons. The extraordinary attachment of these children to each other was the theme of Corsica. Arrived at the age of manhood, they bound themselves by a solemn oath that not even death itself should separate them. This vow each registered in his own blood on a parchment they exhanged; the conditions prescribed were that he who died first should appear to the other, not only at the moment of his death, but also as a warning to foretell it.

ALFRED. An oath more easily made than kept.

FABIEN. In three months after, one of the two brothers was waylaid and murdered in an ambuscade. At that very moment, the other, residing in this very house, being seized with a vague sense of danger, was engaged in writing to him, and as he impressed his seal upon the burning wax, he heard a sigh behind him. He turned and saw his brother standing by his side, his hand upon his shoulder, although he felt no touch or weight. Mechanically he offered the letter to the figure, but it shook its head mournfully, and waving its arm to the wall, the masonry seemed to obey the gesture — it opened, and the living man beheld the murder in all its harrowing identity.

ALFRED. It was a dream.

FABIEN. The archives of justice at Bastia attest its truth, for on the deposition of the surviving brother, the murderers were detected and arrested. Terrified by what they thought the intervention of heaven, they confessed that the crime had been perpetrated exactly as seen in the vision, and at the very same hour.

ALFRED. This is strange indeed, and terrible. Do you fear, then, that Louis is dead?

FABIEN. No, he lives; but I fear he is wounded.

ALFRED. How? By whom?

FABIEN. This morning, on my way to the mountains — ah, my mother returns — do not speak of this before her, I entreat you.

ALFRED. Rely on my discretion.

(*Enter* MADAME DEI FRANCHI, GRIFFO, MARIA, *and* SERVANTS *carrying the supper, which they place on the table*.)

MADAME. Now gentlemen, when you are disposed, supper is ready. Well, Fabien?

FABIEN. Well, mother, my passing gloom has vanished — I am gay and joyous. Monsieur de Meynard, take your seat. (ALFRED *hands* MADAME *to table — they seat themselves,* GRIFFO *and* MARIA *waiting*.) And so you have come to visit Corsica? You do well not to postpone your visit. In a few years, our laws, our manners, will exist no longer. All will be swept away before the modern mania of improvement; we are degenerating hourly from our ancient habits.

ALFRED. But in this house, at least, I find a noble picture of the earlier times.

FABIEN. Yes, in my mother always. But for me, I am at this moment engaged in an action my ancestors would have deemed disgraceful to them.

ALFRED. You? Impossible.

FABIEN. You'll wonder more when I explain it. Our peasantry in this district have been long divided into two factions, who hate each other mortally — the Colonnas and the Orlandos; but for the first time in Corsica, a quarrel has been compromised. Surrounded by muskets, rapiers, and stilettos, I am selected as the arbiter of peace; this evening is fixed for the formality of pacification.

ALFRED. And how originated this famous quarrel, which your good offices have put an end to?

FABIEN. Like many others, from a very trifling cause — so insignificant I cannot name it without smiling. A hen!

ALFRED. A hen!

FABIEN. Yes, a wretched barn door hen. Ten years ago this hen escaped from the farm yard of the Orlandos to that of the Colonnas. The first demanded the hen, the others said it was theirs. During the dispute, the aged grandmother of the Colonnas, who held the fowl, wrung its neck and threw it in the face of the mother of the Orlandos. One of the Orlandos seized the hen and was about to throw it back when a Colonna, who had a loaded carbine, fired, and shot him on the spot.

ALFRED. And how many lives have been sacrificed in this silly altercation?

FABIEN. The killed are nine, the wounded five.

ALFRED. And all for a poor hen! No doubt both parties are worn out, and entreated you to interfere.

FABIEN. Far from it. They would have exterminated each other, rather than have made the slightest overture. Our prefect wrote to Louis, who is gentleness itself, to say that if *I* interfered all might be reconciled. He pledged his word for me, and I was bound in honour to redeem it. This evening, in this hall, the ceremony will take place. (*Bells are rung at a distance.*) Hark! the village bell announces the hour when all are summoned to attend.

(GRIFFO *enters R.*)

GRIFFO. Monsieur Fabien, here's one without desires to speak with you.

FABIEN. Who is he?

GRIFFO. Orlando.

FABIEN. In right good time. (*Going to R.*) Come in, honest Orlando.

(ORLANDO *appears at the door R, dragged in by* GRIFFO.)

ORLANDO. I beg pardon, but —

FABIEN. But what?

ORLANDO. Why this — that is — I don't exactly know — but —

FABIEN. Come in, man, come in.

ORLANDO. Oh, yes — come in, that's easily said, and easily done too — but when I am in —

FABIEN. Well, what then?

ORLANDO. Monsieur Fabien dei Franchi, it chokes a man to be reconciled to an enemy.

FABIEN. Remember, Orlando, you have given your word.

ORLANDO. Yes, yes, I have — Oh, if I hadn't!

FABIEN. Recollect, too, your side has had the advantage. Five Colonnas killed, against four Orlandos.

ORLANDO. That's some consolation — but nevertheless —

(MARIA *enters L, with the dessert.*)

MARIA. Monsieur Fabien, some one without enquires for you.

FABIEN. Where?

MARIA (*pointing to the L door*). There!

FABIEN. Who is it?

MARIA. A Colonna.

FABIEN. Good; desire him to walk in. Griffo, go round by that door and lock it on the outside. (*Exit* GRIFFO *R, locks door on the outside, and re-enters C.*) I repeat it, Orlando, you have the advantage.

ORLANDO. But mind, he must bring a hen with him.

FABIEN. Decidedly.

ORLANDO. A white hen.

FABIEN. Oh, white or black, that makes no difference.

ORLANDO. White, white, nothing but white.

FABIEN. Well, it shall be white.

ORLANDO. And alive.

FABIEN. And alive.

ORLANDO. If it should be dead, remember, the contract fails.

FABIEN. Be satisfied — it *shall* be alive.

ORLANDO. He must offer his hand first.

FABIEN. No, you both offer at the same time; you agreed to that.

ORLANDO. I don't remember that part of the agreement.

FABIEN. How! can an Orlando's memory fail, when he has passed his word?

ORLANDO (*with a deep sigh*). Ah! If I hadn't! It's very hard, nevertheless. But five dead Colonnas against four Orlandos, that's something.

(MARIA *appears at the door L, pushing in* COLONNA.)

MARIA. Go in, I tell you.

COLONNA. Well, if I must, I must.

(ORLANDO *has crept towards the door R, and endeavours to get out, but finding it fastened on the outside, he resumes his confidence, and eyes* COLONNA *fiercely*.)

FABIEN (*to* COLONNA). Remember, you have given your word.

COLONNA. You see, Monsieur Fabien, here's the point: there has been one killed more on our side than on the other — the terms are not equal.

FABIEN. Granted so far; but there are four Orlandos wounded against one Colonna.

COLONNA. Wounded don't count.

FABIEN. It is too late now to argue. Have you brought the hen?

COLONNA. The hen?

FABIEN. You remember your promise; come, you must have brought it.

COLONNA. Yes, yes.

FABIEN. Where is it?

COLONNA. Here.

FABIEN. Here! Where?

COLONNA. In my pocket.

FABIEN. Of course a white one?

COLONNA. Yes, white, certainly. There's one small black spot —

FABIEN. No matter, I'll take that on myself. It is alive?

COLONNA. It was when I started, but on the way I sat down once or twice, and perhaps —

FABIEN. Produce it. (*To* GRIFFO.) Lock that door on the outside as you did the other. (*Exit* GRIFFO *L, locks door on the outside, and re-enters C.*) Hold your fowl in your hand and be ready.

COLONNA. As I bring the fowl, he must be the first to offer his hand.

FABIEN. Not so; both together, that's the agreement.

COLONNA. Is it positively so written down?

FABIEN. Positively. Come, Colonna.

COLONNA (*with a deep sigh*). Oh! If I hadn't promised! But a Colonna must keep his word.

FABIEN (*to* ORLANDO). Who is your surety?

ORLANDO. Andrea Mari.

FABIEN (*to* COLONNA). And yours?

COLONNA. My surety? I forgot that entirely.

ORLANDO (*turning round to go out*). A failure on his side! I declare the treaty void.

FABIEN (*holding him*). No, no, he has one here. Monsieur Alfred de Meynard, will you act as surety to Colonna?

ALFRED. With all my heart.

FABIEN. The preliminaries are complete. Throw open the gate, and admit the company.

(MADAME DEI FRANCHI *and* ALFRED *rise from table;* GRIFFO *opens the doors at the back. Enter the* JUDGE OF THE PEACE, *who carries several olive branches in his hand, and the* MALE *and* FEMALE RELATIONS *and* FRIENDS *of the two adversaries.*)

JUDGE (*after taking his place at the head of the table*). My worthy friends, we are assembled here by Monsieur Fabien dei Franchi, in his ancestral mansion, to witness one of those delightful scenes which are acceptable above, and do honour to the human heart. (ORLANDO *and* COLONNA *growl.*) Receive each of you the peaceful olive branch, and vow oblivion for the past and friendship for the future.

COLONNA. Oblivion, *perhaps*; friendship, *never*.

ORLANDO (*to* FABIEN). You hear him!

COLONNA. Diavolo! 'Tis I, not thou, must restore the hen.

FABIEN (*presenting an olive branch to* ORLANDO). Friendship for the future, Orlando.

ORLANDO. I'll make an effort.

FABIEN (*presenting another branch to* COLONNA). Colonna, friendship for the future.

COLONNA. Well, I'll try.

FABIEN. Good; that point's disposed of. Now shake hands.

(*They pause.* FABIEN *goes to fetch* ORLANDO, *whom he brings forward to the middle of the stage, then goes for* COLONNA — *whilst he is bringing* COLONNA, ORLANDO *regains his place — he makes a sign to* ALFRED, *who leads* ORLANDO *forward on one side, whilst* FABIEN *leads* COLONNA *on the other.*)

FABIEN. Your hands, I say. (*They shake hands unwillingly.*)

JUDGE (*reads*). 'Before us, Antonio Sanola, Justice of the Peace for the district of Sullacaro, it has been solemnly and formally agreed between Carbano Orlando, and Marco Colonna, that from this day forth, the 22nd of March, 1841, the vendetta declared between them since the 11th of February, 1830, shall cease for ever. In token of which they have severally signed these presents, before the principal inhabitants of the village, their respective sureties, friends and relatives; and which are further ratified by Monsieur Fabien dei Franchi, elected as arbitrator, and by me, Antonio Sanola, judge of the district as aforesaid.'

FABIEN. Now then, Colonna, restore the hen.

(COLONNA *makes a movement as if to strike* ORLANDO *in the face; but under the stern look of* FABIEN *he restrains himself, and presents it with tolerable civility.*)

JUDGE. Now, gentlemen, your signatures.

ORLANDO. I can't sign; I don't know how to write.

JUDGE. Then you must affix your mark. A cross will do.

(ORLANDO, *after many difficulties, is persuaded to make his cross —* COLONNA, *who contrives to write his name in a vile scrawl, resumes his place in high triumph at his superiority in penmanship over his rival — After this, the* JUDGE *requires the witnesses to sign — During this time,* FABIEN *goes up to* ORLANDO, *who is examining the hen.*)

FABIEN. Orlando, I congratulate you. No more quarrels between you and Colonna.

ORLANDO. Excellenza! the hen is miserably thin.

COLONNA (*aside to* FABIEN). It isn't a hen; it's a little cock.

(*All having signed the paper, exeunt* PEASANTS *with the* JUDGE, ORLANDO *and* COLONNA *last.*)

ORLANDO. If I hadn't given my hand — but we shall see. (*Exit.*)

COLONNA. If I hadn't restored the hen — but time will show. (*Exit.*)

FABIEN (*to* ALFRED). Well, sir, you have seen our social manners in Corsica; judge whether we are entitled to rank with civilized nations.

ALFRED. At least I have a new incident to add to my adventures.

MADAME. You will relate to our dear Louis how his brother has redeemed his pledge.

ALFRED. I shall not fail to do so.

MADAME. It grows late; you are doubtless fatigued. Griffo, conduct our guest to his apartment.

FABIEN. I have some particular orders for Griffo; select another servant.

MADAME. In that case, I will attend on him myself.

ALFRED. Impossible, Madame, I cannot suffer it.

MADAME. In the old times the lady of the castle always acted as chamberlain, and in Corsica we are still in the sixteenth century.

ALFRED. If you are peremptory, I must obey. (*To* FABIEN.) Good night. Remember, we were interrupted; you owe me the remainder of a story.

FABIEN. Yes, tomorrow.

(*Exeunt* MADAME DEI FRANCHI, ALFRED *and* MARIA.)

FABIEN. Griffo.

GRIFFO. Monsieur?

FABIEN. You must instantly set out for Ajaccio; there wait the arrival of a letter from Paris. The moment you receive it, gallop back as if life and death were on your speed.

GRIFFO. You fear something has happened to your brother?

FABIEN. Griffo, he is wounded. I must know whether his wound is slight or dangerous.

GRIFFO. Have you received a warning?

FABIEN. Yes; this morning on my way to the mountains I felt a sudden pain as if a sword had pierced my chest. I looked round and saw no one. I laid my hand upon the place; there was no wound. My heart felt crushed, and the name of my brother leaped unbidden to my lips. I looked at my watch; it was ten minutes after nine. (*He turns involuntarily towards the clock.*) Look, look, the clock! It points to the same hour, although it must be close on midnight — the clock has stopped.

(MADAME DEI FRANCHI *re-enters.*)

MADAME (*returning*). Yes, I noticed it before. The clock stopped this morning, and without apparent cause.

FABIEN. This morning! They must have forgot to wind it up.

MADAME. No, on the contrary, it was wound up the day before yesterday.

FABIEN. There's no mistaking this; 'tis a second warning.

MADAME. What say you, Fabien?

FABIEN. Nothing, nothing. Good night, dearest mother.

MADAME. Bless you, my son; good night. If evil hovers o'er us, may Providence avert it. (*Exit.*)

FABIEN. To horse! To horse! Griffo, lose not a moment. At all hazards, I will write to Louis. Put the letter in the post the moment you arrive; 'twill catch the steamer which leaves tomorrow. Haste, haste. I'll bring the letter before your foot is in the stirrup. (*Exit* GRIFFO.) The sudden pain in my side — the strange coincidence between my watch and the clock — (*throws off his coat and waistcoat.*) But perhaps 'tis nothing after all. (*He remains in his shirt sleeves, sits at the table and writes.*) 'My brother, my dearest Louis, if this finds you still alive, write instantly — though but two words — to reassure me. I have received a terrible admonition — write — write.'

(*He folds the letter and seals it; at the same time* LOUIS DEI FRANCHI *appears, without his coat or waistcoat, as his brother is, but with a blood stain upon his breast; he glides across the stage, ascending gradually through the floor at the same time, and lays his hand on* FABIEN's *left shoulder.*)

FABIEN (*turning round*). My brother! — dead!

(MADAME DEI FRANCHI *enters.*)

MADAME (*at the door*). Who uttered that word?

LOUIS. Silence — look there!

(LOUIS DEI FRANCHI *waves his arm, passes through the wall, and disappears; at the same moment the scene at the back opens and discloses a glade in the Forest of Fontainebleau. On one side, a young man who is wiping the blood from his sword with a handkerchief; two seconds are near him. On the other side,* LOUIS DEI FRANCHI, *stretched upon the ground, supported by his two seconds and a surgeon.*)

Picture.

ACT TWO: SCENE ONE

The masked ball at the Opera, in Paris. MASKS, DOMINOES *and*
OFFICERS, *in ball costume, walking about, accosting each other
and chatting. During the scene, ball quadrilles are played.*

(*Enter* CORALIE, *followed by* MONTGIRON.)
MONTGIRON. Stay, my angel! One word.
CORALIE. Let it be a short one.
MONTGIRON. Love! Is that short enough?
CORALIE (*going*). Short and sweet, but it has too long a meaning.
MONTGIRON. Not so fast, my pretty Coralie.
CORALIE (*unmasking*). Oh, you know me. Well, Baron, what now?
MONTGIRON. I give a supper tonight after the ball; will you join
   us?
      (*Enter* ESTELLE *and* VERNER.)
CORALIE (*catching at a domino who is passing*). I say, Estelle,
   here's the Baron has a supper tonight, and is in want of guests.
ESTELLE (*unmasking*). Let him address his invitations to us ladies
   of the ballet.
CORALIE. And we'll undertake to provide a full company.
ESTELLE. So you may ice your champagne with confidence, my
   dear Baron.
MONTGIRON. Then I may depend on you?
      (*Enter* BEAUCHAMP.)
CORALIE. Here is my security. Monsieur Beauchamp, you are to
   retain me in custody until — oh, by the by, what hour?
MONTGIRON. Three o'clock precisely.
CORALIE. Until three o'clock; at which disgracefully late hour,
   you are to surrender me at the table of the Baron de Montgiron.
BEAUCHAMP. Accepted!
ESTELLE. Monsieur Verner, till then I confide myself to your
   sense of propriety.
VERNER. Agreed.

(*All remask and join the crowd. Enter* LOUIS DEI FRANCHI; *he advances, looking anxiously round, like a man who is seeking somebody*.)

LOUIS (*stopping and looking at his watch*). It is close on half-past one; that was the time named, and this the place. The anonymous letter I have received assured me she would be here. I have traversed these passages, I have examined every domino that passed me, but I cannot find her. Perhaps I have been deceived — oh, would it were so! Émilie, dear Émilie, for you I have suffered much, and will endure still more.

(*As* LOUIS *disappears in the crowd,* MONTGIRON *returns with* GIORDANO MARTELLI *and several* GENTLEMEN.)

MONTGIRON (*to* GENTLEMEN). Yes, yes, every one his own master at present, but remember you sup with me at three o'clock.

GENTLEMEN. At three! We understand.

(*They shake hands with* MONTGIRON *and* GIORDANO, *and withdraw to the crowd.* LOUIS *returns*.)

LOUIS (*to himself*). I seek in vain; I cannot find her.

MONTGIRON. Louis.

GIORDANO. Louis dei Franchi!

LOUIS (*much surprised*). Giordano! My friend, my countryman!

GIORDANO. My dear Louis, I rejoice to meet you.

LOUIS. I thought you were in Algiers with your regiment.

GIORDANO. I arrived in Paris this morning, on leave of absence.

MONTGIRON. And now, like a true Anacreon, he seeks the Opera, to blend the myrtle with his laurels.

GIORDANO. And you? How chances it I meet you in Paris?

MONTGIRON. He is studying the law — Dupin, Vattel and Grotius; that accounts for his melancholy and abstracted air. Come, cheer up, man. Tonight you must be one of us, and sup with me; you'll meet all our own set: Beauchamp, Verner, Château-Renaud.

LOUIS (*quickly*). Château-Renaud!

MONTGIRON. You know him?

LOUIS. I have met him once or twice.

MONTGIRON. Oh, he's in great request; a most accomplished fellow, acknowledged as the best swordsman in France, and by his own account resistless with the fair. He kills a reputation or an antagonist with equal sang-froid.

LOUIS (*aside*). Should it be so? Can I have wronged her?

MONTGIRON. Well, we may reckon on you?

LOUIS. You must excuse me, I have an appointment here; besides, I am not in spirits for such a party.

MONTGIRON. An appointment! Oh, bring the fair lady with you.

LOUIS. You mistake me. I am not here to seek proofs of love, but to save one who seeks her own destruction.

MONTGIRON. Louis, are you serious?

LOUIS. I am indeed. Thank you once again, but I must decline. (*Exit.*)

GIORDANO. Poor fellow, I hope he hasn't got into a scrape.

MONTGIRON. Oh no, a love affair; six days will settle it.

GIORDANO. Who is the lady to whom he refers?

MONTGIRON. I cannot tell. Louis is reserved, and not a talker like Château-Renaud.

(*Enter* CHÂTEAU-RENAUD.)

RENAUD (*entering*). I beg pardon, but I heard my name. I fear I interrupt you.

MONTGIRON. Oh, not in the least. 'Tis of you we were speaking.

RENAUD. Then I am one too many here.

MONTGIRON. No, no, pray stay. (*Introducing them.*) Monsieur de Château-Renaud, the Baron Giordano Martelli, Captain in the First Chasseurs of Africa: (*they bow.*) both distinguished heroes, one in the field of Mars, the other in that of Venus.

RENAUD. Now, Montgiron, positively you give me a reputation I do not deserve. How I have ever earned the character you honour me with, I cannot imagine.

MONTGIRON. Indeed! That's strange, for they do say you gave it to yourself.

RENAUD. Who says so?

MONTGIRON. It was mentioned here not five minutes ago.

RENAUD. Ah! By whom?

MONTGIRON. First, I believe, by me.

RENAUD. You said that I boasted of success!

MONTGIRON. Yes, and I added, which you did not always achieve.

RENAUD. The devil you did! Name a single instance.

MONTGIRON. Fifty, if you please.

RENAUD. For example, name one.

MONTGIRON. Well, without going very far —

RENAUD. Name — name —

MONTGIRON. Madame de l'Esparre.

RENAUD. Émilie de l'Esparre!

MONTGIRON. Yes. They say you have compromised her name, although she never gave you the least encouragement.

RENAUD. That is the general opinion, is it?

MONTGIRON. It is.

115

RENAUD. Then you take me for a coxcomb, a braggart, a would-be Don Juan?

GIORDANO. Gentlemen!

RENAUD (*to* GIORDANO). Fear nothing, my dear sir; this is no quarrel, 'tis a simple wager. (*To* MONTGIRON.) Will you bet?

MONTGIRON. On what?

RENAUD. That I prove to you this very night my influence with the lady you have named.

MONTGIRON. How will you prove it?

RENAUD. You shall see her in a few minutes, leaning on my arm, here at this very ball.

MONTGIRON. Oh, that proves nothing.

(LOUIS *has entered during this conversation.*)

RENAUD. Well — but if I brought her to your house to supper?

MONTGIRON. That's quite another matter — but there I defy you.

RENAUD. Do you? Name your wager.

MONTGIRON. A thousand francs. We'll give you till four o'clock.

RENAUD. By which hour I engage to bring Madame de l'Esparre to your bachelor party. If I am one moment late, I lose.

MONTGIRON. Agreed.

RENAUD. Adieu till then. (*Exit.*)

LOUIS (*coming forward*). My dear Baron, you were kind enough to invite me to your supper, which I declined. Will you permit me now to accept your invitation?

MONTGIRON. Bravo! Our party then will be complete, if Château-Renaud keeps his word. You will not fail, gentlemen?

LOUIS *and* GIORDANO. We shall be there. (*Exeunt.*)

A curtain descends — Music — It rises and discovers

ACT TWO: SCENE TWO

A retired part of the Opera House.

(*Enter* CHÂTEAU-RENAUD *and* ÉMILIE.)

ÉMILIE. You requested my presence here; I am come, although at the risk of my motives being misinterpreted by you and by the world.

RENAUD. What have you to fear? Behind that mask and domino, no one can recognise you.

ÉMILIE. Once seen, the tongue of slander would assail me; if known, I am ruined. I have obeyed the conditions you insisted on; now keep your promise and restore to me those letters.

RENAUD. Oh certainly, since you insist upon it.

ÉMILIE. You will then return them? Give them to me and let me go.

RENAUD. What! suffer you to leave so quickly, when I have agreed to your desire that this should be our last interview? No, you must first hear me — you must first tell me —

ÉMILIE. What can I say more?

RENAUD. Tell me at least the cause of this sudden change, this rupture which drives me to despair. Why did you ever encourage my addresses? Why did you ever flatter me with hope, to make me feel more bitterly the disappointment? Why write those letters, pledges of returned affection, and now so coldly ask their restitution?

ÉMILIE. I have given you a right to speak thus to me, to think me wavering — fickle — nay, contemptible. I will not deny that you possessed my early love. My first affections, as you know, were yours; my father saw and crushed our hopes at once. The fate of my poor sister — the ill-assorted marriage of Louise — was ever present to his mind. A marriage which cost him a daughter, me a sister, for from that hour I have never seen her. Where is she now? Perhaps deserted, struggling with misery and

117

want. Ill-founded rumours, or some other causes of which I am ignorant, taught his distempered mind to see in you a copy of my sister's husband. To snatch me from the fate he so much dreaded, he made me the companion of his journey into Corsica. On my return, his stern resolution — regardless of the feelings of my heart — obliged me to accept the hand of a man of rank and wealth. The disparity of our years, our total want of sympathy, rendered it impossible for me to love, although I might respect and honour him. It is now a sacred duty I owe to the Admiral de l'Esparre, as well as to myself, to claim from you the evidences of our plighted troth.

RENAUD. You demand of me no trifling sacrifice.

ÉMILIE. Be not deluded by a thought so vain, so false, as to suppose I can again receive you with the feelings that inspired those letters. Cease to claim possession of a heart which, with all its sufferings, all its anguish, belongs now to another. Such sentiments are unworthy of you, and their avowal tends to degrade us both.

RENAUD. Who has dared to impugn my actions thus?

ÉMILIE. Those letters have been seen by others, and most injurious comments made upon them. Thus, through the thoughtlessness of vanity, you assist to wound the honour you are bound to guard.

RENAUD. Émilie! This is the mere impulse of caprice —

ÉMILIE. Oh no; what seems to you caprice is in my mind almost remorse.

RENAUD. You act not from your own impulse; you have been urged on to this.

ÉMILIE. I cannot disregard the warning of a friend.

RENAUD. And this friend, this devoted, meddling friend, doubtless is Louis dei Franchi.

ÉMILIE. It matters not.

RENAUD. If I have heard rightly, you knew him before your marriage; you received his visits constantly. He loved you. Perhaps his passion was returned.

ÉMILIE. This is insulting. The letters — I implore you — the letters.

RENAUD. Well, I have promised to restore them, and I will keep my word. I have them not about me; they are at my residence.

ÉMILIE. Sir! You have deceived me! In reliance on your promise to restore them here, where I have consented most reluctantly to meet you, and for the last time, it may be I have already compromised my position. This last evasion is too palpable. You may no longer love, but you shall at least respect me.

RENAUD. Émilie, you are ungrateful. Listen to me; you have named your sister; you know not how eagerly I have sought to find her, to restore her to your arms. I am at last successful —

ÉMILIE. Oh, heavens!

RENAUD. I have promised that you shall see her this very night. She awaits your coming.

ÉMILIE. You do not deceive me?

RENAUD. This is too much! I have a carriage at the door and will escort you to her lodgings instantly. There I will leave you, while I hasten to procure those letters you insist on my restoring, and thus at the same moment give you a double proof of my respect and my devotion.

ÉMILIE. Haste, haste! I am ready. Forgive me if I doubted you.

RENAUD. I do, I do! (*Looks at his watch.*) Ten minutes to four. I shall win my wager, and preserve my reputation. (*Exeunt.*)

A curtain descends — Music — It is raised for

ACT TWO: SCENE THREE

The house of MONTGIRON. *A bachelor's saloon, very elegantly furnished; entrance door at the back; through a doorway placed on the left, another apartment is seen, in which there is a table richly covered; on the right a chimney-piece, with a cloak over it.*
Enter SERVANT *from the back, showing in* LOUIS *and* GIORDANO.

SERVANT. This way, gentlemen.

GIORDANO. The Baron de Montgiron has not yet returned from the Opera, I presume?

SERVANT. No, sir. My master ordered supper at four precisely. Do you wish for anything, gentlemen?

GIORDANO. No thank you; you can leave us.

(SERVANT *bows and retires. In the meantime,* LOUIS *has seated himself and appears absorbed in his own reflections.*
GIORDANO *regards him for some minutes in silence; at length he approaches him and takes his hand.*)

Louis, pardon me, but I see you are unhappy. Before others I said nothing; now that we are alone, tell me your secret. The grief that is confided to another loses half its bitterness. I am your friend, your countryman; you do not doubt me?

LOUIS. No, Giordano. I will trust you with the frankness of a brother. I love, and I am wretched.

GIORDANO (*sitting down near* LOUIS). Ah, I guessed as much.

LOUIS. This love first dawned in Corsica. A breeze as soft and balmy as the odour of our orange groves wafted it towards my heart; a rude tempest has torn it from me. When the object of my affection left Ajaccio, knowing she had gone to Paris I resolved to follow her. I left my home, my country, my parent, and my noble generous broher, who loved her also, but who sacrificed his own feelings from regard to mine. I came here full of hope, rejoicing to be near her. I came too late; she was already married to another.

120

GIORDANO. Married!

LOUIS. Yes, married without affection; married at the very moment when I thought to offer her my hand.

GIORDANO. And have you seen her since?

LOUIS. Chance threw me into the society of her husband. He sought my company and invited me to his house.

GIORDANO. A dangerous guest.

LOUIS. Oh, no, you know me not. The sainted shrine is not more safe from desecration by the kneeling pilgrim, than is the wife of him whose proffered friendship I accepted. I resolved to stifle my unhappy passion, and become worthy of his confidence. But I mistook my strength, and ceased my visits. (*He rises.*)

GIORDANO. What cause did you assign for your absence?

LOUIS. I needed none; he was ordered on a foreign service. During her husband's absence she lived almost in seclusion, when there appeared a man who seemed to assume a fatal influence over her, and whom I at once recognised as an enemy. That man was Monsieur de Château-Renaud.

GIORDANO. Château-Renaud! I thought so.

LOUIS. I see that like myself you are a believer in first impressions. At first sight of this man I started involuntarily, and when introduced we scarcely spoke to each other.

GIORDANO. You have given me a clue to the sequel; the lady of your love is Madame de l'Esparre?

LOUIS. You have guessed truly. 'Tis she — 'tis Émilie! This Château-Renaud, unrestrained by heart or conscience in the pursuit of pleasure, saw no obstacles, felt no compunction, nay more — he has boasted publicly that having once been an accepted lover he still retains that character, though she is married to another. The idle gossip of the world reached me in my lone retreat. I wrote to Émilie, claiming the freedom of a friend, and pointed out the selfish vanity by which she was compromised. From her I received no answer, but from an unknown quarter was informed that I should meet her at this ball. Impelled by the fatality that governs me, I came, and was a witness of the shameful wager in which her name and honour are involved. (*He lifts his hand to his eyes.*)

GIORDANO (*after a moment's silence*). Louis, be advised; let us leave this place before the party meets.

LOUIS. I feel, Giordano, that you are right. It were better that I should avoid this scene; but do we always act as reason dictates? I cannot go. I *must* remain.

GIORDANO. Summon your pride; reflect. If this woman dares to present herself here tonight, and in this company, she is unworthy the attentions of an honourable man.

LOUIS. Yes, I am resolved. If she comes, she will find me here. If she raises her eyes, she will meet mine, and she will blush.

(*Boisterous laughter without.*)

GIORDANO. Hark! They are coming.

(*Enter* MONTGIRON, BEAUCHAMP *with* CORALIE, VERNER *with* ESTELLE, CELESTINA, *and other gentlemen and ladies; the ladies still in character dresses and masks.*)

MONTGIRON. This way, ladies; you are welcome to my poor habitation.

CORALIE. Why, Baron, you are lodged like an eastern sultan.

ESTELLE (*flopping into a spring chair*). What a delicious chair.

CELESTINA. What beautiful furniture! I hope it is all paid for.

BEAUCHAMP. Montgiron has an old aunt with heavy dividends.

VERNER. What a lucky fellow! I have an old aunt with nothing but ill temper.

MONTGIRON. Off with your masks, ladies; disguise is useless here.

(*They take off their masks, place their bouquets, and arrange their toilets.*)

CORALIE. Where is the supper?

ALL. Ay, where is the supper?

MONTGIRON. You must excuse me, ladies; we are not quite ready. We cannot sup until the clock strikes four. A circumstance —

CORALIE. Nothing happened to the champagne, I hope?

ESTELLE. Oh, I should expire!

(SERVANTS *enter with wine and biscuits, which they hand round.*)

MONTGIRON. Our number is not complete. I have promised to wait for Château-Renaud.

ALL. Château-Renaud!

CORALIE (*dipping biscuit in wine*). Here's to his speedy arrival.

MONTGIRON. Until four o'clock. A wager depends on it.

ALL. A wager!

MONTGIRON. He has laid me a thousand francs that he will bring here to join our party, a certain lady of our acquaintance.

LOUIS (*aside*). This is torture.

MONTGIRON. If he is one minute late, he loses.

ESTELLE. How preciously proper she must be!

CORALIE. I wish somebody would ask me to supper, and bet me a thousand francs I wouldn't come.

CELESTINA. Who is the heroine?

BEAUCHAMP. A vestal of the lamp.

VERNER. A Joan of Arc at least.

MONTGIRON. There is no breach of confidence in telling you. 'Tis Madame —

LOUIS (*rises, and places his hand upon the arm of* MONTGIRON). Montgiron, will you accord me one favour?

MONTGIRON. A favour, my dear Louis?

LOUIS. Do not name the lady you expect.

CORALIE. Why not?

LOUIS. Because, Mademoiselle, that lady is married to a friend of mine.

BEAUCHAMP. A married woman! The wager improves.

MONTGIRON. The husband is at this moment cruising off the coast of Mexico.

LOUIS. In a few weeks he will return to Paris, and I would have him spared all knowledge of his wife's imprudence.

ESTELLE. Poor fellow! I pity him.

CORALIE. Serve him right.

CELESTINA. Certainly.

CORALIE. 'Twill teach him not to go cruising on the coast of Jericho again.

ESTELLE. Mexico, you dunce.

CORALIE. Well, I suppose it makes no difference to his wife. A husband six thousand miles off is the same thing as none at all.

MONTGIRON. I respect your scruples, Louis. Since you desire it, we will treat the lady in question with the most profound discretion. Ladies — gentlemen — whether Château-Renaud comes alone or not, whether he win or lose his wager, I pledge you all to silence on this adventure.

GENTLEMEN. Oh, certainly — we promise it.

MONTGIRON (*to the* LADIES). And you?

LADIES. We swear!

LOUIS. I thank you.

BEAUCHAMP. I would advise Château-Renaud to make haste; it wants but three minutes of his time.

VERNER (*looking at the clock*). Is your clock right?

MONTGIRON. To a minute. I sent word to set it by his watch; the rest is his affair.

GIORDANO (*aside to* LOUIS). Courage, Louis; she will not come.

LOUIS (*constantly looking at the clock*). It wants one minute yet. How slowly move those fatal hands — and yet my life hangs upon their speed. Will they never achieve the goal? Will the hour never strike to release me from this agony?

(*A moment of silence. The first chime of the clock, striking four, is heard.*)

GIORDANO. Louis, you wronged her.

(LOUIS *takes a glass, and is about to lift it to his mouth; the clock continues to strike. At the third chime, a loud ringing is heard from the bell in the ante-chamber.*)

LOUIS (*putting down his glass, and starting*). 'Tis he!

GIORDANO. Perhaps she's not with him.

MONTGIRON (*springing towards the door at the back*). Is he alone? (*He disappears for a moment, and all eyes are turned with great curiosity towards the back.*)

LOUIS (*seizing the arm of* GIORDANO). No, she's there. Her footfall strikes upon my heart.

GIORDANO. Courage.

(MONTGIRON *returns.*)

MONTGIRON. Enter, Madame, I entreat you.

(CHÂTEAU-RENAUD *enters with* ÉMILIE, *masked.*)

RENAUD. Come in, dear Émilie. You needn't unveil unless you like. Bear witness, all of you, it was striking four when we arrived.

MONTGIRON. You have fairly won. Gentlemen, I have lost my wager.

ÉMILIE. Won! He has won. What? Ah, I am betrayed; my fears were well founded. My presence here, then, was the subject of a wager.

RENAUD. Émilie — I —

ÉMILIE (*to* MONTGIRON). Speak, sir. You seem to be the master here; I turn to you for a reply.

MONTGIRON. I confess, Madame, that Monsieur de Château-Renaud induced me to hope that you would honour us with your company.

ÉMILIE. To win this infamous wager, he has stooped to falsehood and to treachery. It was to visit a suffering relative he feigned to conduct me; I came on an errand of charity and affection. (*All express disbelief.*) Oh, I fear not to face you now. If there be any here whose brows should wear a blush, I know 'tis not the wife of the Admiral de l'Esparre. (*She unmasks.*)

RENAUD. Madame, you treat the jest too seriously. Since you are here, you will surely stay?

ÉMILIE. I recognise at least one friend, and in his hands I place myself. Monsieur Louis dei Franchi, will you afford me your protection to conduct me home?

LOUIS (*springing towards her*). My life is yours.

RENAUD. One moment. Allow me to observe, sir, that *I* brought this lady here, and *I* alone will escort her hence.

ÉMILIE. Gentlemen, I place myself beneath the shelter of your honour; you will shield me from further insult.

LOUIS (*placing himself between her and* CHÂTEAU-RENAUD). Fear nothing, Madame, I am by your side.

RENAUD (*after having repressed a movement of violence, very calm*). 'Tis well. I know now to whom I may look for explanation.

LOUIS (*coolly*). If you allude to me, sir, I shall be at home in half an hour.

RENAUD. In less than that you will find a friend to represent me.

ÉMILIE. A duel!

LOUIS (*with disdain*). A challenge in the presence of a lady! Oh, sir, it lacked but this to give a finish to your character. (*Offering his arm to Émilie.*) Come, Madame, my blood to the last drop is yours; my life is nothing to the honour, the happiness, you have now conferred upon me.

(ÉMILIE *takes his arm, they go up, bow to the company, and exeunt.*)

RENAUD (*with an air of forced gaiety*). Well, gentlemen, I suppose I have lost after all. But I shall sup with none the worse appetite.

(SERVANT *enters.*)

SERVANT. Supper is ready.

ALL. Come.

GIORDANO (*aside, going to procure his hat*). Not I. This is no place for me; I will seek Louis, and see this matter terminated.

(*The rest all move towards the room where the supper is prepared, and* GIORDANO *goes off at the back.*)

Curtain descends — Music — Curtain rises, and discovers

ACT TWO: SCENE FOUR

A glade in the Forest of Fontainebleau. LOUIS DEI FRANCHI *discovered, lying on the ground wounded, attended by his seconds* MONTGIRON *and* GIORDANO; *a* SURGEON *is near him and examines his wound; on the other side,* CHÂTEAU-RENAUD *wiping his sword; two other seconds,* BEAUCHAMP *and* VERNER, *are near him. It is an exact reproduction of the tableau that terminated the first act.*

GIORDANO (*to* SURGEON). Well, sir, what hope?

SURGEON. None; the lungs are pierced. (*Looking at his watch.*) Ten minutes past nine! He has not five minutes to live.

GIORDANO (*with great emotion*). My poor friend!

LOUIS (*coming to himself*). Giordano, where are you?

GIORDANO. Here, Louis, by your side. Speak; what would you? Have you no wish to be conveyed to your mother — to your brother Fabien?

LOUIS. No, no; they will know all.

GIORDANO. When?

LOUIS. Tonight.

GIORDANO. Tonight! And by what means?

LOUIS. By me. Your hand, Giordano; yours, sir — Émilie, farewell. (*He sinks back exhausted and dies. During the utterance of these last words, the back of the scene opens slowly and discovers the chamber of the first act, the clock marking the hour, ten minutes after nine;* MADAME DEI FRANCHI *and* FABIEN, *looking exactly as they did before.*)

FABIEN. Pray for Louis, dearest mother. I go to avenge him.

126

ACT THREE

The glade in the Forest of Fontainebleau where LOUIS *was killed.*
BOISSEC *discovered making faggots and singing. The noise of a
carriage on the road is heard at a distance.* BOISSEC *pauses in his
work and looks through the trees.*

BOISSEC. Click, clack! What a cloud of dust! And how they do
scamper along yonder — a post chaise tearing away at full
gallop. It's a fine thing to be rich. But what is the postillion
about? He's taking them right against a heap of stones. If that
man isn't drunk, I'm not sober. He'll upset them, ten to one.
(*Loud crash without, as of the chaise being overturned.*) A hollow
bet, won already. There's an end of your journey, whoever you
are. (*Still looking, whilst he is filling his pipe.*) Ah! Two gentlemen get out and shake themselves. They are looking about for
assistance. These gentry often give a great deal of trouble, and
pay nothing for it. I'll pretend not to see them; but they see me,
and are making signs. (*Shouts of 'Hullo' without.*) Now they
call. I'm blind and deaf. (*He resumes his work and sings.*)
  (*Enter* CHÂTEAU-RENAUD *and* MONTGIRON.)
RENAUD. I say, my good fellow. (BOISSEC *continues, without
noticing him.*) My good friend — (*Slapping him on the back.*)
Are you deaf?
BOISSEC (*turning half round*). Did you speak to me, sir?
RENAUD. Yes, I did.
BOISSEC. Beg pardon, but I was so busy with my work. (*He
resumes chopping and humming.*)
MONTGIRON. Listen to me. If we take you from your work, we
will gladly repay you for your lost time.
BOISSEC (*taking his pipe out of his mouth, and bowing*). The case
is altered. Gentlemen, I am at your service.
MONTGIRON. The axletree of our carriage is broke. Do you know
any wheelwright in Fontainebleau who could mend it?

127

BOISSEC. A first rate one — my cousin. He should have been a coachmaker in Paris, but there's no such thing as justice in this world.

MONTGIRON. Fly, then, and bring him here with his tools instantly.

BOISSEC. 'Tis a good mile to his shop.

MONTGIRON. Ten francs are yours if you dispatch.

BOISSEC (*eagerly*). Ten francs! I'm off like a flash of lightning. (*He goes a few steps and returns.*) I beg pardon, have you broke any bones in your tumble?

MONTGIRON. No, no.

BOISSEC. Because, you see, my cousin is a famous veterinary surgeon also, and can set an arm or a leg with any man in Paris.

MONTGIRON. We have no need of his skill in that line.

BOISSEC. Ah, I'm sorry for that. (*Pretends to go, then returns.*) I beg pardon again, but an upset in the dust makes people thirsty. My cousin sells capital wine, almost as good as (*aside*) vinegar.

MONTGIRON. Begone, I tell you, or the ten francs will dwindle to five.

BOISSEC (*going*). Au revoir. (*Exit.*)

(MONTGIRON *goes up to* CHÂTEAU-RENAUD, *who during this dialogue has seated himself upon a fallen tree, and supports his head with his hand.*)

MONTGIRON. Château-Renaud, what ails you, man?

RENAUD. If I were superstitious, I should give up this journey.

MONTGIRON. It has commenced badly enough, that must be admitted.

RENAUD. We should have done far better to have remained in Paris.

MONTGIRON. I think differently, and have determined to be missing for the present. Your duel with Louis, in spite of our precautions, has taken wind. The Attorney General and the Minister of Police are making tender enquiries after us.

RENAUD (*walking about uneasily*). I care little for their enquiries.

MONTGIRON. But I tell you they are serious this time, and resolved to make an example. Unfortunately, this is not your first affair —

RENAUD. And for a trifling mishap or two like this —

MONTGIRON. You would wish to figure in a court of justice? I have no such ambition. We should be acquitted perhaps; but in the meantime, three months in prison, on spare diet, is anything but amusing. Besides, you have forgot another trifling inconvenience.

RENAUD. Indeed! Of what nature?

128

MONTGIRON. Louis dei Franchi is dead — but he has left a brother.

RENAUD. Well, what of him?

MONTGIRON. Only this: he is a true Corsican. As soon as he hears of what has happened, he will traverse the world to obtain revenge.

RENAUD. I see no reason, because I have fought with one brother, why I should run the gauntlet through the whole family.

MONTGIRON. In France, no; in Corsica, yes. Take my advice and keep out of the way for a few weeks, until this unhappy affair has blown over.

RENAUD. Well, as you wish it, and our plans are formed, let us proceed. I cannot conceal the sensations which oppress me. I am pursued by some fatality. For the first time I feel as if urged on by some controlling influence to something fatal.

MONTGIRON (*laughing*). You, Château-Renaud, grown superstitious?

RENAUD. 'Tis weak, I own; but the strongest minds are sometimes moved by trifles — the breaking of a mirror, or the howling of a dog. I have laughed at all this a hundred times, and now I am shaken by the overturn of our post chaise. And in what locality? In the Forest of Fontainebleau, in the very glade where five days since — (*looking round him and with terror.*) Say — do you not recognise the spot — this path — that tree —

MONTGIRON (*looking round*). Yes, 'tis the very place. The accident is strange.

RENAUD. Montgiron, there's more than *accident* in this; 'tis destiny — perhaps the hand of Providence.

MONTGIRON. Our man returns.

(*Enter* BOISSEC.)

Well, friend, you have lost no time. Is the blacksmith at work?

BOISSEC. Look yonder, and you can see him. In a few minutes all will be right again.

MONTGIRON. Here's the money I promised you.

BOISSEC. Thank you, sir. With ten francs in my pocket, I am a gentleman for the rest of the day. (*The sound of a carriage is heard.*) Ah, another carriage! If it would only break down like the first, I might double the ten francs. Good day, Messieurs, and a pleasant journey. (*He takes up his hatchet, lifts his faggots on his shoulder, and goes off, singing.*)

RENAUD (*agitated*). Let us leave this spot. Let us get beyond the forest — it feels like a grave. In the whisper of the wind I hear the dying sigh of Louis, and at every turn I dread to meet his ghost.

129

MONTGIRON. What folly!

RENAUD. It may be folly, but I cannot conquer it. Let us be gone. (*As they are going up, enter* FABIEN *in a cloak.*)

FABIEN. Stay!

MONTGIRON. What do I see?

RENAUD (*with terror, to* FABIEN). What would you?

FABIEN. Can you not guess?

RENAUD. Louis dei Franchi!

FABIEN. No. Not Louis — but his brother.

RENAUD. His brother!

MONTGIRON (*aside*). My fears are realised.

FABIEN (*with calm but terrible sternness, advancing towards* CHÂTEAU-RENAUD, *who retreats from him*). You take me for the spectre of your victim. No; I am one more terrible, more implacable. I am Fabien dei Franchi, come from the wilds of Corsica to demand of you: where is my brother?

RENAUD (*with a sort of arrogance*). Of me? What have I to do with him?

FABIEN. You answer as the first murderer. What have you done with him? I'll tell you that. Five days since, at the remotest end of Corsica, I learned how I had lost a loved — an only brother; how you drew your serpent slime across his path, blighted the bright vision of his days, tried to bring dishonour on a woman it was the devoted object of his life to guard. By a base lie you decoyed that woman into a snare from which he rescued her. Then, taking advantage of a mere bravo's skill, you murdered him. (MONTGIRON *and* CHÂTEAU-RENAUD *appear indignant.*) Yes! I repeat my words — you are the assassin of my brother.

RENAUD. Assassin!

FABIEN. Aye; for when a man is deadly with his weapon and goads another man he knows to be less practised than himself to quarrel, he fights him not, he murders him.

MONTGIRON. Hold, gentlemen, I entreat you. Monsieur Fabien dei Franchi, I cannot comprehend you. Five days ago, you say, you were in Corsica. How is it possible these sad details could reach you in so short a space of time?

FABIEN. The dead travel quickly.

MONTGIRON. We are not children, sir, to be terrified with nursery tales.

FABIEN (*coldly*). On the same evening of my brother's death I was informed of all; nay more — I *saw* it all. In five days I have traversed two hundred and eighty leagues. When I reached your house, they told me you had just left Paris. I ascertained the route you had taken. I saw your carriage overturned and I exclaimed 'The hand of the avenger is upon him'.

RENAUD (*with resolution*). Well, sir, I am found. What would you with me?

FABIEN. A mortal combat. Know you not that a Corsican race is like the fabled Hydra? Kill one — another supplies his place. You have shed my brother's blood; I am here to demand yours, or yield my own.

RENAUD. You wish to take my life! And how?

FABIEN. Not after the usual practice of my country, from behind a wall or across a hedge, but in the manner sanctioned here, according to rule — according to fashion. (*Throwing open his cloak.*) You see I am in proper costume.

RENAUD. I would have avoided this most earnestly; I was flying from it. But if I accept the challenge, it is on one condition.

FABIEN. Name it.

RENAUD. That the quarrel ceases here, and that I am not again to be called upon by another brother or some distant cousin. Let this be the last encounter.

FABIEN. The last it *shall* be. I am the only living relative of Louis, and after me, Monsieur de Château-Renaud, be assured none will trouble you.

RENAUD. Name your hour, place, and weapons.

FABIEN. The hour? I have sworn it should be at the moment when I met you. The weapons? With a sword you killed my brother; with a sword you shall encounter me. The place? The spot where we now stand.

RENAUD. This spot?

FABIEN. Yes, this spot. You chose it five days since. At the foot of that tree my brother fell; the traces of his blood remain there still.

RENAUD (*with resolution*). Since you are determined, be it so. (*Throws off his coat.*) The sooner all this ends, the better.

MONTGIRON (*passing between them*). Gentlemen, this cannot be. The duel is impossible; at least at present. Here is but one witness, and you are both unarmed.

FABIEN. You are mistaken, sir; I come prepared. (*Calling at the back.*) Meynard, approach.

(*Enter* ALFRED DE MEYNARD *in a cloak, carrying two swords.*)

Here is my second — here are arms for both.

MONTGIRON (*going up to* ALFRED). Meynard! Perhaps we may yet find means —

131

FABIEN. (*taking off his coat and waistcoat*). Monsieur de Meynard, sir, knows his duty.

RENAUD. (*who has removed his waistcoat*). I am ready.

FABIEN. Meynard, request Monsieur de Château-Renaud to take his choice.

    (ALFRED *presents the swords to* CHÂTEAU-RENAUD, *who selects one.*)

RENAUD. Now sir. (*A clock at a distance strikes nine.*)

FABIEN. (*coldly*). If you have any last instructions for your friend, you have still an opportunity.

RENAUD. Why shall I use it?

FABIEN. Because, as surely as yon sky is over us, in ten minutes you take your place there, where my brother fell.

RENAUD. This is no time for empty boasting, sir.

FABIEN. (*very calm*). Gentlemen, bear witness for me. Do I look like an empty boaster? Now sir — on guard!

    (*They fight for several minutes, in which* CHÂTEAU-RENAUD *exerts himself to kill or wound* FABIEN, *but is foiled by his coolness and skill.*)

Pause for a moment, you are out of breath.

RENAUD. (*to* MONTGIRON). His wrist is made of iron. (*After a moment or two.*) When you are ready.

FABIEN. I am always ready.

    (*They fight. The sword of* CHÂTEAU-RENAUD *is broken.*)

MONTGIRON. (*springing forward*). Gentlemen, the sword of Château-Renaud is broken. The duel is over, the arms are no longer equal.

FABIEN. You are mistaken again, sir. (*Breaking his sword beneath his heel.*) I have made them equal. (*To* CHÂTEAU-RENAUD, *pointing to the broken blade.*) Take up that fragment, and let us try once more.

MONTGIRON. Are you still implacable?

FABIEN. As destiny itself.

    (ALFRED *assists* FABIEN *to tie the end of his sword round his wrist with a handkerchief.* MONTGIRON *fastens* CHÂTEAU-RENAUD's *sword in the same manner.*)

RENAUD. (*aside to* MONTGIRON). He will kill me, Montgiron; I feel convinced of it. You will continue your journey alone. In eight days write to my mother, and say I had a fall from my horse. In a fortnight tell her I am dead. If she learned the fatal news abruptly, she would die herself.

MONTGIRON. Château-Renaud, you are mad.

RENAUD. No. I am not mad, but in two minutes I am a dead man.

(*During this* MONTGIRON *has tied the sword round* CHÂTEAU-RENAUD's *wrist.*)

ALFRED. Gentlemen, are you ready?

(CHÂTEAU-RENAUD *and* FABIEN *close in mortal combat.* CHÂTEAU-RENAUD *overthrows him, but just as he is going to strike,* FABIEN *plunges his weapon into his heart.*)

RENAUD (*falling back close to the tree near which* LOUIS *fell*). Montgiron, I was a true prophet. Farewell. (*Dies.*)

FABIEN. (*rising*). My mother, I have kept my word. Louis! Louis! I can weep for him now.

(*He passes behind a tree up stage; then advances, with face covered by his hands, and sinks weeping upon the fallen tree. A pause.* LOUIS DEI FRANCHI *appears, rising gradually through the earth and placing his hand on the shoulder of his brother.*)

LOUIS. Mourn not, my brother. We shall meet again.

THE OCTOROON

First performed at the Winter Garden Theatre in New York on 6 December 1859.

George Peyton	MR A. H. DAVENPORT
Salem Scudder	MR J. JEFFERSON
Mr Sunnyside	MR G. HOLLAND
Jacob M'Closky	MR T. B. JOHNSTON
Wahnotee	MR DION BOUCICAULT
Lafouche	MR STODDART
Captain Ratts	MR HARRISON
Colonel Pointdexter	MR RUSSELL
Jules Thibodeaux	
Judge Caillou	
Jackson	
Old Pete	MR G. JAMIESON
Paul (*a boy slave*)	MISS BURKE
Solon	
Mrs Peyton	
Zoe	MISS AGNES ROBERTSON
Dora Sunnyside	
Grace	
Minnie	
Dido	

ACT ONE

The scene opens on a view of the Plantation Terrebonne, in Louisiana. A branch of the Mississippi is seen winding through the estate. A low-built but extensive planter's dwelling, surrounded with a veranda, and raised a few feet from the ground, occupies the left side. On the right stand a table and chairs. GRACE is discovered sitting at breakfast-table with the Negro children.

SOLON (*enters, from the house*). Yah! you bomn'ble fry — git out — a gen'leman can't pass for you.

GRACE (*seizing a fly whisk*). Hee! — ha git out! (*She drives the children away. In escaping, they tumble against SOLON, who falls with the tray; the children steal the bananas and rolls that fall about.*)

PETE (*who is lame, enters; he carries a mop and pail*). Hey! laws a massey! why, clar out! drop dat banana! I'll murder this yer crowd. (*He chases children about; they leap over railing at back.*)

(*Exit SOLON.*)

Dem little niggers is a judgment upon dis generation.

GEORGE (*enters, from the house*). What's the matter, Pete?

PETE. It's dem black trash, Mas'r George; dis ere property wants claring; dem's getting too numerous round: when I gets time I'll kill some on 'em, sure!

GEORGE. They don't seem to be scared by the threat.

PETE. Stop, you varmin! stop till I get enough of you in one place!.

GEORGE. Were they all born on this estate?

PETE. Guess they nebber was born — dem tings! what, dem? — get away! Born here — dem darkies? What, on Terrebonne! Don't b'lieve it, Mas'r George; dem black tings never was born at all; dey swarmed one mornin' on a sassafras tree in the swamp; I cotched 'em; dey ain't no 'count. Don't believe

137

dey'll turn out niggers when dey're growed; dey'll come out sunthin' else.

GRACE. Yes, Mas'r George, dey was born here; and old Pete is fonder on 'em dan he is of his fiddle on a Sunday.

PETE. What? dem tings — dem? get away. (*Makes blow at the children.*) Born here! dem darkies! What, on Terrebonne? Don't b'lieve it, Mas'r George — no. One morning dey swarmed on a sassafras tree in de swamp, and I cotched 'em all in a sieve — dat's how dey come on top of dis yearth — git out, you — ya, ya! (*Laughs.*)

(*Exit* GRACE.)

MRS PEYTON (*enters from the house*). So, Pete, you are spoiling those children as usual!

PETE. Dat's right, missus! gib it to ole Pete! he's allers in for it. Git away dere! Ya! if dey ain't all lighted, like coons, on dat snake fence, just out of shot. Look dar! Ya, ya! Dem debils. Ya!

MRS PEYTON. Pete, do you hear?

PETE. Git down dar! I'm arter you! (*Hobbles off.*)

MRS PEYTON. You are out early this morning, George.

GEORGE. I was up before daylight. We got the horses saddled, and galloped down the shell road over the Piney Patch; then coasting the Bayou Lake, we crossed the long swamps, by Paul's Path, and so came home again.

MRS PEYTON (*laughing*). You seem already familiar with the names of every spot on the estate.

(*Enter* PETE, *who arranges breakfast.*)

GEORGE. Just one month ago I quitted Paris. I left that siren city as I would have left a beloved woman.

MRS PEYTON. No wonder! I dare say you left at least a dozen beloved women there, at the same time.

GEORGE. I feel that I departed amid universal and sincere regret. I left my loves and my creditors equally inconsolable.

MRS PEYTON. George, you are incorrigible. Ah! you remind me so much of your uncle, the judge.

GEORGE. Bless his dear old handwriting, it's all I ever saw of him. For ten years his letters came every quarter-day, with a remittance and a word of advice in his formal cavalier style; and then a joke in the postscript, that upset the dignity of the foregoing. Aunt, when he died, two years ago, I read over those letters of his, and if I didn't cry like a baby —

MRS PEYTON. No, George; say you wept like a man. And so you really kept those foolish letters?

GEORGE. Yes; I kept the letters, and squandered the money.

MRS PEYTON (*embracing him*). Ah! why were you not my son — you are so like my dear husband.

SCUDDER (*enters*). Ain't he! Yes — when I saw him and Miss Zoe galloping through the green sugar crop, and doing ten dollars' worth of damage at every stride, says I, how like his old uncle he do make the dirt fly.

GEORGE. O, aunt! what a bright, gay creature she is!

SCUDDER. What, Zoe! Guess that you didn't leave anything female in Europe that can lift an eyelash beside that gal. When she goes along, she just leaves a streak of love behind her. It's a good drink to see her come into the cotton fields — the niggers get fresh on the sight of her. If she ain't worth her weight in sunshine you may take one of my fingers off, and choose which you like.

MRS PEYTON. She need not keep us waiting breakfast, though. Pete, tell Miss Zoe that we are waiting.

PETE. Yes, missus. Why, Minnie, why don't you run when you hear, you lazy crittur?

(MINNIE *runs off*.)

Dat's de laziest nigger on dis yere property. (*Sitting down*.) Don't do nuffin.

MRS PEYTON. My dear George, you are left in your uncle's will heir to this estate.

GEORGE. Subject to your life interest and an annuity to Zoe, is it not so?

MRS PEYTON. I fear that the property is so involved that the strictest economy will scarcely recover it. My dear husband never kept any accounts, and we scarcely know in what condition the estate really is.

SCUDDER. Yes, we do, ma'am; it's in a darned bad condition. Ten years ago the judge took as overseer a bit of Connecticut hardware called M'Closky. The judge didn't understand accounts — the overseer did. For a year or two all went fine. The judge drew money like Bourbon whisky from a barrel, and never turned off the tap. But out it flew, free for everybody or anybody to beg, borrow, or steal. So it went, till one day the judge found the tap wouldn't run. He looked in to see what stopped it, and pulled out a big mortgage. 'Sign that,' says the overseer; 'it's only a formality.' 'All right,' says the judge, and away went a thousand acres; so at the end of eight years, Jacob M'Closky, Esquire, finds himself proprietor of the richest half of Terrebonne —

GEORGE. But the other half is free.

SCUDDER. No, it ain't; because, just then, what does the judge do, but hire another overseer — a Yankee — a Yankee named Salem Scudder.

MRS PEYTON. O, no, it was —

SCUDDER. Hold on, now! I'm going to straighten this account clear out. What was this here Scudder? Well, he lived in New York by sittin' with his heels up in front of French's Hotel, and inventin' —

GEORGE. Inventing what?

SCUDDER. Improvements — anything, from a stay-lace to a fire-engine. Well, he cut that for the photographing line. He and his apparatus arrived here, took the judge's likeness and his fancy, who made him overseer right off. Well, sir, what does this Scudder do but introduces his inventions and improvements on this estate. His new cotton gins broke down, the steam sugar-mills burst up, until he finished off with his folly what Mr M'Closky with his knavery began.

MRS PEYTON. O, Salem! how can you say so? Haven't you worked like a horse?

SCUDDER. No, ma'am, I worked like an ass — an honest one, and that's all. Now, Mr George, between the two overseers, you and that good lady have come to the ground; that is the state of things, just as near as I can fix it.

(ZOE sings without.)

GEORGE. 'Tis Zoe.

SCUDDER. O, I have not spoiled that anyhow. I can't introduce any darned improvement there. Ain't that a cure for old age; it kinder lifts the heart up, don't it?

MRS PEYTON. Poor child! what will become of her when I am gone? If you haven't spoiled her, I fear I have. She has had the education of a lady.

GEORGE. I have remarked that she is treated by the neighbours with a kind of familiar condescension that annoyed me.

SCUDDER. Don't you know that she is the natural daughter of the judge, your uncle, and that old lady thar just adored anything her husband cared for; and this girl, that another woman would 'a' hated, she loves as if she'd been her own child.

GEORGE. Aunt, I am prouder and happier to be your nephew and heir to the ruins of Terrebonne, than I would have been to have had half Louisiana without you.

ZOE (enters from the house). Am I late? Ah! Mr Scudder, good morning.

SCUDDER. Thank'ye. I'm from fair to middlin', like a bamboo cane, much the same all the year round.

140

ZOE. No; like a sugar cane; so dry outside, one would never think there was so much sweetness within.

SCUDDER. Look here: I can't stand that gal! if I stop here, I shall hug her right off. (*He sees* PETE, *who has set his pail down up stage, and gone to sleep on it.*) If that old nigger ain't asleep, I'm blamed. Hillo! (*He kicks pail from under* PETE, *and lets him down. Exit.*)

PETE. Hi! Debbel's in de pail! Whar's breakfass?

(*Enter* SOLON *and* DIDO *with coffeepot and dishes.*)

DIDO. Bless'ee, Missey Zoe, here it be. Dere's a dish of penpans — jess taste, Mas'r George — and here's fried bananas; smell 'em do, sa glosh.

PETE. Hole yer tongue, Dido. Whar's de coffee? (*He pours it out.*) If it don't stain de cup, your wicked ole life's in danger, sure! dat right! black as nigger; clar as ice. You may drink dat, Mas'r George. (*Looks off.*) Yah! here's Mas'r Sunnyside, and Missey Dora, jist drove up. Some of you niggers run and hole de hosses; and take dis, Dido. (*He gives her coffeepot to hold, and hobbles off, followed by* SOLON *and* DIDO.)

(*Enter* SUNNYSIDE *and* DORA.)

SUNNYSIDE. Good day, ma'am. (*He shakes hands with George.*) I see we are just in time for breakfast. (*He sits.*)

DORA. O, none for me; I never eat. (*She sits.*)

GEORGE (*aside*). They do not notice Zoe. (*Aloud*) You don't see Zoe, Mr Sunnyside.

SUNNYSIDE. Ah! Zoe, girl; are you there?

DORA. Take my shawl, Zoe. (ZOE *helps her.*) What a good creature she is.

SUNNYSIDE. I dare say, now, that in Europe you have never met any lady more beautiful in person, or more polished in manners, than that girl.

GEORGE. You are right, sir; though I shrank from expressing that opinion in her presence, so bluntly.

SUNNYSIDE. Why so?

GEORGE. It may be considered offensive.

SUNNYSIDE (*astonished*). What? I say, Zoe, do you hear that?

DORA. Mr Peyton is joking.

MRS PEYTON. My nephew is not acquainted with our customs in Louisiana, but he will soon understand.

GEORGE. Never, Aunt! I shall never understand how to wound the feelings of any lady; and, if that is the custom here, I shall never acquire it.

DORA. Zoe, my dear, what does he mean?

ZOE. I don't know.

GEORGE. Excuse me, I'll light a cigar. (*He goes up.*)

DORA (*aside to* ZOE). Isn't he sweet! O, dear, Zoe, is he in love with anybody?

ZOE. How can I tell?

DORA. Ask him, I want to know; don't say I told you to inquire, but find out. Minnie, fan me, it is so nice — and his clothes are French, ain't they?

ZOE. I think so; shall I ask him that too?

DORA. No, dear. I wish he would make love to me. When he speaks to one he does it so easy, so gentle; it isn't bar-room style; love lined with drinks, sighs tinged with tobacco — and they say all the women in Paris were in love with him, which I feel *I* shall be. Stop fanning me; what nice boots he wears.

SUNNYSIDE (*to* MRS PEYTON). Yes, ma'am, I hold a mortgage over Terrebonne; mine's a ninth, and pretty near covers all the property, except the slaves. I believe Mr M'Closky has a bill of sale on them. O, here he is.

(*Enter* M'CLOSKY.)

SUNNYSIDE. Good morning, Mr M'Closky.

M'CLOSKY. Good morning, Mr Sunnyside; Miss Dora, your servant.

DORA (*seated*). Fan me, Minnie.— (*Aside*) I don't like that man.

M'CLOSKY (*aside*). Insolent as usual. — (*Aloud*) You begged me to call this morning. I hope I'm not intruding.

MRS PEYTON. My nephew, Mr Peyton.

M'CLOSKY. O, how d'ye do, sir? (*He offers his hand,* GEORGE *bows coldly. Aside*) A puppy — if he brings any of his European airs here we'll fix him. — (*Aloud*) Zoe, tell Pete to give my mare a feed, will ye?

GEORGE (*angrily*). Sir!

M'CLOSKY. Hillo! did I tread on ye?

MRS PEYTON. What is the matter with George?

ZOE (*takes fan from* MINNIE). Go, Minnie, tell Pete; run! (*Exit* MINNIE.)

MRS PEYTON. Grace, attend to Mr M'Closky.

M'CLOSKY. A julep, gal, that's my breakfast, and a bit of cheese.

GEORGE (*aside to* MRS PEYTON). How can you ask that vulgar ruffian to your table!

MRS PEYTON. Hospitality in Europe is a courtesy: here, it is an obligation. We tender food to a stranger, not because he is a gentleman, but because he is hungry.

GEORGE. Aunt, I will take my rifle down to the Atchafalaya. Paul has promised me a bear and a deer or two. I see my little

142

Nimrod yonder, with his Indian companion. Excuse me, ladies.
Ho! Paul! (*He enters house.*)

PAUL (*outside*). I'ss, Mas'r George.
(*Enter* PAUL *with the Indian.*)

SUNNYSIDE. It's a shame to allow that young cub to run over the
swamps and woods, hunting and fishing his life away instead of
hoeing cane.

MRS PEYTON. The child was a favourite of the judge, who
encouraged his gambols. I couldn't bear to see him put to work.

GEORGE (*returning with rifle*). Come, Paul, are you ready?

PAUL. I'ss Mas'r George. O, golly! ain't that a pooty gun.

M'CLOSKY. See here, you imp; if I catch you, and your redskin
yonder, gunning in my swamps, I'll give you rats, mind. Them
vagabonds, when the game's about, shoot my pigs.
(GEORGE *goes into house.*)

PAUL. You gib me rattan, Mas'r Clostry, but I guess you take a
berry long stick to Wahnotee. Ugh, he make bacon of you.

M'CLOSKY. Make bacon of me, you young whelp! Do you mean
that I'm a pig? Hold on a bit. (*He seizes whip and holds* PAUL.)

ZOE. O, sir! don't, pray, don't.

M'CLOSKY (*slowly lowering his whip*). Darn you, redskin, I'll
pay you off some day, both of ye. (*He returns to table and
drinks.*)

SUNNYSIDE. That Indian is a nuisance. Why don't he return to
his nation out West?

M'CLOSKY. He's too fond of thieving and whiskey.

ZOE. No; Wahnotee is a gentle, honest creature, and remains here
because he loves that boy with the tenderness of a woman.
When Paul was taken down with the swamp fever the Indian
sat outside the hut, and neither ate, slept, nor spoke for five
days, till the child could recognise and call him to his bedside.
He who can love so well is honest — don't speak ill of poor
Wahnotee.

MRS PEYTON. Wahnotee, will you go back to your people?

WAHNOTEE. Sleugh.

PAUL. He don't understand; he speaks a mash-up of Indian and
Mexican. Wahnotee Patira na sepau assa wigiran?

WAHNOTEE. Weal Omenee.

PAUL. Says he'll go if I'll go with him. He calls me Omenee, the
Pigeon, and Miss Zoe is Ninemoosha, the Sweetheart.

WAHNOTEE (*pointing to* ZOE). Ninemoosha.

ZOE. No, Wahnotee, we can't spare Paul.

PAUL. If Omenee remain, Wahnotee will die in Terrebonne.

143

(*During the dialogue,* WAHNOTEE *has taken* GEORGE's *gun.*)

GEORGE (*enters*). Now I'm ready. (GEORGE *tries to regain his gun;* WAHNOTEE *refuses to give it up;* PAUL *quietly takes it from him and remonstrates with him.*)

DORA. Zoe, he's going; I want him to stay and make love to me; that's what I came for today.

MRS PEYTON. George, I can't spare Paul for an hour or two; he must run over to the landing; the steamer from New Orleans passed up the river last night, and if there's a mail they have thrown it ashore.

SUNNYSIDE. I saw the mailbags lying in the shed this morning.

MRS PEYTON. I expect an important letter from Liverpool; away with you, Paul; bring the mailbags here.

PAUL. I'm 'most afraid to take Wahnotee to the shed, there's rum there.

WAHNOTEE. Rum!

PAUL. Come, then, but if I catch you drinkin', O, laws a mussey, you'll get snakes! I'll gib it you! now mind. (*Exits with Indian.*)

GEORGE. Come, Miss Dora, let me offer you my arm.

DORA. Mr George, I am afraid, if all we hear is true, you have led a dreadful life in Europe.

GEORGE. That's a challenge to begin a description of my feminine adventures.

DORA. You have been in love, then?

GEORGE. Two hundred and forty-nine times! Let me relate you the worst cases.

DORA. No! no!

GEORGE. I'll put the naughty parts in French.

DORA. I won't hear a word! O, you horrible man! go on. (GEORGE *and* DORA *go into the house.*)

M'CLOSKY. Now, ma'am, I'd like a little business, if agreeable. I bring you news; your banker, old Lafouche, of New Orleans, is dead; the executors are winding up his affairs, and have foreclosed on all overdue mortgages, so Terrebonne is for sale. Here's the *Picayune* (*Producing paper*) with the advertisement.

ZOE. Terrebonne for sale!

MRS PEYTON. Terrebonne for sale, and you, sir, will doubtless become its purchaser.

M'CLOSKY. Well, ma'am, I s'pose there's no law agin my bidding for it. The more bidders, the better for you. You'll take care, I guess, it don't go too cheap.

MRS PEYTON. O, sir, I don't value the place for its price, but for the many happy days I've spent here; that landscape, flat and uninteresting though it may be, is full of charm for me; those poor people, born around me, growing up about my heart, have bounded my view of life; and now to lose that homely scene, lose their black, ungainly faces! O, sir, perhaps you should be as old as I am, to feel as I do, when my past life is torn away from me.

M'CLOSKY. I'd be darned glad if somebody would tear my past life away from *me*. Sorry I can't help you, but the fact is, you're in such an all-fired mess that you couldn't be pulled out without a derrick.

MRS PEYTON. Yes, there is a hope left yet, and I cling to it. The house of Mason Brothers, of Liverpool, failed some twenty years ago in my husband's debt.

M'CLOSKY. They owed him over fifty thousand dollars.

MRS PEYTON. I cannot find the entry in my husband's accounts; but you, Mr M'Closky, can doubtless detect it. Zoe, bring here the judge's old desk; it is in the library.

(*Exit* ZOE *to the house*.)

M'CLOSKY. You don't expect to recover any of this old debt, do you?

MRS PEYTON. Yes; the firm has recovered itself, and I received a notice two months ago that some settlement might be anticipated.

SUNNYSIDE. Why, with principal and interest this debt has been more than doubled in twenty years.

MRS PEYTON. But it may be years yet before it will be paid off, if ever.

SUNNYSIDE. If there's a chance of it, there's not a planter round here who wouldn't lend you the whole cash, to keep your name and blood amongst us. Come, cheer up, old friend.

MRS PEYTON. Ah! Sunnyside, how good you are; so like my poor Peyton. (*Exit* MRS PEYTON *and* SUNNYSIDE *to the house*.)

M'CLOSKY. Curse their old families — they cut me — a bilious, conceited, thin lot of dried-up aristocracy. I hate 'em. Just because my grandfather wasn't some broken-down Virginia transplant, or a stingy old Creole, I ain't fit to sit down to the same meat with them. It makes my blood so hot I feel my heart hiss. I'll sweep these Peytons from this section of the country. Their presence keeps alive the reproach against me that I ruined them. Yet, if this money should come! Bah! There's no chance of it. Then, if they go, they'll take Zoe — she'll follow them. Darn that girl; she makes me quiver when I think of her; she's took me for all I'm worth.

145

(*Enter* ZOE *from house, with the desk.*)

M'CLOSKY. O, here, do you know what the annuity the old judge left you is worth today? Not a picayune.

ZOE. It is surely worth the love that dictated it; here are the papers and accounts. (*Putting the desk on the table.*)

M'CLOSKY. Stop, Zoe; come here! How would you like to rule the house of the richest planter on Atchafalaya — eh? or say the word, and I'll buy this old barrack, and you shall be mistress of Terrebonne.

ZOE. O, sir, do not speak so to me!

M'CLOSKY. Why not! look here, these Peytons are bust; cut 'em; I am rich, jine me; I'll set you up grand, and we'll give these first families here our dust, until you'll see their white skins shrivel up with hate and rage; what d'ye say?

ZOE. Let me pass! O, pray, let me go!

M'CLOSKY. What, you won't, won't ye? If young George Peyton was to make you the same offer, you'd jump at it pretty darned quick, I guess. Come, Zoe, don't be a fool; I'd marry you if I could, but you know I can't; so just say what you want. Here, then, I'll put back these Peytons in Terrebonne, and they shall know you done it; yes, they'll have you to thank for saving them from ruin.

ZOE. Do you think they would live here on such terms?

M'CLOSKY. Why not? We'll hire out our slaves, and live on their wages.

ZOE. But I'm not a slave.

M'CLOSKY. No; if you were I'd buy you, if you cost all I'm worth.

ZOE. Let me pass!

M'CLOSKY. Stop.

SCUDDER (*enters*). Let her pass.

M'CLOSKY. Eh?

SCUDDER. Let her pass! (*He takes out his knife. Exit* ZOE *to house.*)

M'CLOSKY. Is that you, Mr Overseer? (*He examines paper.*)

SCUDDER. Yes, I'm here, somewhere, interferin'.

M'CLOSKY (*sitting*). A pretty mess you've got this estate in —

SCUDDER. Yes — me and Co. — we done it; but, as you were senior partner in the concern, I reckon you got the big lick.

M'CLOSKY. What d'ye mean?

SCUDDER. Let me proceed by illustration. (*Sits.*) Look thar! (*Points with his knife off.*) D'ye see that tree? — it's called a live oak, and is a native here; beside it grows a creeper; year after year that creeper twines its long arms round and round the tree — sucking the earth dry all about its roots — living on its life — overrunning its branches, until at last the live oak withers and dies out. Do you know what the niggers round here call that sight? they call it the Yankee hugging the Creole.

M'CLOSKY. Mr Scudder, I've listened to a great many of your insinuations, and now I'd like to come to an understanding what they mean. If you want a quarrel! —

SCUDDER. No, I'm the skurriest crittur at a fight you ever see; my legs have been too well brought up to stand and see my body abused; I take good care of myself, I can tell you.

M'CLOSKY. Because I heard that you had traduced my character.

SCUDDER. Traduced! Whoever said so lied. I always said you were the darndest thief that ever escaped a white jail to misrepresent the North to the South.

M'CLOSKY (*raises hand to back of his neck*). What!

SCUDDER. Take your hand down — take it down. (M'CLOSKY *lowers his hand.*) Whenever I gets into company like yours, I always start with the advantage on my side.

M'CLOSKY. What d'ye mean?

SCUDDER. I mean that before you could draw that bowie knife, you wear down your back, I'd cut you into shingles. Keep quiet, and let's talk sense. You wanted to come to an understanding, and I'm coming thar as quick as I can. Now, Jacob M'Closky, you despise me because you think I'm a fool; I despise you because I know you to be a knave. Between us we've ruined these Peytons; you fired the judge, and I finished off the widow. Now, I feel bad about my share in the business. I'd give half the balance of my life to wipe out my part of the work. Many a night I've laid awake and thought how to pull them through, till I've cried like a child over the sum I couldn't do; and you know how darned hard 'tis to make a Yankee cry.

M'CLOSKY. Well, what's that to me?

SCUDDER. Hold on, Jacob, I'm coming to that — I tell ye, I'm such a fool — I can't bear the feeling, it keeps at me like a skin complaint, and if this family is sold up —

M'CLOSKY. What then?

SCUDDER (*rising*). I'd cut my throat — or yours — yours I'd prefer.

M'CLOSKY. Would you now? why don't you do it?

SCUDDER. 'Cos I's skeered to try! I never killed a man in my life — and civilisation is so strong in me I guess I couldn't do it — I'd like to, though!

M'CLOSKY. And all for the sake of that old woman and that young

147

puppy — eh? No other cause to hate — to envy me — to be jealous of me — eh?

SCUDDER. Jealous? what for?

M'CLOSKY. Ask the colour in your face: d'ye think I can't read you, like a book? With your New England hypocrisy, you would persuade yourself that it was this family alone you cared for; it ain't — you know it ain't — 't is the 'Octoroon'; and you love her as I do; and you hate me because I'm your rival — that's where the tears come from, Salem Scudder, if you ever shed any — that's where the shoe pinches.

SCUDDER. Wal, I do like the gal; she's a —

M'CLOSKY. She's in love with young Peyton; it made me curse whar it made you cry, as it does now; I see the tears on your cheeks now.

SCUDDER. Look at 'em Jacob, for they are honest water from the well of truth. I ain't ashamed of it — I do love the gal; but I ain't jealous of you, because I believe the only sincere feeling about you is your love for Zoe, and it does your heart good to have her image thar; but I believe you put it thar to spile. By fair means I don't think you can get her, and don't you try foul with her, 'cause if you do, Jacob, civilisation be darned, I'm on you like a painter, and when I'm drawed out I'm pizin.

(*Exit* SCUDDER *to house.*)

M'CLOSKY. Fair or foul, I'll have her — take that home with you! (*He opens desk.*) What's here — judgments? yes, plenty of 'em; bill of costs: account with Citizens' Bank — what's this? "Judgment, $40,000, 'Thibodeaux against Peyton,'" — surely, that is the judgment under which this estate is now advertised for sale — (*He takes up paper and examines it.*) yes, 'Thibodeaux against Peyton, 1838.' Hold on! whew! this is worth taking to — in this desk the judge used to keep one paper I want — this should be it. (*Reads.*) 'The free papers of my daughter Zoe, registered February 4th, 1841.' Why, Judge, wasn't you lawyer enough to know that while a judgment stood against you it was a lien on your slaves? Zoe is your child by a quadroon slave, and you didn't free her; blood! if this is so, she's mine! this old Liverpool debt — that may cross me — if it only arrive too late — if it don't come by this mail — Hold on! this letter the old lady expects — that's it; let me only head off that letter, and Terrebonne will be sold before they can recover it. That boy and the Indian have gone down to the landing for the post-bags; they'll idle on the way as usual? my mare will take me across the swamp, and before they can reach the shed, I'll

have purified them bags — ne'er a letter shall show this mail.
Ha, ha! — (*Calls.*) Pete, you old turkey-buzzard, saddle my
mare. Then, if I sink every dollar I'm worth in her purchase,
I'll own that Octoroon.

ACT TWO

The wharf with goods, boxes, and bales scattered about — a camera on a stand; DORA *being photographed by* SCUDDER, *who is arranging photographic apparatus,* GEORGE *and* PAUL *looking on at back.*

SCUDDER. Just turn your face a leetle this way — fix your — let's see — look here.

DORA. So?

SCUDDER. That's right. (*Putting his head under the darkening apron.*) It's such a long time since I did this sort of thing, and this old machine has got so dirty and stiff, I'm afraid it won't operate. That's about right. Now don't stir.

PAUL. Ugh! she looks as though she war gwine to have a tooth drawed!

SCUDDER. I've got four plates ready, in case we miss the first shot. One of them is prepared with a self-developing liquid that I've invented. I hope it will turn out better than most of my notions. Now fix yourself. Are you ready?

DORA. Ready!

SCUDDER. Fire! — one, two, three. (SCUDDER *takes out watch.*)

PAUL. Now it's cooking; laws mussey! I feel it all inside, as if I was at a lottery.

SCUDDER. So! (*Throws down apron.*) That's enough. (*Withdrawing slide, turns and sees* PAUL.) What! what are you doing there, you young varmint! Ain't you took them bags to the house yet?

PAUL. Now, it ain't no use trying to get mad, Mas'r Scudder. I'm gwine! I only come back to find Wahnotee; whar is dat ign'ant Injiun?

SCUDDER. You'll find him scenting round the rum store, hitched up by the nose. (*Goes into the room.*)

PAUL (*calling at the door*). Say, Mas'r Scudder, take me in dat telescope?

150

SCUDDER (*inside the room*). Get out, you cub! clar out!

PAUL. You got four of dem dishes ready. Gosh, wouldn't I like to hab myself took! What's de charge, Mas'r Scudder? (*He runs off.*)

SCUDDER (*enters from the room*). Job had none of them critters on his plantation, else he'd never ha' stood through so many chapters. Well, that has come out clear, ain't it? (*Showing the plate.*)

DORA. O, beautiful! Look, Mr Peyton.

GEORGE (*looking*). Yes, very fine!

SCUDDER. The apparatus can't mistake. When I travelled round with this machine, the homely folks used to sing out, 'Hillo, mister, this ain't like me!' 'Ma'am,' says I, 'the apparatus can't mistake.' 'But, mister, that ain't my nose.' 'Ma'am, your nose drawed it. The machine can't err — you may mistake your phiz but the apparatus don't.' 'But, sir, it ain't agreeable.' 'No, ma'am, the truth seldom is.'

PETE (*enters, puffing*). Mas'r Scudder! Mas'r Scudder!

SCUDDER. Hillo! what are you blowing about like a steamboat with one wheel for?

PETE. *You* blow, Mas'r Scudder, when I tole you: dere's a man from Noo Aleens just arriv'd at de house, and he's stuck up two papers on de gates: 'For sale — dis yer property,' and a heap of oder tings — an he seen missus, and arter he shown some papers she burst out crying — I yelled; den de corious of little niggers dey set up, den de hull plantation children — de live stock reared up and created a purpiration of lamentation as did de ole heart good to har.

DORA. What's the matter?

SCUDDER. He's come.

PETE. Dass it — I saw 'm!

SCUDDER. The sheriff from New Orleans has taken possession — Terrebonne is in the hands of the law.

ZOE (*enters*). O, Mr Scudder! Dora! Mr Peyton! come home — there are strangers in the house.

DORA. Stay, Mr Peyton: Zoe, a word! (*She leads her forward — aside.*) Zoe, the more I see of George Peyton the better I like him; but he is too modest — that is a very impertinent virtue in a man.

ZOE. I'm no judge, dear.

DORA. Of course not, you little fool; no one ever made love to you, and you can't understand; I mean, that George knows I am an heiress; my fortune would release this estate from debt.

151

ZOE. O, I see!

DORA. If he would only propose to marry me I would accept him, but he don't know that, and he will go on fooling, in his slow European way, until it is too late.

ZOE. What's to be done?

DORA. You tell him.

ZOE. What? that he isn't to go on fooling in his slow —

DORA. No, you goose! twit him on his silence and abstraction — I'm sure it's plain enough, for he has not spoken two words to me all the day; then joke round the subject, and at last speak out.

SCUDDER. Pete, as you came here, did you pass Paul and the Indian with the letter-bags?

PETE. No, sar; but dem vagabonds neber take the 'specable straight road, dey goes by de swamp. (*Exits up the path.*)

SCUDDER. Come, sir!

DORA (*to* ZOE). Now's your time. — (*Aloud*) Mr Scudder, take us with you — Mr Peyton is so slow, there's no getting him on. (*Exit* DORA *and* SCUDDER.)

ZOE. They are gone! — (*Glancing at* GEORGE) Poor fellow, he has lost all.

GEORGE. Poor child! how sad she looks now she has no resource.

ZOE. How shall I ask him to stay?

GEORGE. Zoe, will you remain here? I wish to speak to you.

ZOE (*aside*). Well, that saves trouble.

GEORGE. By our ruin you lose all.

ZOE. O, I'm nothing; think of yourself.

GEORGE. I can think of nothing but the image that remains face to face with me; so beautiful, so simple, so confiding, that I dare not express the feelings that have grown up so rapidly in my heart.

ZOE (*aside*). He means Dora.

GEORGE. If I dared to speak!

ZOE. That's just what you must do, and do it at once, or it will be too late.

GEORGE. Has my love been divined?

ZOE. It has been more than suspected.

GEORGE. Zoe, listen to me, then. I shall see this estate pass from me without a sigh, for it possesses no charm for me; the wealth I covet is the love of those around me — eyes that are rich in fond looks, lips that breathe endearing words; the only estate I value is the heart of one true woman, and the slaves I'd have are her thoughts.

ZOE. George, George, your words take away my breath!

GEORGE. The world, Zoe, the free struggle of minds and hands is before me; the education bestowed on me by my dear uncle is a noble heritage which no sheriff can seize; with that I can build up a fortune, spread a roof over the heads I love, and place before them the food I have earned; I will work —

ZOE. Work! I thought none but coloured people worked.

GEORGE. Work, Zoe, is the salt that gives savour to life.

ZOE. Dora said you were slow; if she could hear you now —

GEORGE. Zoe, you are young; your mirror must have told you that you are beautiful. Is your heart free?

ZOE. Free? of course it is!

GEORGE. We have known each other but a few days, but to me those days have been worth all the rest of my life. Zoe, you have suspected the feeling that now commands an utterance — you have seen that I love you.

ZOE. Me! you love *me*?

GEORGE. As my wife — the sharer of my hopes, my ambitions, and my sorrows; under the shelter of your love I could watch the storms of fortune pass unheeded by.

ZOE. *My* love! *My* love? George, you know not what you say! *I* the sharer of your sorrows — your wife! Do you know what I am?

GEORGE. Your birth — I know it. Has not my dear aunt forgotten it — she who had the most right to remember it? You are illegitimate, but love knows no prejudice.

ZOE (*aside*). Alas! he does not know, he does not know! and will despise me, spurn me, loathe me, when he learns who, what, he has so loved — (*Aloud*) George, O, forgive me! Yes, I love you — I did not know it until your words showed me what has been in my heart; each of them awoke a new sense, and now I know how unhappy — how very unhappy I am.

GEORGE. Zoe, what have I said to wound you?

ZOE. Nothing; but you must learn what I thought you already knew. George, you cannot marry me; the laws forbid it!

GEORGE. Forbid it?

ZOE. There is a gulf between us, as wide as your love, as deep as my despair; but, O, tell me, say you will pity me! that you will not throw me from you like a poisoned thing!

GEORGE. Zoe, explain yourself — your language fills me with shapeless fears.

ZOE. And what shall I say? — I — my mother was — no, no — not her! Why should I refer the blame to her? George, do you see

153

that hand you hold? look at these fingers; do you see the nails are of a bluish tinge?

GEORGE. Yes, near the quick there is a faint blue mark.

ZOE. Look in my eyes; is not the same colour in the white?

GEORGE. It is their beauty.

ZOE. Could you see the roots of my hair you would see the same dark, fatal mark. Do you know what that is?

GEORGE. No.

ZOE. That is the ineffaceable curse of Cain. Of the blood that feeds my heart, one drop in eight is black — bright red as the rest may be, that one drop poisons all the flood; those seven bright drops give me love like yours — hope like yours — ambition like yours — life hung with passions like dewdrops on the morning flowers; but the one black drop gives me despair, for I'm an unclean thing — forbidden by the laws — I'm an Octoroon!

GEORGE. Zoe, I love you none the less; this knowledge brings no revolt to my heart, and I can overcome the obstacle.

ZOE. But *I* cannot.

GEORGE. We can leave this country, and go far away where none can know.

ZOE. And your mother, she who from infancy treated me with such fondness, she who, as you said, has most reason to spurn me, can she forget what I am? Will she gladly see you wedded to the child of her husband's slave? No! she would revolt from it, as all but you would; and if I consented to hear the cries of my heart, if I did not crush out my infant love, what would she say to the poor girl on whom she had bestowed so much? No, no!

GEORGE. Zoe, must we immolate our lives on her prejudice?

ZOE. Yes, for I'd rather be black than ungrateful! Ah, George, our race has at least one virtue — it knows how to suffer!

GEORGE. Each word you utter makes my love sink deeper into my heart.

ZOE. And I remained here to induce you to offer that heart to Dora!

GEORGE. If you bid me do so I will obey you —

ZOE. No, no! if you cannot be mine, O, let me not blush when I think of you.

GEORGE. Dearest Zoe! (*Exit* GEORGE *and* ZOE. *As they exit,* M'CLOSKY *rises from behind a rock and looks after them.*)

M'CLOSKY. She loves him! I felt it — and how she can love! (*Advances.*) That one black drop of blood burns in her veins

154

and lights up her heart like a foggy sun. O, how I lapped up her words, like a thirsty bloodhound! I'll have her, if it costs me my life! Yonder the boy still lurks with those mail-bags; the devil still keeps him here to tempt me, darn his yellow skin! I arrived just too late, he had grabbed the prize as I came up. Hillo! he's coming this way, fighting with his Injiun. (*Conceals himself.*)

PAUL (*enters, wrestling with* WAHNOTEE). It ain't no use now: you got to gib it up!

WAHNOTEE. Ugh!

PAUL. It won't do! You got dat bottle of rum hid under your blanket — gib it up now, you — Yar! (*Wrenching it from him*) You nasty, lying Injiun! It's no use you putting on airs; I ain't gwine to sit up wid you all night and you drunk. Hillo! war's de crowd gone? And dar's de 'paratus — O, gosh, if I could take a likeness ob dis child! Uh — uh, let's have a peep. (*Looking through camera*) O, golly! yar, you Wahnotee! you stan' dar, I see you. Ta demine usti. (*He looks at* WAHNOTEE *through the camera;* WAHNOTEE *springs back with an expression of alarm.*)

WAHNOTEE. No tue Wahnotee.

PAUL. Ha, ha! he tinks it's a gun. You ign'ant Injiun, it can't hurt you! Stop, here's dem dishes — plates — dat's what he call 'em, all fix: I see Mas'r Scudder do it often — tink I can take likeness — stay dere, Wahnotee.

WAHNOTEE. No, carabine tue.

PAUL. I must operate and take my own likeness too — how debbel I do dat? Can't be ober dar an' here too — I ain't twins. Ugh! ach! 'Top; you look, you Wahnotee; you see dis rag, eh? Well when I say go, den lift dis rag like dis, see! den run to dat pine tree up dar (*Points.*) and back ag'in, and den pull down de rag so, d'ye see?

WAHNOTEE. Hugh!

PAUL. Den you hab glass ob rum.

WAHNOTEE. Rum!

PAUL. Dat wakes him up. Coute, Wahnotee in omenee dit go Wahnotee, poina la fa, comb a pine tree, la revieut sala, la fa.

WAHNOTEE. Firewater!

PAUL. Yes, den a glass ob firewater; now den. (*Throwing mailbags down and sitting on them*) Pret, now den go.

(WAHNOTEE *raises the apron and runs off.* PAUL *sits for his picture —* M'CLOSKY *appears.*)

M'CLOSKY. Where are they? Ah, yonder goes the Indian!

PAUL. De time he gone just 'bout enough to cook dat dish plate.

M'CLOSKY. Yonder is the boy — now is my time! What's he doing; is he asleep? (*Advancing*) He is sitting on my prize! darn his carcass! I'll clear him off there — he'll never know what stunned him. (*He takes Indian's tomahawk and steals to* PAUL.)

PAUL. Dam dat Injiun! is dat him creeping dar? I daren't move fear to spile myself. (M'CLOSKY *strikes him on the head — he falls dead.*)

M'CLOSKY. Horraw; the bags are mine — now for it! — (*Opening the mail-bags*) What's here? Sunnyside, Pointdexter, Jackson, Peyton; here it is — the Liverpool postmark, sure enough! — (*Opening letter — reads.*) 'Madam, we are instructed by the firm of Mason and Co., to inform you that a dividend of forty per cent. is payable on the first proximo, this amount in consideration of position, they send herewith, and you will find enclosed by draft to your order, on the Bank of Louisiana, which please acknowledge — the balance will be paid in full, with interest, in three, six, and nine months — your drafts on Mason Brothers at those dates will be accepted by La Palisse and Compagnie, N. O., so that you may command immediate use of the whole amount at once, if required. Yours, etc., James Brown.' What a find! this infernal letter would have saved all. (*During the reading of the letter, he remains nearly motionless under the focus of the camera.*) But now I guess it will arrive too late — these darned U.S. mails are to blame. The Injiun! he must not see me. (*Exits rapidly.*)

(WAHNOTEE *runs on, and pulls down the apron. He sees* PAUL, *lying on the ground, and speaks to him, thinking that he is shamming sleep. He gesticulates and jabbers to him and moves him with his feet, then kneels down to rouse him. To his horror he finds him dead. Expressing great grief he raises his eyes and they fall upon the camera. Rising with a savage growl, he seizes the tomahawk and smashes the camera to pieces. Going to* PAUL *he expresses in pantomime grief, sorrow, and fondness, and takes him in his arms to carry him away.*)

ACT THREE

A room in MRS PEYTON's *house showing the entrance on which an auction bill is pasted.* SOLON *and* GRACE *are there.*

PETE (*outside*). Dis way — dis way.
    (*Enter* PETE, POINTDEXTER, JACKSON, LAFOUCHE, *and* CAILLOU.)
PETE. Dis way, gen'l'men; now, Solon — Grace — dey's hot and tirsty — sangaree, brandy, rum.
JACKSON. Well, what d'ye say, Lafouche — d'ye smile?
    (*Enter* THIBODEAUX *and* SUNNYSIDE.)
THIBODEAUX. I hope we don't intrude on the family.
PETE. You see dat hole in dar, sar? I was raised on dis yar plantation — nebber see no door in it — always open, sar, for stranger to walk in.
SUNNYSIDE. And for substance to walk out.
RATTS (*enters*). Fine southern style that, eh!
LAFOUCHE (*reading the bill*). 'A fine, well-built old family mansion, replete with every comfort.'
RATTS. There's one name on the list of slaves scratched, I see.
LAFOUCHE. Yes; No. 49, Paul, a quadroon boy, aged thirteen.
SUNNYSIDE. He's missing.
POINTDEXTER. Run away, I suppose.
PETE (*indignantly*). No, sar; nigger nebber cut stick on Terrebonne; dat boy's dead, sure.
RATTS. What, Picayune Paul, as we called him, that used to come aboard my boat? — poor little darkey, I hope not; many a picayune he picked up for his dance and nigger songs, and he supplied our table with fish and game from the Bayous.
PETE. Nebber supply no more, sar — nebber dance again. Mas'r Ratts, you hard him sing about de place where de good niggers go, de last time.
RATTS. Well!

157

PETE. Well, he gone dar hisself; why I tink so — 'cause we missed Paul for some days, but nebber tout nothin' till one night dat Injiun Wahnotee suddenly stood right dar 'mongst us — was in his war paint, and mighty cold and grave — he sit down by de fire. 'Whar's Paul?' I say — he smoke and smoke, but nebber look out ob de fire; well knowing dem critters, I wait a long time — den he say, 'Wahnotee great chief'; den I say nothing — smoke anoder time — last, rising to go, he turn round at door, and say berry low — O, like a woman's voice he say, 'Omenee Pangeuk' — dat is, Paul is dead — nebber see him since.

RATTS. That redskin killed him.

SUNNYSIDE. So we believe; and so mad are the folks around, if they catch the redskin they'll lynch him sure.

RATTS. Lynch him! Darn his copper carcass, I've got a set of Irish deck-hands aboard that just loved that child; and after I tell them this, let them get a sight of the redskin, I believe they would eat him, tomahawk and all. Poor little Paul!

THIBODEAUX. What was he worth?

RATTS. Well, near on five hundred dollars.

PETE (scandalised). What, sar! You p'tend to be sorry for Paul, and prize him like dat! Five hundred dollars! (To THIBODEAUX) T'ousand dollars, Massa Thibodeau.

SCUDDER (enters). Gentlemen, the sale takes place at three. Good morning, Colonel. It's near that now, and there's still the sugar-houses to be inspected. Good day, Mr Thibodeaux — shall we drive down that way? Mr Lafouche, why, how do you do, sir? you're looking well.

LAFOUCHE. Sorry I can't return the compliment.

RATTS. Salem's looking a kinder hollowed out.

SCUDDER. What, Mr Ratts, are you going to invest in swamps?

RATTS. No; I want a nigger.

SCUDDER. Hush.

PETE. Eh! wass dat?

SCUDDER. Mr Sunnyside, I can't do this job of showin' round the folks; my stomach goes agin it. I want Pete here a minute.

SUNNYSIDE. I'll accompany them certainly.

SCUDDER (eagerly). Will ye? Thank ye; thank ye.

SUNNYSIDE. We must excuse Scudder, friends. I'll see you round the estate.

(Enter GEORGE and MRS PEYTON.)

LAFOUCHE. Good morning, Mrs Peyton.

(All salute.)

SUNNYSIDE. This way, gentlemen.

RATTS (*aside to* SUNNYSIDE). I say, I'd like to say summit soft to the old woman; perhaps it wouldn't go well, would it?

THIBODEAUX. No; leave it alone.

RATTS. Darn it, when I see a woman in trouble, I feel like selling the skin off my back.

(*Exit* THIBODEAUX, SUNNYSIDE, RATTS, POINTDEXTER, GRACE, JACKSON, LAFOUCHE, CAILLOU, SOLON.)

SCUDDER (*aside to* PETE). Go outside there; listen to what you hear, then go down to the quarters and tell the boys, for I can't do it. O, get out.

PETE. He said 'I want a nigger.' Laws, a mussey! What am goin' to cum ob us! (*Exits slowly, as if trying to conceal himself.*)

GEORGE. My dear aunt, why do you not move from this painful scene? Go with Dora to Sunnyside.

MRS PEYTON. No, George; your uncle said to me with his dying breath, 'Nellie, never leave Terrebonne,' and I never *will* leave it, till the law compels me.

SCUDDER. Mr George, I'm going to say somethin' that has been chokin' me for some time. I know you'll excuse it. Thar's Miss Dora — that girl's in love with you; yes, sir, her eyes are startin' out of her head with it: now her fortune would redeem a good part of this estate.

MRS PEYTON. Why, George, I never suspected this!

GEORGE. I did, Aunt, I confess, but —

MRS PEYTON. And you hesitated from motives of delicacy?

SCUDDER. No, ma'am; here's the plan of it. Mr George is in love with Zoe.

GEORGE. Scudder!

MRS PEYTON. George!

SCUDDER. Hold on, now! things have got so jammed in on top of us, we ain't got time to put kid gloves on to handle them. He loves Zoe, and has found out that she loves him. (*Sighing*) Well, that's all right; but as he can't marry her, and as Miss Dora would jump at him —

MRS PEYTON. Why didn't you mention this before?

SCUDDER. Why, because *I* love Zoe, too, and I couldn't take that young feller from her; and she's jist living on the sight of him, as I saw her do; and they so happy in spite of this yer misery around them, and they reproachin' themselves with not feeling as they ought. I've seen it, I tell you; and darn it, ma'am, can't you see that's what's been a hollowing me out so — I beg your pardon.

159

MRS PEYTON. O, George — my son, let me call you — I do not speak for my own sake, nor for the loss of the estate, but for the poor people here: they will be sold, divided, and taken away — they have been born here. Heaven has denied me children; so all the strings of my heart have grown around and amongst them, like the fibres and roots of an old tree in its native earth. O, let all go, but save them! With them around us, if we have not wealth, we shall at least have the home that they alone can make —

GEORGE. My dear mother — Mr Scudder — you teach me what I ought to do; if Miss Sunnyside will accept me as I am, Terrebonne shall be saved: I will sell myself, but the slaves shall be protected.

MRS PEYTON. *Sell* yourself, George! Is not Dora worth any man's —

SCUDDER. Don't say that, ma'am; don't say that to a man that loves another gal. He's going to do an heroic act; don't spile it.

MRS PEYTON. But Zoe is only an Octoroon.

SCUDDER. She's won this race agin the white, anyhow; it's too late now to start her pedigree. (*As* DORA *enters*) Come, Mrs Peyton, take my arm. Hush! here's the other one: she's a little too thoroughbred — too much of the greyhound; but the heart's there, I believe.

(*Exeunt* SCUDDER *and* MRS PEYTON.)

DORA. Poor Mrs Peyton.

GEORGE. Miss Sunnyside, permit me a word: a feeling of delicacy has suspended upon my lips an avowal, which —

DORA (*aside*). O, dear, has he suddenly come to his senses?

(*Enter* ZOE, *stopping at back.*)

GEORGE. In a word, I have seen and admired you!

DORA (*aside*). He has a strange way of showing it. European, I suppose.

GEORGE. If you would pardon the abruptness of the question, I would ask you. Do you think the sincere devotion of my life to make yours happy would succeed?

DORA (*aside*). Well, he has the oddest way of making love.

GEORGE. You are silent?

DORA. Mr Peyton, I presume you have hesitated to make this avowal because you feared, in the present condition of affairs here, your object might be misconstrued, and that your attention was rather to my fortune than myself. (*A pause*) Why don't he speak? — I mean, you feared I might not give you credit for sincere and pure feelings. Well, you wrong me. I don't think you capable of anything else but —

GEORGE. No, I hesitated because an attachment I had formed before I had the pleasure of seeing you had not altogether died out.

DORA (*smiling*). Some of those sirens of Paris, I presume. (*Pausing*) I shall endeavour not to be jealous of the past; perhaps I have no right to be. (*Pausing*) But now that vagrant love is — eh, faded — is it not? Why don't you speak, sir?

GEORGE. Because, Miss Sunnyside, I have not learned to lie.

DORA. Good gracious — who wants you to?

GEORGE. I do, but I can't do it. No, the love I speak of is not such as you suppose — it is a passion that has grown up here since I arrived; but it is a hopeless, mad, wild feeling, that must perish.

DORA. Here! since you arrived! Impossible: you have seen no one; whom can you mean?

ZOE (*advancing*). Me.

GEORGE. Zoe!

DORA. You!

ZOE. Forgive him, Dora; for he knew no better until I told him. Dora, you are right. He is incapable of any but sincere and pure feelings — so are you. He loves me — what of that? You know you can't be jealous of a poor creature like me. If he caught the fever, were stung by a snake, or possessed of any other poisonous or unclean thing, you could pity, tend, love him through it, and for your gentle care he would love you in return. Well, is he not thus afflicted now? I am his love — he loves an Octoroon.

GEORGE. O, Zoe, you break my heart!

DORA. At college they said I was a fool — I must be. At New Orleans, they said, 'She's pretty, very pretty, but no brains.' I'm afraid they must be right; I can't understand a word of all this.

ZOE. Dear Dora, try to understand it with your heart. You love George; you love him dearly; I know it; and you deserve to be loved by him. He will love you — he must. His love for me will pass away — it shall. You heard him say it was hopeless. O, forgive him and me!

DORA (*weeping*). O, why did he speak to me at all then? You've made me cry, then, and I hate you both! (*Exits through room.*)

(*Enter* MRS PEYTON *and* SCUDDER, M'CLOSKY *and* POINTDEXTER.)

M'CLOSKY. I'm sorry to intrude, but the business I came upon will excuse me.

161

MRS PEYTON. Here is my nephew, sir.

ZOE. Perhaps I had better go.

M'CLOSKY. Wal, as it consarns you, perhaps you better had.

SCUDDER. Consarns Zoe?

M'CLOSKY. I don't know; she may as well hear the hull of it. Go on, Colonel — Colonel Pointdexter, ma'am — the mortgagee, auctioneer, and general agent.

POINTDEXTER. Pardon me, madam, but do you know these papers? (*He hands the papers to* MRS PEYTON.)

MRS PEYTON (*taking them*). Yes, sir; they were the free papers of the girl Zoe; but they were in my husband's secretary. How came they in your possession?

M'CLOSKY. I — I found them.

GEORGE. And you purloined them?

M'CLOSKY. Hold on, you'll see. Go on, Colonel.

POINTDEXTER. The list of your slaves is incomplete — it wants one.

SCUDDER. The boy Paul — we know it.

POINTDEXTER. No, sir, you have omitted the Octoroon girl, Zoe.

MRS PEYTON. ⎤ Zoe!
ZOE. ⎦ Me!

POINTDEXTER. At the time the judge executed those free papers to his infant slave, a judgment stood recorded against him; while that was on record he had no right to make away with his property. That judgment still exists: under it and others this estate is sold today. Those free papers ain't worth the sand that's on 'em.

MRS PEYTON. Zoe a slave! It is impossible!

POINTDEXTER. It is certain, madam: the judge was negligent, and doubtless forgot this small formality.

SCUDDER. But the creditors will not claim the gal?

M'CLOSKY. Excuse me; one of the principal mortgagees has made the demand.

(*Exeunt* M'CLOSKY *and* POINTDEXTER.)

SCUDDER. Hold on yere, George Peyton; you sit down there. You're trembling so, you'll fall down directly. This blow has staggered me some.

MRS PEYTON. O, Zoe, my child! don't think too hard of your poor father.

ZOE. I shall do so if you weep. See, I'm calm.

SCUDDER. Calm as a tombstone, and with about as much life. I see it in your face.

GEORGE. It cannot be! It shall not be!

SCUDDER. Hold your tongue — it must. Be calm — darn the

things; the proceeds of this sale won't cover the debts of the estate. Consarn those Liverpool English fellers, why couldn't they send something by the last mail? Even a letter, promising something — such is the feeling round amongst the planters. Darn me, if I couldn't raise thirty thousand on the envelope alone, and ten thousand more on the postmark.

GEORGE. Zoe, they shall not take you from us while I live.

SCUDDER. Don't be a fool; they'd kill you, and then take her, just as soon as — stop: old Sunnyside, he'll buy her; that'll save her.

ZOE. No, it won't; we have confessed to Dora that we love each other. How can she then ask her father to free me?

SCUDDER. What in thunder made you do that?

ZOE. Because it was the truth, and I had rather be a slave with a free soul, than remain free with a slavish, deceitful heart. My father gives me freedom — at least he thought so. May Heaven bless him for the thought, bless him for the happiness he spread around my life. You say the proceeds of the sale will not cover his debts. Let me be sold then, that I may free his name. I give him back the liberty he bestowed upon me; for I can never repay him the love he bore his poor Octoroon child, on whose breast his last sigh was drawn, into whose eyes he looked with the last gaze of affection.

MRS PEYTON. O, my husband! I thank Heaven you have not lived to see this day.

ZOE. George, leave me! I would be alone a little while.

GEORGE. Zoe! (*Turns away, overpowered.*)

ZOE. Do not weep, George. Dear George, you now see what a miserable thing I am.

GEORGE. Zoe!

SCUDDER. I wish they could sell *me*! I brought half this ruin on this family, with my all-fired improvements. I deserve to be a nigger this day — I feel like one, inside. (*Exit* SCUDDER.)

ZOE. Go now, George — leave me — take her with you.

(*Exit* MRS PEYTON *and* GEORGE.)

A slave! a slave! Is this a dream — for my brain reels with the blow? He said so. What! then I shall be sold — sold! and my master — O! (*She falls on her knees, with her face in her hands.*) No — no master but one. George — George — hush — they come! save me! No, (*Looks off.*) 't is Pete and the servants — they come this way. (*Enters the inner room.*)

(*Enter* PETE, GRACE, MINNIE, SOLON, DIDO, *and all the* NEGROES.)

163

PETE. Cum yer now — stand round, 'cause I've got to talk to you darkies — keep dem chil'n quiet — don't make no noise, de missus up dar har us.

SOLON. Go on, Pete.

PETE. Gen'l'men, my coloured frens and ladies, dar's mighty bad news gone round. Dis yer prop'ty to be sold — old Terrebonne — whar we all been raised, is gwine — dey's gwine to tak it away — can't stop here nohow.

ALL. O-o! — O-o!

PETE. Hold quiet, you trash o' niggers! Tink anybody wants you to cry? Who's you to set up screeching? — Be quiet! But dis ain't all. Now, my culled brethren, gird up your lines, and listen — hold on yer bref — it's a comin'. We t'ought dat de niggers would belong to de ole missus, and if she lost Terrebonne, we must live dere allers, and we would hire out, and bring our wages to ole Missus Peyton.

ALL. Ya! ya! Well —

PETE. Hush! I tell ye, 't ain't so — we can't do it — we've got to be sold —

ALL. Sold!

PETE. Will you hush? she will har you. Yes! I listen dar jess now — dar was ole lady cryin' — Mas'r George — ah! you seen dem big tears in his eyes. O, Mas'r Scudder, he didn't cry zackly; both ob his eyes and cheek look like de bad Bayou in low season — so dry dat I cry for him. (*Raising his voice*) Den say de missus, ''T ain't for de land I keer, but for dem poor niggers — dey'll be sold — dat wot stagger me.' 'No,' say Mas'r George, 'I'd rather sell myself fuss; but dey shan't suffer, nohow — I see 'em dam fuss.'

ALL. O, bless 'um! Bless Mas'r George.

PETE. Hole yer tongues. Yes, for you, for me, for dem little ones, dem folks cried. Now, den, if Grace dere wid her chil'n were all sold, she'll begin screechin' like a cat. She didn't mind how kind old judge was to her; and Solon, too, he'll holler, and break de ole lady's heart.

GRACE. No, Pete; no, I won't. I'll bear it.

PETE. I don't tink you will any more, but dis here will; 'cause de family spile Dido, dey has. She nebber was worth much a' dat nigger.

DIDO. How dar you say dat, you black nigger, you? I fetch as much as any odder cook in Louisiana.

PETE. What's de use of your takin' it kind, and comfortin' de missus' heart, if Minnie dere, and Louise, and Marie, and Julie is to spile it?

164

MINNIE. We won't, Pete; we won't.

PETE (*to the men*). Dar, do ye hear dat, ye mis'able darkies; dem gals is worth a boat load of kinder men dem is. Cum, for de pride of de family, let every darky look his best for the judge's sake — dat ole man so good to us, and dat ole woman — so dem strangers from New Orleans shall say, dem's happy darkies, dem's a fine set of niggers; every one say when he's sold, 'Lor' bless dis yer family I'm gwine out of, and send me as good a home.'

ALL. We'll do it, Pete; we'll do it.

PETE. Hush! hark! I tell ye dar's somebody in dar. Who is it?

GRACE. It's Missy Zoe. See! see!

PETE. Come along; she har what we say, and she's cryin' for us. None o' ye ign'rant niggers could cry for yerselves like dat. Come here quiet: now quiet.

(*Exeunt* PETE *and all the* NEGROES, *slowly*.)

ZOE (*who is supposed to have overheard the last scene, enters*). O! must I learn from these poor wretches how much I owe, and how I ought to pay the debt? Have I slept upon the benefits I received, and never saw, never felt, never knew that I was forgetful and ungrateful? O, my father! my dear, dear father! forgive your poor child. You made her life too happy, and now these tears will flow. Let me hide them till I teach my heart. O, my — my heart! (*Exits, with a low, wailing, suffocating cry*.)

(*Enter* M'CLOSKY, LAFOUCHE, JACKSON, SUNNYSIDE, *and* POINTDEXTER.)

POINTDEXTER (*looking at his watch*). Come, the hour is past. I think we may begin business. Where is Mr Scudder?

JACKSON. I want to get to Ophelensis tonight.

DORA (*enters*). Father, come here.

SUNNYSIDE. Why, Dora, what's the matter? Your eyes are red.

DORA. Are they? Thank you. I don't care, they were blue this morning, but it don't signify now.

SUNNYSIDE. My darling! Who has been teasing you?

DORA. Never mind. I want you to buy Terrebonne.

SUNNYSIDE. Buy Terrebonne! What for?

DORA. No matter — buy it!

SUNNYSIDE. It will cost me all I'm worth. This is folly, Dora.

DORA. Is my plantation at Comptableau worth this?

SUNNYSIDE. Nearly — perhaps.

DORA. Sell it, then, and buy this.

SUNNYSIDE. Are you mad, my love?

DORA. Do you want *me* to stop here and *bid* for it?

165

SUNNYSIDE. Good gracious, no!

DORA. Then I'll do it if you don't.

SUNNYSIDE. I will! I will! But for Heaven's sake go — here comes
the crowd. (*Exit* DORA.) What on earth does that child mean or
want?

> (*Enter* SCUDDER, GEORGE, RATTS, CAILLOU, PETE, GRACE,
> MINNIE, *and all the* NEGROES. *A large table is in the centre
> of the background.* POINTDEXTER *mounts the table with
> his hammer, his clerk sitting at his feet. The Negro mounts
> the table from behind. The rest sit down.*)

POINTDEXTER. Now, gentlemen, we shall proceed to business. It
ain't necessary for me to dilate, describe or enumerate;
Terrebonne is known to you as one of the richest bits of sile in
Louisiana, and its condition reflects credit on them as had to
keep it. I'll trouble you for that piece of baccy, Judge — thank
you — so, gentlemen, as life is short, we'll start right off. The
first lot on here is the estate in block, with its sugar-houses,
stock, machines, implements, good dwelling-houses and
furniture. If there is no bid for the estate and stuff, we'll sell
it in smaller lots. Come, Mr Thibodeaux, a man has a chance
once in his life — here's yours.

THIBODEAUX. Go on. What's the reserve bid?

POINTDEXTER. The first mortgagee bids forty thousand dollars.

THIBODEAUX. Forty-five thousand.

SUNNYSIDE. Fifty thousand.

POINTDEXTER. When you have done joking, gentlemen, you'll
say one hundred and twenty thousand. It carried that easy on
mortgage.

LAFOUCHE. Then why don't you buy it yourself, Colonel?

POINTDEXTER I'm waiting on your fifty thousand bid.

CAILLOU. Eighty thousand.

POINTDEXTER. Don't be afraid: it ain't going for that, Judge.

SUNNYSIDE. Ninety thousand.

POINTDEXTER. We're getting on.

THIBODEAUX. One hundred —

POINTDEXTER. One hundred thousand bid for this mag —

CAILLOU. One hundred and ten thousand —

POINTDEXTER. Good again — one hundred and —

SUNNYSIDE. Twenty.

POINTDEXTER And twenty thousand bid. Squire Sunnyside is
going to sell this at fifty thousand advance tomorrow. (*Looking
round*) Where's that man from Mobile that wanted to give
one hundred and eighty thousand?

THIBODEAUX. I guess he ain't left home yet, Colonel.

POINTDEXTER I shall knock it down to the Squire — going — gone — for one hundred and twenty thousand dollars. (*Raising hammer*) Judge, you can raise the hull on mortgage — going for half its value. (*Knocking on the table*) Squire Sunnyside, you've got a pretty bit o' land, Squire. Hillo, darkey, hand me a smash dar.

SUNNYSIDE. I got more than I can work now.

POINTDEXTER. Then buy the hands along with the property. Now, gentlemen, I'm proud to submit to you the finest lot of field hands and house servants that was ever offered for competition: they speak for themselves, and do credit to their owners. (*Reading*) 'No. 1, Solon, a guest boy, and a good waiter.'

PETE. That's my son — buy him, Mas'r Ratts; he's sure to sarve you well.

POINTDEXTER. Hold your tongue!

RATTS. Let the old darkey alone — eight hundred for that boy.

CAILLOU. Nine.

RATTS. A thousand.

SOLON. Thank you, Mas'r Ratts: I die for you, sar; hold up for me, sar.

RATTS. Look here, the boy knows and likes me, Judge; let him come my way?

CAILLOU. Go on — I'm dumb.

POINTDEXTER. One thousand bid. He's yours, Captain Ratts, *Magnolia* steamer.

(SOLON *goes and stands behind* RATTS.)

'No. 2, the yellow girl, Grace, with two children — Saul, aged four, and Victoria, five.' (*They get on table.*)

SCUDDER. That's Solon's wife and children, Judge.

GRACE (*to* RATTS). Buy me, Mas'r Ratts, do buy me, sar?

RATTS. What in thunder should I do with you and those devils on board my boat?

GRACE. Wash, sar — cook, sar — anyting.

RATTS. Eight hundred agin, then — I'll go it.

JACKSON. Nine.

RATTS. I'm broke, Solon — I can't stop the Judge.

THIBODEAUX. What's the matter, Ratts? I'll lend you all you want. Go it, if you're a mind to.

RATTS. Eleven.

JACKSON. Twelve.

SUNNYSIDE. O, O!

SCUDDER (*to* JACKSON). Judge, my friend. The Judge is a little deaf. Hello! (*Speaking in his ear trumpet*) This gal and them children belong to that boy Solon there. You're bidding to separate them, Judge.

JACKSON. The devil I am! (*Rising*) I'll take back my bid, Colonel.

POINTDEXTER. All right, Judge; I thought there was a mistake. I must keep you, Captain, to the eleven hundred.

RATTS. Go it.

POINTDEXTER. Eleven hundred — going — going — sold! 'No. 3, Pete, a house servant.'

PETE. Dat's me — yer, I'm comin' — stand around dar. (*Tumbles upon the table.*)

POINTDEXTER. Aged seventy-two.

PETE. What's dat? A mistake, sar — forty-six.

POINTDEXTER. Lame.

PETE. But don't mount to nuffin — kin work cannel. Come, Judge, pick up. Now's your time, sar.

JACKSON. One hundred dollars.

PETE. What, sar? me! for me — look ye here! (*He dances.*)

GEORGE. Five hundred.

PETE. Mas'r George — ah, no, sar — don't buy me — keep your money for some udder dat is to be sold. I ain't no 'count, sar.

POINTDEXTER. Five hundred bid — it's a good price. He's yours, Mr George Peyton. (PETE *goes down.*) 'No. 4, the Octoroon girl, Zoe.'

(*Enter* ZOE, *very pale, and stands on table.* M'CLOSKY *who hitherto has taken no interest in the sale, now turns his chair.*)

SUNNYSIDE (*rising*). Gentlemen, we are all acquainted with the circumstances of this girl's position, and I feel sure that no one here will oppose the family who desires to redeem the child of our esteemed and noble friend, the late Judge Peyton.

ALL. Hear! bravo! hear!

POINTDEXTER. While the proceeds of this sale promises to realise less than the debts upon it, it is my duty to prevent any collusion for the depreciation of the property.

RATTS. Darn ye! You're a man as well as an auctioneer, ain't ye?

POINTDEXTER. What is offered for the slave?

SUNNYSIDE. One thousand dollars.

M'CLOSKY. Two thousand.

SUNNYSIDE. Three thousand.

M'CLOSKY. Five thousand.

GEORGE. Demon!

SUNNYSIDE. I bid seven thousand, which is the last dollar this family possesses..

M'CLOSKY. Eight.

THIBODEAUX. Nine.

ALL. Bravo!

M'CLOSKY. Ten. It's no use, Squire.

SCUDDER. Jacob M'Closky, you shan't have that girl. Now, take care what you do. Twelve thousand.

M'CLOSKY. Shan't I! Fifteen thousand. Beat that any of ye.

POINTDEXTER. Fifteen thousand bid for the Octoroon.

DORA (enters). Twenty thousand.

ALL. Bravo!

M'CLOSKY. Twenty-five thousand.

ALL (groan). O! O!

GEORGE. Yelping hound — take that. (He rushes on M'CLOSKY. M'CLOSKY draws his knife.)

SCUDDER (darting between them). Hold on, George Peyton — stand back. This is your own house; we are under your uncle's roof; recollect yourself. And, strangers, ain't we forgetting there's a lady present? (The knives disappear.) If we can't behave like Christians, let's try and act like gentlemen. Go on, Colonel.

LAFOUCHE. He didn't ought to bid against a lady.

M'CLOSKY. O, that's it, is it? Then I'd like to hire a lady to go to auction and buy my hands..

POINTDEXTER. Gentlemen, I believe none of us have two feelings about the conduct of that man; but he has the law on his side — we may regret, but we must respect it. Mr M'Closky has bid twenty-five thousand dollars for the Octoroon. Is there any other bid? For the first time, twenty-five thousand — last time! (Brings hammer down.) To Jacob M'Closky, the Octoroon girl, Zoe, twenty-five thousand dollars.

ACT FOUR

The wharf. The steamer, Magnolia, *alongside, a bluff rock.* RATTS *discovered, superintending the loading of ship. Enter* LAFOUCHE *and* JACKSON.

JACKSON. How long before we start, captain?

RATTS. Just as soon as we put this cotton on board.

    (*Enter* PETE, *with a lantern, and* SCUDDER, *with notebook.*)

SCUDDER. One hundred and forty-nine bales. Can you take any more?

RATTS. Not a bale. I've got engaged eight hundred bales at the next landing, and one hundred hogsheads of sugar at Patten's Slide — that'll take my guards under — hurry up thar.

VOICE (*outside*). Wood's aboard.

RATTS. All aboard then.

    (*Enter* M'CLOSKY.)

SCUDDER. Sign that receipt, Captain, and save me going up to the clerk.

M'CLOSKY. See here — there's a small freight of turpentine in the fore hold there, and one of the barrels leaks; a spark from your engines might set the ship on fire, and you'll go with it.

RATTS. You be darned! Go and try it, if you've a mind to.

LAFOUCHE. Captain, you've loaded up here until the boat is sunk so deep in the mud she won't float.

RATTS (*calling off*). Wood up thar, you Pollo — hang on to the safety valve — guess she'll crawl off on her paddles. (*Shouts heard.*)

JACKSON. What's the matter?

SOLON (*enters*). We got him!

SCUDDER. Who?

SOLON. The Injiun!

SCUDDER. Wahnotee? Where is he? D'ye call running away from a fellow catching him?

170

RATTS. Here he comes.

ALL. Where? Where?

(*Enter* WAHNOTEE. *They are all about to rush on him.*)

SCUDDER. Hold on! stan' round thar! no violence — the crittur don't know what we mean.

JACKSON. Let him answer for the boy then.

M'CLOSKY. Down with him — lynch him.

ALL. Lynch him!

(*Exit* LAFOUCHE.)

SCUDDER. Stan' back, I say! I'll nip the first that lays a finger on him. Pete, speak to the redskin.

PETE. Whar's Paul, Wahnotee? What's come ob de child?

WAHNOTEE. Paul wunce — Paul pangeuk.

PETE. Pangeuk — dead!

WAHNOTEE. Mort!

M'CLOSKY. And you killed him? (*They approach him.*)

SCUDDER. Hold on!

PETE. Um, Paul reste?

WAHNOTEE. Hugh vieu. (*Goes.*) Paul reste ci!

SCUDDER. Here, stay! (*Examines the ground.*) The earth has been stirred here lately.

WAHNOTEE. Weenee Paul. (*He points down, and shows by pantomime how he buried* PAUL.)

SCUDDER. The Injiun means that he buried him there! Stop! here's a bit of leather. (*Drawing out the mail-bags.*) The mail-bags that were lost! (*Sees the tomahawk in* WAHNOTEE'*s belt — draws it out and examines it.*) Look! here are marks of blood — look thar, redskin, what's that?

WAHNOTEE. Paul! (*Makes a sign that* PAUL *was killed by a blow on the head.*)

M'CLOSKY. He confesses it; the Indian got drunk, quarrelled with him, and killed him.

LAFOUCHE (*re-enters with smashed apparatus*). Here are evidences of the crime; this rum-bottle half emptied — this photographic apparatus smashed — and there are marks of blood and footsteps around the shed.

M'CLOSKY. What more d'ye want — ain't that proof enough? Lynch him!

ALL. Lynch him! Lynch him!

SCUDDER. Stan' back, boys! He's an Injiun — fair play.

JACKSON. Try him, then — try him on the spot of his crime.

ALL. Try him! Try him!

LAFOUCHE. Don't let him escape!

171

RATTS. I'll see to that. (*Drawing revolver*) If he stirs, I'll put a bullet through his skull, mighty quick.

M'CLOSKY. Come, form a court then, choose a jury — we'll fix this varmin.

(*Enter* THIBODEAUX *and* CAILLOU.)

THIBODEAUX. What's the matter?

LAFOUCHE. We've caught this murdering Injiun, and are going to try him.

(WAHNOTEE *sits, rolled in blanket.*)

PETE. Poor little Paul — poor little nigger!

SCUDDER. This business goes agin me, Ratts — 't ain't right.

LAFOUCHE. We're ready; the jury's impanelled — go ahead — who'll be accuser?

RATTS. M'Closky.

M'CLOSKY. Me?

RATTS. Yes; you was the first to hail Judge Lynch.

M'CLOSKY. Well, what's the use of argument whar guilt sticks out so plain; the boy and Injiun were alone when last seen.

SCUDDER. Who says that?

M'CLOSKY. Everybody — that is, I heard so.

SCUDDER. Say what you know — not what you heard.

M'CLOSKY. I know then that the boy was killed with that tomahawk — the redskin owns it — the signs of violence are all round the shed — this apparatus smashed — ain't it plain that in a drunken fit he slew the boy, and when sober concealed the body yonder?

ALL. That's it — that's it.

RATTS. Who defends the Injiun?

SCUDDER. I will; for it is agin my natur' to b'lieve him guilty; and if he be, this ain't the place, nor you the authority to try him. How are we sure the boy is dead at all? There are no witnesses but a rum bottle and an old machine. Is it on such evidence you'd hang a human being?

RATTS. His own confession.

SCUDDER. I appeal against your usurped authority. This lynch law is a wild and lawless proceeding. Here's a pictur' for a civilised community to afford; yonder, a poor, ignorant savage, and round him a circle of hearts, white with revenge and hate, thirsting for his blood: you call yourselves judges — you ain't — you're a jury of executioners. It is such scenes as these that bring disgrace upon our Western life.

M'CLOSKY. Evidence! Evidence! Give us evidence. We've had talk enough; now for proof.

172

ALL. Yes, yes! Proof, proof!

SCUDDER. Where am I to get it? The proof is here, in my heart.

PETE (*who has been looking about the camera*). 'Top, sar! 'Top a bit! O, laws-a-mussey, see dis! here's a pictur' I found stickin' in that yar telescope machine, sar! look, sar!

SCUDDER. A photographic plate.

(PETE *holds his lantern up.*)

What's this, eh? two forms! The child — 't is he! dead — and above him — Ah! ah! Jacob M'Closky, 't was you murdered that boy!

M'CLOSKY. Me?

SCUDDER. You! You slew him with that tomahawk; and as you stood over his body with the letter in your hand, you thought that no witness saw the deed, that no eye was on you — but there was, Jacob M'Closky, there was. The eye of the Eternal was on you — the blessed sun in heaven, that, looking down, struck upon this plate the image of the deed. Here you are, in the very attitude of your crime!

M'CLOSKY. 'T is false!

SCUDDER. 'T is true! the apparatus can't lie. Look there, jurymen. (*Showing plate to jury*) Look there. O, you wanted evidence — you called for proof — Heaven has answered and convicted you.

M'CLOSKY. What court of law would receive such evidence? (*Going.*)

RATTS. Stop! *This* would! You called it yourself; you wanted to make us murder that Injiun; and since we've got our hands in for justice, we'll try it on *you*. What say ye? shall we have one law for the redskin and another for the white?

ALL. Try him! Try him!

RATTS. Who'll be accuser?

SCUDDER. I will! Fellow citizens, you are convened and assembled here under a higher power than the law. What's the law? When the ship's abroad on the ocean, when the army is before the enemy, where in thunder's the law? It is in the hearts of brave men, who can tell right from wrong, and from whom justice can't be bought. So it is here, in the wilds of the West, where our hatred of crime is measured by the speed of our executions — where necessity is law! I say, then, air you honest men? air you true? Put your hands on your naked breasts, and let every man as don't feel a real Amercian heart there, bustin' up with freedom, truth, and right, let that man step out — that's the oath I put to ye — and then say, Darn ye, go it!

ALL. Go on! Go on!

173

SCUDDER. No! I won't go on; that man's down. I won't strike him, even with words. Jacob, your accuser is that picter of the crime — let that speak — defend yourself.

M'CLOSKY (*drawing knife*). I will, quicker than lightning.

RATTS. Seize him, then!

(*They rush on* M'CLOSKY, *and disarm him.*)

He can fight though he's a painter: claws all over.

SCUDDER. Stop! Search him, we may find more evidence.

M'CLOSKY. Would you rob me first, and murder me afterwards?

RATTS (*searching him*). That's his programme — here's a pocket-book.

SCUDDER (*opening it*). What's here? Letters! Hello! To 'Mrs Peyton, Terrebonne, Louisiana, United States.' Liverpool postmark. Ho! I've got hold of the tail of a rat — come out. (*Reads.*) What's this? A draft for eighty-five thousand dollars, and credit on Palisse and Co., of New Orleans, for the balance. Hi! the rat's out. You killed the boy to steal this letter from the mail-bags — you stole this letter, that the money should not arrive in time to save the Octoroon; had it done so, the lien on the estate would have ceased, and Zoe be free.

ALL. Lynch him! Lynch him! Down with him!

SCUDDER. Silence in the court: stand back, let the gentlemen of the jury retire, consult, and return their verdict.

RATTS. I'm responsible for the crittur — go on.

PETE (*to* WAHNOTEE). See, Injiun; look dar, (*Showing him the plate*) see dat innocent; look, dar's de murderer of poor Paul.

WAHNOTEE. Ugh! (*Examining the plate.*)

PETE. Ya! as he? Closky tue Paul — kill de child with your tomahawk dar: 't wasn't you, no — ole Pete allus say so. Poor Injiun lub our little Paul.

(WAHNOTEE *rises and looks at* M'CLOSKY — *he is in his war paint and fully armed.*)

SCUDDER. What say ye, gentlemen? Is the prisoner guilty, or is he not guilty?

ALL. Guilty!

SCUDDER. And what is to be his punishment?

ALL. Death! (*All advance.*)

WAHNOTEE (*crosses to* M'CLOSKY). Ugh!

SCUDDER. No, Injiun; we deal out justice here, not revenge. 'T ain't you he has injured, 't is the white man, whose laws he has offended.

RATTS. Away with him — put him down the aft hatch, till we rig his funeral.

174

M'CLOSKY. Fifty against one! O! if I had you one by one alone in the swamp, I'd rip ye all. (*He is borne off in boat, struggling.*)

SCUDDER. Now, then, to business.

PETE (*re-enters from boat*). O, law, sir, dat debil Closky, he tore hisself from de gen'lam, knock me down, take my light, and trows it on de turpentine barrels, and de shed's all afire!
(*Fire seen.*)

JACKSON.(*re-entering*). We are catching fire forward: quick, cut free from the shore.

RATTS. All hands aboard there — cut the starn ropes — give her headway!

ALL. Ay, ay!
(*Cry of 'Fire' heard — engine bells heard — steam whistle noise.*)

RATTS. Cut all away, for'ard — overboard with every bale afire.
(*The steamer moves off with the fire still blazing.*)

M'CLOSKY (*re-enters, swimming*). Ha! have I fixed ye? Burn! burn! that's right. You thought you had cornered me, did ye? As I swam down, I thought I heard something in the water, as if pursuing me — one of them darned alligators, I suppose — they swarm hereabout — may they crunch every limb of ye. (*Exits.*)
(WAHNOTEE *is seen swimming. He finds trail and follows* M'CLOSKY. *The steamer floats on at back, burning.*)

ACT FIVE: SCENE ONE

Negroes' quarters.

ZOE (*enters*). It wants an hour yet to daylight — here is Pete's hut — (*Knocks.*) He sleeps — no: I see a light.

DIDO (*enters from hut*). Who dat?

ZOE. Hush, Aunty 'T is I — Zoe.

DIDO. Missey Zoe? Why you out in de swamp dis time ob night; you catch de fever sure — you is all wet.

ZOE. Where's Pete?

DIDO. He gone down to de landing last night wid Mas'r Scudder; not come back since — kint make it out.

ZOE. Aunty, there is sickness up at the house; I have been up all night beside one who suffers, and I remembered that when I had the fever you gave me a drink, a bitter drink, that made me sleep — do you remember it?

DIDO. Didn't I? Dem doctors ain't no 'count; dey don't know nuffin.

ZOE. No; but you, Aunty, you are wise — you know every plant, don't you, and what it is good for?

DIDO. Dat you drink is fust rate for red fever. Is de folks' head bad?

ZOE. Very bad, Aunty; and the heart aches worse, so they can get no rest.

DIDO. Hold on a bit, I get you de bottle. (*Exits.*)

ZOE. In a few hours that man, my master, will come for me: he has paid my price, and he only consented to let me remain here this one night, because Mrs Peyton promised to give me up to him today.

DIDO (*re-enters with phial*). Here 't is — now you give one timble-full — dat's nuff.

ZOE. All there is there would kill one, wouldn't it?

DIDO. Guess it kill a dozen — nebber try.

ZOE. It's not a painful death, Aunty, is it? You told me it produced a long, long sleep.

DIDO. Why you tremble so? Why you speak so wild? What you's gwine to do, missey?

ZOE. Give me the drink.

DIDO. No. Who dat sick at de house?

ZOE. Give it to me.

DIDO. No. You want to hurt yourself. O, Miss Zoe, why you ask old Dido for dis pizen?

ZOE. Listen to me. I love one who is here, and he loves me — George. I sat outside his door all night — I heard his sighs — his agony — torn from him by my coming fate; and he said, 'I'd rather see her dead than his!'

DIDO. Dead!

ZOE. He said so — then I rose up, and stole from the house, and ran down to the bayou: but its cold, black, silent stream terrified me — drowning must be so horrible a death. I could not do it. Then, as I knelt there, weeping for courage, a snake rattled beside me. I shrunk from it and fled. Death was there beside me, and I dared not take it. O! I'm afraid to die; yet I am more afraid to live.

DIDO. Die!

ZOE. So I came here to you; to you, my own dear nurse; to you, who so often hushed me to sleep when I was a child; who dried my eyes and put your little Zoe to rest. Ah! give me the rest that no master but One can disturb — the sleep from which I shall awake free! You can protect me from that man — do let me die without pain.

DIDO. No, no — life is good for young t'ing like you.

ZOE. O! good, good nurse: you will, you will.

DIDO. No — g' way.

ZOE. Then I shall never leave Terrebonne — the drink, nurse; the drink; that I may never leave my home — my dear, dear home. You will not give me to that man? Your own Zoe, that loves you, Aunty, so much, so much. (*She gets the phial.*) Ah! I have it.

DIDO. No, missey. O! no — don't.

ZOE. Hush! (*Runs off.*)

DIDO. Here, Solon, Minnie, Grace.
(*They enter.*)

ALL. Was de matter?

DIDO. Miss Zoe got de pizen. (*Exits.*)

ALL. O! O! (*Exeunt.*)

ACT FIVE: SCENE TWO

In a canebrake bayou, on a bank, with a canoe nearby, M'CLOSKY *is seen asleep.*

M'CLOSKY. Burn, burn! blaze away! How the flames crack. I'm not guilty; would ye murder me? Cut, cut the rope — I choke — choke — Ah! (*Wakes.*) Hello! where am I? Why, I was dreaming — curse it! I can never sleep now without dreaming. Hush! I thought I heard the sound of a paddle in the water. All night, as I fled through the canebrake, I heard footsteps behind me. I lost them in the cedar swamp — again they haunted my path down the bayou, moving as I moved, resting when I rested — hush! there again! — no; it was only the wind over the canes. The sun is rising. I must launch my dug-out, and put for the bay, and in a few hours I shall be safe from pursuit on board of one of the coasting schooners that run from Galveston to Matagorda. In a little time this darned business will blow over, and I can show again. Hark! there's that noise again! If it was the ghost of that murdered boy haunting me! Well — I didn't mean to kill him, did I? Well, then, what has my all-cowardly heart got to skeer me so far? (*He gets in canoe and rows off.* WAHNOTEE *appears in another canoe. He gets out and finds trail and paddles off after* M'CLOSKY.)

ACT FIVE: SCENE THREE

A cedar swamp. Enter SCUDDER *and* PETE.

SCUDDER. Come on, Pete, we shan't reach the house before midday.

PETE. Nebber mind, sa, we bring good news — it won't spile for de keeping.

SCUDDER. Ten miles we've had to walk, because some blamed varmin onhitched our dug-out. I left it last night all safe.

PETE. P'r'aps it floated away itself.

SCUDDER. No; the hitching line was cut with a knife.

PETE. Say, Mas'r Scudder, s'pose we go in round by de quarters and raise de darkies, den dey cum long wid us, and we 'proach dat ole house like Gin'ral Jackson when he took London out dar.

SCUDDER. Hello, Pete, I never heard of that affair.

PETE. I tell you, sa — hush!

SCUDDER. What?

PETE. Was dat? — a cry out dar in the swamp — dar again!

SCUDDER. So it is. Something forcing its way through the undergrowth — it comes this way — it's either a bear or a runaway nigger. (*He draws a pistol.* M'CLOSKY *rushes on, and falls at* SCUDDER*'s feet.*)

SCUDDER. Stand off — what are ye?

PETE. Mas'r Clusky.

M'CLOSKY. Save me — save me! I can go no farther. I heard voices.

SCUDDER. Who's after you?

M'CLOSKY. I don't know, but I feel it's death! In some form, human, or wild beast, or ghost, it has tracked me through the night. I fled; it followed. Hark! there it comes — it comes — don't you hear a footstep on the dry leaves!

SCUDDER. Your crime has driven you mad.

M'CLOSKY. D'ye hear it — nearer — nearer — ah!

179

(WAHNOTEE *rushes on, and attacks* M'CLOSKY.)

SCUDDER. The Injiun! By thunder.

PETE. You'se a dead man, Mas'r Clusky — you got to b'lieve dat.

M'CLOSKY. No — no. If I must die, give me up to the law; but save me from the tomahawk. You are a white man; you'll not leave one of your own blood to be butchered by the redskin?

SCUDDER. Hold on now, Jacob; we've got to figure on that — let us look straight at the thing. Here we are on the selvage of civilisation. It ain't our side, I believe, rightly; but Nature has said that where the white man sets his foot, the red man and the black man shall up sticks and stand around. But what do we pay for that possession? In cash? No — in kind — that is, in protection, forbearance, gentleness, in all them goods that show the critters the difference between the Christian and the savage. Now, what have you done to show them the distinction? For, darn me, if I can find out.

M'CLOSKY. For what I have done, let me be tried.

SCUDDER. You have been tried — honestly tried and convicted. Providence has chosen your executioner. I shan't interfere.

PETE. O, no; Mas'r Scudder, don't leave Mas'r Closky like dat — don't, sa — 't ain't what good Christian should do.

SCUDDER. D' ye hear that, Jacob? This old nigger, the grandfather of the boy you murdered, speaks for you — don't that go through you? D' ye feel it? Go on, Pete, you've waked up the Christian here, and the old hoss responds. (*He throws bowie knife to* M'CLOSKY.) Take that, and defend yourself.

(*Exeunt* SCUDDER *and* PETE. WAHNOTEE *faces him. They fight,* M'CLOSKY *runs off,* WAHNOTEE *follows him. — Screams outside.*)

ACT FIVE: SCENE FOUR

Parlour at Terrebonne.

ZOE (*enters*). My home, my home! I must see you no more. Those little flowers can live, but I cannot. Tomorrow they'll bloom the same — all will be here as now, and I shall be cold. O! my life, my happy life; why has it been so bright?
    (*Enter* MRS PEYTON *and* DORA.)

DORA. Zoe, where have you been?

MRS PEYTON. We felt quite uneasy about you.

ZOE. I've been to the Negro quarters. I suppose I shall go before long, and I wished to visit all the places, once again, to see the poor people.

MRS PEYTON. Zoe, dear, I'm glad to see you more calm this morning.

DORA. But how pale she looks, and she trembles so.

ZOE. Do I? (*Enter* GEORGE.) Ah! he is here.

DORA. George, here she is.

ZOE. I have come to say good bye, sir; two hard words — so hard, they might break many a heart; mightn't they?

GEORGE. O, Zoe! can you smile at this moment?

ZOE. You see how easily I have become reconciled to my fate — so it will be with you. You will not forget poor Zoe! but her image will pass away like a little cloud that obscured your happiness a while — you will love each other? you are both too good not to join your hearts. Brightness will return amongst you. Dora, I once made you weep; those were the only tears I caused anybody. Will you forgive me?

DORA. Forgive you — (*Kisses her.*)

GEORGE. Zoe, you are pale. Zoe! — she faints!

ZOE. No; a weakness, that's all — a little water. (DORA *gets some water.*) I have a restorative here — will you pour it in the glass? (DORA *attempts to take it.*) No; not you — George. (GEORGE

181

pours the contents of the phial into glass.) Now, give it to me. George, dear George, do you love me?

GEORGE. Do you doubt it, Zoe?

ZOE. No! (*She drinks.*)

DORA. Zoe, if all I possess would buy your freedom, I would gladly give it.

ZOE. I am free! I had but one Master on earth, and he has given me my freedom!

DORA. Alas! but the deed that freed you was not lawful.

ZOE. Not lawful — no — but I am going to where there is no law — where there is only justice.

GEORGE. Zoe, you are suffering — your lips are white — your cheeks are flushed.

ZOE. I must be going — it is late. Farewell, Dora. (*Retires.*)

PETE (*outside*). Whar's Missus — whar's Mas'r George?

GEORGE. They come.

SCUDDER (*enters*). Stand around and let me pass — room thar! I feel so big with joy, creation ain't wide enough to hold me. Mrs Peyton, George Peyton, Terrebonne is yours. It was that rascal M'Closky — but he got rats, I swow — he killed the boy, Paul, to rob this letter from the mail-bags — the letter from Liverpool you know — he sot fire to the shed — that was how the steamboat got burned up.

MRS PEYTON. What d' ye mean?

SCUDDER. Read — read that. (*He gives letter to them.*)

GEORGE. Explain yourself.

SUNNYSIDE (*enters*). Is it true?

SCUDDER. Every word of it, Squire. Here, you tell it, since you know it. If I was to try, I'd bust.

MRS PEYTON. Read, George. Terrebonne is yours.

(*Enter* PETE, DIDO, SOLON, MINNIE, *and* GRACE.)

PETE. War is she — war is Miss Zoe?

SCUDDER. What's the matter?

PETE. Don't ax me. Whar's de gal? I say.

SCUDDER. Here she is — Zoe! — water — she faints.

PETE. No — no. 'T ain't no faint — she's a dying, sa: she got pizon from old Dido here, this mornin'.

GEORGE. Zoe!

SCUDDER. Zoe! is this true? — no, it ain't — darn it, say it ain't. Look here, you're free, you know; nary a master to hurt you now: you will stop here as long as you're a mind to, only don't look so.

DORA. Her eyes have changed colour.

PETE. Dat's what her soul's gwine to do. It's going up dar, whar dere's no line atween folks.

GEORGE. She revives.

ZOE (*on the sofa*). George — where — where —

GEORGE. O, Zoe! what have you done?

ZOE. Last night I overheard you weeping in your room, and you said, 'I'd rather see her dead than so!'

GEORGE. Have I then prompted you to this?

ZOE. No; but I loved you so, I could not bear my fate; and then I stood between your heart and hers. When I am dead she will not be jealous of your love for me, no laws will stand between us. Lift me; so — (GEORGE *raises her head.*) — let me look at you, that your face may be the last I see of this world. O! George, you may, without a blush, confess your love for the Octoroon. (*She dies.* GEORGE *lowers her head gently and kneels beside her.*)

THE ENGLISH HAPPY ENDING

ACT FOUR

SCENE. *The wharf. — The Steamer 'Magnolia' alongside, L. — A bluff rock,* R.U.E. RATTS *discovered, superintending the loading of ship. Enter* LAFOUCHE *and* JACKSON, L.

JACKSON. How long before we start, captain?

RATTS. Just as soon as we put this cotton on board.
   (*Enter* PETE, *with lantern, and* SCUDDER, *with notebook,* R.)

SCUDDER. One hundred and forty-nine bales. Can you take any more?

RATTS. Not a bale. I've got engaged eight hundred bales at the next landing, and one hundred hogsheads of sugar at Patten's Slide — that'll take my guards under — hurry up thar!

VOICE   (*outside*). Wood's aboard.

RATTS. All aboard then.
   (*Enter* M'CLOSKY, R.)

SCUDDER. Sign that receipt, captain, and save me going up to the clerk.

M'CLOSKY. See here — there's a small freight of turpentine in the fore-hold there, and one of the barrels leaks; a spark from your engines might set the ship on fire, and you'd go with it.

RATTS. You be darned! Go and try it if you've a mind to.

LAFOUCHE. Captain, you've loaded up here until the boat is sunk so deep in the mud she won't float.

RATTS (*calls off*). Wood up thar, you Pollo — hang on to the safety valve — guess she'll crawl off on her paddles. (*Shouts heard,* R.)

JACKSON. What's the matter?
   (*Enter* SOLON, R.)

SOLON. We got him!

SCUDDER. Who?

184

SOLON. The Inginn!

SCUDDER. Wahnotee? where is he? d'ye call running away from a fellow catching him?

RATTS. Here he comes.

OMNES. Where? where?

(*Enter* WAHNOTEE, R., *they are all about to rush on him.*)

SCUDDER. Hold on! stan' round thar! no violence — the critter don't know what we mean.

JACKSON. Let him answer for the boy then.

M'CLOSKY. Down with him — lynch him.

OMNES. Lynch him!

(*Exit* LAFOUCHE, R.)

SCUDDER. Stan' back, I say! I'll nip the first that lays a finger on him. Pete, speak to the redskin.

PETE. Whar's Paul, Wahnotee? What's come ob de child?

WAHNOTEE. Paul wunce — Paul pangeuk.

PETE. Pangeuk — dead.

WAHNOTEE. Mort!

M'CLOSKY. And you killed him? (*They approach again.*)

SCUDDER. Hold on!

PETE. Um, Paul reste?

WAHNOTEE. Hugh vieu — (*Goes* L.) — Paul reste ci!

SCUDDER. Here, stay! (*Examines the ground.*) The earth has been stirred here lately.

WAHNOTEE. Weenee Paul. (*Points down and shows by pantomime how he buried* PAUL.)

SCUDDER. The Inginn means that he buried him there! Stop, here's a bit of leather. (*Draws out mail-bags.*) The mail-bags that were lost! (*Sees tomahawk in* WAHNOTEE*'s belt — draws it out and examines it.*) Look! here are marks of blood — look thar, red-skin, what's that?

WAHNOTEE. Paul! (*Makes sign that* PAUL *was killed by a blow on the head.*)

M'CLOSKY. He confesses it; the Indian got drunk, quarrelled with him, and killed him.

(*Re-enter* LAFOUCHE, R., *with smashed apparatus.*)

LAFOUCHE. Here are evidences of the crime; this rum bottle half emptied — this photographic apparatus smashed — and there are marks of blood and footsteps around the shed.

M'CLOSKY. What more d'ye want — ain't that proof enough? Lynch him!

OMNES. Lynch him! Lynch him!

SCUDDER. Stan' back, boys! he's an Inginn — fair play.

185

JACKSON. Try him, then — try him on the spot of his crime.

OMNES. Try him! try him!

LAFOUCHE. Don't let him escape!

RATTS. I'll see to that. (*Draws revolver.*) If he stirs, I'll put a bullet through his skull, mighty quick.

M'CLOSKY. Come — form a court, then, choose a jury — we'll fix this varmin.

(*Enter* THIBODEAUX *and* CAILLOU, L.)

THIBODEAUX. What's the matter?

LAFOUCHE. We've caught this murdering Inginn, and are going to try him.

(WAHNOTEE *sits* L., *rollen in blanket.*)

PETE. Poor little Paul — poor little nigger!

SCUDDER. This business goes agin me, Ratts — 'taint right.

LAFOUCHE. We're ready, the jury is empannelled — go ahead — who'll be accuser?

RATTS. M'Closky.

M'CLOSKY. Me!

RATTS. Yes; you was the first to hail Judge Lynch.

M'CLOSKY (R). Well, what's the use of argument, whar guilt sticks out so plain; the boy and Inginn were alone when last seen.

SCUDDER (L. C). Who says that?

M'CLOSKY. Everybody — that is, I heard so.

SCUDDER. Say what you know — not what you heard.

M'CLOSKY. I know then, that the boy was killed with that tomahawk — the redskin owns it — the signs of violence are all round the shed — this apparatus smashed — ain't it plain that in a drunken fit he slew the boy, and when sober concealed the body yonder?

OMNES. That's it — that's it.

RATTS. Who defends the Indian?

SCUDDER. I will; for it's agin my natur' to b'lieve him guilty; and if he be, this ain't the place, nor you the authority, to try him. How are we sure the boy is dead at all? There are no witnesses but a rum-bottle and an old machine. Is it on such evidence you'd hang a human being?

RATTS. His own confession.

SCUDDER. I appeal against your usurped authority; this lynch law is a wild and lawless proceeding. Here's a picture for a civilised community to afford; yonder, a poor ignorant savage, and round him a circle of hearts, white with revenge and hate, thirsting for his blood; you call yourselves judges — you ain't — you're a jury of executioners. It is such scenes as these that bring disgrace upon our Western life.

M'CLOSKY. Evidence! Evidence! give us evidence, we've had talk enough; now for proof.

OMNES. Yes, yes! Proof, proof!

SCUDDER. Where am I to get it? the proof is here, in my heart!

PETE (*who has been looking about the camera*). Top sar! top a bit! Oh, laws-a-mussey, see dis, here's a pictur' I found sticking in that yar telescope machine, sar! look, sar!

SCUDDER. A photographic plate. (PETE *holds lantern up.*) What's this, eh? two forms! the child — 'tis he! dead — and above him — Ah, ah! Jacob M'Closky — 'twas you murdered that boy!

M'CLOSKY. Me?

SCUDDER. You! You slew him with that tomahawk, and as you stood over his body with the letter in your hand, you thought that no witness saw the deed, that no eye was on you; but there was, Jacob M'Closky, there was — the eye of the Eternal was on you — the blessed sun in heaven, that, looking down, struck upon this plate the image of the deed. Here you are, in the very attitude of your crime!

M'CLOSKY. 'Tis false!

SCUDDER. 'Tis true! the apparatus can't lie. Look there, jurymen — (*shows plate to jury*) — look there. Oh, you wanted evidence — you called for proof — heaven has answered and convicted you.

M'CLOSKY. What court of law would receive such evidence? (*Going.*)

RATTS. Stop, *this* would — you called it yourself; you wanted to make us murder that Inginn, and since we've got our hands in for justice, we'll try it on you. What say ye? Shall we have one law for the redskin and another for the white?

OMNES. Try him! try him!

RATTS. Who'll be accuser?

SCUDDER. I will! Fellow citizens, you have convened and assembled here under a higher power than the law. What's the law? When the ship's abroad on the ocean — when the army is before the enemy — where in thunder's the law? It is in the hearts of brave men who can tell right from wrong, and from whom justice can't be bought. So it is here, in the Wilds of the West, where our hatred of crime is measured by the speed of our executions — where necessity is law! — I say, then, air you honest men? air you true? put your hands on your naked breasts, and let every man as don't feel a real American heart there, bustin' up with freedom, truth and right, let that man step out — that's the oath I put to ye — and then say, darn ye, go it!

187

OMNES. Go on — Go on.

SCUDDER. No! I won't go on, that man's down, I won't strike him even with words. Jacob, your accuser is that picter of the crime — let that speak — defend yourself.

M'CLOSKY (*draws knife*). I will, quicker than lightning.

RATTS. Seize him, then! (*They rush on* M'CLOSKY *and disarm him.*) He can fight though — he's a painter, claws all over.

SCUDDER. Stop! Search him, we may find more evidence.

M'CLOSKY. Would you rob me first, and murder me afterwards?

RATTS (*searching him*). That's his programme — here's a pocket-book.

SCUDDER (*opens it*). What's here? Letters! Hello! to 'Mrs Peyton, Terrebonne, Louisiana, United States' Liverpool post mark. Ho! I've got hold of the tail of a rat — come out. (*Reads.*) What's this? — a draft for 85,000 dollars and credit on Palisse and Co., of New Orleans, for the balance. Hi! the rat's out — you killed the boy to steal this letter from the mail-bags — you stole this letter that the money should not arrive in time to save the Octoroon; had it done so, the lien on the estate would have ceased, and Zoe be free.

OMNES. Lynch him! — lynch him! — down with him!

SCUDDER. Silence in the court — stand back, let the gentlemen of the jury retire, consult, and return their verdict.

RATTS. I'm responsible for the crittur — go on.

PETE (*to* WAHNOTEE). See, Inginn, look dar. (*Shows him plate.*) See dat innocent, look, dare's the murderer of poor Paul.

WAHNOTEE. Ugh! (*Examines plate.*)

PETE. Ya! as he? Closky tue Paul — kill de child with your tomahawk dar, 'twasn't you, no — ole Pete allus say so. Poor Inginn lub our little Paul.

(WAHNOTEE *rises and looks at* M'CLOSKY — *he is in his war paint and fully armed.*)

SCUDDER. What say ye, gentlemen? Is the prisoner guilty, or is he not guilty?

OMNES. Guilty!

SCUDDER. And what is to be his punishment?

OMNES. Death!

WAHNOTEE (*crosses to* M'CLOSKY). Ugh!

SCUDDER. The Inginn, by thunder!

PETE (*to* M'CLOSKY). You's a dead man, mas'r; you've got to b'lieve dat.

M'CLOSKY. No! If I must die, give me up to the laws, but save me from the tomahawk of the savage; you are a white man, you'll not leave one of your own blood to be butchered by the scalping knife of the redskin.

SCUDDER. Hold on now, Jacob, we've got to figure that out; let us look straight at the thing. Here we are on the confines of civilisation; it ain't our sile, I believe, rightly; Natur' has said that where the white mans sets his foot the red man and the black man shall up sticks and stan' round. Now, what do we pay for that possession? In cash? No – in kind – that is, in protection and forbearance, in gentleness, and in all them goods that show the critturs the difference between the Christian and the Savage. Now what have you done to show 'em the distinction? for darn me if I can find out.

M'CLOSKY. For what I've done let me be tried.

SCUDDER. Oh, you have been fairly and honestly tried, and convicted: Providence has chosen your executioner – I shan't interfere.

PETE. Oh! sar! hi, Mas'r Scudder, don't leave Mas'r 'Closky like dat – don't, sar – tain't what a good Christian would do.

SCUDDER. D'ye hear that, Jacob? – this old nigger, the grandfather of the boy your murdered, speaks for you – don't that go through ye – d'ye feel it? Go on, Pete, you've woke up the Christian here, and the old hoss responds.

WAHNOTEE (*placing his hand on* M'CLOSKY's *head*). Wahnotee!

SCUDDER. No, Inginn, we deal justice here, not revenge; tain't you he has injured, 'tis the white man, whose laws he has offended.

RATTS. Away with him! put him down the hatch till we rig his funeral.

M'CLOSKY. Fifty against one! Oh! if you were alone – if I had ye one by one in the swamp, I'd rip ye all.

PETE (*lighting him off*, R). Dis way, Mas'r 'Closky, take care, sar. (*Exit with* M'CLOSKY *and* JACKSON *to steamer*.)

LAFOUCHE. Off with him quick – here come the ladies. (*Enter* MRS CLAIBORNE, R 1 E.)

MRS CLAIBORNE. Shall we soon start, Captain?

RATTS. Yes, ma'am; we've only got a – Take my hand, ma'am, to steady you – a little account to square, and we're off.

MRS CLAIBORNE. A fog is rising.

RATTS. Swamp mist; soon clear off. (*Hands her to steamer*.)

MRS CLAIBORNE. Good night.

RATTS. Good night, ma'am – good night.

SCUDDER. Now to business.

(PETE *appears on deck*.)

189

PETE. Oh! law, sar. Dat debbel, 'Closky — he tore hisself from de gentleman — knock me down — take away my light, and throwed it on de turpentine barrels — de ship's on fire!

(*All hurry off to ship — alarm bell rings — loud shouts; a hatch in the deck is opened —a glare of red —and* M'CLOSKY *emerges from the aperture; he is without his coat, and carries a bowie knife; he rushes down —* WAHNOTEE *alone is watching him from* R. U. E.)

M'CLOSKY. Ha, ha, ha! I've given them something to remember how they treated Jacob M'Closky. Made my way from one end of the vessel to the other, and now the road to escape is clear before me — and thus to secure it! (*He goes to* R. C., *and is met by* WAHNOTEE, *who silently confronts him.*)

WAHNOTEE. Paul.

M'CLOSKY. Devils! — you here! — stand clear!

WAHNOTEE. Paul.

M'CLOSKY. You won't! — die, fool!

(*Thrusts at him —*WAHNOTEE, *with his tomahawk, strikes the knife out of his hand;* M'CLOSKY *starts back;* WAHNOTEE *throws off his blanket, and strikes at* M'CLOSKY *several times, who avoids him; at last he catches his arm, and struggles for the tomahawk, which falls; a violent struggle and fight takes place, ending with the triumph of* WAHNOTEE, *who drags* M'CLOSKY *along the ground, takes up the knife and stabs him repeatedly;* GEORGE *enters, bearing* ZOE *in his arms — all the* CHARACTERS *rush on — noise increasing — The steam vessel blows up —grand Tableau, and*

CURTAIN

THE COLLEEN BAWN

OR

THE BRIDES OF GARRYOWEN

A DOMESTIC DRAMA

in Three Acts

founded on Gerald Griffin's Irish story

THE COLLEGIANS

DRAMATIS PERSONAE

first performed at Miss Laura Keene's Theatre, New York,
27 March 1860

Myles-na-Coppaleen	MR DION BOUCICAULT
Hardress Cregan, *Son of Mrs Cregan*	MR H.F. DALY
Danny Mann,	MR CHARLES WHEATLEIGH
the Hunchbacked Servant	
Kyrle Daly, *College Friend to Hardress*	MR CHARLES FISHER
Father Tom, *Parish Priest of Garryowen*	MR D.W. LEESON
Mr Corrigan, *a Pettifogging Attorney*	MR J.G. BURNETT
Bertie O'Moore	MR HENRY
Hyland Creagh	MR LEVICK
Servant	MR GOODRICH
Corporal	MR CLARKE
Eily O'Connor, *the Colleen Bawn*	MISS AGNES ROBERTSON
Anne Chute, *the Colleen Ruadh*	MISS LAURA KEENE
Mrs Cregan	MADAM PONISI
Sheelah	MISS MARY WELLS
Kathleen Creagh	MISS JOSEPHINE HENRY
Ducie Blennerhasset	MISS HAMILTON

In consequence of the production of this Drama, and others by the same Author, in the United States of America, with which there is no existing International Treaty of Copyright, Vice-Chancellor Wood decreed that no property *could exist* in their representation in this Country; therefore the Assignees of the Author, in whom his property was vested at his bankruptcy, have no title whatever in or to them, and *The Colleen Bawn*, with the Dramas named on the title page of the Play are Performance Free.

T.H.L.

ACT ONE: SCENE ONE

Night — Torc Cregan — the Residence of MRS CREGAN *on the Banks of Killarney. House; window facing Audience — stage open at back. Music — seven bars before curtain. Enter* HARDRESS CREGAN, *from house.*

HARDRESS (*going up*). Hist! Danny, are you there?
    (DANNY *appearing from below, at back.*)
DANNY. Is it yourself, Masther Hardress?
HARDRESS. Is the boat ready?
DANNY. Snug under the blue rock, sir.
HARDRESS. Does Eily expect me tonight?
DANNY. Expict is it? Here is a lether she bade me give yuz; sure the young thing is never aisy when you are away. Look, masther, dear, do ye see that light, no bigger than a star beyant on Muckross Head?
HARDRESS. Yes, it is the signal which my dear Eily leaves burning in our chamber.
DANNY. All night long she sits beside that light, wid her face fixed on that lamp in your windy above.
HARDRESS. Dear, dear Eily, after all here's asleep, I will leap from my window, and we'll cross the lake.
DANNY (*searching*). Where did I put that lether?
    (*Enter* KYRLE DALY *from house.*)
KYRLE. Hardress, who is that with you?
HARDRESS. Only Danny Mann, my boatman.
KYRLE. That fellow is like your shadow.
DANNY. Is it a cripple like me, that would be the shadow of an illegant gintleman like Mr Hardress Cregan?
KYRLE. Well, I mean that he never leaves your side.
HARDRESS. And he never *shall* leave me. Ten years ago he was a fine boy — we were foster-brothers and playmates — in a moment of passion, while we were struggling, I flung him from

the gap rock into the reeks below, and thus he was maimed for life.

DANNY. Arrah! whist aroon! wouldn't I die for yez? didn't the same mother foster us? Why, wouldn't ye brake my back if it plazed ye, and welkim! Oh, Masther Kyrle, if ye'd seen him nursin' me for months, and cryin' over me, and keenin'! Sin' that time, sir, my body's been crimpin' up smaller and smaller every year, but my heart is gettin' bigger for him every day.

HARDRESS. Go along, Danny.

DANNY. Long life t'ye sir! I'm off. (*Runs up and descends rocks.*)

KYRLE. Hardress, a word with you. Be honest with me — do you love Anne Chute?

HARDRESS. Why do you ask?

KYRLE. Because we have been fellow-collegians and friends through life, and the five years that I have passed at sea have strengthened, but have not cooled, my feelings towards you. (*Offers hand.*)

(*Enter* MRS CREGAN, *from house.*)

HARDRESS. Nor mine for you, Kyrle. You are the same noble fellow as ever. You ask me if I love my cousin Anne?

MRS CREGAN (*between them*). And I will answer you, Mr Daly.

HARDRESS. My mother!

MRS CREGAN. My son and Miss Chute are engaged. Excuse me, Kyrle, for intruding on your secret, but I have observed your love for Anne with some regret. I hope your heart is not so far gone as to be beyond recovery.

KYRLE. Forgive me, Mrs Cregan, but are you certain that Miss Chute really is in love with Hardress?

MRS CREGAN. Look at him! I'm sure no girl could do that and doubt it.

KYRLE. But I'm not a girl, ma'am; and sure, if you are mistaken —

HARDRESS. My belief is that Anne does not care a token for me, and likes Kyrle better.

MRS CREGAN. You are an old friend of my son, and I may confide to you a family secret. The extravagance of my husband left this estate deeply involved. By this marriage with Anne Chute we redeem every acre of our barony. My son and she have been brought up as children together, and I don't know their true feelings yet.

HARDRESS. Stop, mother, I know this: I would not wed my cousin if she did not love me, not if she carried the whole County Kerry in her pocket, and the barony of Kenmare in the crown of her hat.

MRS CREGAN. Do you hear the proud blood of the Cregans?

HARDRESS. Woo her, Kyrle, if you like, and win her if you can. I'll back you.

(*Enter* ANNE CHUTE, *from house.*)

ANNE. So will I — what's the bet?

MRS CREGAN. Hush!

ANNE. I'd like to have a bet on Kyrle.

HARDRESS. Well, Anne, I'll tell you what it was.

MRS CREGAN. Hardress!

ANNE. Pull in one side, aunt, and let the boy go on.

HARDRESS. Kyrle wanted to know if the dark brown colt, Hardress Cregan, was going to walk over the course for the Anne Chute Stakes, or whether it was a scrub-race open to all.

ANNE. I'm free-trade — coppleens, mules and biddys.

MRS CREGAN. How can you trifle with a heart like Kyrle's?

ANNE. Trifle! his heart can be no trifle, if he's all in proportion.

(*Enter* SERVANT *from house.*)

SERVANT. Squire Corrigan, ma'am, begs to see you.

MRS CREGAN. At this hour, what can the fellow want? Show Mr Corrigan here.

(*Exit* SERVANT *into house.*)

I hate this man; he was my husband's agent, or what the people here call a middle-man — vulgarly polite, and impudently obsequious.

HARDRESS. Genus squireen — a half sir, and a whole scoundrel.

ANNE. I know — a potatoe on a silver plate: I'll leave you to peel him. Come, Mr Daly, take me for a moonlight walk, and be funny.

KYRLE. Funny, ma'am, I'm afraid I am —

ANNE. You are heavy, you mean; you roll through the world like a hogshead of whiskey; but you only want tapping for pure spirits to flow out spontaneously. Give me your arm. Hold that glove now. You are from Ballinasloe, I think?

KYRLE. I'm Connaught to the core of my heart.

ANNE. To the roots of your hair, you mean. I bought a horse at Ballinasloe fair that deceived me; I hope you won't turn out to belong to the same family.

KYRLE. What did he do?

ANNE. Uh! like you, he looked well enough — deep in the chest as a pool — a-dhiol, and broad in the back, as the Gap of Dunloe — but after two days' warm work he came all to pieces, and Larry, my groom, said he'd been stuck together with glue.

KYRLE. Really, Miss Chute! (*Music* – *Exeunt.*)

195

HARDRESS (*advancing, laughing*). That girl is as wild as a coppleen — she won't leave him a hair on the head .(*Goes up.*)
  (*Enter* SERVANT, *showing in* CORRIGAN *from house. Exit* SERVANT.)

CORRIGAN. Your humble servant, Mrs Cregan — my service t'ye, 'Squire — it's a fine night entirely .

MRS CREGAN. May I ask to what business, sir, we have the honour of your call?

CORRIGAN (*aside*). Proud as Lady Beelzebub, and as grand as a queen. (*Aloud*) True for you, ma'am; I would not have come but for a divil of a pinch I'm in entirely. I've got to pay £8,000 tomorrow, or lose the Knockmakilty farms.

MRS CREGAN. Well, sir?

CORRIGAN. And I wouldn't throuble ye —

MRS CREGAN. Trouble me, sir?

CORRIGAN. Iss, m'am — ye'd be forgettin' now that mortgage I have on this property. It ran out last May, and by rights —

MRS CREGAN. It will be paid next month.

CORRIGAN. Are you reckonin' on the marriage of Mister Hardress and Miss Anne Chute?

HARDRESS (*advancing*). Mr Corrigan, you forget yourself.

MRS CREGAN. Leave us, Hardress, awhile. (HARDRESS *retires.*) Now, Mr Corrigan, state, in as few words as possible, what you demand.

CORRIGAN. Mrs Cregan, ma'am, you depend on Miss Anne Chute's fortune to pay me the money, but your son does not love the lady, or, if he does, he has a mighty quare way of shewing it. He has another girl on hand, and betune the two he'll come to the ground, and so bedad will I.

MRS CREGAN. That is false — it is a calumny, sir!

CORRIGAN. I wish it was, ma'am. D'ye see that light over the lake? — your son's eyes are fixed on it. What would Anne Chute say if she knew that her husband, that is to be, had a mistress beyant — that he slips out every night after you're all in bed, and like Leandher, barrin' the wettin', he sails across to his sweetheart?

MRS CREGAN. Is this the secret of his aversion to the marriage? Fool! fool! what madness, and at such a moment.

CORRIGAN. That's what I say, and no lie in it.

MRS CREGAN. He shall give up this girl — he must!

CORRIGAN. I would like to have some security for that. I want by tomorrow — Anne Chute's written promise to marry him or my £8,000.

196

MRS CREGAN. It is impossible, sir; you hold ruin over our heads .

CORRIGAN. Madam, it's got to hang over your head or mine .

MRS CREGAN. Stay, you know that what you ask is out of our power — you know it — therefore this demand only covers the true object of your visit .

CORRIGAN. 'Pon my honour! and you are as 'cute, ma'am, as you are beautiful!

MRS CREGAN. Go on, sir .

CORRIGAN. Mrs Cregan, I'm goin' to do a foolish thing — now, by gorra I am! I'm richer than ye think, maybe, and if you'll give me your *personal* security, I'll take it .

MRS CREGAN. What do you mean?

CORRIGAN. I mean that I'll take a lien for life on *you,* instead of the mortgage I hold on the Cregan property. (*Aside*) That's nate, I'm thinkin'.

MRS CREGAN. Are you mad?

CORRIGAN. I am — mad in love with yourself, and that's what I've been these fifteen years.
     (*Music through dialogue till* ANNE CHUTE *is off.*)

MRS CREGAN. Insolent wretch! my son shall answer and chastise you. (*Calls*) Hardress!

HARDRESS (*advancing*) Madam.
     (*Enter* ANNE CHUTE *and* KYRLE.)

CORRIGAN.   ⎧ Miss Chute!
HARDRESS. (*together*) ⎨ Well, mother?
ANNE.   ⎩ Well, sir?

MRS CREGAN (*aside*). Scoundrel! he will tell her all and ruin us! (*Aloud*) Nothing. (*Turns aside.*)

CORRIGAN. Your obedient.

ANNE. Oh! (*Crosses with* KYRLE *and exit — Music ceases.*)

CORRIGAN. You are in my power, ma'am. See, now, not a sowl but myself knows of this secret love of Hardress Cregan, and I'll keep it as snug as a bug in a rug, if you'll only say the word.

MRS CREGAN. Contemptible hound, I loathe and despise you!

CORRIGAN. I've known that fifteen years, but it hasn't cured my heart ache.

MRS CREGAN. And you would buy my aversion and disgust!

CORRIGAN. Just as Anne Chute buys your son, if she knew but all. Can he love his girl beyant, widout haten this heiress he's obliged to swallow? — ain't you sthriven to sell him? But you didn't feel the hardship of being sold till you tried it on yourself.

MRS CREGAN. I beg you, sir, to leave me.

CORRIGAN. That's right, ma'am — think over it, sleep on it. Tomorrow I'll call for your answer. Good evenin' kindly.

(*Music — Exit* CORRIGAN *in house.*)

MRS CREGAN. Hardress.

HARDRESS. What did he want?

MRS CREGAN. He came to tell me the meaning of yonder light upon Muckross Head.

HARDRESS. Ah! has it been discovered. Well, mother, now you know the cause of my coldness, my indifference for Anne.

MRS CREGAN. Are you in your senses, Hardress? Who is this girl?

HARDRESS. She is known at every fair and pattern in Munster as the Colleen Bawn — her name is Eily O'Connor.

MRS CREGAN. A peasant girl — a vulgar barefooted beggar.

HARDRESS. Whatever she is, love has made her my equal, and when you set your foot upon her you tread upon my heart.

MRS CREGAN. 'Tis well, Hardress. I feel that perhaps I have no right to dispose of your life and your happiness — no, my dear son — I would not wound you — heaven knows how well I love my darling boy, and you shall feel it. Corrigan has made me an offer by which you may regain the estate, and without selling yourself to Anne Chute.

HARDRESS. What is it? Of course you accepted it?

MRS CREGAN. No, but I will accept, yes, for your sake — I — I will. He offers to cancel this mortgage if — if — I will consent to — become his wife.

HARDRESS. You — you, mother? Has he dared —

MRS CREGAN. Hush! he is right. A sacrifice must be made — either you or I must suffer. Life is before you — my days are well nigh past — and for your sake, Hardress — for yours; my pride, my only one. Oh! I would give you more than my life.

HARDRESS. Never — never! I will not, cannot accept it. I'll tear that dog's tongue from his throat that dared insult you with the offer.

MRS CREGAN. Foolish boy, before tomorrow night we shall be beggars — outcasts from this estate. Humiliation and poverty stand like spectres at yonder door — tomorrow they will be realities. Can you tear out the tongues that will wag over our fallen fortunes? You are a child, you cannot see beyond your happiness.

HARDRESS. Oh! mother, mother, what can be done? My marriage with Anne is impossible.

(*Enter* DANNY MANN, *up rock, at back.*)

198

DANNY. Whisht, if ye plaze — ye're talkin' so loud she'll hear ye say that — she's comin'.

MRS CREGAN. Has this fellow overheard us?

HARDRESS. If he has, he is mine, body and soul. I'd rather trust him with a secret than keep it myself.

MRS CREGAN. I cannot remain to see Anne; excuse me to my friends. The night perhaps will bring counsel, or at least resolution to hear the worst! Good night, my son. (*Music — Exit into house.*)

DANNY. Oh! masther, she doesn't know the worst! She doesn't know that you are married to the Colleen Bawn.

HARDRESS. Hush! what fiend prompts you to thrust that act of folly in my face.

DANNY. Thrue for ye, masther! I'm a dirty mane scut to remind ye of it.

HARDRESS. What will my haughty, noble mother say, when she learns the truth! how can I ask her to receive Eily as a daughter? Eily, with her awkward manners, her Kerry brogue, her ignorance of the usages of society. Oh! what have I done?

DANNY. Oh! vo — vo, has the ould family come to this! Is it the daughter of Mihil-na-Thradrucha, the ould rope-maker of Garryowen, that 'ud take the flure as your wife?

HARDRESS. Be silent, scoundrel! How dare you speak thus of my love? — wretch that I am to blame her? — poor, beautiful, angel-hearted Eily.

DANNY. Beautiful is it! Och — wurra — wurra, deelish! The looking-glass was never made that could do her justice; and if St. Patrick wanted a wife, where would he find an angel that 'ud compare with the Colleen Bawn. As I row her on the lake, the little fishes come up to look at her; and the wind from heaven lifts up her hair to see what the devil brings her down here at all — at all.

HARDRESS. The fault is mine — mine alone — I alone will suffer!

DANNY. Oh! why isn't it mine? Why can't I suffer for yez, masther dear? Wouldn't I swally every tear in your body, and every bit of bad luck in your life, and then wid a stone round my neck, sink myself and your sorrows in the bottom of the lower lake.

HARDRESS (*placing hand on* DANNY). Good Danny, away with you to the boat — be ready in a few moments, we will cross to Muckross Head. (*Looks at light at back.*)

(*Music — Exit* HARDRESS *into house.*)

DANNY. Never fear, sir. Oh! it isn't that spalpeen, Corrigan, that shall bring ruin on that ould place. Lave Danny alone. Danny, the fox, will lade yez round and about, and cross the scint. (*Takes off his hat — sees letter.*) Bedad, here's the letter from the Colleen Bawn that I couldn't find awhile ago — it's little use now. (*Goes to lower window, and reads by light from house.*) 'Come to your own Eily, that has not seen you for two long days. Come, acushla agrah machree. I have forgotten how much you love me — Shule, shule agrah. — Colleen Bawn'. Divil an address is on it.

    (*Enter* KYRLE *and* ANNE.)

ANNE. Have they gone?

KYRLE. It is nearly midnight.

ANNE. Before we go in, I insist on knowing who is this girl that possesses your heart. You confess that you are in love — deeply in love.

KYRLE. I do confess it — but not even your power can extract that secret from me — do not ask me, for I could not be false, yet dare not be true. (*Exit* KYRLE *into house.*)

ANNE. He loves me — oh! he loves me — the little bird is making a nest in my heart. Oh! I'm faint with joy.

DANNY (*as if calling after him*). Sir, sir!

ANNE. Who is that?

DANNY. I'm the boatman below, an' I'm waitin' for the gintleman.

ANNE. What gentleman?

DANNY. Him that's jist left ye, ma'am — I'm waitin' on him.

ANNE. Does Mr Kyrle Daly go out boating at this hour?

DANNY. It's not for me to say, ma'am, but every night at twelve o'clock I'm here wid my boat under the blue rock below, to put him across the lake to Muckross Head. I beg your pardon, ma'am, but here's a paper ye dropped on the walk beyant — if it's no vally I'd like to light my pipe wid it. (*Gives it.*)

ANNE. A paper I dropped! (*Goes to window — reads.*)

DANNY (*aside*). Oh, Misther Corrigan, you'll ruin masther will ye? asy now, and see how I'll put the cross on ye.

ANNE. A love-letter from some peasant girl to Kyrle Daly! Can this be the love of which he spoke? have I deceived myself?

DANNY. I must be off, ma'am; here comes the signal. (*Music.*)

ANNE. The signal?

DANNY. D'ye see yonder light upon Muckross Head? It is in a cottage windy; that light goes in and out three times winkin' that way, as much as to say, 'Are ye comin?' Then if the light in that room there (*Points at house above*) answers by a wink, it manes No! but if it goes out entirely, his honour jumps from the parlour windy into the garden behind and we're off. Look! (*Light in cottage disappears.*) That's one. (*Light appears*) Now again. (*Light disappears*) That's two. (*Light appears*) What did I tell you? (*Light disappears*) That's three, and here it comes again. (*Light appears*) Wait now, and ye'll see the answer. (*Light disappears from window*) That's my gentleman. (*Music change*) You see he's goin' — good night, ma'am.

ANNE. Stay, here's money; do not tell Mr Daly that I know of this.

DANNY. Divil a word — long life t'ye. (*Goes up.*)

ANNE. I was not deceived; he meant me to understand that he loved me! Hark! I hear the sound of some one who leaped heavily on the garden walk. (*Goes to house — looking at back.*)

(*Enter* HARDRESS *wrapped in a boat cloak.*)

DANNY (*going down*). All right, yer honour.

ANNE (*hiding*). It is he, 'tis he. (*Mistaking* HARDRESS *for* DALY — *closed in.*)

ACT ONE: SCENE TWO

The Gap of Dunloe. Hour before sunrise. Enter CORRIGAN.

CORRIGAN. From the rock above I saw the boat leave Torc Cregan. It is now crossing the lake to the cottage. Who is this girl? What is this mysterious misthress of young Cregan? — that I'll find out.

    (MYLES *sings outside.*)
               'Oh! Charley Mount is a pretty place,
                  In the month of July — '

CORRIGAN. Who's that? — 'Tis that poaching scoundrel — that horse stealer, Myles-na-Coppaleen. Here he comes with a keg of illicit whiskey, as bould as Nebuckadezzar.

    (*Enter* MYLES *singing, with keg on his shoulder.*)

CORRIGAN. Is that you, Myles?

MYLES. No! it's my brother.

CORRIGAN. I know ye, my man.

MYLES. Then why the divil did ye ax?

CORRIGAN. You may as well answer me kindly — civility costs nothing.

MYLES. Ow now! don't it? Civility to a lawyer manes six-and-eight-pence about.

CORRIGAN. What's that on your shoulder?

MYLES. What's that to you?

CORRIGAN. I am a magistrate, and can oblige you to answer.

MYLES. Well! it's a boulster belongin' to my mother's feather bed.

CORRIGAN. Stuff'd with whiskey!

MYLES. Bedad! how would I know what it's stuff'd wid? I'm not an upholsterer.

CORRIGAN. Come, Myles, I'm not so bad a fellow as ye may think.

MYLES. To think of that now!

CORRIGAN. I am not the mane creature you imagine!

MYLES. Ain't ye now, sir? You keep up appearances mighty well, indeed.

CORRIGAN. No, Myles! I am not that blackguard I've been represented.

MYLES (*sits on keg*). See that now — how people take away a man's character. You are another sort of blackguard entirely.

CORRIGAN. You shall find me a gentleman — liberal, and ready to protect you.

MYLES. Long life t'ye, sir.

CORRIGAN. Myles, you have come down in the world lately; a year ago you were a thriving horse-dealer, now you are a lazy, ragged fellow.

MYLES. Ah, it's the bad luck, sir, that's in it.

CORRIGAN. No, it's the love of Eily O'Connor that's in it — it's the pride of Garryowen that took your heart away, and made ye what ye are — a smuggler and a poacher.

MYLES. Thim's hard words.

CORRIGAN. But they are true. You love like a wild beast in some cave or hole in the rocks above; by night your gun is heard shootin' the otter as they lie out on the stones, or you snare the salmon in your nets; on a cloudy night your whiskey still is going — you see, I know your life.

MYLES. Better than the priest, and devil a lie in it.

CORRIGAN. Now, if I put ye in a snug farm — stock ye with pigs and cattle, and rowl you up comfortable — d'ye think the Colleen Bawn wouldn't jump at ye?

MYLES. Bedad, she'd make a lape I b'leve — and what would I do for all this luck?

CORRIGAN. Find out for me who it is that lives at the cottage on Muckross Head.

MYLES. That's asy — it's Danny Mann — no less and his ould mother Sheelah.

CORRIGAN. Yes, Myles, but there's another — a girl who is hid there.

MYLES. Ah, now!

CORRIGAN. She only goes out at night.

MYLES. Like the owls.

CORRIGAN. She's the misthress of Hardress Cregan.

MYLES (*seizing* CORRIGAN). Thurra mon dhiol, what's that?

CORRIGAN. Oh, lor! Myles — Myles — what's the matter — are you mad?

MYLES. No — that is — why — why did ye raise your hand at me in that way?

CORRIGAN. I didn't.

MYLES. I thought ye did — I'm mighty quick at takin' thim hints, bein' on me keepin' agin' the gaugers — go on — I didn't hurt ye.

CORRIGAN. Not much.

MYLES. You want to find out who this girl is?

CORRIGAN. I'll give £20 for the information — there's ten on account. (*Gives money.*)

MYLES. Long life t'ye; that's the first money I iver got from a lawyer, and bad luck to me but there's a cure for the evil eye in thim pieces.

CORRIGAN. You will watch tonight?

MYLES. In five minutes I'll be inside the cottage itself.

CORRIGAN. That's the lad.

MYLES. (*aside*). I was goin' there.

CORRIGAN. And tomorrow you will step down to my office with the particulars?

MYLES. Tomorrow you shall breakfast on them.

CORRIGAN. Good night, entirely. (*Exit* CORRIGAN.)

MYLES. I'll give ye a cowstail to swally, and make ye think it's a chapter in St. Patrick, ye spalpeen! When he called Eily the misthress of Hardress Cregan, I nearly sthretched him — begorra, I was full of sudden death that minute! Oh, Eily! acushla agrah asthore machree! as the stars watch over Innisfallen, and as the wathers go round it and keep it, so I watch and keep round you, avourneen!

(*Song* — MYLES)

> Oh, Limerick is beautiful, as everybody knows,
> The river Shannon's full of fish, beside that city flows;
> But it is not the river, nor the fish that preys upon my mind,
> Nor with the town of Limerick have I any fault to find.
> The girl I love is beautiful, she's fairer than the dawn;
> She lives in Garryowen, and she's called the Colleen Bawn.
> As the river, proud and bold, goes by that famed city,
> So proud and cold, widout a word, that Colleen goes by me!
> Oh, hone! Oh, hone!

> Oh, if I was the Emperor of Russia to command,
> Or Julius Caesar, or the Lord Lieutenant of the land,
> I'd give up all my wealth, my manes, I'd give up my army,
> Both the horse, the fut, and the Royal Artillery;
> I'd give the crown from off my head, the people on their knees,
> I'd give my fleet of sailing ships upon the briny seas,

And a beggar I'd go to sleep, a happy man at dawn,
If by my side, fast for my bride, I'd the darlin' Colleen Bawn.
Oh, hone! Oh, hone!

I must reach the cottage before the masther arrives; Father Tom is there waitin' for this keg o' starlight — it's my tithe; I call every tenth keg 'his riverince'. It's worth money to see the way it does the old man good, and brings the wather in his eyes; it's the only place I ever see any about him — heaven bless him! (*Sings.*)
(*Exit* MYLES — *Music.*)

ACT ONE: SCENE THREE

Interior of EILY *'s Cottage on Muckross Head — fire burning;
table; armchair; stools; basin, sugar spoon, two jugs, tobacco,
plate, knife, and lemon on table.* FATHER TOM *discovered
smoking in armchair,* EILY *in balcony, watching over lake.*

FATHER TOM. (*sings*). 'Tobacco is an Injun weed'. And every weed
    wants wathering to make it come up; but tobacco bein' an Injun
    weed that is accustomed to a hot climate, water is entirely, too
    cold for its warrum nature — it's whiskey and water it wants. I
    wonder if Myles has come; I'll ask Eily. (*Calls*) Eily alanna! Eily
    a suilish machree!

EILY (*turning*). Is it me, Father Tom?

FATHER TOM. Has he come?

EILY. No, his boat is half a mile off yet.

FATHER TOM. Half a mile! I'll choke before he's here.

EILY. Do you mean Hardress?

FATHER TOM. No, dear! Myles-na-Coppaleen — cum spiritu
    Hiberneuse — which manes in Irish, wid a keg of poteen.
    (*Enter* MYLES.)

MYLES. Here I am, your riverince, never fear. I tould Sheelah to
    hurry up with the materials, knowin' ye'd be dhry and hasty.
    (*Enter* SHEELAH, *with kettle of water.*)

SHEELAH. Here's the hot water.

MYLES. Lave it there till I brew Father Tom a pint of mother's
    milk.

SHEELAH. We'el thin, ye'll do your share of the work, and not a
    ha'porth more.

MYLES. Didn't I bring the sperrits from two miles and more? and
    I deserve to have the pref'rence to make the punch for his
    riverince.

SHEELAH. And didn't I watch the kettle all night, not to let it
    off the boil? — there now.

MYLES (*quarrelling with* SHEELAH). No, you didn't, &c.

SHEELAH (*quarrelling*). Yes, I did, &c.

EILY. No, no; I'll make it, and nobody else.

FATHER TOM. Asy now, ye bocauns, and whist; Myles shall put in the whiskey, Sheelah shall put in the hot water, and Eily, my Colleen, shall put the sugar in the cruiskeen. A blessin' on ye all three that loves the ould man. (MYLES *takes off his hat* — WOMEN *curtsey* — *they make punch*) See now, my children, there's a moral in everything, e'en in a jug of punch. There's the sperrit, which is the sowl and strength of the man. (MYLES *pours spirit from keg*) That's the whiskey. There's the sugar, which is the smile of woman; (EILY *puts sugar*) without that, life is without taste or sweetness. Then there's the lemon, (EILY *puts lemon*) which is love; a squeeze now and again does a boy no harm; but not too much. And the hot water (SHEELAH *pours water*) which is adversity — as little as possible if ye plaze that makes the good things better still.

MYLES. And it's complate, ye see, for it's a woman that gets into hot wather all the while. (*Pours from jug to jug.*)

SHEELAH. Myles, if I hadn't the kettle, I'd bate ye.

MYLES. Then, why didn't ye let me make the punch? There's a guinea for your riverince that's come t'ye — one in ten I got awhile ago — it's your tithe — put a hole in it, and hang it on your watch chain, for it's a mighty grate charm entirely.

(*They sit,* SHEELAH *near fire,* COLLEEN *on stool beside her,* FATHER TOM *in chair,* MYLES *on stool.*)

FATHER TOM. Eily, look at that boy, and tell me, haven't ye a dale to answer for?

EILY. He isn't as bad about me as he used to be; he's getting over it.

MYLES. Yes, darlin', the storm has passed over, and I've got into settled bad weather.

FATHER TOM. Maybe, afther all, ye'd have done better to have married Myles there, than be the wife of a man that's ashamed to own ye.

EILY. He isn't — he's proud of me. It's only when I spake like the poor people, and say or do anything wrong, that he's hurt; but I'm gettin' clane of the brogue, and learnin' to do nothing — I'm to be changed entirely.

MYLES. Oh! if he'd lave me yer own self, and only take away wid him his improvements. Oh! murder — Eily, aroon, why wasn't ye twins, an' I could have one of ye, only nature couldn't make two like ye — it would be onreasonable to ax it.

207

EILY. Poor Myles, do you love me still so much?

MYLES. Didn't I lave the world to folly ye, and since then there's been neither night nor day in my life — I lay down on Glenna Point above, where I see this cottage, and I lived on the sight of it. Oh! Eily, if tears were pison to the grass there wouldn't be a green blade on Glenna Hill this day.

EILY. But you knew I was married, Myles.

MYLES. Not thin, aroon — Father Tom found me that way, and sat beside, and lifted up my soul. Then I confessed to him, and, sez he, 'Myles, go to Eily, she has something to say to you — say I sent you'. I came, and ye tould me ye were Hardress Cregan's wife, and that was a great comfort entirely. Since I knew that (*Drinks — voice in cup*) I haven't been the blackguard I was.

FATHER TOM. See the beauty of the priest, my darlin' — *videte et admirate* — see and admire it. It was at confession that Eily tould me she loved Cregan, and what did I do? — sez I, 'Where did you meet your sweetheart?' 'At Garryowen', sez she. 'Well', says I; 'that's not the place'. 'Thrue, your riverince, it's too public entirely', sez she. 'Ye'll mate him only in one place', sez I; 'and that's the stile that's behind my chapel', for, d'ye see, her mother's grave was forenint the spot, and there's a sperrit round the place, (MYLES *drinks*) that kept her pure and strong. Myles, ye thafe, drink fair.

SHEELAH. Come now, Eily, couldn't ye cheer up his riverince wid the tail of a song?

EILY. Hardress bid me not sing any ould Irish songs, he says the words are vulgar.

SHEELAH. Father Tom will give ye absolution.

FATHER TOM. Put your lips to that jug; there's only the sthrippens left. Drink! and while that thrue Irish liquor warms your heart, take this wid it. May the brogue of ould Ireland niver forsake your tongue — may her music niver lave yer voice — and may a true Irishwoman's virtue niver die in your heart!

MYLES. Come, Eily, it's my liquor — haven't ye a word to say for it?

(*Song,* EILY — '*Cruiskeen Lawn*'.)

Let the farmer praise his grounds
As the huntsman doth his hounds,
And the shepherd his fresh and dewy morn;
But I, more blest than they,
Spend each night and happy day,
With my smilin' little Cruiskeen Lawn, Lawn, Lawn.
Chorus (*repeat*) Gramachree, mavourneen, slanta gal avourneen,

Gramachree ma Cruiskeen Lawn, Lawn, Lawn,
With my smiling little Cruiskeen Lawn.
(*Chorussed by* MYLES, FATHER TOM *and* SHEELAH.)

(MYLES.)

And when grim Death appears
In long and happy years,
To tell me that my glass is run,
I'll say, begone, you slave,
For great Bacchus gave me lave
To have another Cruiskeen Lawn — Lawn — Lawn.
Gramachree, &c., &c.

HARDRESS (*without*). Ho! Sheelah — Sheelah!

SHEELAH (*rising*). Whist! it's the master.

EILY (*frightened*). Hardress! oh, my! what will he say if he finds us here — run, Myles — quick, Sheelah — clear away the things.

FATHER TOM. Hurry now, or we'll get Eily in throuble. (*Takes keg* — MYLES *takes jugs* — SHEELAH *kettle*)

HARDRESS. Sheelah, I say!
(*Exeunt* FATHER TOM *and* MYLES *quickly*.)

SHEELAH. Comin', Sir, I'm puttin' on my petticoat. (*Exit* SHEELAH *quickly*.)
(*Enter* HARDRESS *and* DANNY — DANNY *immediately goes off*.)

EILY. Oh, Hardress, asthore!

HARDRESS. Don't call me by those confounded Irish words — what's the matter? you're trembling like a bird caught in a trap.

EILY. Am I, mavou — no I mean — is it tremblin' I am, dear?

HARDRESS. What a dreadful smell of tobacco there is here, and the fumes of whiskey punch too, the place smells like a shebeen. Who has been here?

EILY. There was Father Tom an' Myles dhropped in.

HARDRESS. Nice company for my wife — a vagabond.

EILY. Ah! who made him so but me, dear? Before I saw you, Hardress, Myles coorted me, and I was kindly to the boy.

HARDRESS. Damn it, Eily, why will you remind me that my wife was ever in such a position?

EILY. I won't see him again — if yer angry, dear, I'll tell him to go away, and he will, because the poor boy loves me.

HARDRESS. Yes, better than I do you mean?

EILY. No, I don't — oh! why do you spake so to your poor Eily?

HARDRESS. Spake, so! Can't you say speak?

EILY. I'll thry, aroon — I'm sthrivin' — 'tis mighty hard, but what wouldn't I undert-tee-ta — undergo for your sa-se — for your seek.

HARDRESS. Sake — sake!

EILY. Sake — seek — oh, it is to bother people entirely they mixed 'em up! Why didn't they make them all one way?

HARDRESS (*aside*). It is impossible! How can I present her as my wife? Oh! what an act of madness to tie myself to one so much beneath me — beautiful — good as she is —

EILY. Hardress, you are pale — what has happened?

HARDRESS. Nothing — that is nothing but what you will rejoice at.

EILY. What d'ye mane?

HARDRESS. What do I mane! Mean — mean!

EILY. I beg your pardon, dear.

HARDRESS. Well; I mean that after tomorrow there will be no necessity to hide our marriage, for I shall be a beggar, my mother will be an outcast, and amidst all the shame, who will care what wife a Cregan takes?

EILY. And d'ye think I'd like to see you dhragged down to my side — ye don't know me — see now — never all me life again don't let on to mortal that we're married — I'll go as a servant in your mother's house — I'll work for the smile ye'll give me in passing, and I'll be happy, if ye'll only let me stand outside and hear your voice.

HARDRESS. You're a fool. I told you that I was betrothed to the richest heiress in Kerry; her fortune alone can save us from ruin. Tonight my mother discovered my visits here, and I told her who you were.

EILY. Oh! what did she say?

HARDRESS. It broke her heart.

EILY. Hardress! is there no hope?

HARDRESS. None. That is none — that — that I can name.

EILY. There is one — I see it.

HARDRESS. There is. We were children when we were married, and I could get no priest to join our hands but one, and he had been disgraced by his bishop. He is dead. There was no witness to the ceremony but Danny Mann — no proof but his word, and your certificate.

EILY (*takes paper from her breast*). This!

HARDRESS. Eily! if you doubt my eternal love keep that security, it gives you the right to the shelter of my roof; but oh! if you would be content with the shelter of my heart.

EILY. And will it save ye, Hardress? And will your mother forgive me?

HARDRESS. She will bless you — she will take you to her breast.

EILY. But you — another will take you to her breast.

HARDRESS. Oh! Eily, darling — d'ye think I could forget you, machree — forget the sacrifice more than blood you give.

EILY. Oh! When you talk that way to me, ye might take my life, and heart, and all. Oh! Hardress, I love you — take the paper and tare it. (HARDRESS *takes paper*.)

(*Enter* MYLES.)

MYLES. No. I'll be damned if he shall.

HARDRESS. Scoundrel! you have been listening?

MYLES. To every word. I saw Danny wid his ear agin that dure, so as there was only one kay-hole I adopted the windy. Eily, aroon, Mr Cregan will giv' ye back that paper; you can't tare up an oath; will ye help him then to cheat this other girl, and to make her his mistress, for that's what she'll be if ye are his wife. An' after all, what is there agin' the crature? Only the money she's got. Will you stop lovin' him when his love belongs to another? No! I know it by myself; but if ye jine their hands together your love will be an adultery.

EILY. Oh, no!

HARDRESS. Vagabond! outcast! jail bird! dare you prate of honour to me?

MYLES. I am an outlaw, Mr Cregan — a felon may be — but if you do this thing to that poor girl that loves you so much — had I my neck in the rope — or my fut on the deck of a convict ship — I'd turn round and say to ye, 'Hardress Cregan, I make ye a present of the contimpt of a rogue'. (*Snaps fingers*.)

(*Music till end of Act — Enter* FATHER TOM, SHEELAH *and* DANNY — HARDRESS *throws down paper — goes to table — takes hat*.)

HARDRESS. Be it so, Eily, farewell! until my house is clear of these vermin — (DANNY *appears at back*) — you will see me no more.

(*Exit* HARDRESS *followed by* DANNY.)

EILY. Hardress — Hardress! (*Going up*) Don't leave me, Hardress!

FATHER TOM (*intercepts her*). Stop, Eily!

(DANNY *returns and listens*.)

EILY. He's gone — he's gone!

FATHER TOM. Give me that paper, Myles. (MYLES *picks it up, gives it*.) Kneel down there, Eily, before me — put that paper in your breast.

EILY (*kneeling*). Oh! what will I do — what will I do!

FATHER TOM. Put your hand upon it now.

EILY. Oh, my heart — my heart!

FATHER TOM. Be the hush, and spake after me — by my mother that's in heaven.

EILY. By my mother that's in heaven.

FATHER TOM. By the light and the word.

EILY. By the light and the word.

FATHER TOM. Sleepin' or wakin'.

EILY. Sleepin' or wakin'.

FATHER TOM. This proof of my truth.

EILY. This proof of my truth.

FATHER TOM. Shall never again quit my breast.

EILY. Shall never again quit my breast. (EILY *utters a cry and falls — Tableau.*)

END OF ACT ONE

ACT TWO: SCENE ONE

Gap of Dunloe; same as Second Scene, Act I — Music. Enter
HARDRESS *and* DANNY.

HARDRESS. Oh! what a giddy fool I've been. What would I give
to recall this fatal act which bars my fortune?

DANNY. There's something throublin' yez, Masther Hardress.
Can't Danny do something to aise ye? — spake the word and I'll
die for ye.

HARDRESS. Danny, I *am* troubled. I was a fool when I refused to
listen to you at the chapel of Castle Island.

DANNY. When I warned ye to have no call to Eily O'Connor.

HARDRESS. I was mad to marry her.

DANNY. I knew she was no wife for you. A poor thing widout
manners, or money, or book larnin', or a ha'porth of fortin'.
Oh! worra. I told ye dat, but ye bate me off, and here now is
the way of it.

HARDRESS. Well, it's done, and can't be undone.

DANNY. Bedad, I dun know that. Wouldn't she untie the knot
herself — couldn't ye coax her?

HARDRESS. No.

DANNY. Is that her love for you? You that give' up the divil an all
for her. What's *her* ruin to yours? Ruin — goredoutha — ruin is
it? Don't I pluck a shamrock and wear it a day for the glory of
St. Patrick, and then throw it away when it's gone by my likin'.
What, is *she* to be ruined by a gentleman? Whoo! Mighty good,
for the likes o' her.

HARDRESS. She would have yielded, but —

DANNY. Asy now, an I'll tell ye. Pay her passage out to Quaybec,
and put her aboord a three-master widout sayin' a word. Lave
it to me. Danny will clare the road forenint ye.

HARDRESS. Fool, if she still possesses that certificate — the
proof of my first marriage — how can I dare to wed another?

Commit bigamy — disgrace my wife — bastardize my children!

DANNY. Den' by the powers, I'd do by Eily as wid the glove there on her hand; make it come off, as it come on — an' if it fits too tight, take the knife to it.

HARDRESS (*turning to him*). What do you mean?

DANNY. Only gi' me the word, an' I'll engage that the Colleen Bawn will never throuble ye any more; don't ax me any questions at all. Only — if you're agreeable, take off that glove from yer hand and give it me for a token — that's enough.

HARDRESS (*throws off cloak — seizes him — throws him down*). Villain! Dare you utter a word or meditate a thought of violence towards that girl —

DANNY. Oh! murder — may I never die in sin, if —

HARDRESS. Begone! away, at once, and quit my sight. I have chosen my doom; I must learn to endure it — but, blood! and hers! Shall I make cold and still that heart that beats alone for me? — quench those eyes, that look so tenderly in mine? Monster! am I so vile that you dare to whisper such a thought?

DANNY. Oh! masther, divil burn me if I meant any harm.

HARDRESS. Mark me well, now. Respect my wife as you would the queen of the land — whisper a word such as those you uttered to me, and it will be your last. I warn ye — remember and obey. (*Exit* HARDRESS.)

DANNY (*rises — picks up cloak*). Oh! the darlin' creature! would I harrum a hair of her blessed head? — no! Not unless you gave me that glove, and den I'd jump into the bottomless pit for ye. (*Exit* DANNY — *Music — change.*)

ACT TWO: SCENE TWO

Room in MRS CREGAN's *house; window, backed by landscape; door, backed by interior; lights up. Enter* ANNE CHUTE.

ANNE. That fellow runs in my head. (*Looking at window.*) There he is in the garden, smoking like a chimney-pot. (*Calls*) Mr Daly!

KYRLE (*outside window*). Good morning!

ANNE (*aside*). To think he'd smile that way, after going Leandering all night like a dissipated young owl. (*Aloud*) Did you sleep well? (*Aside*) Not a wink, you villian, and you know it.

KYRLE. I slept like a top.

ANNE (*aside*). I'd like to have the whipping of ye. (*Aloud*) When did you get back?

KYRLE. Get back! I've not been out.

ANNE (*aside*). He's not been out! This is what men come to after a cruise at sea — they get sunburnt with love. Those foreign donnas teach them to make fire-places of their hearts, and chimney-pots of their mouths. (*Aloud*) What are you doing down there? (*Aside*) As if he was stretched out to dry.

    (KYRLE *puts down pipe outside.*)
    (*Enter* KYRLE *through window.*)

KYRLE. I have been watching Hardress coming over from Divil's Island in his boat — the wind was dead against him.

ANNE. It was fair for going to Divil's Island last night, I believe.

KYRLE. Was it?

ANNE. You were up late, I think?

KYRLE. I was. I watched by my window for hours, thinking of her I loved — slumber overtook me and I dreamed of a happiness I never can hope for.

ANNE. Look me straight in the face.

KYRLE. Oh! if some fairy could strike us into stone now — and leave us looking for ever into each other s faces, like the blue lake below and the sky above it.

215

ANNE. Kyrle Daly! What would you say to a man who had two loves, one to whom he escaped at night and the other to whom he devoted himself during the day, what would you say?

KYRLE. I'd say he had no chance.

ANNE. Oh! Captain Cautious! Well answered. Isn't he fit to take care of anybody? — his cradle was cut out of a witness box.

(*Enter* HARDRESS *through window.*)

KYRLE. Anne! I don't know what you mean, but that I know that I love you, and you are sporting with a wretchedness you cannot console. I was wrong to remain here so long, but I thought my friendship for Hardress would protect me against your invasion — now I will go.

HARDRESS (*advancing*). No. Kyrle, you will stay. Anne, he loves you, and I more than suspect you prefer him to me. From this moment you are free; I release you from all troth to me; in his presence I do this.

ANNE. Hardress!

HARDRESS. There is a bar between us which you should have known before, but I could not bring myself to confess. Forgive me, Anne — you deserve a better man than I am. (*Exit.*)

ANNE. A bar between us! What does he mean?

KYRLE. He means that he is on the verge of ruin: he did not know how bad things were till last night. His generous noble heart recoils from receiving anything from you but love.

ANNE. And does he think I'd let him be ruined any way? Does he think I wouldn't sell the last rood o' land — the gown off my back, and the hair off my head before that boy that protected and loved me, the child, years ago, should come to a hap'orth of harrum.

KYRLE. Miss Chute!

ANNE. Well, I can't help it. When I am angry the brogue comes out, and my Irish heart will burst through manners, and graces, and twenty stay-laces. I'll give up my fortune, that I will.

KYRLE. You can't — you've got a guardian who cannot consent to such a sacrifice.

ANNE. Have I? then I'll find a husband that will.

KYRLE (*aside*). She means me — I see it in her eyes.

ANNE (*aside*). He's trying to look unconscious. (*Aloud*) Kyrle Daly, on your honour and word as a gentleman, do you love me and nobody else?

KYRLE. Do you think me capable of contaminating your image by admitting a meaner passion into my breast?

ANNE. Yes, I do.

KYRLE. Then you wrong me.

ANNE. I'll prove that in one word. Take care now — it's coming.

KYRLE. Go on.

ANNE (*aside*). Now I'll astonish him. (*Aloud*) Eily!

KYRLE. What's that?

ANNE. 'Shule, shule, agrah!'

KYRLE. Where to?

ANNE. Three winks, as much as to say, 'Are you coming?' and an extinguisher above here means 'Yes'. Now you see I know all about it.

KYRLE. You have the advantage of me.

ANNE. Confess now, and I'll forgive you.

KYRLE. I will — tell me what to confess, and I'll confess it — I don't care what it is.

ANNE (*aside*). If I hadn't eye-proof he'd brazen it out of me. Isn't he cunning? He's one of those that would get fat where a fox would starve.

KYRLE. That was a little excursion into my past life — a sudden descent on my antecedents, to see if you could not surprise an infidelity — but I defy you.

ANNE. You do? I accept that defiance, and mind me, Kyrle, if I find you true, as I once thought, there's my hand; but if you are false in this, Anne Chute will never change her name for yours. (*He kisses her hand.*) Leave me now.

KYRLE. Oh! the lightness you have given to my heart. The number of pipes I'll smoke this afternoon will make them think we've got a haystack on fire. (*Exit* KYRLE *through window.*)

ANNE (*rings bell on table*). Here, Pat — Barney — someone.

(*Enter* SERVANT.)

Tell Larry Dolan, my groom, to saddle the black mare, Fireball, but not bring her round the house — I'll mount in the stables.

(*Exit* SERVANT.)

I'll ride over to Muckross Head, and draw that cottage; I'll know what's there. It mayn't be right, but I haven't a big brother to see after me — and self-protection is the first law of nature. (*Exit* ANNE.)

(*Music — Enter* MRS CREGAN *and* HARDRESS.)

MRS CREGAN. What do you say, Hardress?

HARDRESS. I say, mother, that my heart and faith are both already pledged to another, and I cannot break my engagement.

MRS CREGAN. And this is the end of all our pride!

HARDRESS. Repining is useless — thought and contrivance are of no avail — the die is cast.

217

MRS CREGAN. Hardress — I speak not for myself, but for you — and I would rather see you in your coffin than married to this poor, lowborn, silly, vulgar creature. I know you, my son, you will be miserable, when the infatuation of first love is past; when you turn from her and face the world, as one day you must do, you will blush to say, 'This is my wife'. Every word from her mouth will be a pang to your pride — you will follow her movements with terror — the contempt and derision she excites will rouse you first to remorse, and then to hatred — and from the bed to which you go with a blessing, you will rise with a curse.

HARDRESS. Mother! mother! (*Throws himself in chair.*)

MRS CREGAN. To Anne you have acted a heartless and dis-honourable part — her name is already coupled with yours at every fireside in Kerry.

(*Enter* SERVANT.)

SERVANT. Mr Corrigan, ma'am.

MRS CREGAN. He comes for his answer. Shew him in. (*Exit* SERVANT.) The hour has come, Hardress — what answer shall I give him?

HARDRESS. Refuse him — let him do his worst.

MRS CREGAN. And face beggary! On what shall we live? I tell you the prison for debt is open before us. Can you work? No! Will you enlist as a soldier and send your wife into service? We are ruined — d'ye hear — ruined. I must accept this man only to give you and yours a shelter, and under Corrigan's roof I may not be ashamed perhaps to receive your wife.

(*Enter* SERVANT, *shewing in* MR CORRIGAN.)

CORRIGAN. Good morning, ma'am; I am punctual you perceive.

MRS CREGAN. We have considered your offer, sir, and we see no alternative — but — but —

CORRIGAN. Mrs Cregan, I'm proud, ma'am, to take your hand.

HARDRESS (*starting up*). Begone — begone, I say — touch her and I'll brain you.

CORRIGAN. Squire! Sir! Mr Hardress.

HARDRESS. Must I hurl you from the house?

(*Enter two* SERVANTS.)

MRS CREGAN. Hardress, my darling boy, restrain yourself.

CORRIGAN. Good morning ma'am. I have my answer. (*To* SERVANT) Is Miss Chute within?

SERVANT. No, sir, she's galloped out of the stable yard.

CORRIGAN. Say I called to see her. I will wait upon her at this hour tomorrow. (*Looking at the* CREGANS) Tomorrow! tomorrow! (*Exit followed by* SERVANTS.)

MRS CREGAN. Tomorrow will see us in Limerick Jail, and this house in the hands of the sheriff.

HARDRESS. Mother! heaven guide and defend me; let me rest for awhile — you don't know all yet, and I have not the heart to tell you.

MRS CREGAN. With you, Hardress, I can bear anything — anything — but your humiliation and your unhappiness —

HARDRESS. I know it, mother, I know it. (*Exit — Music.*)
(DANNY *appears at window.*)

DANNY. Whisht — missiz — whisht.

MRS CREGAN. Who's there?

DANNY. It's me sure, Danny — that is — I know the throuble that's in it. I've been through it all wid him.

MRS CREGAN. You know, then —?

DANNY. Everything, ma'am; and, shure, I sthruv hard and long to impache him for doing id.

MRS CREGAN. Is he, indeed, so involved with this girl that he will not give her up?

DANNY. No; he's got over the worst of it, but she holds him tight, and he feels kindly and soft-hearted for her, and darn't do what another would.

MRS CREGAN. Dare not?

DANNY. Sure she might be packed off across the wather to Ameriky, or them parts beyant? Who'd ever ax a word afther her? — barrin' the masther, who'd murdher me if he knew I whispered such a thing.

MRS CREGAN. But would she go?

DANNY. Ow, ma'am, wid a taste of persuasion, we'd mulvather her aboord. But there's another way again, and if ye'd only coax the masther to send me his glove, he'd know the manin' of that token, and so would I.

MRS CREGAN. His glove?

DANNY. Sorra a haporth else. If he'll do that, I'll take my oath ye'll hear no more of the Colleen Bawn.

MRS CREGAN. I'll see my son. (*Exit.*)

DANNY. Tare an' 'ouns, that lively girl, Miss Chute, has gone the road to Muckross Head; I've watched her — I've got my eye on all of them. If she sees Eily — ow, ow, she'll get the ring itself in that helpin' of kale-canon. Be the piper, I'll run across the lake, and, maybe, get there first; she's got a long round to go, and the wind rising — a purty blast entirely. (*Goes to window — Music.*)
(*Re-enter* MRS CREGAN, *with glove.*)

MRS CREGAN (*aside*). I found his gloves in the hall, where he had thrown them in his hat.

DANNY. Did ye ax him, ma'am?

MRS CREGAN I did — and here is the reply. (*Holds out glove.*)

DANNY. He has changed his mind, then?

MRS CREGAN. He has entirely.

DANNY. And — and — I am — to — do it?

MRS CREGAN. That is the token.

DANNY. I know it — I'll keep my promise. I'm to make away with her?

MRS CREGAN. Yes, yes — take her away — away with her! (*Exit* MRS CREGAN.)

DANNY. Never fear, ma'am. (*Going to window.*) He shall never see or hear again of the Colleen Bawn. (*Exit* DANNY *through window.*)

ACT TWO: SCENE THREE

Exterior of EILY'*s Cottage; Cottage, set pieces, backed by Lake;*
table and two seats. SHEELAH *and* EILY *discovered knitting.*

SHEELAH. Don't cry, darlin' — don't alaina!

EILY. He'll never come back to me — I'll never see him again,
Sheelah!

SHEELAH. Is it lave his own wife?

EILY. I've sent him a letther by Myles, and Myles has never come
back — I've got no answer — he won't spake to me — I am
standin' betune him and fortune — I'm in the way of his
happiness. I wish I was dead!

SHEELAH. Whisht! be the husht! what talk is that? when I'm
tuk sad that way, I go down to the chapel and pray a turn — it
lifts the cloud off my heart.

EILY. I can't pray; I've tried, but unless I pray for him, I can't
bring my mind to it.

SHEELAH. I never saw a colleen that loved as you love; sorra come
to me, but I b'lieve you've got enough to supply all Munster, and
more left over than would choke ye if you wern't azed of it.

EILY. He'll come back — I'm sure he will; I was wicked to doubt.
Oh! Sheelah! what becomes of the girls he doesn't love. Is there
anything goin' on in the world where he isn't?

SHEELAH. There now — you're smilin' again.

EILY. I'm like the first mornin' when he met me — there was dew
on the young day's eye — a smile on the lips o' the lake. Hardress
will come back — oh, yes! he'll never leave his poor Eily all alone
by herself in this place. Whisht now, an' I'll tell you. (*Music.*)
(*Song — Air, 'Pretty Girl Milking her Cow'.*)

> 'Twas on a bright morning in summer,
> I first heard his voice speaking low,
> As he said to a colleen beside me,

221

'Who's that pretty girl milking her cow?'
And many times after he met me,
And vow'd that I always should be
His own little darling alanna,
Mavourneen a sweelish machree.
I haven't the manners or graces
Of the girls in the world where ye move,
I haven't their beautiful faces,
But I have a heart that can love.
If it plase ye, I'll dress in satins,
And jewels I'll put on my brow,
But don't ye be after forgettin'
Your pretty girl milking her cow.

SHEELAH. Ah, the birds sit still on the boughs to listen to her, and the trees stop whisperin'; she leaves a mighty big silence behind her voice, that nothin' in nature wants to break. My blessin' on the path before her — there's an angel at the other end of it. (*Exit* SHEELAH *into cottage*.)

EILY (*repeats last line of song*).

(*Enter* ANNE CHUTE.)

ANNE. There she is.

(EILY *sings till facing* ANNE — *stops* — *they examine each other*.)

ANNE. My name is Anne Chute.

EILY. I am Eily O'Connor.

ANNE. You are the Colleen Bawn — the pretty girl.

EILY. And you are the Colleen Ruaidh.

ANNE (*aside*). She is beautiful.

EILY (*aside*). How lovely she is.

ANNE. We are rivals.

EILY. I am sorry for it.

ANNE. So am I, for I feel that I could have loved you.

EILY. That's always the way of it; everybody want to love me, but there's something spoils them off.

ANNE. (*showing letter*). Do you know that writing?

EILY. I do, ma'am, well, though I don't know how you came by it.

ANNE. I saw your signals last night — I saw his departure, and I have come here to convince myself of his falsehood to me. But now that I have seen you, you have no longer a rival in his love, for I despise him with all my heart, who could bring one so beautiful and simple as you are to ruin and shame!

EILY. He didn't — no — I am his wife! Oh, what have I said!

ANNE. What?

EILY. Oh, I didn't mane to confess it — no, I didn't! but you wrung it from me in defence of him.

ANNE. You his wife?

(*Enter* DANNY.)

DANNY (*at back — aside*). The divil! they're at it — an' I'm too late!

ANNE. I cannot believe this — shew me your certificate.

EILY. Here it is.

DANNY (*advances between them*). Didn't you swear to the priest that it should niver lave your breast?

ANNE. Oh! you're the boatman.

DANNY. Iss, ma'am!

ANNE. Eily, forgive me for doubting your goodness, and your purity. I believe you. Let me take your hand. (*Crosses to her.*) While the heart of Anne Chute beats you have a friend that won't be spoiled off, but you have no longer a rival, mind that. All I ask of you is that you will never mention this visit to Mr Daly — and for you (*To* DANNY.) this will purchase your silence. (*Gives money.*) Goodbye! (*Exit* ANNE.)

DANNY. Long life t'ye. (*Aside*) What does it mane? Hasn't she found me out.

EILY. Why did she ask me never to spake to Mr Daly of her visit here? Sure I don't know any Mr Daly.

DANNY. Didn't she spake of him before, dear?

EILY. Never!

DANNY. Nor didn't she name Master Hardress?

EILY. Well, I don't know; she spoke of him and of the letter I wrote to him, but I b'lieve she never named him intirely.

DANNY (*aside*). The divil's in it for sport; she's got 'em mixed up.

(*Enter* SHEELAH *from cottage.*)

SHEELAH. What bring you back, Danny?

DANNY. Nothing! but a word I have from the masther for the Colleen here.

EILY. Is it the answer to the letter I sent by Myles?

DANNY. That's it, jewel, he sent me wid a message.

SHEELAH. Somethin' bad has happened. Danny, you are as pale as milk, and your eye is full of blood — yez been drinkin'.

DANNY. Maybe I have.

SHEELAH. You thrimble, and can't spake straight to me. Oh! Danny, what is it, avick?

DANNY. Go on now, an' stop yer keenin'.

EILY. Faith, it isn't yourself that's in it, Danny; sure there's nothing happened to Hardress.

DANNY. Divil a word, good or bad, I'll say while the mother's there.

SHEELAH. I'm goin'. (*Aside*) What's come to Danny this day, at all, at all; bedad, I don't know my own flesh and blood. (*Runs into cottage.*)

DANNY. Sorro' and ruin has come on the Cregans; they're broke intirely.

EILY. Oh, Danny.

DANNY. Whisht, now! You are to meet Masther Hardress this evenin', at a place on the Divil's Island, beyant. Ye'll niver breath a word to mortal to where yer goin', d'ye mind, now; but slip down, unbeknown, to the landin' below, where I'll have the boat waitin' for yez.

EILY. At what hour?

DANNY. Just after dark, there's no moon tonight, an' no one will see us crossin' the water. (*Music till end of scene.*)

EILY. I will be there; I'll go down only to the little chapel by the shore, and pray there 'till ye come. (*Exit* EILY *into cottage.*)

DANNY. I'm wake and cowld! What's this come over me? Mother, mother acushla.

(*Enter* SHEELAH.)

SHEELAH. What is it, Danny?

DANNY (*staggering to table*). Give me a glass of spirits! (*Falls in chair.*)

ACT TWO: SCENE FOUR

The old Weir Bridge, or a Wood on the verge of the Lake. Enter
ANNE CHUTE.

ANNE. Married! the wretch is married! and with that crime
already on his conscience he was ready for another and similar
piece of villany. It's the Navy that does it. It's my belief those
sailors have a wife in every place they stop at.

MYLES (*sings outside*).
    'Oh! Eily astoir, my love is all crost,
     Like a bud in the frost'.

ANNE. Here's a gentleman who has got my complaint — his love
is all crost, like a bud in the frost.
 (*Enter* MYLES.)

MYLES.
 'And there's no use at all in my goin' to bed,
  For it's drames, and not sleep, that comes into my head,
  And it's all about you', &c. &c.

ANNE. My good friend, since you can't catch your love, d'ye
think you could catch my horse? (*Distant thunder.*)

MYLES. Is it a black mare wid a white stockin' on the fore off leg?

ANNE. I dismounted to unhook a gate — a peal of thunder
frightened her, and she broke away.

MYLES. She's at Torc Cregan stables by this time — it was an admiration to watch her stride across the Phil Dolan's bit of plough.

ANNE. And how am I to get home?

MYLES. If I had four legs, I wouldn't ax betther than to carry ye,
an' a proud baste I'd be. (*Thunder — rain.*)

ANNE. The storm is coming down to the mountain — is there no
shelter near?

MYLES. There may be a corner in this ould chapel. (*Rain*) Here
comes the rain — murdher! ye'll be wet through. (*Music — pulls
off coat.*) Put this round yez.

225

ANNE. What will you do? You'll catch your death of cold.

MYLES (*taking out bottle*). Cowld is it. Here's a wardrobe of top coats. (*Thunder*) Whoo! this is a fine time for the water — this way, ma'am. (*Exeunt* MYLES *and* ANNE.)

(*Enter* EILY, *cloak and hood.*)

EILY. Here's the place where Danny was to meet me with the boat. Oh! here he is.

(*Enter* DANNY.)

How pale you are!

DANNY. The thunder makes me sick.

EILY. Shall we not wait till the storm is over?

DANNY. If it comes on bad we can put into the Divil's Island Cave.

EILY. I feel so happy that I am going to see him, yet there is a weight about my heart that I can't account for.

DANNY (*aside*). I can. [(*Aloud.*)] Are you ready now?

EILY. Yes; come — come.

DANNY (*staggering*). I'm wake yet. My throat is dry — if I'd a draught of whiskey now.

EILY. Sheelah gave you a bottle.

DANNY. I forgot — it's in the boat. (*Rain.*)

EILY. Here comes the rain — we shall get wet.

DANNY. There's the masther's boat cloak below.

EILY. Come, Danny, lean on me. I'm afraid you are not sober enough to sail the skiff.

DANNY. Sober! The dhrunker I am the better I can do the work I've got to do.

EILY. Come, Danny, come — come! (*Exeunt* EILY *and* DANNY — *Music ceases.*)

(*Re-enter* ANNE CHUTE *and* MYLES.)

MYLES. It was only a shower, I b'lieve — are ye wet, ma'am?

ANNE. Dry as a biscuit.

MYLES. Ah! then it's yerself is the brave and beautiful lady — as bould an' proud as a ship before the blast. (ANNE *looks off.*)

ANNE. Why, there is my mare, and who comes with —

MYLES. It's Mr Hardress Cregan himself.

ANNE. Hardress here?

MYLES. Eily gave me a letter for him this morning.

(*Enter* HARDRESS.)

HARDRESS. Anne, what has happened? Your horse galloped wildly into the stable — we thought you had been thrown.

MYLES. Here is the letther Eily tould me to give him. (*To* HARDRESS) I beg your pardon, sir, but here's the taste of a letther — I was axed to give your honour. (*Gives letter.*)

226

HARDRESS (*aside*). From Eily!

ANNE. Thanks, my good fellow, for your assistance.

MYLES. Not at all, ma'am. Sure, there isn't a boy in the County Kerry that would not give two thumbs off his hands to do a service to the Colleen Ruaidh, as you are called among us — iss indeed, ma'am. (*Going — aside*) Ah! then it's the purty girl she is in them long clothes. (*Exit* MYLES.)

HARDRESS (*reads, aside*). 'I am the cause of your ruin; I can't live with that thought killin' me. If I do not see you before night you will never again be throubled with your poor Eily'. Little simpleton! she is capable of doing herself an injury.

ANNE. Hardress! I have been very blind and very foolish, but today I have learned to know my own heart. There's my hand, I wish to seal my fate at once. I know the delicacy which prompted you to release me from my engagement to you. I don't accept that release; I am yours.

HARDRESS. Anne, you don't know all.

ANNE. I know more than I wanted, that's enough. I forbid you ever to speak on this subject.

HARDRESS. You don't know my past life.

ANNE. And I don't want to know. I've had enough of looking into past lives; don't tell me anything you wish to forget.

HARDRESS. Oh, Anne — my dear cousin; if I could forget — if silence could be oblivion. (*Exeunt* HARDRESS *and* ANNE.)

ACT TWO: SCENE FIVE

Exterior of MYLES' *Hut. Enter* MYLES *singing 'Brian O' Linn'.*

"Brian O' Linn had no breeches to wear,
So he bought him a sheepskin to make him a pair;
The skinny side out, the woolly side in,
'They are cool and convanient', said Brian O' Linn''.

MYLES (*locks door of cabin*). Now I'll go down to my whiskey-still. It is under my feet this minute, bein' in a hole in the rocks they call O'Donoghue's stables, a sort of water cave; the people around here think that the cave is haunted with bad spirits, and they say that of a dark stormy night strange onearthly noises is heard comin' out of it — it is me singing 'The Night before Larry was stretched'. Now I'll go down to that cave, and wid a sod of live turf under a kettle of worty, I'll invoke them sperrits — and what's more they'll come. (*Exit* MYLES *singing — Music till* MYLES *begins to speak next scene.*)

ACT TWO: SCENE SIX

A Cave; through large opening at back is seen the Lake and moon; rocks — flat rock; gauze waters all over stage; rope hanging. Enter MYLES *singing, top of rock.*

MYLES. And this is a purty night for my work! The smoke of my whiskey-still will not be seen; there's my distillery beyant in a snug hole up there, (*Unfastens rope*) and here's my bridge to cross over to it. I think it would puzzle a gauger to folly me; this is a patent of my own — a tight-rope bridge. (*Swings across.*) Now I tie up my drawbridge at this side till I want to go back — what's that — it was an otter I woke from a nap he was taken on that bit of rock there — ow! ye divil! if I had my gun I'd give ye a leaden supper. I'll go up and load it, maybe I'll get a shot; them stones is the place where they lie out of a night, and many a one I've shot of them. (*Music — disappears up rock.*)

    (*A small boat with* DANNY *and* EILY *appears and works on to rock.*)

EILY. What place is this you have brought me to?

DANNY. Never fear — I know where I'm goin' — step out on that rock — mind yer footin'; 'tis wet there.

EILY. I don't like this place — it's like a tomb.

DANNY. Step out, I say; the boat is laking.

    (EILY *steps on to rock.*)

EILY. Why do you spake to me so rough and cruel?

DANNY. Eily, I have a word to say t'ye, listen now, and don't thrimble that way.

EILY. I won't, Danny — I won't.

DANNY. Wonst, Eily, I was a fine brave boy, the pride of my ould mother, her white haired darlin' — you wouldn't think it to look at me now. D'ye know how I got changed to this?

EILY. Yes, Hardress told me.

DANNY. He done it — but I loved him before it, an' I loved him afther it — not a dhrop of blood I have, but I'd pour out like wather for the masther.

EILY. I know what you mean — as he has deformed your body — ruined your life — made ye what ye are.

DANNY. Have you, a woman, less love for him than I, that you wouldn't give him what he wants of you, even if he broke your heart as he broke my back, both in a moment of passion? Did I ax him to ruin himself and his ould family, and all to mend my bones? No! I loved him, and I forgave him that.

EILY. Danny, what d'ye want me to do?
    (DANNY *steps out on rock.*)

DANNY. Give me that paper in your breast? (*Boat floats off slowly.*)

EILY. I can't — I've sworn never to part with it! You know I have!

DANNY. Eily, that paper stands between Hardress Cregan and his fortune; that paper is the ruin of him. Give it, I tell yez.

EILY. Take me to the priest; let him lift the oath off me. Oh! Danny, I swore a blessed oath on my two knees, and ye would ax me to break that?

DANNY (*seizes her hands*). Give it up, and don't make me hurt ye.

EILY. I swore by my mother's grave, Danny. Oh! Danny, dear, don't. Don't, acushla, and I'll do anything. See now, what good would it be; sure, while I live I'm his wife. (*Music changes.*)

DANNY. Then you've lived too long. Take your marriage lines wid ye to the bottom of the lake. (*He throws her from rock backwards into the water, with a cry; she reappears, clinging to rock.*)

EILY. No! save me. Don't kill me. Don't, Danny, I'll — do anything, only let me live.

DANNY. He wants ye dead. (*Pushes her off.*)

EILY. Oh! Heaven help me. Danny — Danny — Dan — (*Sinks.*)

DANNY (*looking down*). I've done it. She's gone. (*Shot is fired; he falls — rolls from the rock into the water.*)
    (MYLES *appears with gun on rock.*)

MYLES. I hit one of them bastes that time. I could see well, though it was so dark. But there was somethin' moving on that stone. (*Swings across.*) Divil a sign of him. Stop! (*Looks down.*) What's this? it's a woman — there's something white there.

(*Figure rises near rock — kneels down; tries to take the hand of figure.*) Ah! that dress; it's Eily. My own darlin' Eily. (*Pulls off waistcoat — jumps off rock.* EILY *rises — then* MYLES *and* EILY *rise up — he turns, and seizes rock —* EILY *across left arm.*)

END OF ACT TWO

ACT THREE: SCENE ONE

Interior of an Irish Hut; door and small opening; Truckle bed and bedding, on which DANNY MANN *is discovered; table with jug of water; lighted candle stuck in bottle; two stools —* SHEELAH *at table — Music.*

DANNY (*in his sleep*). Gi'me the paper, thin — screeching won't save ye — down, down! (*Wakes*) Oh, mother, darlin' — mother!

SHEELAH (*waking*). Eh! did ye call me, Danny?

DANNY. Gi'me a dhrop of wather — it's the thirst that's killin' me.

SHEELAH (*takes jug*). The fever's on ye mighty bad.

DANNY (*drinks, falls back, groans*). Oh, the fire in me won't go out! How long have I been here?

SHEELAH. Ten days this night.

DANNY. Ten days dis night! have I been all that time out of my mind?

SHEELAH. Iss, Danny. Ten days ago, that stormy night, ye crawled in at that dure, wake an' like a ghost.

DANNY. I remind me now.

SHEELAH. Ye tould me that ye'd been poachin' salmon, and had been shot by the keepers.

DANNY. Who said I hadn't?

SHEELAH. Divil a one! Why did ye make me promise not to say a word about it? didn't ye refuse even to see a doctor itself?

DANNY. Has any one axed after me?

SHEELAH. No one but Mr Hardress.

DANNY. Heaven bless him.

SHEELAH. I told him I hadn't seen ye, and here ye are this day groanin' when there's great doin's up at Castle Chute. Tomorrow the masther will be married to Miss Anne.

DANNY. Married! but — the — his —

SHEELAH. Poor Eily, ye mane?

232

DANNY. Hide the candle from my eyes, it's painin' me, shade it off. Go on, mother.

SHEELAH. The poor Colleen! Oh, vo, Danny, I knew she'd die of the love that was chokin' her. He didn't know how tindher she was, when he give her the hard word. What was that message the masther sent to her, that ye wouldn't let me hear? It was cruel, Danny, for it broke her heart entirely; she went away that night, and, two days after, a cloak was found floatin' in the reeds, under Brikeen Bridge; nobody knew it but me. I turned away, and never said — The crature is drowned, Danny, and wo to them as dhruv her to it. She has no father, no mother to put a curse on him, but there's the Father above that niver spakes till the last day, and then — (*She turns and sees* DANNY *gasping, his eyes fixed on her, supporting himself on his arm.*) Danny! Danny! he's dyin' — he's dyin'. (*Runs to him.*)

DANNY. Who said that? Ye lie! I never killed her — sure he sent me the glove — where is it?

SHEELAH. He's ravin' again.

DANNY. The glove, he sent it to me full of blood. Oh! master, dear, there's your token. I tould ye I would clear the path forenist ye.

SHEELAH. Danny, what d'ye mane?

DANNY. I'll tell ye how I did it, masther; 'twas dis way, but don't smile like dat, don't, sir! She wouldn't give me de marriage lines, so I sunk her, and her proofs wid her! She's gone! she came up wonst, but I put her down agin! Never fear — she'll never throuble yer agin, never, never. (*Lies down, mutters —* SHEELAH *on her knees, in horror and prayer.*)

SHEELAH. 'Twas he! he! — my own son — he's murdered her, and he's dyin' — dyin', wid blood on his hands! Danny! Danny! Spake to me!

DANNY. A docther! will dey let me die like a baste, and never a docther?

SHEELAH. I'll run for one that'll cure ye. Oh! weerasthrue, Danny! Is it for this I've loved ye? No, forgive me, acushla, it isn't your own mother that 'ud add to yer heart-breakin' and pain. I'll fetch the docther, avick. (*Music — puts on cloak and pulls hood over her head.*) Oh! hone — oh! hone! (*Exit* SHEELAH *— a pause — knock — pause — knock.*)

(*Enter* CORRIGAN.)

CORRIGAN. Sheelah! Nobody here? — I'm bothered entirely. The cottage on Muckross Head is empty — not a sowl in it but a cat. Myles has disappeared, and Danny gone — vanished, bedad, like a fog. Sheelah is the only one remaining. I called to see Miss Chute; I was kicked out. I sent her a letther; it was returned to me unopened. Her lawyer has paid off the mortgage, and taxed my bill of costs — the spalpeen! (DANNY *groans.*) What's that? Some one asleep there. 'Tis Danny!

DANNY. A docther — gi'me a doctor!

CORRIGAN. Danny here — concealed, too! Oh! there's something going on that's worth peepin' into. Whist! there's footsteps comin'. If I could hide a bit. I'm a magistrate, an' I ought to know what's goin' on — here's a turf hole wid a windy in it. (*Exit* CORRIGAN.)

    (*Enter* SHEELAH *and* FATHER TOM.)

SHEELAH (*goes to* DANNY). Danny!

DANNY. Is that you, mother?

SHEELAH. I've brought the docther, asthore.

    (DANNY *looks up.*)

DANNY. The priest!

SHEELAH (*on her knees*). Oh! my darlin', don't be angry wid me, but dis is the docther you want; it isn't in your body where the hurt is; the wound is in your poor sowl — there's all the harrum.

FATHER TOM. Danny, my son — (*Sits*) — it's sore-hearted I am to see you down this way.

SHEELAH. And so good a son he was to his ould mother.

DANNY. Don't say that — don't. (*Covering his face.*)

SHEELAH. I will say it — my blessin' on ye — see that, now, he's cryin'.

FATHER TOM. Danny, the hand of death is on ye. Will ye lave your sins behind ye here below, or will ye take them with ye above, to show them on ye? Is there anything ye can do that'll mend a wrong? leave that legacy to your friend, and he'll do it. Do ye want pardon of any one down here — tell me, avick; I'll get it for ye, and send it after you — may be ye'll want it.

DANNY (*rising up on arm*). I killed Eily O'Connor.

SHEELAH (*covers her face with her hands*). Oh! oh!

FATHER TOM. What harrum had ye agin the poor Colleen Bawn?
    (CORRIGAN *takes notes.*)

DANNY. She stud in *his* way, and he had my heart and sowl in his keeping.

FATHER TOM. Hardress!

DANNY. Hisself! I said I'd do it for him, if he'd give me the token.

FATHER TOM. Did Hardress employ you to kill the girl?

DANNY. He sent me the glove; that was to be the token that I was to put her away, and I did — I — in the Pool a Dhiol. She wouldn't gi'me the marriage lines; I threw her in and then I was kilt.

FATHER TOM. Killed! by whose hand?

DANNY. I don't know, unless it was the hand of heaven.

FATHER TOM (*rising, goes down — aside*). Myles-na-Coppaleen is at the bottom of this; his whiskey still is in that cave, and he has not been seen for ten days past. (*Aloud — goes to* DANNY.) Danny, after ye fell, how did ye get home?

DANNY. I fell in the wather; the current carried me to a rock; how long I was there half drowned I don't know, but on wakin' I found my boat floatin' close by, an' it was still dark, I got in and crawled here.

FATHER TOM (*aside*). I'll go and see Myles — there's more in this than has come out.

SHEELAH. Won't yer riverince say a word of comfort to the poor boy? — he's in great pain entirely.

FATHER TOM. Keep him quiet, Sheelah. (*Music.*) I'll be back again with the comfort for him. Danny, your time is short; make the most of it. (*Aside*) I'm off to Myles-na-Coppaleen. Oh, Hardress (*Going up*) Cregan, ye little think what a bridal day ye'll have! (*Exit.*)

CORRIGAN (*who has been writing in note-book, comes out — at back*). I've got down every word of the confession. Now, Hardress Cregan, there will be guests at your weddin' tonight ye little dhrame of. (*Exit.*)

DANNY (*rising up*). Mother, mother! the pain is on me. Wather — quick — wather!

(SHEELAH *runs to table — takes jug — give it to* DANNY — *he drinks —* SHEELAH *takes jug —* DANNY *struggles — falls back on bed — close on picture.*)

ACT THREE: SCENE TWO

Chamber in Castle Chute. Enter KYRLE DALY *and* SERVANT.

KYRLE. Inform Mrs Cregan that I am waiting upon her.
    (*Enter* MRS CREGAN.)
MRS CREGAN. I am glad to see you, Kyrle.
    (*Exit* SERVANT.)
KYRLE. You sent for me, Mrs Cregan. My ship sails from Liverpool tomorrow. I never thought I could be so anxious to quit my native land.
MRS CREGAN. I want you to see Hardress. For ten days past he shuns the society of his bride. By night he creeps out alone in his boat on the lake — by day he wanders round the neighbourhood pale as death. He is heartbroken.
KYRLE. Has he asked to see me?
MRS CREGAN. Yesterday he asked where you were.
KYRLE. Did he forget that I left your house when Miss Chute, without a word of explanation, behaved so unkindly to me?
MRS CREGAN. She is not the same girl since she accepted Hardress. She quarrels — weeps — complains, and has lost her spirits.
KYRLE. She feels the neglect of Hardress.
ANNE (*without*). Don't answer me. Obey! and hold your tongue.
MRS CREGAN. Do you hear? she is rating one of the servants.
ANNE (*without*). No words — I'll have no sulky looks neither!
    (*Enter* ANNE, *dressed as a bride, with veil and wreath in her hand.*)
ANNE. Is that the veil and wreath I ordered? How dare you tell me that. (*Throws it off.*)
MRS CREGAN. Anne!
    (ANNE *sees* KYRLE — *stands confused.*)
KYRLE. You are surprised to see me in your house, Miss Chute?
ANNE. You are welcome, sir.
KYRLE (*aside*). She looks pale! She's not happy — that's gratifying.

236

ANNE. He doesn't look well — that's some comfort.

MRS CREGAN. I'll try to find Hardress. (*Exit* MRS CREGAN.)

KYRLE. I hope you don't think I intrude — that is — I came to see Mrs Cregan.

ANNE (*sharply*). I don't flatter myself you wished to see me, why should you?

KYRLE. Anne, I am sorry I offended you; I don't know what I did, but no matter.

ANNE. Not the slightest.

KYRLE. I released your neighbourhood of my presence.

ANNE. Yes, and you released the neighbourhood of the presence of somebody else — she and you disappeared together.

KYRLE. She!

ANNE. Never mind.

KYRLE. But I do mind. I love Hardress Cregan as a brother, and I hope the time may come, Anne, when I can love you as a sister.

ANNE. Do you? I don't.

KYRLE. I don't want the dislike of my friend's wife to part my friend and me.

ANNE. Why should it? I'm nobody.

KYRLE. If you were my wife, and asked me to hate any one, I'd do it — I couldn't help it.

ANNE. I believed words like that once when you spoke them, but I have been taught how basely you can deceive.

KYRLE. Who taught you?

ANNE. Who? — your wife.

KYRLE. My what?

ANNE. Your wife — the girl you concealed in the cottage on Muckross Head. Stop now, don't speak — save a falsehood, however many ye have to spare. I saw the girl — she confessed.

KYRLE. Confessed that she was my wife?

ANNE. Made a clean breast of it in a minute, which is more than you could do with a sixteen-foot waggon and a team of ten in a week.

KYRLE. Anne, hear me; this is a frightful error — the girl will not repeat it.

ANNE. Bring her before me and let her speak.

KYRLE. How do I know where she is?

ANNE. Well, bring your boatman then, who told me the same.

KYRLE. I tell you it is false; I never saw — never knew the girl!

ANNE. You did not? (*Shews* EILY'S *letter.*) Do you know that? You dropped it, and I found it.

KYRLE (*takes letter*). This! (*Reads.*)

(*Enter* HARDRESS.)

ANNE. Hardress! (*Turns aside.*)

KYRLE. Oh! (*Suddenly struck with the truth — glances towards* ANNE — *finding her looking away, places letter to* HARDRESS.) Do you know that? you dropped it.

HARDRESS (*conceals letter*). Eh? — Oh!

KYRLE. 'Twas he. (*Looks from one to the other.*) She thinks me guilty; but if I stir to exculpate myself, he is in for it.

HARDRESS. You look distressed, Kyrle. Anne, what is the matter?

KYRLE. Nothing, Hardress. I was about to ask Miss Chute to forget a subject which was painful to her, and to beg of her never to mention it again — not even to you, Hardress.

HARDRESS. I am sure she will deny you nothing.

ANNE. I will forget, sir; (*Aside*) but I will never forgive him — never.

KYRLE (*aside*). She loves me still, and he loves another, and I am the most miserable dog that ever was kicked. (*Aloud*) Hardress, a word with you. (*Exit* KYRLE *and* HARDRESS.)

ANNE. And this is my wedding day. There goes the only man I ever loved. When he's here near by me, I could give him the worst treatment a man could desire, and when he goes he takes the heart and all of me off with him, and I feel like an unfurnished house. This is pretty feelings for a girl to have, and she in her regimentals. Oh! if he wasn't married — but he is, and he'd have married me as well — the malignant! Oh! if he had, how I'd have made him swing for it — it would have afforded me the happiest moment of my life. (*Music — exit* ANNE.)

ACT THREE: SCENE THREE

Exterior of MYLES' *Hut. Enter* FATHER TOM.

FATHER TOM. Here's Myles' shanty. I'm nearly killed with climbin' the hill. I wonder is he at home? Yes, the door is locked inside. (*Knocks.*) Myles — Myles, are ye at home?
MYLES (*outside*). No — I'm out.
(*Enter* MYLES.)
MYLES. Arrah! is it yourself, Father Tom, that's in it?
FATHER TOM. Let us go inside, Myles — I've a word to say t'ye.
MYLES. I — I've lost the key.
FATHER TOM. Sure it's sticken inside.
MYLES. Iss — I always lock the dure inside and lave it there when I go out, for fear on losin' it.
FATHER TOM. Myles, come here to me. It's lyin' ye are. Look me in the face. What's come to ye these ten days past — three times I've been to your door and it was locked, but I heard ye stirrin' inside.
MYLES. It was the pig, yer riverince.
FATHER TOM. Myles, why did yer shoot Danny Mann?
MYLES. Oh, murther, who tould you that?
FATHER TOM. Himself.
MYLES. Oh, Father Tom, have ye seen him?
FATHER TOM. I've just left him.
MYLES. Is it down there ye've been?
FATHER TOM. Down where?
MYLES. Below, where he's gone to — where would he be, afther murthering a poor crature?
FATHER TOM. How d'ye know that?
MYLES. How! How did I? — whisht, Father Tom, it was his ghost.
FATHER TOM. He is not dead, but dyin' fast, from the wound ye gave him.
MYLES. I never knew 'twas himself 'till I was tould.

239

FATHER TOM. Who tould you?

MYLES. Is it who?

FATHER TOM. Who? who? — not Danny, for he doesn't know who killed him.

MYLES. Wait, an' I'll tell you. It was nigh twelve that night, I was comin' home — I know the time, betoken Murty Dwyer made me step in his shebeen, bein' the wake of the ould Callaghan, his wife's uncle — and a dacent man he was. 'Murty', ses I —

FATHER TOM. Myles, you're desavin' me.

MYLES. Is it afther desavin' yer riverence I'd be?

FATHER TOM. I see the lie in yer mouth. Who tould ye it was Danny Mann ye killed?

MYLES. You said so awhile ago.

FATHER TOM. Who tould ye it was Danny Mann?

MYLES. I'm comin' to it. While I was at Murty's, yer riverince, as I was a-tellin' you — Dan Dayley was there — he had just kim'd in. 'Good morrow, — good day' — ses he. 'Good morrow, good Dan, ses I', — jest that ways entirely — 'it's an opening to the heart to see you'. Well, yer riverince, as I ware sayin', — 'long life an' good wife to ye, Masther Dan', ses I. 'Thank ye, ses he, and the likes to ye, anyway'. The moment I speck them words, Dan got heart, an' up an' tould Murty about his love for Murty's darter — the Colleen Rue. The moment he heard that, he puts elbows in himself, an' stood lookin' at him out on the flure. 'You flog Europe, for boldness', ses he — 'get out of my sight', ses he, — 'this moment', ses he, — 'or I'll give yer a kick that will rise you from poverty to the highest pitch of affluence', ses he — 'away out o' that, you notorious delinquent; single yer freedom and double yer distance', ses he. Well, Dan was forced to cut an' run. Poor boy, I was sorry for his trouble; there isn't a better son nor brother this moment goin' the road than what he is — said — said — there wasn't a better, an', an' — oh! Father Tom, don't ax me; I've got an oath on my lips. (*Music.*) Don't be hard on a poor boy.

FATHER TOM. I lift the oath from ye. Tell me, avick, oh! tell me. Did ye search for the poor thing — the darlin' soft-eyed Colleen? Oh! Myles, could ye lave her to lie in the cowld lake all alone?

(*Enter* EILY *from door.*)

MYLES. No, I couldn't.

FATHER TOM (*turns — sees* EILY). Eily! Is it yerself, and alive — an' not — not — Oh! Eily, mavourneen. Come to my heart. (*Embraces* EILY.)

MYLES. D'ye think ye'd see me alive if she wasn't? I thought ye knew better — it's at the bottom of the Pool a Dhiol I'd be this minute if she wasn't to the fore.

FATHER TOM. Speak to me — let me hear your voice.

EILY. Oh! father, father, won't ye take me, far far away from this place.

FATHER TOM. Why, did ye hide yourself, this way?

EILY. For fear *he'd* see me.

FATHER TOM. Hardress. You knew then that he instigated Danny to get rid of ye?

EILY. Why didn't I die — why am I alive now for him to hate me?

FATHER TOM. D'ye know that in a few hours he is going to marry another.

EILY. I know it, Myles told me — that's why I'm hiding myself away.

FATHER TOM. What does she mean?

MYLES. She loves him still — that's what she manes.

FATHER TOM. Love the wretch who sought your life!

EILY. Isn't it his own? It isn't his fault if his love couldn't last as long as mine. I was a poor, mane creature — not up to him any way; but if he's only said, 'Eily, put the grave between us and make me happy', sure I'd lain down, wid a big heart, in the loch.

FATHER TOM. And you are willing to pass a life of seclusion that he may live in his guilty joy?

EILY. If I was alive wouldn't I be a shame to him an' a ruin — ain't I in his way? Heaven help me — why would I trouble him? Oh! he was in great pain o' mind entirely when he let them put a hand on me — the poor darlin'.

FATHER TOM. And you mean to let him believe you dead?

EILY. Dead an' gone: then perhaps, his love for me will come back, and the thought of his poor, foolish little Eily that worshipped the ground he stood on, will fill his heart awhile.

FATHER TOM. And where will you go?

EILY. I don't know. Anywhere. What matters?

MYLES. Love makes all places alike.

EILY. I'm alone in the world now.

FATHER TOM. The villain — the monster! He sent her to heaven because he wanted her there to blot out with her tears the record of his iniquity. Eily, ye have but one home, and that's my poor house. You are not alone in the world — there's one beside ye, your father, and that's myself.

MYLES. Two — bad luck to me, two. I am her mother; sure I brought her into the world a second time.

FATHER TOM. Whist! look down there, Myles — what's that on the road?

MYLES. It's the sogers — a company of red-coats. What brings the army out? — who's that wid them? — it is ould Corrigan, and they are going towards Castle Chute. There's mischief in the wind.

FATHER TOM. In with you, an' keep close awhile; I'll go down to the castle and see what's the matter.

EILY. Promise me that you'll not betray me — that none but yourself and Myles shall ever know I'm livin'; promise me that, before you go.

FATHER TOM. I do, Eily; I'll never breathe a word of it — it is as sacred as an oath. (*Exit — music.*)

EILY (*going to cottage*). Shut me in, Myles, and take the key wid ye, this time. (*Exit in cottage.*)

MYLES (*locks door*). There ye are like a pearl in an oyster; now I'll go to my bed as usual on the mountain above — the bolster is stuffed wid rocks, and I'll have a cloud round me for a blanket. (*Exit* MYLES.)

ACT THREE: SCENE FOUR

Outside of Castle Chute. Enter CORRIGAN *and six* SOLDIERS.

CORRIGAN. Quietly, boys; sthrew yourselves round the wood —
some of ye at the gate beyant — two more this way — watch
the windies; if he's there to escape at all, he'll jump from a
windy. The house is surrounded.
> (*Quadrille music under stage — Air, 'The Boulanger'.*)
Oh, oh! they're dancin' — dancin' and merry-making, while
the net is closin' around 'em. Now Masther Hardress Cregan —
I was kicked out, was I; but I'll come this time wid a call that
ye'll answer wid your head instead of your foot. My letters
were returned unopened; but here's a bit of writin' that ye'll
not be able to hand back so easy.
> (*Enter* CORPORAL.)

CORPORAL. All right, sir.

CORRIGAN. Did you find the woman, as I told ye?

CORPORAL. Here she is, sir.
> (*Enter* SHEELAH, *guarded by two* SOLDIERS.)

SHEELAH (*crying*). What's this? Why am I thrated this way —
what have I done?

CORRIGAN. You are wanted awhile — it's your testimony we
require. Bring her this way. Follow me! (*Exit.*)

SHEELAH (*struggling*). Let me go back to my boy. Ah! good
luck t'ye, don't kape me from my poor boy! (*Struggling.*) Oh!
you dirty blackguards, let me go — let me go! (*Exit* SHEELAH
and SOLDIERS.)

ACT THREE: SCENE FIVE

Ballroom in Castle Chute. Steps; platform — balustrades on top; backed by moonlight landscape; doors; table; writing materials, books, papers on; chairs; chandeliers lighted. LADIES *and* GENTLEMEN, WEDDING GUESTS *discovered*, HYLAND CREAGH, BERTIE O'MOORE, DUCIE, KATHLEEN CREAGH, ADA CREAGH, PATSIE O'MOORE, BRIDESMAIDS *and* SERVANTS *discovered. — Music going on under stage.*

HYLAND. Ducie, they are dancing the Boulanger, and they can't see the figure unless you lend them the light of your eyes.

KATHLEEN. We have danced enough; it is nearly seven o'clock.

DUCIE. Mr O'Moore; when is the ceremony to commence?

O'MOORE. The execution is fixed for seven — here's the scaffold, I presume. (*Points to table.*)

HYLAND. Hardress looks like a criminal. I've seen him fight three duels, and he never shewed such a pale face as he exhibits tonight.

DUCIE. He looks as if he was frightened at being so happy.

HYLAND. And Kyrle Daly wears as gay an appearance.

(*Enter* KYRLE DALY, *down steps.*)

DUCIE. Hush! here he is.

KYRLE. That need not stop your speech, Hyland. I don't hide my love for Anne Chute, and it is my pride, and no fault of mine if she has found a better man.

HYLAND. He is not a better man.

KYRLE. He is — she thinks so — what she says becomes the truth.

(*Enter* MRS CREGAN.)

MRS CREGAN. Who says the days of chivalry are over? Come, gentlemen, the bridesmaids must attend the bride. The guests will assemble in the hall.

(*Enter* SERVANT *with letter and card on salver.*)

244

SERVANT. Mr Bertie O'Moore, if you plase. A gentleman below asked me to hand you this card.

O'MOORE. A gentleman; what can he want. (*Reads card.*) Ah! indeed; this is a serious matter, and excuses the intrusion.

HYLAND. What's the matter?

O'MOORE. A murder has been committed.

ALL. A murder?

O'MOORE. The perpetrator of the deed has been discovered, and the warrant for his arrest requires my signature.

HYLAND. Hang the rascal. (*Goes up with* DUCIE.)

O'MOORE. A magistrate, like a doctor, is called on at all hours.

MRS CREGAN. We can excuse you for such a duty, Mr O'Moore.

O'MOORE. This is the result of some brawl at a fair I suppose. Is Mr Corrigan below?

MRS CREGAN (*starting*). Corrigan?

O'MOORE. Shew me to him.

(*Exit* O'MOORE *and* SERVANT — GUESTS *go up and off.*)

MRS CREGAN. Corrigan here! What brings that man to this house? (*Exit* MRS CREGAN.)

(*Enter* HARDRESS, *down steps, pale.*)

HARDRESS (*sits*). It is in vain — I cannot repress the terror with which I approach these nuptials — yet, what have I to fear? Oh! my heart is bursting with its load of misery.

(*Enter* ANNE, *down steps.*)

ANNE. Hardress! what is the matter with you?

HARDRESS (*rising*). I will tell you — yes, it may take this horrible oppression from my heart. At one time I thought you knew my secret: I was mistaken. — The girl you saw at Muckross Head —

ANNE. Eily O'Connor.

HARDRESS. Was my wife!

ANNE. Your wife?

HARDRESS. Hush! Maddened with the miseries this act brought upon me, I treated her with cruelty — she committed suicide.

ANNE. Merciful powers!

HARDRESS. She wrote to me bidding me farewell for ever, and the next day her cloak was found floating in the lake. (ANNE *sinks in chair.*) Since then I have neither slept nor waked — I have but one thought, one feeling; my love for her, wild and maddened, has come back upon my heart like a vengeance.

(*Music — tumult heard.*)

ANNE. Heaven defend our hearts, what is that?

(*Enters* MRS CREGAN, *deadly pale — locks door behind her.*)

MRS CREGAN. Hardress! my child!

HARDRESS. Mother!

ANNE. Mother, he is here. Look on him — speak to him — do not gasp and stare on your son in that horrid way. Oh! mother, speak, or you will break my heart.

MRS CREGAN. Fly — fly! (HARDRESS *going.*) Not that way. No — the doors are defended! there is a soldier placed at every entrance! You — you are trapped and caught — what shall we do? — the window in my chamber — come — come — quick —

ANNE. Of what is he accused?

HARDRESS. Of murder. I see it in her face. (*Noise.*)

MRS CREGAN. Hush! they come — begone! Your boat is below that window. Don't speak! when oceans are between you and danger — write! Till then not a word. (*Forcing him off, — noise.*)

ANNE. Accused of murder! He is innocent!

MRS CREGAN. Go to your room! Go quickly to your room, you will betray him — you can't command your features.

ANNE. Dear mother, I will.

MRS CREGAN. Away, I say — you will drive me frantic, girl. My brain is stretched to cracking. Ha! (*Noise.*)

ANNE. There is a tumult in the drawing-room.

MRS CREGAN. They come! You tremble! Go — take away your puny love — hide it where it will not injure him — leave me to face this danger!

ANNE. He is not guilty.

MRS CREGAN. What's that to me, woman? I am his mother — the hunters are after my blood! Sit there — look away from this door. They come!

(*Knocking loudly — crash — door opened — enter* CORPORAL *and* SOLDIERS *who cross stage, facing up to charge —* GENTLEMEN *with drawn swords on steps;* LADIES *on at back —* O'MOORE, — *enter* CORRIGAN — KYRLE *on steps.*)

CORRIGAN. Gentlemen, put up your swords, the house is surrounded by a military force, and we are here in the king's name.

ANNE. Gentlemen, come on, there was a time in Ireland when neither king nor faction could call on Castle Chute without a bloody welcome.

GUESTS. Clear them out!

KYRLE (*interposing*). Anne, are you mad. Put up your swords — stand back there — speak — O'Moore, what does this strange outrage mean?

(SOLDIERS *fall back —* GENTLEMEN *on steps —* KYRLE *comes forward.*)

O'MOORE. Mrs Cregan, a fearful charge is made against your son; I know — I believe he is innocent. I suggest, then, that the matter be investigated here at once, amongst his friends, so that this scandal may be crushed in its birth.

KYRLE. Where is Hardress?

CORRIGAN. Where? — why he's escaping while we are jabbering here. Search the house.

(*Exit two* SOLDIERS.)

MRS CREGAN. Must we submit to this, sir? Will you, a magistrate, permit —

O'MOORE. I regret, Mrs Cregan, but as a form —

MRS CREGAN. Go on, sir!

CORRIGAN (*at door*). What room is this? 'tis locked —

MRS CREGAN. That is my sleeping chamber.

CORRIGAN. My duty compels me.

MRS CREGAN (*throws key down on ground*). Be it so, sir.

CORRIGAN (*picks up key — unlocks door*). She had the key — he's there. (*Exit* CORRIGAN, CORPORAL *and two* SOLDIERS.)

MRS CREGAN. He has escaped by this time.

O'MOORE. I hope Miss Chute will pardon me for my share in this transaction — believe me, I regret —

ANNE. Don't talk to me of your regret, while you are doing your worst. It is hate, not justice, that brings this accusation against Hardress, and this disgrace upon me.

KYRLE. Anne!

ANNE. Hold *your* tongue — his life's in danger, and if I can't love him, I'll fight for him, and that's more than any of you men can do. (*To* O'MOORE.) Go on with your dirty work. You have done the worst now — you have dismayed our guests, scattered terror amid our festival, and made the remembrance of this night, which should have been a happy one, a thought of gloom and shame.

MRS CREGAN. Hark! I hear — I hear his voice. It cannot be.

(*Re-enter* CORRIGAN.)

CORRIGAN. The prisoner is here!

MRS CREGAN. Ah, (*Utters a cry*) is he? Dark bloodhound, have you found him? May the tongue that tells me so be withered from the roots, and the eye that first detected him be darkened in its socket!

KYRLE. Oh, madam! for heaven's sake!

ANNE. Mother! mother!

MRS CREGAN. What! shall it be for nothing he has stung the mother's heart, and set her brain on fire?

247

(*Enter* HARDRESS, *handcuffed, and two* SOLDIERS.)

MRS CREGAN. I tell you that my tongue may hold its peace, but there is not a vein in all my frame but curses him. (*Turns — sees* HARDRESS; *falls on his breast.*) My boy! my boy!

HARDRESS. Mother, I entreat you to be calm. Kyrle, there are my hands, do you think there is blood upon them?

(KYRLE *seizes his hand —* GENTLEMEN *press around him, take his hand, and retire up.*)

HARDRESS. I thank you, gentlemen; your hands acquit me. Mother, be calm — sit there. (*Points to chair.*)

ANNE. Come here, Hardress; your place is here by me.

HARDRESS. Now, sir, I am ready.

CORRIGAN. I will lay before you, sir, the deposition upon which the warrant issues against the prisoner. Here is the confession of Daniel or Danny Mann, a person in the service of the accused, taken on his death-bed; in articulo mortis, you'll observe.

O'MOORE. But not witnessed.

CORRIGAN (*calling*). Bring in that woman.

(*Enter* SHEELAH *and two* SOLDIERS.)

I have witnesses. Your worship will find the form of law in perfect shape.

O'MOORE. Read the confession, sir.

CORRIGAN (*reads*). 'The deponent being on his death-bed, in the presence of Sheelah Mann and Thomas O'Brien, parish priest of Kinmare, deposed and said —'

(*Enter* FATHER TOM.)

Oh, you are come in time, sir.

FATHER TOM. I hope I am.

CORRIGAN. We may have to call your evidence.

FATHER TOM. I have brought it with me.

CORRIGAN. 'Deposed and said, that he, deponent, killed Eily O'Connor; that said Eily was the wife of Hardress Cregan and stood in the way of his marriage with Miss Anne Chute; deponent offered to put away the girl, and his master employed him to do so'.

O'MOORE. Sheelah, did Danny confess this crime?

SHEELAH. Divil a word — it's a lie from end to end, that ould thief was niver in my cabin — he invented the whole of it — sure you're the divil's own parverter of the truth!

CORRIGAN. Am I? Oh, oh! Father Tom will scarcely say as much? (*To him.*) Did Danny Mann confess this in your presence?

FATHER TOM. I decline to answer that question!

CORRIGAN. Aha! you must — the law will compel you!

FATHER TOM. I'd like to see the law that can unseal the lips of the priest, and make him reveal the secrets of heaven.

ANNE. So much for your two witnesses. Ladies stand close. Gentlemen, give us room here. (BRIDESMAIDS *down*.)
  (*Exit* FATHER TOM.)

CORRIGAN. We have abundant proof, your worship — enough to hang a whole county. Danny isn't dead yet. Deponent agreed with Cregan that if the deed was to be done, that he, Cregan, should give his glove as a token.

MRS CREGAN. Ah!

HARDRESS. Hold! I confess that what he has read is true. Danny did make the offer, and I repelled his horrible proposition.

CORRIGAN. Aha! but you gave him the glove?

HARDRESS. Never, by my immortal soul — never!

MRS CREGAN (*advancing*). But I — I did! (*Movement of surprise.*) I, your wretched mother — I gave it to him — I am guilty! thank heaven for that! remove those bonds from his hands and put them here on mine.

HARDRESS. 'Tis false, mother, you did not know his purpose — you could not know it.
  (CORPORAL *takes off handcuffs.*)

MRS CREGAN. I will not say anything that takes the welcome guilt from off me.
  (*Enter* MYLES *from steps.*)

MYLES. Won't ye, ma'am? Well; if ye won't, I will.

ALL. Myles!

MYLES. Save all here. If you plaze, I'd like to say a word; there's been a murder done, and I done it.

ALL. You!

MYLES. Myself. Danny was killed by my hand. (*To* CORRIGAN.) Wor yez any way nigh that time?

CORRIGAN (*quickly*). No.

MYLES (*quickly*). That's lucky; then take down what I'm sayin'. I shot the poor boy — but widout manin' to hurt him. It's lucky I killed him that time, for it's lifted a mighty sin off the sowl of the crature.

O'MOORE. What does he mean?

MYLES. I mane, that if you found one witness to Eily O'Connor's death, I found another that knows a little more about it, and here she is.
  (*Enter* EILY *and* FATHER TOM *down steps.*)

ALL. Eily!

MYLES. The Colleen Bawn herself!

EILY. Hardress!

HARDRESS. My wife — my own Eily.

EILY. Here, darlin', take the paper, and tear it if you like. (*Offers him the certificate.*)

HARDRESS. Eily, I could not live without you.

MRS CREGAN. If ever he blamed you, it was my foolish pride spoke in his hard words — he loves you with all his heart. Forgive me, Eily.

EILY. Forgive.

MRS CREGAN. Forgive your mother, Eily.

EILY (*embracing her*). Mother!

(MRS CREGAN, HARDRESS, EILY, FATHER TOM *group together* — ANNE, KYRLE, *and* GENTLEMEN — LADIES *together* — *their backs to* CORRIGAN — CORRIGAN *takes bag, puts in papers, looks about, puts on hat, buttons coat, slinks up stage, runs up stairs and off* — MYLES *points off after him* — *several* GENTLEMEN *run after* CORRIGAN.)

ANNE. But what's to become of me, is all my emotion to be summoned for nothing? Is my wedding dress to go to waste, and here's all my blushes ready? I must have a husband.

HYLAND and GENTLEMEN. Take me.

O'MOORE. Take me.

ANNE. Don't all speak at once! Where's Mr Daly!

KYRLE. Here I am, Anne!

ANNE. Kyrle, come here! You said you loved me, and I think you do.

KYRLE. Oh!

ANNE. Behave yourself now. If you'll ask me, I'll have you.

KYRLE (*embracing* ANNE). Anne! (*Shouts outside.*)

ALL. What's that?

MYLES (*looking off at back*). Don't be uneasy! it's only the boys outside that's caught ould Corrigan thryin' to get off, and they've got him in the horsepond.

KYRLE. They'll drown him.

MYLES. Nivir fear, he wasn't born to be drownded — he won't sink — he'll rise out of the world, and divil a fut nearer heaven he'll get than the top o' the gallows.

EILY (*to* HARDRESS). And ye won't be ashamed of me?

ANNE. I'll be ashamed of him if he does.

EILY. And when I spake — no — speak —

ANNE. Spake is the right sound. Kyrle Daly, pronounce that word.

KYRLE. That's right; if you ever spake it any other way I'll divorce ye — mind that.

FATHER TOM. Eily, darlin', in the middle of your joy, sure you would not forget one who never forsook you in your sorrow.

EILY. Oh, Father Tom!

FATHER TOM. Oh, it's not myself I mane.

ANNE. No, it's that marauder there, that lent me his top coat in the thunder storm. (*Pointing to* MYLES.)

MYLES. Bedad, ma'am, your beauty left a linin' in it that has kept me warm ever since.

EILY. Myles, you saved my life — it belongs to you. There's my hand, what will you do with it?

MYLES (*takes her hand and* HARDRESS'). Take her, wid all my heart. I may say that, for ye can't take her widout. I am like the boy who had a penny to put in the poor-box — I'd rather keep it for myself. It's a shamrock itself ye have got, sir; and like that flower she'll come up every year fresh and green forenint ye. When he cease to love her may dyin' become ye, and when ye *do* die, lave yer money to the poor, your widdy to me, and we'll both forgive ye. (*Joins hands.*)

EILY. I'm only a poor simple girl, and it's frightened I am to be surrounded by so many —

ANNE. Friends, Eily, friends.

EILY. Oh, if I could think so — if I could hope that I had established myself in a little corner of their hearts, there wouldn't be a happier girl alive than THE COLLEEN BAWN.

CURTAIN

OH, LIMERICK IS BEAUTIFUL

Oh, Limerick is beautiful, as everyone knows,
The river Shannon's full of fish, beside that city flows;
But it is not the river, nor the fish that preys upon my mind,
Nor with the town of Limerick have I any fault to find.
The girl I love is beautiful, she's fairer than the dawn;
She lives in Garryowen, and she's called the Colleen Bawn.
As the river, proud and bold, goes by that famed city,
So proud and cold, widout a word, that Colleen goes by me!

        Oh, hone! Oh, hone!

Oh, if I was the Emperor of Russia to command,
Or Julius Caesar, or the Lord Lieutenant of the land,
I'd give up all my wealth, my manes, I'd give up my army,
Both the horse, the fut, and the Royal Artillery;
I'd give the crown from off my head, the people on their knees,
I'd give my fleet of sailing ships upon the briny seas,
And a beggar I'd go to sleep, a happy man at dawn,
If by my side, fast for my bride, I'd the darlin' Colleen Bawn.

        Oh, hone! Oh, hone!

CRUISKEEN LAWN

Let the farmer praise his grounds,
As the huntsman doth his hounds,
And the shepherd his fresh and dewy morn;
But I, more blest than they,
Spend each night and happy day,
With my smilin' little Cruiskeen Lawn, Lawn, Lawn.
Chorus
Gramachree, mavourneen, slanta gal avourneen,
Gramachree ma Cruiskeen Lawn, Lawn, Lawn,
With my smiling little Cruiskeen Lawn.

And when grim Death appears
In long and happy years,
To tell me that my glass is run,
I'll say, begone, you slave,
For great Bacchus gave me lave
To have another Cruiskeen Lawn — Lawn — Lawn.

Chorus
Gramachree, &c. &c.

PRETTY GIRL MILKING HER COW

'Twas on a bright morning in summer,
I first heard his voice speaking low,
As he said to a colleen beside me,
"Who's that pretty girl milking her cow?"
And many times after he met me,
And vow'd that I always should be
His own little darling alanna,
Mavourneen a sweelish machree.

I haven't the manner or graces
Of the girls in the world where ye move,
I haven't their beautiful faces,
But I have a heart that can love.
If it plase ye, I'll dress in satins,
And jewels I'll put on my brow,
But don't ye be after forgettin'
Your pretty girl milking her cow.

BRIAN O'LINN

Brian O'Linn had no breeches to wear,
So he bought him a sheepskin to make him a pair;
The skinny side out, the woolly side in,
"They are cool and convanient", said Brian O'Linn.

THE SHAUGHRAUN

AN ORIGINAL DRAMA

In Three Acts

DRAMATIS PERSONAE

*first performed at Wallack's Theatre, New York, on
14 November 1874.*

Captain Molineux, *a young English Officer, commanding a detachment at Ballyragget*	MR H.J. MONTAGUE
Robert Ffolliott, *a young Irish Gentleman — under sentence as a Fenian — in love with Arte O'Neal*	MR C.A. STEVENSON
Father Dolan, *the Parish Priest of Suil-a-beg, his tutor and guardian*	MR JOHN GILBERT
Corry Kinchela, *a Squireen*	MR EDWARD ARNOTT
Harvey Duff, *a Police Agent in disguise of a peasant, under the name of Keach*	MR HARRY BECKETT
Conn, *the Shaughraun, the soul of every fair, the life of every funeral, the first fiddle at all weddings and patterns*	MR DION BOUCICAULT
Sergeant Jones, *of the 41st*	MR W.J. LEONARD
Sullivan	MR C.E. EDWIN
Reilly	MR E.M. HOLLAND
Mangan	MR J.F. JOSEPHS
Doyle	MR J. PECK
Donovan	MR G. ATKINS
Arte O'Neal, *in love with Robert*	MISS JEFFRIES LEWIS
Claire Ffolliott, *a Sligo Lady*	MISS ADA DYOS
Mrs O'Kelly, *Conn's Mother*	MADAME PONISI
Moya, *Father Dolan's Niece, in love with Conn*	MRS JANE BURKE
Biddy (Bridget) Madigan, *a Keener*	MRS SEFTON
Nancy Malone, *a Keener*	MISS E. BLAISDELL

(Reilly, Mangan, Doyle, Donovan — **Peasants**)

Peasants, Soldiers, Constabulary

ACT ONE: SCENE ONE

Suil-a-beg — the Cottage of ARTE O'NEAL — *the Stage is a Yard in the rear of the Cottage — the Dairy window is seen facing audience. Door in return of Cottage — the ruins of Suil-a-more Castle cover a bold headland in the half distance — the Atlantic bounds the picture — Sunset — Music.* CLAIRE FFOLLIOTT *at work at a churn.*

CLAIRE. Phoo! How my arms ache! (*Sings.*)
>Where are you going, my pretty maid?
>I'm going a-milking, sir, she said.
>(*Enter* MRS O'KELLY *from house.*)

MRS O'KELLY. Sure, miss, this is too hard work entirely for the likes of you!

CLAIRE. Go on, now, Mrs O'Kelly, and mind your own business. Do you think I'm not equal to making the butter come?

MRS O'KELLY. It's yourself can make the butter come. You have only got to look at the milk and the butter will rise. But, oh, miss! who's this coming up the cliff? It can't be a vision!

CLAIRE. 'Tis one of the officers from Ballyragget.

MRS O'KELLY. Run in quick, before he sees you, and I'll take the churn.

CLAIRE. Not I! — I'll stop where I am. If he was the Lord Lieutenant himself I'd not stir or take a tuck out of my gown. Go tell the mistress.

MRS O'KELLY. And is this the way you will receive the quality? (*Exit house.*)

CLAIRE (*sings, working*).
>Then what is your fortune, my pretty maid?

He is stopping to reconnoitre. (*Sings again.*)
>What is your fortune, my pretty maid?

Here he comes. (*Continues to sing.*)
>My face is my fortune, sir, she said.

259

CLAIRE. There's no lie in that, any way; and a mighty small income I've got.

(*Enter* MOLINEUX, *looking about.*)

MOLINEUX. My good girl.

CLAIRE. Sir to you. (*Aside*) He takes me for the dairymaid.

MOLINEUX. Is this place called Swillabeg?

CLAIRE. No; it is called Shoolabeg.

MOLINEUX. Beg pardon; your Irish names are so unpronounceable. You see, I'm an Englishman.

CLAIRE. I remarked your misfortune. Poor creature, you couldn't help it.

MOLINEUX. I do not regard it as a misfortune.

CLAIRE. Got accustomed to it, I suppose. Were you born so?

MOLINEUX. Is your mistress at home?

CLAIRE. My mistress. Oh, 'tis Miss O'Neal you mane!

MOLINEUX. Delicious brogue — quite delicious! Will you take her my card?

CLAIRE. I'm afeard the butter will spoil if I lave it now.

MOLINEUX. What is your pretty name?

CLAIRE. Claire! What's yours?

MOLINEUX. Molineux — Captain Molineux. Now, Claire, I'll give you a crown if you will carry my name to your mistress.

CLAIRE. Will you take my place at the churn while I go?

MOLINEUX. How do you work the infernal thing? (*Crosses to her.*)

CLAIRE. Take hould beside me, and I'll show you. (*He takes handle of churn beside her, they work together.*) There, that's it! Beautiful! You were intended for a dairymaid!

MOLINEUX. I know a dairymaid that was intended for me.

CLAIRE. That speech only wanted a taste of the brogue to be worthy of an Irishman.

MOLINEUX (*kissing her*). Now I'm perfect.

CLAIRE (*starting away*). What are you doing?

MOLINEUX. Tasting the brogue. Stop, my dear; you forget the crown I promised you. Here it is. (*He hands her the money.*) Don't hide your blushes, they become you.

CLAIRE. Never fear — I'll be even wid your honour yet. Don't let — (*Up to porch*) — the butther spoil while I'm gone. (*Going, and looking at card.*) What's your name again — Mulligrubs?

MOLINEUX. No; Molineux.

CLAIRE. I ax your pardon. You see I'm Irish, and the English names are so unpronounceable. (*Exit house.*)

MOLINEUX (*churning gravely*). She's as fresh and fragrant as one of her own pats of |butter. If the mistress be as sweet as the

260

maid, I shall not regret being stationed in this wilderness. Deuced hard work this milk pump! There is a strange refinement about that Irish girl. When I say strange, I am no judge, for I've never done the agricultural shows. I have never graduated in dairymaids, but this one must be the cream of the dairy. Confound this piston-rod; I feel like a Chinese toy!

(*Enter* ARTE O'NEAL *followed by* CLAIRE.)

ARTE. What can he want? (*Advancing.*) What is he doing?

CLAIRE. I have not the slightest idea. (*Crosses to behind.*)

ARTE. Captain Molineux.

MOLINEUX (*confused*). Oh, a thousand pardons! I was just a-amusing myself. I am — a — very fond of machinery, and so — (*Bows*) Miss O'Neal, I presume?

ARTE (*introducing* CLAIRE). My cousin, Miss Claire Ffolliott.

MOLINEUX. Miss Ffolliott! Really I took her for a — (*Aside*) Oh, lord! what have I done?

ARTE (*aside*). Claire has been at some mischief here.

CLAIRE (*at churn, and aside to* MOLINEUX). Don't hide your blushes, they become you.

MOLINEUX (*aside*). Spare me!

ARTE. I hope you come to tell me how I can be of some service to you.

MOLINEUX. I have just arrived with a detachment of our regiment at Ballyragget. The government received information that a schooner carrying a distinguished Fenian hero was hovering about the coast, intending to land her passengers in this neighbourhood. So a gunboat has been sent round to these waters, and we are under orders to co-operate with her. Deuced bore, not to say ridiculous — there is no foundation for the scare — but we find ourselves quartered here without any resources.

ARTE. But I regret I cannot extend to you the hospitalities of Suil-a-beg. An unmarried girl is unable to play the hostess.

CLAIRE. Even two unmarried girls couldn't play the hostess.

MOLINEUX. But you own the finest shooting in the west of Ireland. The mountains are full of grouse, and the streams about here are full of salmon!

CLAIRE. The captain would beg leave to sport over your domain — shall I spare you the humiliation of confessing that you are not mistress in your own house, much less lady of the manor. Do you see that ruin yonder! Oh — 'tis the admiration of the traveller, and the study of painters, who come from far and near to copy it. It was the home of my forefathers when they kept open house for the friend — the poor — or the stranger. The mortgagee has put up a gate now, so visitors pay sixpence a head to admire the place, and their guide points across to this cabin where the remains of the ould family, two lonely girls, live. God knows how — you ask leave to kill game on Suil-a-more and Keim-an-eigh. (*Crosses to the dairy window.*) Do you see that salmon? It was snared last night in the Pool-a-Bricken by Conn, the Shaughraun. He killed those grouse at daylight on the side of Maurnturk. That's our daily food, and we owe it to a poacher.

MOLINEUX. You have to suffer bitterly indeed for ages of family imprudence, and the Irish extravagance of your ancestors.

ARTE. Yes, sir, the extravagance of their love for their country, and the imprudence of their fidelity to their faith!

MOLINEUX. But surely you cannot be without some relatives!

CLAIRE. I have a brother — the heir to this estate.

MOLINEUX. Is he abroad?

CLAIRE. Yes, he is a convict working out his sentence in Australia!

MOLINEUX. Oh, I beg pardon. I did not know. (*To* ARTE.) Have you any relatives?

ARTE. Yes, I am the affianced wife of her brother!

MOLINEUX (*confused*). Really, ladies, I have to offer a thousand apologies.

ARTE. I do not accept one — it carries insult to the man I love.

MOLINEUX. At least you will allow me to regret having aroused such distressing memories?

CLAIRE. Do you think they ever sleep?

MOLINEUX. No! — naturally — of course not — I meant — (*Aside*) I am astray on an Irish bog here, and every step I take gets me deeper in the mire.

CLAIRE (*aside*). How confused he is. That's a good fellow, although he is an Englishman.

ARTE. I am very sorry we have not the power to grant you a privilege, which, you see, we do not enjoy.

KINCHELA (*outside*). Holloo! Is there nobody at home? (*Music.*)

ARTE. Here comes a gentleman who can oblige you.

KINCHELA (*outside*). Holloo! one of you! Don't you hear me? Bridget come — come and hould my pony.

MOLINEUX. Who is this stentorian gentleman?

CLAIRE. Mr Corry Kinchela; one who has trimmed his fortunes with prudence, and his conscience with economy.

(*Enter* CORRY KINCHELA.)

262

KINCHELA. Where the devil is everybody? Oh, there you are! I had to stable my own horse! Oh, my service to you, sir! — I believe I've the honour of addressing Captain Molineux. I'm just back from Dublin, and thought I'd stop on my road to tell you the court has decreed the sale of this estate, undher foreclosure, and in two months you'll have to turn out.

ARTE. In two months, then, even this poor shelter will be taken from us.

KINCHELA. I'm afeard the rightful owner will want to see the worth of his money! But never fear, two handsome girls like yourselves will not be long wanting a shelter — or — a welcome. Eh, captain? oh! ho! It will be pick and choose for them anywhere, I'm thinking.

MOLINEUX (aside). This fellow is awfully offensive to me.

KINCHELA. I've been away for the last few weeks, so I've not been able to pay my respects to you officers, and invite you all to sport over this property. You are right welcome, captain. My name is Kinchela — Mr Corry Kinchela — of Ballyragget House, where I'll be proud to see my tablecloth under your chin. I don't know why one of these girls didn't introduce me.

MOLINEUX. They paid me the compliment of presuming that I had no desire to form your acquaintance.

KINCHELA. What! do you know, sir, that you are talking to a person of position and character?

MOLINEUX. I don't care a straw for your position, and I don't like your character. (Back turned to KINCHELA.)

KINCHELA. Do you mean to insult me, sir?

MOLINEUX. I am incapable of it.

KINCHELA. Ah!

MOLINEUX. In the presence of ladies; but I believe I should be entitled to do so, for you insulted them in mine. (Turning to CLAIRE.) I ask your pardon for the liberty I took with you when I presented myself.

CLAIRE (offering her hand). The liberty you took with him when he presented himself clears the account.

KINCHELA. We'll meet again, sir.

MOLINEUX. I hope not. Good evening. (To ARTE, shaking hands.)

ARTE. I would delay you, captain; but you have a long way across the mountain, and the darkness is falling; the road is treacherous.

(MOLINEUX goes up to CLAIRE, shakes hands with her again, and exits.)

KINCHELA. The devil guide him to pass the night in a bog-hole up to his neck. Listen hither, you, too. (Crosses to CLAIRE.) Sure,

I don't want to be too hard upon you. To be sure the sale of this place will never cover my mortgage on it; it will come to me every acre of it. (*Turns to* ARTE.) Bedad, the law ought to throw your own sweet self in as a makeweight to square my account. (*She turns away; he turns to* CLAIRE.) See now, there's your brother, Robert Ffolliott, going to rot over there in Australia, and here in a few weeks you both will be without a roof over your heads. Now, isn't it a cruel thing entirely to let this go on when, if that girl would only say the word, I'd make her Mrs Kinchela. (CLAIRE *gets to porch.*) And I've got a hoult of the ear of our county member; shure he'll get Robert the run of the country — as free as a fish in a pond he'll be over there. And, stop now — (*To* ARTE) — you shall send him a £1,000 that I'll give you on your wedding day.

ARTE. I'd rather starve with Robert Ffolliott in a jail than own the county of Sligo if I'd to carry you as a mortgage on it.

KINCHELA. Do you think the boy cares what becomes of you, or who owns you? Not a ha'porth! How many letters have you had from him for the last past year?

ARTE (*up by* CLAIRE). Alas! not one.

KINCHELA. Not one! (*Aside*) I know that, for I've got them all safe under lock and key. (*Aloud*) See that now; not one thought, not a sign from him, and here I am, every day in the week, like a dog at your door. It is too hard on me entirely. I've some sacret schaming behind my back to ruin me entirely in your heart —

(*Enter* FATHER DOLAN *from house.*)

I know that it is the same that's sending over to Robert Ffolliott the money, without which he'd starve outright beyant there. I'd like to find out who it is.

FATHER DOLAN (*at porch*). I am the man, Mr Kinchela!

KINCHELA. Father Dolan, may I ask, sir, on what grounds you dare to impache me in the good opinion of these girls?

FATHER DOLAN. Certainly. (*Turns to* ARTE.) Miss O'Neal — Claire, my dear — will you leave me awhile — (*Music*) — alone with Mr Kinchela; he wants to know the truth about himself.

CLAIRE. And you can't insult him in the presence of ladies. Come, Arte.

(ARTE *crosses to door, turns, curtseys to* KINCHELA, *and exit.* CLAIRE *follows, with a look at him.*)

FATHER DOLAN. The father of young Ffolliott bequeathed to you and to me the care of his infant son — heaven forgive me if I grew so fond of my darling charge, I kept no watch over you, my partner, in the trust. Year after year you dipped the estate with your sham improvements and false accounts; you reduced the rents to impoverish the income, so it might not suffice to pay the interest on the mortgages.

KINCHELA. Go on, sir; this is mighty fine — go on. I wish I had a witness by, I'd make you pay for this. Is there anything more?

FATHER DOLAN. There is; you hope to buy the lad's inheritance for an old song when it is sold. Thus you fulfil the trust confided to you by your benefactor, his poor father, whose hand you held when he expired in my arms — thus you have kept the oath to the dead!

KINCHELA. Would not every acre of it have escheated to the Crown, as the estate of a convicted felon, only I saved it for young Ffolliott by getting his family to make it over before the sentence was pronounced upon him?

FATHER DOLAN. Yes; to make it over to you in trust for these two girls, his sister and his betrothed.

KINCHELA. To be sure, wasn't you by, and helped to persuade him? More betoken, you were a witness to the deed.

FATHER DOLAN. I was. I helped you to defraud the orphan boy, and since then have been a witness how you have robbed these helpless women. Oh! beware, Kinchela! When these lands were torn from Owen Roe O'Neal in the old times, he laid his curse on the spoilers, for Suil-a-more was the dowry of his bride, Grace Ffolliott. Since then many a strange family have tried to hold possession of the place; but every year one of them would die — the land seemed to swallow them up one by one. Till the O'Neals and Ffolliotts returned none other thrived upon it.

KINCHELA. Sure that's the raison I want Arte O'Neal for my wife. Won't that kape the ould blood to the fore? Ah, ah, sir! why wouldn't you put in the good word for me to the girl? Do I ask betther than to give back all I have to the family? Sure there's nothing, sir, done that can't be mended that way.

FATHER DOLAN. I'd rather rade the service over her grave, and hear the sods falling on her coffin, than spake the holy words to make her your wife. Corry Kinchela, I know it was by your means and to serve this end, my darling boy — her lover — was denounced and convicted.

KINCHELA. 'Tis false!

FATHER DOLAN. It is true! But the truth is locked in my soul, and heaven keeps the key. (*Up to porch.*)

KINCHELA (*aside*). Some false-hearted cur has confessed again me.

(*Aloud*) Very well, sir. Then out of that house these girls shall turn, homeless and beggars.

FATHER DOLAN. Not homeless, while I have a roof over me — not beggars, I thank God, who gives me the crust to share with them. (*Exit into house.*)

KINCHELA. How could he know I had any hand in bringing young Ffolliott to the dock? Who can have turned tail on me?

(*Enter* HARVEY DUFF.)

HARVEY DUFF. Whisht, sir!

KINCHELA. Who's there? — Harvey Duff?

HARVEY DUFF. I saw your coppaleen beyant under the hedge, and I knew yourself was in it. I've great news entirely for you — news enough to burst a budget —

KINCHELA. You are always finding a mare's nest.

HARVEY DUFF. I've found one now wid a divil's egg in it.

KINCHELA. Well, out with it.

HARVEY DUFF. There was a fire last night on Rathgarron Head. You know what that means?

KINCHELA. A signal to some smuggler at sea that the coast is clear, and to run in and land his cargo.

HARVEY DUFF. Divil a keg was landed from that ship, barrin' only one man that was put ashore — not a boy was on the strand to meet the boat, nor a car, nor a skip to hurry off the things — only one thing, and that was Conn, the Shaughraun — 'twas himself that lighted the signal — 'twas him that stud up to his middle in the salt say to carry the man ashore. I seen it all as I lay on the flat of my stomach on the edge of the cliff, and looked down on the pair o' them below.

KINCHELA. Well, what's all this to me?

HARVEY DUFF. Wait, sure. I'm hatching the egg for you. 'Who's that', ses I to myself, 'that Conn would carry in his two arms as tindher as a mother would hould a child? — who's that', ses I, 'that he's capering all around for all the world like a dog that's just onloosed? — who's that he's houlding by the two hands of him, as if 'twas Moya Dolan herself he'd got before him instead of a ragged sailor boy?'

KINCHELA. Well, did you find out who it was?

HARVEY DUFF. Maybe I didn't get snug behind the bushes beside the pathway up the cliff. They passed close to me, talking low; but I heard his voice, and saw the man as plain as I see you now.

KINCHELA. Saw whom?

HARVEY DUFF. Robert Ffolliott. 'Twas himself I tell you.

KINCHELA. Are you sure?

HARVEY DUFF. Am I sure? Do you think I can mistake the face
that turned upon me in the coort when they sentenced him on
my evidence, or the voice that said 'if there's justice in heaven,
you and I will meet again on this side of the grave? — then',
ses he, 'have your soul ready', and the look he fixed upon me
shrivelled up my soul inside like a boiled cockle that ye might
pick out with a pin. Am I sure? I wish I was as sure of heaven.

KINCHELA. He has escaped from the penal settlement — ay, that's
it — and where would he go to straight but here, into the trap
baited with the girl he loves?

HARVEY DUFF. There'll be a price offered for him, sir — and your
honour will put it in my way to airn an honest penny. Wouldn't
they hang him this time? Egorra! I'd be peaceable if he was
only out of the way for good.

KINCHELA. Listen to me — d'ye know what took me to Dublin?
I heard that the Queen had resolved to release the Fenian
prisoners under sentence.

HARVEY DUFF. Murther alive — I'm a corpse.

KINCHELA. I saw the secretary — he mistook me fear for hope
— 'It is thrue', ses he, 'I'm expecting every day to get the
despatch, I wish you joy'.

HARVEY DUFF. Be jabers I'd have liked to seen your face when
you got that polthogue in the gob.

KINCHELA. Robert Ffolliott returned! a free man, he will throw
his estates into Chancery.

HARVEY DUFF. Where will he throw me!

KINCHELA. He's a fugitive convict still, can't we deal with him?

HARVEY DUFF. If his own people around here get to know he's
among them, why a live coal in a keg of gunpowdher would
not give an 'idaya' of the County Sligo.

KINCHELA. I know it — high and low they love him as they hate
me — bad cess to them.

HARVEY DUFF. Oh, nivir fear — he'll keep in the dark for his own
sake. (*Music*)

KINCHELA. Keep a watch on the Shaughraun — find out where the
pair o' em lie in hiding. Bring me the news to Ballyragget
House — meanwhile, I'll think what's best to be done — be off,
quick! (*Exit* HARVEY DUFF.) Robert Ffolliott here — tare an'
ages — I'm ruined, horse and foot — I'll have all Connaught and
the Coort of Chancery on me back. Harvey Duff is right — 'tis
life or death with me and him — well, it shall be life with you,
Arte O'Neal — and death to him that parts us. (*Exit.*)

ACT ONE: SCENE TWO

The Devil's Jowl — A cleft in the rocks on the sea coast. Enter ROBERT FFOLLIOTT.

ROBERT. It must be past the hour when Conn promised to return. How often he and I have climbed these rocks together in search of the sea-birds' eggs — and waded for cockles in the strand below. Dear faithful truant to ramble with you — how many a lecture from my dear old tutor, Father Dolan, who told me I ought to be ashamed of my love for the Shaughraun. Ah! my heart was not so much to blame after all.

MOLINEUX (*outside*). Holloa!

ROBERT. That's not his voice.

MOLINEUX (*still outside*). Holloa!

ROBERT. Why it's a man in the uniform of an officer — he has seen me. (*Calls.*) Take care, sir, don't take that path — turn to the right — round that boulder — that's the road — Egad, another step and he would have gone over the cliff. He is some stranger who has lost his way.

MOLINEUX (*entering*). What an infernal country! First I was nearly smothered in a bog, and then, thanks to you my good fellow, I escaped breaking my neck. Do you know the way to Ballyragget? How far is it to the barracks?

ROBERT. Two miles.

MOLINEUX. Irish miles, of course.

ROBERT. I shall be happy to show you the road but regret I cannot be your guide. The safest for a stranger is by the cliff to Suil-a-beg.

MOLINEUX. But I have just come from there.

ROBERT. From Suil-a-beg?

MOLINEUX. I shall not regret to revisit the place — charming spot — I've just passed there the sweetest hour of my life.

ROBERT. You saw the lady of the house I presume?

268

MOLINEUX. Pardon me, sir, I mistook your yachting costume — perhaps you are acquainted with Miss Ffolliott.

ROBERT. Yes; but we have not met for some time. I thought you referred to Arte — I mean Miss O'Neal.

MOLINEUX. Oh, she is charming, of course; but Miss Ffolliott is an angel. She has so occupied my thoughts that I have lost my way — in fact, instead of going straight home, I have been revolving in an orbit round that house by a kind of centrifugal attraction, of which she is the centre.

ROBERT. But surely you admired Miss O'Neal?

MOLINEUX. Oh, she is well enough, bright little thing but besides Claire Ffolliott —

ROBERT. I prefer the beauty of Miss O'Neal.

MOLINEUX. I don't admire your taste.

ROBERT. Well, let us drink to each of them.

MOLINEUX. With pleasure, if you can supply the opportunity. (ROBERT *pulls out his flask, and fills cup.*) Ah! I see you are provided. Allow me to present myself — Captain Molineux, of the 49th. Here's to Miss Claire Ffolliott.

ROBERT. Here's to Miss Arte O'Neal. (*They drink.*)

MOLINEUX. I beg your pardon — I did not catch your name.

ROBERT. I did not mention it. (*A pause.*)

MOLINEUX. This liquor is American whiskey, I perceive.

ROBERT. Do you find anything wrong about it?

MOLINEUX. Nothing whatever. (*He offers his cup to be filled again.*) But it reminds me of a duty I have to perform. We have orders to capture a dangerous person who will be, or has been, landed on this coast lately, and as these rocks are just the kind of place where he might find refuge —

ROBERT. Not at all unlikely — I'll keep a look-out for him.

MOLINEUX. I propose to revisit this spot again tonight with a file of men. Here's your health.

ROBERT. Sir, accept my regards. Here's good luck to you.

MOLINEUX. Good night. (*Music — a whistle heard outside.*) What's that?

ROBERT. 'Tis a ring at the bell. A friend of mine is waiting for me on the cliff above. (*Aside*) 'Tis Conn!

MOLINEUX. Oh, I beg pardon! Farewell. (*Going.*)

ROBERT. Stop. You might not fare well if you ascend that path alone.

MOLINEUX. Why not?

ROBERT. Because my friend's at the top of it, and if he saw you coming out alone — (*Aside*) — he would think I had been caught, and egad! the Shaughraun might poach the Captain!

MOLINEUX. Well, if he met me, what then?

ROBERT. You see the poor fellow is mad on one point — he can't bear the sight of one colour, and that is red. His mother was frightened by a mad bull, and the minute Conn sees a bit of scarlet, such, for example, as your coat there, the bull breaks out in him, and he might toss you over the cliff; so, by your leave —

MOLINEUX. This is the most extraordinary country I was ever in. (*Exeunt, arm-in-arm.*)

ACT ONE: SCENE THREE

Exterior of FATHER DOLAN's *Cottage — Night — Lighted window.*
Enter MOYA *with pail, which she puts down.*

MOYA. There! now I've spancelled the cow and fed the pig, my
uncle will be ready for his tay. Not a sign of Conn for the past
three nights. What's come to him?
    (*Enter* MRS O'KELLY.)
MRS O'KELLY. Is that yourself, Moya? I've come to see if that
vagabond of mine has been round this way.
MOYA. Why would he be here — hasn't he a home of his own.
MRS O'KELLY. The shebeen is his home when he's not in gaol.
His father died o' drink, and Conn will go the same way.
MOYA. I thought your husband was drowned at sea?
MRS O'KELLY. And, bless him, so he was.
MOYA (*aside*). Well, that's a quare way of dying o' drink.
MRS O'KELLY. The best of men he was, when he was sober — a
betther never dhrawed the breath o' life.
MOYA. But you say he never was sober.
MRS O'KELLY. Nivir! An' Conn takes afther him!
MOYA. Mother.
MRS O'KELLY. Well.
MOYA. I'm afeard I'll take afther Conn.
MRS O'KELLY. Heaven forbid, and purtect you agin him. You are
a good, dacent girl, an' desarve the best of husbands.
MOYA. Them's the only ones that gets the worst. More betoken
yourself, Mrs O'Kelly.
MRS O'KELLY. Conn nivir did an honest day's work in his life —
but dhrinkin', an fishin', an' shootin', an' sportin', and love-
makin'.
MOYA. Sure, that's how the quality pass their lives.
MRS O'KELLY. That's it. A poor man that spoorts the sowl of a
gentleman is called a blackguard.

271

CONN (*entering*). There's somebody talking about me.

MOYA (*running to him*). Conn!

CONN. My darlin', was the mother makin' little of me, don't believe a word that comes out o' her! She's jealous — a devil a haperth less. She's choking wid it this very minute, just bekase she sees my arms about ye. She's as proud of me as an ould hen that's got a duck for a chicken. Hould your whist now! Wipe your mouth, an' give me a kiss!

MRS O'KELLY (*embracing him*). Oh, Conn, what have you been afther? The polis were in my cabin today about ye. They say you stole Squire Foley's horse.

CONN. Stole his horse! Sure the baste is safe and sound in his paddock this minute.

MRS O'KELLY. But he says you stole it for the day to go huntin'.

CONN. Well, here's a purty thing, for a horse to run away with a man's characther like this! Oh, wurra! May I never die in sin, but this was the way of it. I was standing by ould Foley's gate, when I heard the cry of the hounds comin' across the tail end of the bog, and there they wor, my dear, spread out like the tail of a paycock, an' the finest dog fox you'd ever seen sailing ahead of them up the boreen, and right across the churchyard. It was enough to raise the inhabitants. Well, as I looked, who should come up and put his head over the gate beside me but the Squire's brown mare, small blame to her. Divil a thing I said to her, nor she to me, for the hounds had lost their scent, we knew by their whelp and whine as they hunted among the grave-stones, when, whish! the fox went by us. I leapt on the gate, an' gave a shriek of a view holloo to the whip; in a minute the pack caught the scent again, an' the whole field came roarin' past. The mare lost her head, an' tore at the gate. 'Stop', ses I, 'ye devil!' and I slipped the taste of a rope over her head an' into her mouth. Now mind the cunnin' of the baste, she was quiet in a minute. 'Come home now', ses I, 'asy' and I threw my leg across her. Be gabers! No sooner was I on her bare back than whoo! Holy rocket! She was over the gate, an' tearin like mad afther the hounds. 'Yoicks!' ses I, 'Come back the thief of the world, where are you takin' me to?' as she went through the huntin' field an' laid me besides the masther of the hounds, Squire Foley himself. He turned the colour of his leather breeches. 'Mother of Moses!' ses he, 'Is that Conn the Shaughraun on my brown mare?' 'Bad luck to me!' ses I 'It's no one else!' 'You sthole my horse', says the Squire. 'That's a lie!' ses I, 'For it was your horse sthole me!'

MOYA. An' what did he say to that?

CONN. I couldn't sthop to hear, for just then we took a stone wall and a double ditch together, and he stopped behind to keep an engagement he had in the ditch.

MRS O'KELLY. You'll get a month in jail for this.

CONN. Well, it was worth it.

MRS O'KELLY. An' what brings you here? Don't you know Father Dolan has forbidden you the house?

CONN. The Lord bless him! I know it well, but I've brought something wid me tonight that will get me absolution. I've left it with the ladies at Suil-a-beg, but they will bring it up here to share wid his riverence.

MRS O'KELLY. What is it at all?

CONN. Go down, mother, an' see, an' when you see it, kape your tongue betune your teeth, if one of your sex can.

MRS O'KELLY. Well, but you're a quare mortil. (*Exit.*)

MOYA. Oh, Conn! I'm afeared my uncle won't see you. (FATHER DOLAN *inside calls* 'MOYA'.) There! he's calling me. (*Going, taking pail.*)

CONN. Go in an' tell him I'm sthravagin outside till he's soft. Now put on your sweetest lip, darlin'.

MOYA. Never fear! sure he does be always telling me my heart is too near my mouth.

CONN. Ah! I hope nobody will ever measure the distance but me, my jewel. (*Music.*)

MOYA. Ah! Conn, do you see those flowers? I picked 'em by the way-side as I came along, and I put them in my breast. They are dead already; the life and fragrance have gone out of them; killed by the heat of my heart. So it may be with you, if I picked you and put you there. (*Pause*) Won't the life go out of your love? hadn't I better lave you where you are?

CONN. For another girl to make a posy of me. Ah — (*taking pail*) — my darling Moya! sure if I was one of those flowers, and you were to pass me by like that, I do believe that I'd pluck myself and walk afther you on my own stalk. (*Exeunt.*)

ACT ONE: SCENE FOUR

A room in FATHER DOLAN's *House. Fireplace. Window at back door. Lamp on table.* FATHER DOLAN *reading, sits armchair.*

FATHER DOLAN. What keeps Moya so long outside? Moya! —
  (*Enter* MOYA *with tea things; they are on a tray, and she has a kettle in her hand.*)
MOYA. Yes, uncle, here's your tay, I was waiting for the kettle to boil.
  (*Puts things on table, gives* FATHER DOLAN *a cup of tea, then to fire with kettle.*)
FATHER DOLAN. I thought I heard voices outside!
MOYA. It was only the pig!
FATHER DOLAN. And I heard somebody singing.
MOYA. It was the kettle, uncle.
FATHER DOLAN. Go tell that pig not to come here till he's cured, and if I hear any strange kettles singing round here my kettle will boil over.
MOYA. Sure uncle! I never knew that happen but you put your fire out. (*At fire kneeling.*)
FATHER DOLAN. See, now, Moya, that ragamuffin Conn will be your ruin. What makes you so fond of the rogue?
MOYA. All the batins I got for him when I was a child an' the hard words you gave me since.
FATHER DOLAN. Has he one good quality undher heaven? If he has I'll forgive him.
MOYA. He loves me.
FATHER DOLAN. Love! Oh, that word covers more sin than charity. I think I hear it raining, Moya, and I would not keep a dog out in such a night.
MOYA. Oh! (*Laughs behind his back.*)
FATHER DOLAN. You may let him stand out of the wet (MOYA *beckons on* CONN, *who enters*) but don't let him open his mouth.

274

Gi' me a cup of tay, Moya; I hope it will be stronger than the last.

MOYA. Oh! what will I do? He wants his tay stronger, and I've no more tay in the house. (*A pause.* CONN *pours whiskey into tea-pot. She gives cup of tea.*)

FATHER DOLAN. Well, haven't you a word to say for yourself?

CONN. Divil a one, your riverence!

FATHER DOLAN. You are going to ruin?

CONN. I am, bad luck to me!

FATHER DOLAN. And you want to take a dacent girl along with you. (*Still reading.*)

CONN. I'm a vagabone entirely.

FATHER DOLAN. What sort of a life do you lead? What is your occupation? Stealing salmon out of the river of a night! (*Puts down book and takes up cup of tea.*)

CONN. No, sir; I'm not so bad as that, but I'll confess to a couple of throut. Sure the salmon is out of sayson. (*He pulls two trout out of his bag, and gives them to* MOYA, *who takes them.*)

FATHER DOLAN. And don't you go poaching the grouse on the hill-side.

CONN. I do! divil a lie in it. (*Pulls out four grouse.*)

FATHER DOLAN. D'ye know where all this leads to?

CONN. Well, along with the grouse I'll go to pot.

(MOYA *laughs and removes the game and fish. She receives trout on tray, from which she has taken the tea-things.* MOYA *returns and busies herself at dresser.*)

FATHER DOLAN. Bless me, Moya! — Moya! this tay is very strong, and has a curious taste.

CONN. Maybe the wather is to blame in regard of being smoked.

FATHER DOLAN. And it smells of whiskey.

CONN. It's not the tay you smell, sir, it's me.

FATHER DOLAN. That reminds me. (*Rising, puts down tea and takes up book.*) Didn't you give me a promise last Aister — a blessed promise, made on your two knees — that you would lave off dhrink?

CONN. I did, barrin' one thimbleful a day, just to take the cruelty out o' the wather.

FATHER DOLAN. One thimbleful. I allowed that concession, no more.

CONN. God bless ye, ye did; an' I kep' my word.

FATHER DOLAN. Kept your word! how dare you say that! Didn't I find you ten days after stretched out drunk as a fiddler at Tim O'Malley's wake!

CONN. Ye did, bad luck to me!

FATHER DOLAN. And you took only one thimbleful?

CONN. Divil a dhrop more — see this. Ah, will ye listen to me, sir? I'll tell you how it was. When they asked me to the wake, I wint — oh, I wouldn't decave you, I wint. Thcre was the Mulcaheys, and thc Malones, and the —

FATHER DOLAN. I don't want to hear about that. Come to the drink —

CONN. Av coorse — egorra! I came to that soon enough. Well, sir, when afther blessing the keeners, and the rest o' 'em, I couldn't despise a drink out of respect for the corpse — long life to it! 'But, boys', ses I, 'I'm on a puniance', scs I. 'Is there a thimble in the house', ses I, 'for a divil a dhrop more than the full an it will pass my lips this blessed day'.

FATHER DOLAN. Ah!

CONN. Well, as the divil's luck would have it, there was only one thimble in the place, and that was a tailor's thimble, an' they couldn't get it full. (FATHER DOLAN, *to conceal his laughter, goes up, puts his book in recess, then comes down.*) Egorra! but they got me full first.

FATHER DOLAN (*at table*). Ah, Conn, I'm afeard liquor is not the worst of your doings. We lost sight of you lately for more than six months. In what jail did you pass that time?

CONN. I was on my thravels.

FATHER DOLAN. Where?

CONN. Round the world. See, sir. Afther masther was tuck an' they sint him away the heart seemed to go out o' me entirely. I stand by the say — look over it, an' see the ships sailin' away to where he may be, till the longing grew too big for my body — an' one night I jumped into the coastguard boat, stuck up the sail, and wint to say.

FATHER DOLAN. Bless the boy, you didn't think you could get to Australia in a skiff. (*Rises and stands back to fire.*)

CONN. I didn't think at all — I wint. All night I tossed about, an' the next day and that night, till at daylight I came across a big ship. 'Sthop', ses I — 'take me aboard — I'm out of my coorse'. They whipped me on deck, an' took me before the Captain. 'Where do you come from?' ses he. 'Suil-a-beg', ses I. 'I'll be obleeged to you to lave me anywhere handy by there'. 'You'll have to go to Melbourne first', ses he. 'Is that anywhere in the County Sligo?' 'Why, ye omadhaun', ses he, 'you won't see home for six months'. Then I set up a wierasthru. 'Poor devil', ses the Captain; 'I'm sorry for you, but you must cross the ocean. What sort of work can ye do best?' 'I can play the fiddle', ses I. 'Take him forrad, and be good to him', ses he. An' so they did. That's how I got my passage to Australia.

FATHER DOLAN. You rogue, you boarded that ship on purpose.

MOYA. Ay, to get nearer to the young masther. And did you find him, Conn? (*Goes to him.*)

CONN. I did. And oh, sir, when he laid eyes on me, he put his two arums around my neck, an' sobbed an' clung to me like when we were children together. 'What brings you here?' ses he. 'To bring you back wid me', ses I. 'That's impossible', ses he; 'I am watched'. 'So is the salmon in the Glenamoy', ses I; 'but I get 'em. So is the grouse on Keim-an-Eigh; but I poach 'em. And now I've come to poach you', ses I. An' I did it. (*Music.*)

(*Enter* ROBERT FFOLLIOTT *with* CLAIRE *and* ARTE.)

FATHER DOLAN. Is this the truth you are telling me? You found him? (*After an irrepressible gesture, and an inarticulate attempt to bless* CONN.)

CONN. Safe, and in fine condition. (*Seizes* MOYA, *and stops her mouth as she is about to utter a cry on seeing* ROBERT.)

FATHER DOLAN. Escaped and free! Tell me —

CONN. Oh, egorra! he must speak for himself now.

ROBERT. Father Dolan! (*Throws off disguise and embraces him.*)

FATHER DOLAN. Robert, my darling boy! Oh, blessed day! Do I hold you to my heart again? (*He embraces him.*)

CONN (*aside to* MOYA). There's nobody looking. (*Kisses her.*)

MOYA. Conn, behave.

ARTE. He has been hiding on the sea shore among the rocks a whole day and two nights.

CLAIRE. All alone, with sea-weed for his bed. (*Goes up to fire.*)

MOYA. Oh, if I'd only known that!

CONN. An' nothin' to eat but a piece of tobacco an' a cockle.

ARTE. And he wouldn't stop at Suil-a-beg to taste a morsel; he would come over here to see you.

FATHER DOLAN. Come near the fire. Moya, hurry now, and put food on the table. Sit ye down; let me see you all around me once again. (MOYA *brings in food.*) And to think I cannot offer you a glass of wine, nor warm your welcome with a glass of liquor! I have not got a bottle in the house. (CONN *pulls out his bottle, and puts it on the table.*) The rogue — (*They form a group round the fire.*)

ROBERT. We may thank poor Conn, who contrived my escape. I made my way across to America.

CLAIRE. But how did you escape, Conn?

CONN. Oh, asy enough; they turned me out.

ARTE. Turned you out!

CONN. As if I wor a stray cat. 'Very well', says I, 'Bally-mulligan is my parish. I'm a pauper; send me, or gi' me board wages where I am'. 'No', ses they, 'we've Irish enough here already'. 'Then send me back to Sligo', ses I, an' they did.

CLAIRE. They might take you for a cat, for you seem always to fall upon your legs.

FATHER DOLAN. I can't get over my surprise to see my blessed child there sitting by my side. Now, we'll all drink his health. (*Music — gives glass to* CLAIRE, &c.)

CONN. Which thimble am I to drink out of?

FATHER DOLAN. The tailor's, you reprobate, are you ready? Now, then — (*The face of* HARVEY DUFF *appears at the window*) — here's his health, and long life to him. May heaven keep watch over —

ROBERT (*his glass in hand, slowly pointing to the window*). Look! — look there.

(HARVEY DUFF *disappears; they turn.*)

CLAIRE. What was it?

ARTE. How pale you are!

ROBERT. The face — I saw the face — there at the window — the same I saw when I was in the dock!

CLAIRE. Ah, Robert, you dream.

ROBERT. The police spy — Harvey Duff — the man that denounced me. 'Twas his white face pressed against the glass yonder, glaring at me. (*Exit* CONN.) Can it be a vision?

(FATHER DOLAN *up to window.*)

ARTE. It was. You are weak, dear; eat — recover your strength.

(ROBERT *sits —* ARTE *at his feet.*)

MOYA. It wasn't a face, but an empty stomach.

ROBERT. It gave my heart a turn. You must be right. It was a weakness — the disorder of my brain — it must be so.

FATHER DOLAN. The night is very dark. (*Closes curtains —* CONN *re-enters.*) Well?

CONN. Nothing.

FATHER DOLAN. I thought so. Come, refresh yourself. (*Sits on bench, with his back to the audience.*)

CONN (*aside*). Moya, there was somebody there!

MOYA. How d'ye know! — did ye see him?

CONN. No; but I left Tatthers outside.

MOYA. Your dog. Why didn't he bark?

CONN. He couldn't. I found this in his mouth.

MOYA. What's that?

CONN. The sate of a man's breeches. (*Exit.*)

ROBERT (*eating*). My visit here must be a short one. The vessel that landed me is now standing off and on the coast, awaiting my signal to send in a boat ashore to take me away again.

ARTE. I am afraid your arrival was expected by the authorities. They are on the watch.

ROBERT. I know they are. I've had a chat with them on the subject, and a very nice fellow the authority seemed to be, and a great admirer of my rebel sister there.

CLAIRE. Captain Molineux.

ROBERT. He and I met this morning at the Coot's Nest.

CLAIRE. How dare the fellow talk about me?

ROBERT. Look at her! — she is all ablaze — her face is the colour of his coat!

CLAIRE. I never saw the creature but once.

ROBERT. Then you made good use of your time. I never saw a man in such a condition; he's not a man — he's a trophy. (*Music.*)

CLAIRE. Robert, you are worse than he is.

FATHER DOLAN. I could listen to him all night.

ARTE. So could I.

(*The window is dashed open,* CONN *leaps in.*)

CONN. Sir — quick — away with yeez — hide! the red-coats are on us!

ARTE. Oh, Robert, fly!

MOYA. This way — by the kitchen — through the garden.

CONN. No; the back dure is watched by a couple of them. Is it locked?

MOYA. Fast!

CONN. Give me your coat and hat, I'll make a dash out. Tatthers will attend to one, I'll stretch the other, and the rest will give me chase, thinking it is yourself, and then you can slip off unbeknonst. (*Three knocks.*)

FATHER DOLAN. It is too late!

MOYA. Hide yourself in the old clock-case in the kitchen. There's just enough room in it for him.

ARTE. Quick, Robert, quick! Oh, save yourself if you can! (*Exit with* ROBERT.)

CLAIRE. Oh, I wish I was a man, I wouldn't give him up without a fight! (*Exit.*)

CONN. Egorra, the blood of the old stock is in her. (*Standing by with uplifted chair.*) I'm ready, sir. (*Two knocks.*)

FATHER DOLAN. Conn, put that down, and open the door.

(CONN *opens door.* SERGEANT *and two* SOLDIERS *enter;*
they stand at door. SERGEANT *draws window-curtains, and*
discovers two SOLDIERS *outside, and then exits, saluting*
CAPTAIN MOLINEUX *as he enters.*)

MOLINEUX. I deeply regret to disturb your household at such an
hour, but my duty is imperative.

(*Enter* CLAIRE *and* ARTE.)

A convict escaped from penal servitude has landed on this
coast, and I am charged with his capture. Miss Ffolliott, I am
sorry to be obliged to perform so painful a duty in your
presence, and in yours, Miss O'Neal.

CLAIRE. Especially, sir, when the man you seek is my brother!

ARTE. And my affianced husband!

MOLINEUX. Believe me, I would exchange places with him, if I
could.

(*Enter a* SERGEANT.)

SERGEANT (*saluting*). Please, sir, there's a mad dog, sir, a-sitting at
the back door, and he has bit four of our men awful.

CONN. Tatthers was obliged to perform his painful duty.

CLAIRE. Call off the dog, Conn. Moya, open the back door. (*Exit*
CONN, *with* MOYA.)

MOLINEUX. Your assurance gives me hope that we have been
misled.

ARTE. The house is very small, sir. Here is a bedroom; let your
men search it.

(*Enter* MOYA, CONN *and two* SOLDIERS — *the two* SOLDIERS
remain at door.)

MOYA (*to the two* SOLDIERS). I suppose you've seen there was
never a human being in my kitchen barrin' the cat? My
bedroom is upstairs — maybe you'd like to search that.

MOLINEUX. I shall be obliged, sir, to visit every room — sound
every piece of furniture, from the roof to the cellar; but the
indignity of the proceeding is more offensive to my feelings
than it can be to yours. I will accept your simple assurance
that the person we are in search of is not in your house. Give
me that, and I will withdraw my men.

CLAIRE (*offering her hand to* MOLINEUX). Thank you!

ARTE (*aside, to* FATHER DOLAN). Save him, sir! oh, save him!

FATHER DOLAN (*aside*). Oh, God, help me in this great temptation.

ARTE (*aside*). You will not betray him. Speak — say he is not
here!

MOLINEUX. I await your reply.

CONN (*aside*). I wish he would take my word.

FATHER DOLAN. The lad — the person you seek — my poor boy! Oh, sir, for mercy's sake, don't ask me. He has been here, but —

MOLINEUX. He is gone — he went before we arrived?

ARTE. Yes — yes!

CONN. Yes, sir; he wint away before he came here at all.

MOLINEUX. Have I your word as a priest, sir, that Robert Ffolliott is not under this roof?

(FATHER DOLAN, *after a passionate struggle with himself, turns from* MOLINEUX, *and buries his face in his hands.*)

(ROBERT *enters.*)

ROBERT. No, sir. Robert Ffolliott is here!

(ARTE, *with a suppressed cry, throws herself into* CLAIRE'S *arms.*)

MOLINEUX. I am very sorry for it. (*Goes slowly up to* SERGEANT — ROBERT *embraces* FATHER DOLAN.) Secure your prisoner! (*The* SERGEANT *advances* — ROBERT *meets him, is handcuffed* — SERGEANT *retires two or three paces* — FATHER DOLAN *totters across, and falls on his knees* — ROBERT *raises him and puts him in chair* — *the* SERGEANT *touches* ROBERT *on shoulder, then moves to door* — ROBERT *is passing out, when* ARTE *throws her arms around his neck.*)

FATHER DOLAN. What have I done? — what have I done? (*Sinking into chair.*)

CONN. Be asy, Father. Sure, he'd rather have the iron on his hand, than you the sin upon your sowl! (*Tableau — Slow Act Drop.*)

END OF ACT ONE

ACT TWO: SCENE ONE

Room in Ballyragget House — Music. Enter KINCHELA *and* HARVEY DUFF. *Music.*

KINCHELA. Come in. How pale you are! Did he resist?

HARVEY DUFF. Give me a glass of sperrets!

KINCHELA. Recover yourself. Is he wounded?

HARVEY DUFF. Divil a scratch, but I am.

KINCHELA. Where?

HARVEY DUFF. Nivir mind.

KINCHELA. You are faint; come and sit down.

HARVEY DUFF. No, I'm easier on my feet.

KINCHELA. How did it happen?

HARVEY DUFF. While I was peeping through the key-hole of the kitchen dure.

KINCHELA. I mean how was he taken?

HARVEY DUFF. I did not stop to see, for when he got sight of my face agin the windy, his own turned as white as your shirt. I believe he knew me.

KINCHELA. Impossible! that black wig disguises you completely. You have shaved off your great red whiskers. Your own mother wouldn't know you.

HARVEY DUFF. No, she wouldn't; the last time I went home she pelted me wid the poker. But if the people round here suspected I was Harvey Duff, they would tear me to rags; there wouldn't survive of me a piece as big as the one I left in the mouth of that divil of a dog!

KINCHELA. Don't be afraid, my good fellow. I'll take care of you.

(Gets glass and bottle; HARVEY DUFF *drinks, and returns glass to him before he speaks.)*

HARVEY DUFF. And it is yourself you'll be taking care of at the same time. There's a pair of us, Misther Kinchela, mind me, now. We are harnessed to the same pole, and as I'm dhruv you must travel.

KINCHELA. What do you mean?

HARVEY DUFF. I mane that I have been your parthner in this game to chate young Ffolliott out of his liberty first, then out of his estate, and now out of his wife! Where's my share?

KINCHELA. Your share! Share of what? (*Puts away bottle and glass.*)

HARVEY DUFF. Oh, not the wife. Take her and welcome; but where's my share of the money?

KINCHELA. Were you not handsomely paid at the time for doing your duty?

HARVEY DUFF. My jooty! Was it my jooty to come down here among the people disguised as a Fenian delegate, and pass myself off for a head centre, so that I could swear them in an' denounce 'em? Who gave me the office to trap young Ffolliott? Who was it picked out Andy Donovan, an' sent him in irons across the say, laving his young wife to die in a madhouse?

KINCHELA. Hush! not so loud.

HARVEY DUFF. Do you remember the curse of Bridget Madigan, when her only boy was found guilty on my evidence? Take your share of that, an' give me some of what I have airned.

KINCHELA. You want a share of my fortune?

HARVEY DUFF. A share of our fortune!

KINCHELA. Every penny I possess is invested in this estate. If Robert Ffolliott returns home a free man I could not hould more of it than would stick to my brogues when I was kicked out. Listen to this letter that I found here tonight waiting for me. It is from London. (*Reads.*) 'On Her Majesty's service. The Home Office. In reply to your inquiries concerning Robert Ffolliott, undergoing penal servitude, I am directed by his lordship to inform you that Her Majesty has been pleased to extend a full pardon to the Fenian prisoners'.

HARVEY DUFF. Pardoned! I'm a corpse!

KINCHELA (*reads*). 'But as Robert Ffolliott has effected his escape, the pardon will not extend to him unless he should reconstitute himself a prisoner'.

HARVEY DUFF. Oh, lor'! that is exactly what he has done. He has gave himself up.

KINCHELA. Was he not captured?

HARVEY DUFF. No, bad luck to it. Our schame to catch him has only qualified him for a pardon.

KINCHELA. What! has an infernal fate played such a trick upon me?

HARVEY DUFF. The divil will have his joke.

KINCHELA. His freedom and return here is your death warrant and my ruin.

HARVEY DUFF. I'll take the next ship to furrin parts.

KINCHELA. Stay! the news is only known to ourselves.

HARVEY DUFF. In a couple of days it will be all over Ireland, and they will let him out! Tare alive! what'll I do? Where will I go? I'll swear an information against meself, and get sent to jail for purtection.

KINCHELA. Listen, I've a plan. Can I rely upon your help?

HARVEY DUFF. I'll do anything short of murder, but I'll get somebody to do that for me. What's to be done?

KINCHELA (*close to* HARVEY DUFF). I'll visit him in prison, and offer him the means to escape. Now what more likely than he should be killed while making the attempt?

HARVEY DUFF. Oh! whew! the soldiers will not dhraw a trigger on him barrin' a magistrate is by to give the ordher.

KINCHELA. But the police will. You will go at once to the police-barracks at Sligo, pick your men, tell 'em you apprehend an attempt at rescue. The late attack on the police-van at Manchester, and the explosion at Clerkenwell prison in London will warrant extreme measures.

HARVEY DUFF. The police won't fire if he doesn't defend himself.

KINCHELA. But he will!

HARVEY DUFF. Where will he get the arms?

KINCHELA. I will provide them for him!

HARVEY DUFF. Corry Kinchela, the divil must be proud of you!

KINCHELA. We must get some of our own people to help, and if the police hesitate, sure it's the duty of every loyal subject to kill a fugitive convict. What men could we depend on at a pinch?

HARVEY DUFF. There's Sullivan an' Doyle.

KINCHELA. Which Doyle?

HARVEY DUFF. Jim Doyle.

KINCHELA. Jim Doyle!

HARVEY DUFF. Yes, the man with the big carbuncle on the end of his nose. Then there's Reilly.

KINCHELA. Reilly? He's transported.

HARVEY DUFF. No, no; he's not.

KINCHELA. Oh, but he will, and you'll be hanged.

HARVEY DUFF. And so will you — an' Mangan, an' all their smuggling crew.

KINCHELA. Where can you find them?

HARVEY DUFF. At the Coot's Nest. They expect a lugger in at every tide.

KINCHELA. Have them ready and sober tonight. Come to me for instructions at midday. (*Going — stops.*) Ah! that will do — he will fall into that trap — (*Rubs his hands*) — it can't fail. (*Exit.*)

HARVEY DUFF (*speaking after* KINCHELA's *exit*). Harvey Duff, take a friend's advice — get out of this place as quick as you can. Take your little pickin's and your passage across the salt say; find some place where a rogue can live peaceably — have some show and a chance of making an honourable living. (*Exit — scene changes — music.*)

ACT TWO: SCENE TWO

Parlour at FATHER DOLAN's — (*as before*). FATHER DOLAN *at fireside*. CLAIRE *looking out of window; window-curtains open.*

FATHER DOLAN. There, my darling, do not sob so bitterly. Sure that will do no good, and only spoil your blue eyes.

ARTE. What's the good of my eyes if I can't see him. Let me cry. God help me! what else can I do? Oh, if I could only see him — speak to him — one minute! Do you think they would let me in?

FATHER DOLAN. I have sent a letter to the Captain. Moya has carried it to the barracks.

ARTE. If Claire had gone instead of Moya — had she pleaded for us, he would not refuse her.

CLAIRE. But I could not go.

ARTE. Why not?

CLAIRE. I could not ask that Englishman a favour.

FATHER DOLAN. You speak unkindly and unjustly. He acted with a gentle forbearance, and a respect for my character and our sorrow, I cannot forget.

CLAIRE. Nor can I.

FATHER DOLAN. It made a deep impression on my heart.

CLAIRE. Yes; a bitter curse on the day I ever laid eyes on him.

ARTE (*rising, and down to her behind table*). Oh, Claire, you wrong him! Surely I have no cause to regard him as a friend; but you did not see the tears in his eyes when I appealed to his mercy —

CLAIRE. Didn't I?

FATHER DOLAN (*still seated*). Poor fellow, he suffered for what he was obliged to do. You should not hate the man.

CLAIRE. I don't! And that's what ails me!

ARTE. Are you mad?

CLAIRE. I am! I've tried to hate him, and I can't! Do you think I was blind to all you saw? I tried to shut my eyes; but I only shut him in. I could not shut him out! I hate his country and his people.

FATHER DOLAN. You were never there.

CLAIRE. Never! and I wish they had never been here, particularly this fellow, who has the impudence to upset all my principles with his chalky smile and bloodless courtesy. I can't stand the ineffable resignation with which he makes a fool of himself and me.

(FATHER DOLAN *goes to fire, and* MOYA *enters.*)

CLAIRE (*eagerly*). Well, have you seen him? Can't you speak?

MOYA. I will when I get my breath. Yes, I saw him, and, oh! how good and —

CLAIRE. Stop that! we know all about that! Where is his answer? — quick!

MOYA. He's bringing it himself!

CLAIRE. Oh! (*Turns away.*) We don't want him here.

ARTE. Did you see the young master?

MOYA. No, miss; nobody was let in to see him.

FATHER DOLAN. What kept you so long then?

MOYA. Conn come back wid me, and knowing you did not want him round here, I was thrying to get away from him — that's what kept me; but he was at my heels all the way, and Tatthers at his heels. A nice sthreel we made along the road.

FATHER DOLAN. Where is he?

MOYA. They are both outside.

FATHER DOLAN. The pair of vagabonds! Why does he not go home?

MOYA. He says the ould woman is no consolation.

CONN (*sings outside*).

> 'If I were dead an' in my grave,
> No other tombstone would I have
> But I'd dig a grave both wide and deep,
> With a jug of punch at my head and feet.
> > Ri tooral loo'.

FATHER DOLAN. Is the fellow so insensible to our sorrow that he sets it to the tune of a jug of punch?

CLAIRE. Don't blame poor Conn. The boy is so full of sport that I believe he would sing at his own funeral.

MOYA. Long life to ye, miss, for the good word.

CONN (*entering, and speaking to his dog*). Lie down now, an' behave.

FATHER DOLAN. Where have you been all night?

CONN. Where would I be but undher his prison windy, keeping up his heart wid the songs and the divarshin!

ARTE. Diversion.

CONN. Sure I had all the soldiers dancing to my fiddle, and I put Tatthers through all his thricks. I had 'em all in fits of laffin' when I made him dancc to my tunes. That's the way the masther knew I was waiting on him. He guessed what I was at, for when I struck up 'Where's the slave?' he answered inside with 'My lodging is on the cowld ground'; then when I made Tatthers dance to 'Tell me the sorrow in your heart' — till I thought they'd have died wid the fun — he sung back 'The girl I left behind me', mainin' yourself, Miss Arte, an' I purtended that the tears runnin' down my nose was with the laffin'.

(MOYA *puts stool by* CONN. *Wipes his eyes with apron.*)

FATHER DOLAN. I did you great wrong. I ask your pardon.

ARTE. What is to be done?

CONN. I've only to whisper five words on the cross-roads and I'd go bail I'd have him out of that before night.

FATHER DOLAN. Yes; you would raise the country to attack the barracks, and rescue him. I will not give countenance to violence.

CLAIRE. 'Tis the shortest way out!

ARTE. Oh, any way but that!

MOYA (*aside to* CONN, *taking up stool*). Come into my kitchen. Have you had nothin' to ate since yesterday?

CONN. Yes, my heart, I've that in my mouth all the night. (*Exit, with* MOYA.)

CLAIRE (*who is watching at window*). Here he comes.

(*A knock. After* MOLINEUX *passes window,* CLAIRE *crosses, and sits by fire, back to audience.*)

FATHER DOLAN. There's a knock at the door.

ARTE. 'Tis he!

CLAIRE. I know that.

FATHER DOLAN. Why did you not let him in? (*Crosses to door.*)

CLAIRE (*aside*). Because I was trying to keep him out.

(FATHER DOLAN *opens door.* MOLINEUX *enters.*)

MOLINEUX. Good day, sir. I ventured to intrude in person to bring you this order, necessary to obtain admission to see Mr. Ffolliott, and that I might entreat you to bear me no ill-will for the painful duty I had to perform last night. (*Hands a paper to* ARTE.)

CLAIRE. Oh, no, sir; you had to deprive us of a limb, and I

suppose you performed the operation professionally well. Do you come for your fee in the form of our gratitude?

FATHER DOLAN. Forgive her, sir! Claire, this is too bad!

MOLINEUX (*awkward*). Oh, no — not at all! Pray don't mention it — I assure you.

ARTE. This paper is signed by Mr. Kinchela — are we indebted to him for the favour?

MOLINEUX. The prisoner is now in the custody of the civil power, and Mr. Kinchela is the magistrate of the district.

FATHER DOLAN (*taking his hat from desk*). Come, Arte, come, Claire.

ARTE (*to* MOLINEUX). We are grateful — (*Giving hands*) — very grateful for your kindness in our affliction. (*Aside to* MOLINEUX, *and pointing to* CLAIRE.) Don't mind her.

(FATHER DOLAN *takes* MOLINEUX's *hand, and then exit with* ARTE.)

MOLINEUX (*aside*). Don't mind her; I wish I did not. (*Aloud*) May I be permitted to accompany you to — (*Advances to table and puts down cap.*)

CLAIRE (*still seated*). To the prison? Do you wish to make the people about here believe I am in custody. A fine figure I'd make hanging on the arm of the policeman who arrested my brother!

MOLINEUX. You cannot make me feel more acutely than I do the misery of my condition. I did not sleep a wink last night.

CLAIRE. And how many winks do you suppose I got?

MOLINEUX. I tried to act with as much tenderness as the nature of my duty would permit.

CLAIRE. That's the worse part of it.

MOLINEUX. Do you reproach me with my gentleness?

CLAIRE. I do! You have not even left us the luxury of complaint.

MOLINEUX. Really, I don't understand you.

CLAIRE. No wonder. I don't understand myself! (*Rising, and at fire.*)

MOLINEUX. Well, if you don't understand yourself, you shall understand me, Miss Ffolliott. You oblige me to take refuge from your cruelty, and place myself under the protection of your generosity. You extort from me a confession that I feel is premature, for our acquaintance has been short.

CLAIRE. And not sweet.

MOLINEUX. I ask your pity for my position last night, when I found myself obliged to arrest the brother of the woman I love.

289

CLAIRE. Captain Molineux, do you mean to insult me? Oh, sir, you know I am a friendless girl, alone in this house — my brother is in jail! I have no protection!

MOLINEUX. Miss Ffolliott — Claire!

(*Enter* CONN, *followed by* MOYA.)

CONN. Did you call, miss?

CLAIRE (*after a pause*). No.

CONN. I thought I heard a screech. (*Music.*)

CLAIRE. Go away! I don't want you.

MOYA (*aside to* CONN). Don't you see what's the matther?

CONN. No.

MOYA. You're an omadhaun. Come out of that, an' I'll tell you. (*Exit with* CONN.)

> (CLAIRE *crosses to bench, sits face to audience, handkerchief to face.*)

CLAIRE. There! what will those pair think of me? Do you see what you have exposed me to? Is it not enough to play the character of executioner of my brother, but you must add to your part this scene of outrage on me! (*Sits down, and weeps passionately.*)

MOLINEUX. Forgive me. I ask it most humbly. If I said I would give my heart's blood to the last to spare you one of those tears, you might feel the avowal was an offence. What can I say? Miss Ffolliott, for mercy sake don't cry so bitterly! — forget what I've done!

CLAIRE. I — I can't!

MOLINEUX. On my knees, I implore your pardon. I'll go away. I'll never see you again.

> (CLAIRE *suddenly and mechanically arrests his movement by catching his arm.* MOLINEUX *kisses her hand.*)

Heaven bless you — farewell!

CLAIRE (*without moving her hand from face*). Don't go.

MOLINEUX (*advances a little*). Did I hear right? You bid me stay?

CLAIRE. Am I mad? (*Rises, and goes to fireplace.*)

MOLINEUX. Miss Ffolliott, I am here.

CLAIRE. I forgive you on one condition.

MOLINEUX. I accept it, whatever it may be.

CLAIRE. Save my brother.

MOLINEUX. I'll do my best. Anything else?

CLAIRE. Never speak of love to me again.

MOLINEUX (*close to her*). Never, never! On my honour I will never breathe a —

CLAIRE. Until he is free.

MOLINEUX. And then may I — may I — (*He stands beside her at fireplace; her head bent down, he steals his arm around her.*)

CLAIRE. Not a word until then.

MOLINEUX. Not a word!

    (CLAIRE *leans her head on his shoulder. Slow close in, as he kisses her.*)

ACT TWO: SCENE THREE

Room in the Barracks. Enter the SERGEANT, *followed by* KINCHELA.

KINCHELA. I am Mr. Kinchela, the magistrate. I wish to see the prisoner; he must be removed to police quarters.

SERGEANT. We shall be glad to get rid of him. It is the police business. Our men don't half like it. (*Exit.*)

KINCHELA. Now I'll know at once by his greeting whether those girls have been speakin' about me.

(*Enter* ROBERT, *followed by* SERGEANT.)

ROBERT. Kinchela, my dear friend, I knew you would not fail me.

KINCHELA (*aside*). 'Tis all right. (*Turns coldly, and with stiff manner.*) Pardon me, Mr. Ffolliott, you forget your position and mine — I bear Her Majesty's commission as justice of the peace, and whatever friendship once united us it ceased when you became a rebel.

ROBERT. Do I hear aright? Your letters to me breathed the most devoted —

KINCHELA (*to* SERGEANT). You can leave us. (SERGEANT *goes out — he suddenly changes his manner.*) My dear young master, forgive me, in the presence of that fellow I was obliged to play the magistrate.

ROBERT. Egad! you took my breath away.

KINCHELA. Didn't I do it well — my devotion to you and the precious charge you left in my care exposes me to suspicion. I am watched, and to preserve my character for loyalty I am obliged to put on airs — Oh! I'm your mortal enemy, mind that.

ROBERT. You!

KINCHELA. Every man, woman, an' child in the County Sligo believes it, and hate me. I've played my part so well that your sister an' Miss O'Neal took offence at my performance.

ROBERT. No — ha! ha!

KINCHELA. Yes! ho! ho! they actually believe I am what I am obliged to appear, and they hate me cordially. I'm the biggest blackguard —

ROBERT. You! my best friend!

KINCHELA. Oh, I don't mind it! The truth is, I'm afeard if I had betrayed my game to them — you know the weakness of the sex — they could not have kept my secret.

ROBERT. But surely Father Dolan?

KINCHELA. He is just as bad.

ROBERT. Forgive them.

KINCHELA. I do.

ROBERT. The time will come when they will repent their usage of you.

KINCHELA. Ay, by my soul it will.

ROBERT. They have no friend, no protector but you; for now my chains will be more firmly riveted than ever.

KINCHELA. Whisht! you must escape.

ROBERT. It is impossible! How? When?

KINCHELA. Tonight! Tomorrow, when you are removed to Sligo jail, it might not be so aisy; but tonight I can help you.

ROBERT. To regain my freedom?

KINCHELA. Is that ship that landed you within reach?

ROBERT. Every night at eight o' clock she runs in shore, and lies-to off the coast; a bonfire lighted on Rathgarron Head is to be the signal for her to send off her skiff under the ruins of St. Bridget's Abbey to take me on board.

KINCHELA. That signal will be fired tonight, and you shall be there to meet the boat.

ROBERT. Do you, indeed, mean this, Kinchela? Will you risk this for my sake?

KINCHELA. I will lay down my life if you want it. (*They embrace.*)

ROBERT. What am I to do?

KINCHELA. Give me your promise that you will not breathe a word to a mortal about the place I am going to propose; neither to your sister, nor to Miss O'Neal, nor, above all, to Father Dolan.

ROBERT. Must I play a part to deceive them?

KINCHELA. My life and liberty are staked in the attempt as well as yours.

ROBERT. I give you the promise.

KINCHELA. Tonight your quarters will be changed to the old Gate Tower. Wait till dark, then use this chisel to pick out the stones

293

that form the back of the fireplace in your room. The wall there is only one course thick. (*He gives* ROBERT *chisel.*)

ROBERT. You are sure?

KINCHELA. Conn, the Shaughraun was shut up in that cell last spring, and he picked his way out through the wall with a two-pronged fork. He was creeping out of the hole he had made when they caught him. The wall has been rebuilt, but the place has not served as a prison since.

ROBERT. Where shall I find myself when I am outside?

KINCHELA. In a yard enclosed by four low walls. There's a door in one of them that's bolted on the inside. Open that, and you are free.

ROBERT. Are there no sentinels posted there?

KINCHELA. No; but if there is, there's a double-barrelled pistol that will clear your road. (*Hands pistol —* ROBERT *examines it.*) (*Aside*) I'll put Duff outside that door; there'll be an end to him.

ROBERT (*returning the pistol*). Take it back. I will not buy my liberty at the price of any man's life. I will take my chance; but, stay, the signal on Rathgarron Head! Who will light the bonfire? (CONN *playing outside.*) Hark! — 'tis Conn! Do you hear? Poor fellow! he is playing 'I'm under your window, darling'. Ah! I can employ him. How will he do it? — how will I send him word?

KINCHELA. You won't betray me?

ROBERT. No, no. (*Writes in his book — repeats as he writes.*) 'Be at Rathgarron Head tonight, beside the tar barrel'. What signal can I give him that he will be able to hear or see across the bay?

KINCHELA (*dictating*). 'When you hear two gunshots on St. Bridget's Abbey, light the fire'.

ROBERT (*writes*). 'When you hear two gunshots —' For that purpose I accept it.

KINCHELA (*gives* ROBERT *the pistol — aside*). No matter for what purpose. He will use it to serve mine. If they hang him for murdering Harvey Duff, I'll be afther killing two birds wid one stone.

ROBERT. Beg the sentry to come here.

KINCHELA. What are you going to do?

ROBERT. You will see. (*Taking out coins.*)

KINCHELA. Here is the Sergeant. (*He enters.*)

ROBERT (*folding money in the paper*). Will you give these few pence to the fiddler outside, and beg the fellow to move on? (*Hands paper to* SERGEANT.)

SERGEANT. The men encourage him about the place. (*Going*) There's Father Dolan and Miss O'Neal outside; they have got a pass to see you.

ROBERT. Show them in. (*Exit* SERGEANT.)

KINCHELA. Now, watch their manner towards me; but you won't mind a word they say against me.

ROBERT. Not I. I know you better. (*Fiddle outside.*) Hush! 'tis Conn. He has got the letter. Listen — 'I'll be faithful and true!' Ay, as the ragged dog at your heels is faithful and true to you, so you have been to me, my dear, devoted, loving playfellow — my wild companion!

(*Enter* ARTE *and* FATHER DOLAN.)

ARTE. Robert! (*Embracing him.*) Mr. Kinchela!

FATHER DOLAN. I am surprised to find you here, sir!

KINCHELA (*aside to* ROBERT). D'ye hear?

ROBERT (*aside to* KINCHELA). All right!.

ARTE. You do not know that man.

KINCHELA. Oh, yes he does. I've made a clane breast of it.

ROBERT. Yes, he has told me all.

KINCHELA. How I brought all of you to ruin, and betrayed my trust, and grew rich and fat on my plundher. I defy you to make me out a bigger blackguard than I've painted myself, so my sarvice to you! (*Exit.*)

FATHER DOLAN. When St. Patrick made a clean sweep of all the venomous reptiles in Ireland, some of the vermin must have found refuge in the bodies of such men as that.

ROBERT. This is the first uncharitable word I ever heard you utter.

FATHER DOLAN. Heaven forgive me for it, and him! You're right, my vocation is to pray for sinners, not revile them.

ARTE. And mine to comfort you, and not to bring our complaints to add to your misfortune.

ROBERT. Hold up your hearts; mine is full of hope.

FATHER DOLAN. Hope; where do you find it?

ROBERT. In her eyes! You might as well ask me where I find love. I was in prison when I stood liberated on American soil. The chains were on my soul when I stretched it longing across the ocean towards my home; but now I am in prison, this narrow cell is Ireland. I breathe my native air, and am free!

FATHER DOLAN. They will send you back again.

ARTE. Ah, sure! the future belongs to heaven, the present is our own.

FATHER DOLAN. I believe I was wrong to come here at all. I feel like a mourning band on a white hat! (*Music.*)

(*Enter* SERGEANT.)

SERGEANT. Sorry to disturb you, sir, but we are ordered to shift your quarters. You will occupy the room in the Old Gate Tower. The guard is waiting, sir, when you are ready. (*Exit.*)

ROBERT. I am prepared to accompany you.

ARTE. Must we leave you?

ROBERT. For the present, but we shall soon meet again. Now will you indulge a strange humour of mine? You know the ruins of St. Bridget's Abbey, where we have so often sat together?

ARTE. Can I ever forget it! We go there often; the place is full of you.

ROBERT. Go there tonight at nine o' clock.

ARTE. I'll offer up a prayer at the old shrine.

ROBERT. Ay, with all my heart, for I may want it.

FATHER DOLAN. What do you mean? There's some mischief going on; I know it by his eye. He used to wear the same look when he was going to give me the slip and be off from his Latin grammar to play truant with Conn the Shaughraun.

ROBERT. Ask me nothing, for I can answer you only one word — hope!

FATHER DOLAN. 'Tis the finest word in the Irish language.

ARTE. There's a finer — faith. (*Embraces* ROBERT.)

FATHER DOLAN. And love is the mother of those heavenly twins. I declare my heart is lifted up between you, as if your young ones were its wings.

ROBERT. Good night, and not for the last time.

(*Enter* SERGEANT.)

ARTE. Good night!

FATHER DOLAN. I leave my heart with you. God bless you!

ROBERT. Remember, tonight at the Abbey.

ARTE (*aside*). At nine o' clock.

ROBERT. I shall be there. (*She utters an exclamation.*) Hush!
(*Exit* FATHER DOLAN *with* ARTE.)
You gave the money to the fiddler?

SERGEANT. Yes, sir!

ROBERT (*aside*). Ah, I forgot! Conn can't read. What will he do to decipher my note — bah! I must trust to his cunning to get at the contents. Now, sergeant, lead me to my new cell in the Gate Tower. (*Exeunt.*)

ACT TWO: SCENE FOUR

MRS O'KELLY's *Cabin — Exterior — Evening.*

CONN (*entering with a paper in his hand*). There's writing upon it. Himself has sent me a letther. Well, this is the first I ever got, and well to be sure, (*Looks at it — turns it over*) I'd know more about it if there was nothing in it; but it's the writin' bothers me.

MRS O'KELLY (*entering*). Is that yourself, Conn?

CONN (*aside*). I wish it was somebody else that had book larnin'.

MRS O'KELLY. What have you there?

CONN. It's a letther the masther is afther writin' to me.

MRS O'KELLY. What's in it?

CONN. Tuppence was in it for postage. (*Aside*) That's all I made out of it.

MRS O'KELLY. I mane what does he say in it?

CONN. Rade it!

MRS O'KELLY. You know I can't.

CONN. Oh, ye ignorant ould woman!

MRS O'KELLY. I know I am; but I took care to send you to school, Conn, though the sixpence a week it cost me was pinched out of my stomach and off my back.

CONN. The Lord be praised that ye had it to spare, anyway.

MRS O'KELLY. Go on, now — it's makin' fun of yer ould mother ye are. Tell me what the young masther says.

CONN. In the letther?

MRS O'KELLY. Yes!

CONN (*aside*). Murther, what'll I do? (*Aloud*) Now, mind, it's a sacret. (*Reads*) 'Collee costhum garanga caravat selibubu luckli rastuck pig'.

MRS O'KELLY. What's that — it's not English!

CONN. No; it's in writin' — now kape that to yourself.

CLAIRE (*entering*). Conn, there is some project on foot tonight to

297

rescue my brother — don't deny it — he has almost confessed as much to Father Dolan. Tell me the truth!

CONN. I would not decaive you. Well, I promised not to say a word about it; but there it is, rade it for yourself.

CLAIRE (*looks at note*). Yes; 'tis his hand.

CONN. I knew it in a minute.

CLAIRE. It is in pencil.

CONN (*to* MRS O'KELLY). I told you it wasn't in English.

CLAIRE (*reads*). 'Be at Rathgarron Head tonight beside the tar-barrel. When you hear two gunshots in St. Bridget's Abbey, light the fire'.

CONN. You wouldn't believe me when I read that to you ten minutes ago. The signal fire that's to tell the ship out at sea beyant there to send a boat ashore to take him off.

MRS O'KELLY. Oh, blessed day! Is it to escape from gaol he'd be thrying?

CLAIRE. He has told my cousin to be in the ruins tonight.

CONN. There's going to be a scrimmage, an' I'm not in it. I'm to be sent away like this. It's too hard on me intirely. Oh, if I could find somebody to take my place and fire the signal! I'd bring him out of gaol this night if I had to carve a hole in the wall wid my five fingers!

CLAIRE. I'll take your place!

CONN. You will!

MRS O'KELLY. Oh, Miss Claire, don't go; there'll be gun-shots and bagginets! This is one of Conn's divilments, and ye'll be all murthered! Oh, weir asthru! what'll I do?

CONN. Will ye hould your whisht?

MRS O'KELLY. No, I won't! I'll go an' inform agin ye before ye get into throuble, and then, maybe, they'll let you off aisy.

CLAIRE. Here comes the Captain. For heaven's sake, pacify her! She will betray us.

CONN. Well, come inside, mother, darlin'! There! I'll stop wid ye. Will that aise your mind? You onsensible ould woman!

MRS O'KELLY. Conn, don't lave me alone in the world! Sure, I've nobody left but yourself, an' if ye're taken from me, I'll be a widdy!

CONN. Then both of us will be two widdys together. Don't ye hear Miss Claire is going to take my place?

MRS O'KELLY. Heaven bless an' purtect every hair of your head, miss! And will ye, indeed, spend one night by the mother's fireside?

CONN. And I'll play all the tunes you love the best on my fiddle till I warm the cockles of your ould heart! (*Sings.*)

> 'Oh, then, Conn, my son, was a fine young man,
> An' to every one cuish he had one shin;
> Till he wint to the wars of a bloody day,
> When a big cannon-ball whipped his two shins away,
> An' my rickety a —' (*Exeunt.*)

(*Enter* ARTE *and* MOLINEUX.)

ARTE. I have invited the Captain to pass the evening at Suil-a-beg, but he will not be persuaded.

MOLINEUX. I may not desert my post till the police arrive from Sligo to relieve me of my charge.

ARTE. But your soldiers are there?

MOLINEUX. Soldiers will not move without orders; besides, my men have such a distaste for this business, that I believe, if left to defend their prisoner against an attempt to rescue him, they would disgrace themselves.

ARTE (*aside to* CLAIRE). Get him away; an attempt will be made tonight.

CLAIRE (*aside*). Leave us!

ARTE. Well, good day, Captain. Come Claire. (*Exit.*)

CLAIRE (*after a pause*). It is a lovely evening.

MOLINEUX. You are not going home.

CLAIRE. Not yet. I shall take a stroll along the shore to Rathgarron Head!

MOLINEUX. Alone?

CLAIRE. I suppose so!

MOLINEUX. Is it far?

CLAIRE. No!

MOLINEUX. Not far — ahem! would you allow me to go part of the road beside you? (*Music.*)

CLAIRE. Pray do not neglect your duty on my account, besides I want to consult my feelings in solitude, uninfluenced by your presence.

MOLINEUX. That sweet confession gives me hope and courage.

CLAIRE. Good night! leave me, light a meditative cigar, and go back to your duty. (*He takes out cigar-case.*) Leave me to wander by the light of the rising moon, and sit down on the rocks beside the sea.

(*He takes match — she lights one and keeps the box.*)

MOLINEUX. How good you are! — an angel!

CLAIRE. Of light. There, good night!

MOLINEUX. Good night! (*She goes off very slowly — he moves away — turns.*) Oh, if I had some excuse to follow her a little way. (*He brushes the light away from the end of his cigar, and calls.*) Miss Ffolliott, pardon me, but my cigar is out, and you have my matches — ha! ha! sorry to trouble you, oh, don't come back, I beg. (*Follows her out.*)

CONN (*leaping out of window and fastening shutters*). I've locked the dure an' barred the shutters!

MRS O'KELLY (*inside*). Conn, let me out!

CONN. Behave now, or I'll tell the neighbours you've been drinking. Good night, mother! (*Runs out.*)

ACT TWO: SCENE FIVE

The interior of prison, large window, old fireplace, small window, door. Through window is seen exterior and courtyard — night.

ROBERT (*discovered listening*). They are relieving guard. (*Drum*) I shall not receive another visit for the night. Now to work — that must be the wall Kinchela spoke of. I see some new brick-work there, but where shall I land? Is there much of a drop into the yard below? (*Looks out of window.*) The wall hides the interior — can I reach this window?

   (*Climbs to large window as* CONN *is seen at small window.*)

CONN. Divil a sowl about this side of the tower. There's a light in his cell. I wondher is he alone? No matter. Where's my iron pick? Now to make a hole in the wall. (*Disappears.*)

ROBERT. The yard seems to be on a level of this chamber. Where's my chisel? (*Begins to work.*) The mortar is as soft as butter. This was done by government contract. It's an ill wind that blows nobody any — what's that? It sounds like somebody at work on the wall. Can it be a rat? (*Listens.*) No, it stops now. (*He works.*) There it goes again. (*He stops.*) Now it stops. It echoes me as if there was some one on the other side. Oh, Lord! my heart sinks at the thought. I'll satisfy myself. (*He goes to large window.*)

CONN (*appearing at small window*). There's a rat in the chimbley! Gorra! maybe I'm all wrong, and himself is not in it at all.

   (*Looks in at window as* ROBERT, *having climbed, looks out.*)

ROBERT. I can't see round the corner, but there seems to be no one there.

CONN. Divil a sowl in it. I wish I could see crooked. Here goes again. (*Disappears.*)

ROBERT. The noise has ceased — it was a rat. (*Works.*) This brick is loose enough to pull out, but if that goes, the rest seem

301

shaky. They will fall together. (*A mass of brickwork falls, and discovers* CONN.) Conn!

CONN. Whisht! Who the devil would it be? Asy, for the love of heaven, now! Come asy! I've left Tatthers in the guardroom with the men. Stop till I break another coorse of bricks for ye.

(*The scene moves — the Prison moves off, showing the exterior of Tower with* CONN *clinging to the walls, and* ROBERT *creeping through the orifice. The walls of the Yard appear to occupy three-fourths of stage.*)

(*Enter* KINCHELA, HARVEY DUFF, *and four* CONSTABULARY. CONN *and* ROBERT *disappear into the Yard.*)

KINCHELA. Whisht! there's a noise in the yard! This door is boulted on the inside; but there's a pile of rubbish shot against the back wall that we can see over. (*To* HARVEY DUFF.) Harvey Duff, you will stand there; the rest come wid me.

(KINCHELA *and four* CONSTABULARY *go up and disappear behind wall.* HARVEY DUFF, *holding a short carbine ready, stands with his back to wall.*)

HARVEY DUFF. Now, my fine fellow — now, Mr. Robert Ffolliott, you said we must meet once again on this side o' the grave, and so we will — ho! ha! (CONN's *head appears over the wall.*) I don't think you'll like this meetin' more than the last.

(CONN, *after signing to* ROBERT, *gets sitting on the wall, with his legs dangling just above* HARVEY DUFF's *head.*)

You tould me to have my sowl ready. I wondher if yours is in good condition. Whisht! I hear the boults moving. He is coming! He is — Conn —

(CONN *drops on* HARVEY DUFF's *shoulders, who falls forward with a cry,* CONN *over him. Door opens.* ROBERT *appears.*)

CONN. Run, sir, run! I've got him safe!

(ROBERT *leaps over* HARVEY DUFF's *body, and runs off. At the same moment* CONSTABULARY *mount the back wall — leap into Yard. The* SERGEANT, *with a light, appears at the breach in the wall of the Prison.*)

SERGEANT. Where is he?

CONN. I've got him — here he is, niver fear! Hould him fast.

(*The* CONSTABULARY *enter by the door in the wall, and seize* HARVEY DUFF, *who is lying on his face.*)

CONN. Don't let him go! Hould him down! (*Runs off as* CONSTABULARY *raise* HARVEY DUFF.)

KINCHELA (*coming round corner*). Where is he? Harvey Duff! Bungling fools, he has escaped!

(HARVEY DUFF *gesticulates faintly, and falls back.*)

ACT TWO: SCENE SIX

The Coot's Nest — Night.

ROBERT (*entering*). Escaped once more, and free! My disguise is secreted here in some nook of the rocks — in Conn's cupboard, as he calls it — but I cannot find it in the darkness. I hope the poor fellow has got clear away. I would not have him hurt for my sake. (*A whistle*) Ah! there he is! (*He whistles*) Thank you, kind Providence, for protecting him. Here he comes — leaping from crag to crag like a goat.

CONN (*entering*). Hurroo! tare an' ages, Masther, jewel, but we did that well! But it goes agin my conscience that I did not crack the skull of that thief when I had him fair and asy under my foot. I'll never get absolution for that!

ROBERT. We must not remain in this place — it is the first they will search. I must make my way to St. Bridget's Abbey at once; there Arte is waiting for me. Where is my great coat, my hat, and beard?

CONN. I have the bundle snug inside. But sure, the Captain knows you in that skin. Didn't he meet you here? It will be no cover for you now. Whisht!

ROBERT. What! Do you hear anything?

CONN. No; but Tatthers does. I left the baste to watch on the cliff above. There agin; d'ye hear him? He's givin' tongue; lie close I'll go see what it is. (*Exit.*)

ROBERT. Yonder is the schooner, creeping in with the tide. I can reach the ruins by the seashore; the rocks will conceal me. Then one brief moment with my darling girl —
    (*Re-enter* CONN, *with the coat, hat, and beard.*)

CONN. Speak low; they are close by.

ROBERT. The constabulary?

CONN. Yes; and wid them those smugglin' thieves, Mangan, Sullivan, and Reilly; they are guidin' the polis — the mongrel curs go do that! They know every hole in these rocks.

ROBERT. But the signal — who will set the match to the tarbarrel on Rathgarron Head?

CONN. Nivir fear, sir. Miss Claire is there by this time, and waitin' beside it, lookin' an' listenin' for the two gunshots your honour will fire in the ruins beyant.

ROBERT. Where is my pistol? (*Feeling in his pocket.*) I cannot find it — gone! No; it cannot be lost. By heaven! it must have fallen from my pocket as I climbed the wall! (*Putting on disguise.*)

CONN. Murther alive! what will we do now?

ROBERT. I must swim out to the schooner.

CONN. It is a mile, an' agin the tide. Stop! will ye lave it to me, and I'll go bail I'll find a way of getting them two shots for me? Ah, do, sir! Only this once give me my head an' let me go.

ROBERT. What do you propose to do?

CONN. Don't you recollect once when the Ballyragget hounds couldn't find a fox, after dhrawing every cover in the country, damn a hair of one could they smell, an' the whole field lookin' blazes. You were masther of the hunt. 'What will we do at all?' says you. 'You shall have a fox', ses I, and I whipt in a red herring into the tail o' me coat and away I wint across the fields.

ROBERT. Ha! ha! I remember it well.

CONN. You, he! an' a devil a one on the whole field but yourself knew that there was a two-legged fox to the fore. Now, I'll give them vagabones another taste of the red herring. I will cut in and cross your scent. I'll lade them off, nivir fear, and be jabers I'll show them the finest run of the huntin' sayson.

ROBERT. How, Conn, how?

CONN. Asy — look where they are coming down the cliff; slip out this way, quick, before they catch sight of us; when we get round the corner we must divide up; you go by the shore below, I'll take the cliff above. (*Exit* ROBERT.) Begorra, it isn't the first time I've played the fox! (*Exit.*)

ACT TWO: SCENE SEVEN

Rathgarron Head. Enter CLAIRE *and* MOLINEUX.

CLAIRE. Here we are at Rathgarron Head — are you not tired?

MOLINEUX. I don't know. If you asked if I was dying I should say I could not tell. I feel as if it was all a dream, in which I am not myself.

CLAIRE. Who are you, then?

MOLINEUX. Somebody much happier than I can ever be. I wish I could describe to you the change that has taken place in me since we met.

CLAIRE. Oh, I can understand it, for I feel the very — (*Stops suddenly.*)

MOLINEUX. Eh! what do you feel?

CLAIRE. Do you see those ruins on yonder headland? That is St. Bridget's Abbey! A lovely ruin! How effective is that picture, with the moon shining on it!

MOLINEUX. Splendid, no doubt; but when I'm beside you I cannot admire ruins or moonshine. The most effective picture is on this headland, and I cannot detach my eyes from the loveliness that is before me.

CLAIRE (*aside*). I cannot stand this. I never played so contemptible a part.

MOLINEUX. What is the matter?

CLAIRE. Go home — go away! Why did you come here?

MOLINEUX. My dear Miss Ffolliott, I hope I have not been intruding on you. If I have, I pray you forgive me. I will retrace my steps. (*Going.*)

CLAIRE. No, stop!

MOLINEUX (*returning*). Yes.

CLAIRE. I encouraged you to follow me.

MOLINEUX. I fear I pressed myself upon you.

CLAIRE (*aside*). Oh! why is he so willingly deceived! His gentleness and truth make me ashamed of the part I play.

MOLINEUX. I have said or done something to offend you. Tell me what it is. It will afford me much pleasure to plead for pardon for what I haven't done.

CLAIRE. You want to know what ails me?

MOLINEUX. Yes.

CLAIRE. Do you see that tar-barrel?

MOLINEUX. Good gracious! what has a tar-barrel got to do with my offence?

CLAIRE. Nothing; but it has everything to do with mine.

MOLINEUX (*aside, after a pause*). I wonder whether there's madness in the family?

CLAIRE. Do you see that tar-barrel?

MOLINEUX. I see something like a tar-barrel in that pile of brush-wood.

CLAIRE. Will you oblige me with a match?

MOLINEUX. Certainly. (*Aside*) There's no doubt about it. So lovely, and yet so afflicted! I feel even more tenderly towards her than I did!

CLAIRE. If I were to ask you to light that bonfire, would you do it?

MOLINEUX. With pleasure. (*Aside*) It is the moon that affects her. I wish I had an umbrella.

CLAIRE. Captain Molineux, my brother has escaped from the prison, guarded by your soldiers. He is now in yonder ruins. This pile of fuel, when lighted, will be the signal for the schooner you see yonder to send a boat ashore to take off the fugitive. I have been a decoy to entice you away from your duty, so that I might deprive your men of the orders they await to pursue my brother, who has broken gaol. Now do you understand my conduct?

MOLINEUX. Miss Ffolliott!

CLAIRE. Now do you understand why every tender word you have spoken has tortured me like poison? Why every throb in your honest heart has been a knife in mine?

MOLINEUX. I thought you were mad. I fear 'tis I have been so.

CLAIRE. You can redeem your professional honour; you can repair the past. I have no means here of lighting that beacon. If the signal is not fired, my brother will be recaptured; but the blood that revolts in my heart against what I am doing is the same that beats in his. He would disdain to owe his liberty to my duplicity and to your infatuation. There's your road. Good night! (CLAIRE *goes out hastily — music.*)

MOLINEUX. So I have been her dupe! No — she was not laughing at me! (*Looks off.*) She is not laughing at me, as one who — see where she has thrown herself on the ground. I hear her sobs. I cannot leave her alone, and in this wild place; and yet what can I do to — poor thing! — I — I don't know how to act. There again — oh, what a moan that was! I cannot let her lie there! (*Hastily exit.*)

ACT TWO: SCENE EIGHT

The Ruins of St. Bridget's Abbey — ARTE *discovered kneeling before the broken shrine,* MOYA *is looking down the cliff.*

MOYA. There is not a sound to be heard barrin' the sheam of the waves as they lick the shore below.

ARTE. I was afraid to come here alone. Even with you beside me I tremble.

MOYA. There's something moving in the strand below. Look, miss, it is a goat! There it is, creeping under the shadow of the rocks.

ARTE. I see nothing!

MOYA. Whisht! I'll give him the offis. (*She sings.*)
    (*Enter* HARVEY DUFF, REILLY, SULLIVAN *and* DOYLE. *They carry carbines.*)

HARVEY DUFF. There they are — there's a pair of them — 'tis Moya with her. The constabulary are giving him chase, but here is where he will run to airth — here's the trap, and there's the bait.

ARTE. There! there he is! and see those men pursue him! Fly, Robert, fly!

MOYA. They will catch him, miss.

ARTE. No; he gains upon them — he has turned the point. He will scale the cliff on this side.

HARVEY DUFF (*seizing* MOYA). Reilly, take hould of her — quick.
    (REILLY *seizes* ARTE — *drags her to front of shrine.*)

ARTE. Who are you, who dare to lay hands on me? Do you know who I am?

HARVEY DUFF. Yes, I do, well enough. You are the sweetheart of the man we want to catch.

ARTE (*crying*). Robert! Robert! beware!

HARVEY DUFF. Stop her screeching — she'll scare him off.

MOYA. Help! murther! thieves! fire!

HARVEY DUFF. Hould your yelp, or I'll choke you — och — gorra — she's bitin' me!

MOYA (*cries*). Don't come here — don't come. (*Stifles her cries with the handkerchief he tears from her head.*)

KINCHELA (*looking over the parapet*). We have lost his track.

HARVEY DUFF. Aye, but we have found it — here he comes — stand close now, an head him off. (KINCHELA *disappears. The figure of* ROBERT FFOLLIOTT *is seen emerging from one side of the ruin. He advances,* SULLIVAN *and* DOYLE *both start out. He looks from side to side.*) Stand and surrender! (*He rushes up the ruins to the window at the back.*) Fire, Sullivan — give it to him. Why don't you fire? (SULLIVAN *fires — the shot takes effect — he falls, and rolls down to a lower platform.*) Ha! ha! that stopped him — he's got it. (*He raises himself, and faintly tries to escape by a breach in the wall.*) Give it to them again! (DOYLE *fires — he falls, and tumbling from one platform to another, rolls on his face on the stage —* REILLY *releasing* ARTE *at second shot.*)

KINCHELA (*appearing*). What are you about? Those two shots are the signal, and see the fire is lighted on Rathgarron Head.

HARVEY DUFF. 'Tis lighted too late!

KINCHELA. No; for there comes the boat from the schooner, and see that man in the water swimming towards her? 'Tis Robert Ffolliott escaped!

HARVEY DUFF. Oho! if that's Robert Ffolliott, I'd like to know who's this?

CONN (*raising himself slowly, and allowing his hat and beard to fall back, and facing* HARVEY DUFF, *with a smile on his blood-stained face*). The Shaughraun!

> (*He falls back.* MOYA, *who has been released by* HARVEY DUFF *in his astonishment, utters a faint cry, and throws herself upon the body. A ray of moonlight striking through the ruined window, falls on the figure of the saint on the Shrine, whose extended arms seem to invoke protection over the prostrate group.*)

END OF ACT TWO

ACT THREE: SCENE ONE

MRS O'KELLY's *Cottage — Music. Enter* FATHER DOLAN *and* CLAIRE.

FATHER DOLAN. Be patient, Claire!

CLAIRE. Patient! My cousin has disappeared — no trace of Arte can be found — Moya has also been spirited away — perhaps murdered, as they murdered Conn!

FATHER DOLAN (*knocking at door*). Mrs O'Kelly, 'tis I — Father Dolan.

(*Enter* MRS O'KELLY.)

MRS O'KELLY. Blessings on your path; it always leads to the poor and to the sore-hearted!

FATHER DOLAN. This is a sad business! Did you hear why they killed your poor boy?

MRS O'KELLY (*sobbing*). Because he'd got a fine shute of clothes on him; they shot at the man that wasn't in it, and they killed my poor boy!

CLAIRE. Did they bring him home insensible?

MRS O'KELLY. No, Miss — they brought him home on a shutter, an' there now he lies wid Tatthers beside him. The cratur' won't let a hand go near the body.

CLAIRE. Poor fellow! he met his death while aiding my brother to escape.

(*Enter* MOLINEUX.)

You see what your men have done?

MRS O'KELLY. It was the polis, not the sodgers, murthered him. Don't blame the Captain, Miss; God bless him, he was in my cabin before daylight — he never spoke a word, but he put five golden pounds in my hand; and, thanks to himself, my Conn will have the finest wake this day, wid Nancy Malone and Biddy Madigan for keeners — There'll be ating and drinking, and six of the O'Kellys to carry him out as grand as a mimber o'

310

parliament — Och hone! — my darlin' boy, it will be a grand day for you, but your poor ould mother will be left alone in her cabin buried alive while yourself is going to glory — och — o-o — hone! (*Exit, crying.*)

MOLINEUX. In the name of Bedlam does she propose to give a dance and a supper party in honour of the melancholy occasion?

CLAIRE. They are only going to wake poor Conn!

FATHER DOLAN. And your five pounds will be spent on whiskey, and cakes, and consolation, and fiddlers, and grief, and meat and drink for the poor.

MOLINEUX. What a compound! You Irish do mix up your —

CLAIRE (*interrupting him*). Never mind what we mix — have you discovered any traces of Arte and Moya? Have you done anything?

MOLINEUX. I've been thinking.

CLAIRE. Thinking! what's the good of thinking? My cousin Arte has been stolen — where is she? The country is full of police and soldiers, and yet two girls have been carried off under your noses — perhaps murdered, for all you know or care — and there you stand like a goose, thinking!

MOLINEUX. Pray don't be so impetuous. You Irish —

CLAIRE. I won't be called 'You Irish'.

MOLINEUX. I beg your pardon; you do make me so nervous.

CLAIRE. Oh, do I! My impetuosity didn't make you nervous last night, did it? No matter; go on — a penny for your thoughts.

MOLINEUX. If Miss O'Neal and Moya were present in the ruins when Conn was shot, they must have been witnesses of the deed. Since then they have disappeared. It struck me that those who killed the boy must have some reason for removing all evidences of the transaction.

CLAIRE. Well?

FATHER DOLAN. He is right.

MOLINEUX. I questioned the constabulary, and find they had no hand in it. The deed was done by a posse of fellows assembled to assist in the pursuit by a police agent named Harvey Duff!

FATHER DOLAN and CLAIRE. Harvey Duff!

MOLINEUX. You know him?

CLAIRE. He has thought it out while we have been blundering. Blinded by our tears, we could not see; deafened by our complaints, we could not hear. (*Seizes both his hands.*) Forgive me!

MOLINEUX. There she goes again! I've done nothing to deserve all this.

311

CLAIRE. Nothing! You have unearthed the fox, you have drawn the badger; now the rogue is in sight our course is clear.

MOLINEUX. It is? I confess I don't see it!

FATHER DOLAN. These two girls were the only witnesses of the deed!

CLAIRE. And that is why they have been carried off?

FATHER DOLAN. No one else was present to prove how Conn was killed.

CONN (*looking out of window*). Yes; I was there!

ALL. Conn alive!

CONN. Whisht! No; I'm dead!

FATHER DOLAN. Why, you provoking vagabond — is this the way you play upon our feelings? Are you hurt?

CONN. I've a crack over the lug, an' a scratch across the small o' me back. Sure, Miss, if I hadn't dhrawed them to shoot, you'd have never had the signal.

MOLINEUX. Brave fellow! how did you escape?

CONN. I'll tell you, sir; but — whoo! gorra! — dead men tell no tales, an' here I am takin' away the characther of the corporation. When the masther got out of jail, there was Kinchela an' his gang waitin' outside to murdther us. We ga' them the slip; and while the masther got off, I led them away afther me to St. Bridget's. Then, afther I got them two shots out of them, I rouled down an' lay as quiet as a sack of pitaties.

CLAIRE. Arte and Moya were in the ruins?

CONN. They were standing by and thrying to screech blue murther. 'Stop their mouths', said a voice that I knew was Kinchela's. Sullivan and Reilly whipt them up and put them on a car that was waitin' outside. After that, sorra a thing I remember till I found myself laid out on a shutter, wid candles all around me, an' whiskey bottles, an' cakes, an' sugar, an' lemon, an' tobacco, an' bacon, an' snuff, an' the devil in all! I thought I was in heaven.

FATHER DOLAN. And that's his idea of heaven! And you let your poor ould mother believe you dead? — you did not relieve her sorrow?

CONN. Would you have me spile a wake afther invitin' all the neighbours?

MOLINEUX. Will you allow me on this occasion to say 'You Irish —'

CLAIRE. Yes, and you need not say any more.

CONN. Then I remember the polis would be wanting me for the share I had in helping the masther to break jail. Ah, sir, don't let on to the mother — she'd never hould her whisht; an' I want to be dead, if you please, to folly up the blackguards that have hould of Moya and Miss O'Neal.

MOLINEUX. Do you know the place where these ruffians resort?

CONN. I'm conceited I do.

FATHER DOLAN. I'll answer for him; he knows every disreputable den in the country.

CONN. What would you do now, if I didn't?

CLAIRE. Here comes your mother with the mourners.

CONN. Hoo! she'll find some of the whiskey gone. (*Disappears.*)

CLAIRE. Now what's to be done?

MOLINEUX. I will proceed at once to Ballyragget House, and see Mr. Kinchela. I will confront him with this evidence.

CLAIRE. You don't know him.

MOLINEUX. I think I do; but he does not know me.

CLAIRE. You will fight him.

MOLINEUX. Oh, no. I looked in his eye; there's no fight there; men who bully women have the courage of the cur — there's no pluck in them. I shall take a guard and arrest him for aiding your brother to escape, that he might murder him safely during his flight.

CLAIRE. Who can prove it?

(*Enter* ROBERT.)

ROBERT. I can!

CLAIRE. Robert! (*Embrace.*)

FATHER DOLAN. Good gracious, what brings you back?

ROBERT. The news I heard on board the schooner. A pardon has been granted to the Fenian prisoners.

CLAIRE. A pardon!

MOLINEUX. I congratulate you, sir. (*Shakes hands with* ROBERT.) Oh, by Jove! Excuse my swearing, but a light breaks in upon me — Kinchela knew of this pardon. I'll go to Ballyragget House at once.

ROBERT. I have just come from there. I went to tax him with his villainy. He has fled.

MOLINEUX. I thought there was no fight in him.

CLAIRE. But Arte is in his power.

ROBERT. Arte in his power! what do you mean?

CLAIRE. He loves her — he has carried her off.

ROBERT. My wife and her fortune. Ha! he played for a high game.

MOLINEUX. And on finding he could not win, he stole half the stakes.

FATHER DOLAN. This man is in league with a desperate crew, half

313

ruffians, half smugglers. Their dens, known only to themselves, are in the bogs and caves of the sea-shore.

ROBERT. I'll unearth him wherever he is. (*Music*.) I'll hunt him with every honest lad of the County Sligo in the pack, and kill him like a rat.

MOLINEUX. I'll send over to Sligo, and get a warrant to arrest the fellow. I like to have the law on my side. If we are to have a hunt, let us have a licence. Where shall I find you?

FATHER DOLAN. At my house.

CLAIRE (*to* ROBERT, *who offers his arm to her*). No, give your arm to Father Dolan.

FATHER DOLAN. Free, and at home! Heaven be praised!

ROBERT. Not free till Arte is so. (*Exit with* FATHER DOLAN.)

CLAIRE (*after watching them off, turns, and advances rapidly to* MOLINEUX). What's your Christian name, or have you English such things amongst you?

MOLINEUX. Yes, my Christian name is Harry!

CLAIRE. Harry!

(*Kissing him. She runs off. He assumes a military position and marches off, whistling 'The British Grenadiers'.*)

VOICES (*outside*). Oh! Ohone! Oh, hould up. Don't give way.

(*Enter* MRS O'KELLY, NANCY MALONE, BIDDY MADIGAN, *and* PEASANTS, DOYLE *and* WOMEN, *six or seven* MEN, *one* WOMAN. *They exeunt at once.*)

MRS O'KELLY. You are kindly welcome. The dark cloud is over the house, but —

NANCY. We come to share the sorrow that's in it this hour.

BIDDY. It will be a fine berryin', Mrs O'Kelly. There will be a grand waste of victuals.

MRS O'KELLY. Step inside, ma'am.

(*They all enter the cabin. Then* REILLY, *followed by* SULLIVAN — *music. The voices of the Keeners are heard inside singing an Irish lament. During this, other* PEASANTS *and* GIRLS *enter in couples, and go into cabin — Scene changes.*)

ACT THREE: SCENE TWO

MRS O'KELLY's *Cabin (interior); Door; fireplace.* CONN *is lying on a shutter, supported by an old table, a three-legged stool, and a keg. Table covered with food and drinking cups, plates of snuff, jugs of punch, lighted candles in bottles, &c. — Tableau of an Irish Wake. A group of women around* CONN. MRS O'KELLY *seated;* MRS MALONE *and* REILLY *near her.* SULLIVAN, DOYLE, *and peasantry (male and female) at table. The* WOMEN *are rocking to and fro during the wail.*

CHORUS — *'The Oolaghaun'*

Male voices —

     Och, Oolaghaun! — och, Oolaghaun!
       Make his bed both wide and deep!
     Och, Oolaghaun! — och, Oolaghaun!
       He's only gone to sleep!

Female voices —

     Why did ye die? — oh, why did ye die?
       And lave us all alone to cry?

Together —

     Why did ye die? — why did ye die?
       Laving us to sigh, och hone!
     Why did ye die? — why did ye die?
       Oolaghaun! — oh, Oolaghaun!

(During the following rhapsody the music of the wail and the chorus subdued recurs as if to animate the Keeners.)

BIDDY. Oh, oh, oho! *(Rocking herself.)* Oh, oo, Oolaghaun!
   The widdy had a son — an only son — wail for the widdy!
ALL *(chorus).*
     Why did ye die? — why did ye die?

315

BIDDY. I see her when she was a fair young girl — a fine girl, wid a child at her breast.

ALL (*chorus*).
> Laving us to sigh! Och, hone!

BIDDY. Then I see a proud woman wid a boy by her side. He was as bould as a bull-calf that runs beside of the cow.

ALL (*chorus*).
> Why did ye die? — why did ye die?

BIDDY. For the girl grew ould as the child grew big, and the woman grew wake as the boy grew strong. (*Rising, and flinging back her hair.*) The boy grew strong, for she fed him wid her heart's blood. Ah, hogoola! Where is he now? Cowld in his bed! Why did ye die? (*Sits.*)

ALL (*chorus*).
> Laving us to sigh! Och, hone!

BIDDY. None was like him — none could compare, and — Good luck to ye, gi' me a dhrop of something to put the sperret in one, for the fire's getting low.

> (SULLIVAN *hands her his jug of punch.*)

MRS O'KELLY. Oh, oh! it's mighty consolin' to hear this. Mrs Malone, you are not ating.

NANCY. No, ma'am, I'm drinkin'. I dhrink now and agin by way of variety. Biddy is not up to herself.

REILLY. Oh! wait till she'll rise on the top of a noggin.

BIDDY (*after drinking places the jug beside her, and rises on low stool*). He was brave! he was brave! he was open-handed! he had the heart of a lion, and the legs of a fox.

> (CONN *takes the jug, empties it quietly, and, unobserved by all, replaces it on stool.*)

BIDDY. His voice was softer than the cuckoo of an evening, and sweeter than the blackbird afther a summer shower. Ye colleens, ye will nivir hear the voice of Conn again. (*Sits and blows her nose.*)

CONN (*aside*). It's a mighty pleasant thing to die like this, once in a way, and hear all the good things said about ye afther you're dead and gone, when they can do you no good.

BIDDY. His name will be the pride of the O'Kellys for evermore.

CONN (*aside*). I was a big blackguard when I was alive.

BIDDY. Noble and beautiful!

CONN (*aside*). Ah! go on out o' that!

BIDDY (*taking up her jug*). Oh, he was sweet and sthrong — Who the devil's been at my jug of punch?

MRS O'KELLY (*sobbing and rising*). Nobody is dhrinkin' — yez all despise the occasion – if yez lave behind ye liquor enough to swim a fly – oh, hoo! There's a hole in your mug, Mr. Donovan, I'd be glad to see it in the bottle – oh, hoo! (*Knock without.*)

SULLIVAN. What's that? (*The door is opened.*)

(*Enter* MOLINEUX – *they all rise.*)

MOLINEUX. I don't come to disturb this – a – melancholy – a-entertainment – I mean a – this festive solemnity.

MRS O'KELLY (*wiping own chair for him with her apron*). Heaven bless you for coming to admire the last of him. Here he is – ain't he beautiful?

MOLINEUX (*aside*). The vagabond is winking at me. I've great mind to kick the keg from under him and send him reeling on the floor. (SULLIVAN *offers him snuff.*)

MRS O'KELLY. How often have I put him to bed as a child, and sung him to sleep! Now he will be put to bed with a shovel, and oh! the song was nivir sung that will awaken him.

MOLINEUX. If any words could put life into him, I came here to speak them. (*Music.*) Robert Ffolliott has been pardoned and has returned home a free man.

ALL. Hurroo! hurroo!

MOLINEUX. But his home is desolate, for the girl he loves has been stolen away. The man who robbed him of his liberty first, then his estate, has now stolen his betrothed.

ALL. Who is it?

MOLINEUX. Mr. Corry Kinchela. The ruffians who shot that brave fellow who lies there were led by Kinchela's agent, Harvey Duff.

ALL. Harvey Duff!

(BIDDY *seizes axe* – MRS O'KELLY *crosses to fire for poker,* DONOVAN *gets scythe and kneels sharpening it with stone* – *Tableaux.*)

(MOLINEUX *first encounters the edge of axe* – *stepping back, confronts* MRS O'KELLY *with the poker* – *which she flourishes savagely* – *and eyes with his glass* DONOVAN *sharpening scythe.*)

BIDDY. Harvey Duff sent my only boy across the say!

DONOVAN. I've a long reckoning agin him; but I've kept it warm in my heart.

MRS O'KELLY. An' I've a short one, and there it lies! (*Pointing to* CONN.)

ALL. Where is he?

MOLINEUX. Kinchela and his men are hiding in some den, where they hold Miss O'Neal and Moya prisoners.

317

ALL. Moya Dolan?

MOLINEUX. The niece of your minister! — the sweetheart of poor Conn! My men shall aid you in the search; but you are familiar with every hole and corner in the county — you must direct it. Robert Ffolliott awaits you all at Suil-a-beg to lead the hunt — that is, after you have paid your melancholy respects to the Shaughraun.

MRS O'KELLY. No; you could not plaze him bether than to go now; bring back the news that you have revenged his murder, an' he'll go under the sod wid a light heart.

ALL. Hurroo! To Suil-a-beg! — To Suil-a-beg.

> (*Exeunt rapidly, all but* REILLY *and* SULLIVAN. MOLINEUX *gives* CONN *a pinch of snuff — he sneezes.* REILLY *and* SULLIVAN *turn and watch him off.*)

REILLY. Sullivan, you must warn Kinchela. Quick! There's not an hour to lose.

SULLIVAN. Where shall I find him?

> (CONN *rises and listens.*)

REILLY. At the Coot's Nest! The lugger came in last night. Tell him to get aboard — take the two women wid him, for he'll have to run for his life.

SULLIVAN. Ay, and, bedad, for ours too! If he's caught we're in for it.

> (CONN *creeps to door, and locks it very quietly.*)

REILLY. I feel the rope around my neck.

SULLIVAN. The other end is chokin' me.

> (*As they turn to go they face* CONN, *they stagger back astonished.*)

BOTH. Murdher, alive!

CONN. That's what I am. Murdher, alive! that will live to see you both hanged for it. (*Advances.*) I'll be at your wake, and begorra I'll give you both a fine characther.

> (SULLIVAN *and* REILLY *rush to the door.*)

Asy, boys, asy! The dure is fast an' here's the key. You're in a fine thrap, ho! ho! You made a mistake last night.

> (SULLIVAN *whispers to* REILLY.)

Take it asy now.

> (*They rush to the table and each seizes a knife.*)

REILLY. Did ye forget ma bouchal that ye're dead?

SULLIVAN (*advancing slowly*). Sure, if we made a mistake last night — we can repair it now!

CONN. Oh — tare an' ages — what'll I do? (*Retreats behind table.*)

REILLY. We'll just lay you out agin comfortable where you wor. Devil a sowl will be the wiser.

CONN. Help! help!

(REILLY *advances and receives the contents of a mug then* SULLIVAN, *who gets the plate of snuff in his eyes.* CONN *jumps over the table, and makes for the window at back.*)

REILLY. Screeching won't save ye! They are miles away by this time.

CONN (*rushing to window, and dashing the shutters open*). Help!

(REILLY *and* SULLIVAN *drag* CONN *back by the hair of his head and throw him down.*)

SULLIVAN. Shut the windy! I'll quiet him!

(MOLINEUX *appears at window.*)

MOLINEUX (*presenting revolver*). Drop those knives! (*A pause.*) Do you hear what I said — drop those knives! (*They let their knives fall.*) Now open the door!

CONN. There's the key! (*Hands it to* REILLY. REILLY *doggedly unlocks the door.* MOLINEUX *appears at door and enters.*) Help me up! (*To* SULLIVAN.) The hangman will do as much for you, one day. (SULLIVAN *helps* CONN *to rise.*)

MOLINEUX. Now! (REILLY *makes a start as if he would escape.*) If you put your head outside the cabin, I'll put a bullet in it! What men are these?

CONN. Two of Kinchela's chickens. They know the road we want to thraval.

MOLINEUX. Take that! (*Hands* CONN *the revolver.*) Do you know how to use it?

CONN. I'll thry! (*Turns to* SULLIVAN.) What part of the world would you like to be sent to? (*Pointing weapon at him.*)

MOLINEUX (*drawing his sword and turning to* REILLY). Attention, my friend! Now put your hands in your pockets! (*Repeats —* REILLY *obeys him.*) Now take me direct to where your employer, Mr. Kinchela, has imprisoned Miss O'Neal; and if, on the road, you take your hands out of your pockets, and attempt to move beyond the reach of my sword, upon my honour, as an officer and a gentleman, I shall cut you down! Forward! (*Exeunt.*)

CONN. Attintion! Put your hand in my pocket. (SULLIVAN *obeys him.*) Now take me straight to where Moya Dolan is shut up; an' if ye stir a peg out o' that on the road, by the piper that played before Julius Caesar, I'll save the country six feet of rope. (*As they go out scene changes.*)

ACT THREE: SCENE THREE

Hogan's Shanty. Enter ARTE *and* MOYA.

ARTE. 'Tis getting dark. Will they keep us another night in this fearful place?

MOYA. I don't care what becomes of me. I wish they would kill me, as they killed Conn — I've nothin' to live for!

ARTE. I have! I'll live to bring Kinchela to the dock, where he brought my Robert. I'll live to tear the mask from his face!

MOYA. I'd like to put my ten commandments on the face of Harvey Duff — the murdherin' villain, if I should only live to see him go up a ladder, and spoil a market.

(*Enter* KINCHELA.)

KINCHELA (*crossing to* ARTE). You look pale; but I see you kape a proud lip still, Miss O'Neal. You despise me now, but afther another month or two, never fear, we'll get on finely together.

ARTE. Do you dream you can keep us here for a month? Why, before a week has passed there's not a sod in the County Sligo but will be turned up to search for us, and then we'll see who'll look the paler, you or I.

KINCHELA. Before midnight you will be safe on board a lugger that lies snug beside this shanty, and before daylight you and I will be on our way to a delightful retirement, where you and I will pass our honeymoon together.

MOYA. And what's to become of me? (*Music.*)

(*Enter* HARVEY DUFF, *with* MANGAN *and* DOYLE.)

HARVEY DUFF. I'll take care of you! The wind is fair, and the tide will serve in an hour. Come, ladies, all on board is the word, if you plaze.

(MANGAN *and* DOYLE *seize* ARTE *and* MOYA.)

ARTE. Kinchela, I implore you not to add this cowardly act to your list of crimes! Release me and this girl, and, on my honour, I will bear no witness against you, nor against any concerned in last night's work.

KINCHELA. It is too late.

ARTE (*struggling with* DOYLE). Kinchela, if you have any respect — any love for me, will you see me outraged thus?

HARVEY DUFF (*aside to* KINCHELA). Ffolliott has returned.

KINCHELA. Ah! Away with them!

MOYA (*to* MANGAN). Lave your hould, I'll go asy!

(*Drops her cloak while struggling with* MANGAN, *she releases herself and boxes his ears.* ARTE *is taken off first by* DOYLE.)

HARVEY DUFF. Robert Ffolliott is pardoned, and he's huntin' the bogs this minute, with half the County Sligo at his back.

KINCHELA. Never fear, they can't discover this place till we are gone. No one ever knew of it but our own fellows.

HARVEY DUFF. And Conn, the Shaughraun.

KINCHELA. He is wiped out.

HARVEY DUFF. We are safe.

KINCHELA. Go, keep watch on the cliff while I get these girls aboard.

HARVEY DUFF. I'll be onaisy in my mind till we are clear o' this. (*Exit.*)

KINCHELA. Robert Ffolliott pardoned, afther all the throuble I took to get him convicted? And this is the way a loyal man is thrated! I am betrayed. No matther; if he can recover his estate, he can't recover his wife. She is mine — mine! She hates me now, but I concait she'll get over that. (*Exit.*)

(*Enter* CONN *and* SULLIVAN.)

CONN. Not a sowl in it — you deceive me!

SULLIVAN. No, they are here! (*Points to the cloak.*) What's that?

CONN. Moya's cloak! (*He picks it up — releases* SULLIVAN, *who creeps off while* CONN *examines cloak.*) 'Tis hers — she's here! Oh, he's slipped out of my pocket — he's off — gone to rouse up the whole pack! What'll I do? Where can I hide until the masther an' the Captain come up? They can't be far behind. If I could get behind one of them big hogsheads, or inside one o' them. Whisht! there was a cry. 'Twas Miss O'Neal's voice. I am only one agin twenty, but I'll make it lively for them while it lasts! (*Exit.*)

ACT THREE: SCENE FOUR

*Shed looking out upon a Rocky Cove. The topmasts of a ship
are seen over the edge of the precipice. Bales, kegs, hogsheads,
naval gear lie about — music — Break of day. Enter* HARVEY DUFF
rapidly. He looks round, and he is very pale.

HARVEY DUFF. Kinchela, hurry — quick!
    (*Enter* KINCHELA.)
KINCHELA. What's the matter?
HARVEY DUFF. I was watching on the cliff above, where I could
    hear the shouts of the people in the glen as they hunted every
    hole in the rocks. I could see Robert Ffolliott and Miss Claire
    hounding them on; when I turned my eyes down here, and on
    this very place where we are standing I saw —
KINCHELA. Who?
HARVEY DUFF. Conn, the Shaughraun!
KINCHELA. You are mad with fright.
HARVEY DUFF. So would you be, if you saw a dead man as plain
    as I saw him. (*Distant cries and shouts.*) D'ye hear them? —
    they are coming close to us!
KINCHELA. Go back to your post on the cliff, and keep watch
    while I get these women on board. We have no time to lose.
    Mangan! Doyle!
HARVEY DUFF (*who has been looking round*). I'll be on my oath
    I saw him here! (*Exit.*)
    (*Enter* MOYA *and* MANGAN.)
MOYA. Where do you want me to go?
KINCHELA. On board that ship below there.
MOYA. Do you think I'm a fly, or a seagull?
KINCHELA. You see this ladder? — by that road you can gain the
    ledge below. There we'll find a basket — we'll send you down
    like a bucket in a well.
MOYA. If I don't choose to go down?

KINCHELA. Then you'll be carried, my beauty!

MOYA. Stand off!

KINCHELA. Tie her hands. Mangan, go get me a taste of rope! (*He seizes her.* MANGAN *exits.*)

MOYA. Help! help! Is there nivir a man within reach of my voice?

KINCHELA. Mangan, bring the rope, curse you!

MOYA. Help! murdher! fire!

> (*A shot is fired from the hogshead.* KINCHELA *throws up his hands, staggers, falls.* MOYA *utters a cry and falls on her knees, covering her face with her hands. The hogshead rises a little — advances to* MOYA, *and covers her like an extinguisher. The legs of* CONN *have been seen under the barrel as it moves. Enter* MANGAN *with the rope,* DOYLE *with* ARTE, SULLIVAN. SULLIVAN *kneels over* KINCHELA.)

MANGAN. Who fired that shot?

DOYLE. She has killed him, and escaped!

ARTE. Brave girl! she has avenged me.

SULLIVAN. He's not dead. See, he moves! There's life in him still. (*Shouts outside.*)

DOYLE. They are coming! away wid ye to the lugger. Quick!

SULLIVAN. Must we lave him here?

DOYLE. We can't carry him down the ladder.

> (*During the foregoing* ARTE *creeps to the back.*)

SULLIVAN. Everyone for himself; the devil take the hindmost. (*Going up to rock piece.*)

ARTE (*who has lifted the end of the ladder*). Stop where you are! (*Throws the ladder over.*) I have been your prisoner; now you are mine! (*Shouts outside nearer.*)

> (*The men look bewildered from side to side, and then rush off.* CONN *pops his head out from the top of the hogshead. and looks out.*)

CONN. Is that you, Miss?

ARTE. Conn, where's Moya?

CONN. She's inside. (*Shouts.*)

> (CONN *disappears, raises the hogshead. They emerge from it.*)

HARVEY DUFF (*outside*). Kinchela, away wid you — quick!

CONN. Stand aside. Here comes the flower of the flock. (*Shouts.*)

> (*They retire —* ARTE *to behind shed.*)
> (HARVEY DUFF *rushes on, very pale.*)

HARVEY DUFF. The crowd are upon us; we are betrayed! What's the matter, man? Up, I tell you! Are you mad or drunk? Stop, then; I'm off. (*Runs to back.*) The ladder gone! — gone! (*Runs to* KINCHELA.) Sphake, man! What will we do? — what does it mean?

(ARTE *appears*, MOYA *from behind hogshead*.)

MOYA. It means that the wind has changed and the tide doesn't serve.

ARTE. It means that you are on your way to a delightful retirement, where you and he will pass your honeymoon together.

HARVEY DUFF (CONN *advances to his side*). The murdher's out.

CONN. And you are in for it. (*Shouts outside.*) D'ye hear them cries — the hounds are on your track, Harvey Duff!

HARVEY DUFF. What will I do? What will I do?

CONN. Say your prayers, if ever you knew any — for your time is come. Look! There they come — down the cliff side. Ha! they've caught sight of you.

(*Shouts* — HARVEY DUFF *rushes up to the edge of the precipice, looks over, wrings his hands in terror*.)

CONN. D'ye see that wild ould woman, wid the knife? that's Bridget Madigan, whose son's life you swore away.

HARVEY DUFF. Save me! — you can — they will tear me into rags. (*To* ARTE, *on his knees*.)

CONN. D'ye know Andy Donovan? that's him with the scythe! You sent his brother across the say! (*Shouts outside.*) Egorra, he knows you! Look at him.

HARVEY DUFF (*on his knees, to* CONN). Spare me! pity me!

CONN. Ay, as you spared me! — as you spared them at whose side you knelt before the altar! — as you pitied them whose salt you ate, but whose blood you dhrank! There's death coming down upon you from above! — there's death waiting for you below! Now, *informer*, take your choice!

(*Shouts* — HARVEY DUFF, *bewildered with fright, and running alternately to the edge of the cliff and back to look at the approaching crowd, staggers like a drunken man, uttering inarticulate cries of fear*.)

(*The crowd, headed by* BIDDY MADIGAN, NANCY MALONE, *rush in. Uttering a scream of terror,* HARVEY DUFF *leaps over the cliff. The crowd pursue him to the edge and lean over. Enter* ROBERT FFOLLIOTT, CLAIRE, FATHER DOLAN *and* CONSTABULARY. *Enter* MOLINEUX *followed by* SERGEANT *and six* SOLDIERS *with* MANGAN, SULLIVAN, *and* DOYLE *in custody*.)

ROBERT (*embracing* ARTE). Arte!

CLAIRE. Has the villain escaped?

MOLINEUX. I've bagged a few; but I've missed the principal offender.

CONN. I didn't — there's my bird.

FATHER DOLAN. Is he dead?

(MOLINEUX *approaches* KINCHELA, *and examines him.*)

MOLINEUX. I fear not; the bullet has entered here, but it has struck something in his breast. (*Draws out a pocket-book.*) This pocket-book has saved his life!

(*He hands it to* FATHER DOLAN, *who opens it, draws out letter, and reads.*)

KINCHELA (*reviving and rising*). Where am I?

MOLINEUX. You are in custody.

KINCHELA. What for?

MOLINEUX. For an attempt to assassinate this gentleman!

KINCHELA. He was a felon, escaping from justice!

FATHER DOLAN. He was a free man, and you knew it, as this letter proves!

(*The crowd utter a cry of rage, and advance towards* KINCHELA. FATHER DOLAN *stands between them and him.* KINCHELA *flies for protection to the* CONSTABULARY.)

KINCHELA. Save me – protect me!

FATHER DOLAN (*facing the crowd*). Stand back! – do you hear me. Must I speak twice?

(*The crowd retire, and lower their weapons.*)

MOLINEUX. Take him away!

KINCHELA. Yes, take me away quick – don't you hear? or them divils won't give you the chance. (*Exit with* CONSTABULARY.)

MRS O'KELLY (*outside*). Where's my boy? Where is he?

CONN. Och, murdher – here's the ould mother! Hide me!

(*Enter* MRS O'KELLY.)

MRS O'KELLY. Where is he – where is my vagabone?

(FATHER DOLAN *brings him forward by the ear.*)

Oh, Conn, ye thief o' of the world – my boy – my darlin'! (*Falls on his neck.*)

CONN. Whisht, mother, don't cry. See this – I'll never be kilt again.

MOYA. Sure, if he hadn't have been murdhered, he couldn't have saved us.

MRS O'KELLY. And after letting me throw all the money away over the wake!

MOLINEUX. Turn the ceremony into a wedding. I really don't see you Irish make much distinction.

CLAIRE. I believe that in England the wedding often turns out the more melancholy occasion of the two.

MOLINEUX. Will you try?

ROBERT. He has earned you, Claire. I give my consent.

ARTE. But what is to become of Conn. Father Dolan will never give his consent.

FATHER DOLAN (*to* CONN). Come here. Will you reform?

CONN. I don't know what that is, but I will!

FATHER DOLAN. Will you mend your ways, and your coat? No; you can't! How do I know but that you will go poaching of a night?

CONN. Moya will go bail I won't.

FATHER DOLAN. And the drink?

MOYA. I will take care there is no hole in the thimble.

FATHER DOLAN. I won't trust either of you — you have deceived me so often. Can you find anyone to answer for you?

CONN. Oh, murdher! What'll I do? Devil a friend I have in the world, barrin Tatthers. (MOYA *whispers in his ear.*) Oh! they won't!

MOYA. Thry! Thry!

CONN (*to the audience*). She says you will go bail for me.

MOYA. I didn't!

CONN. You did!

MOYA. I didn't!

CONN. You are the only friend I have. Long life t'ye! — Many a time have you looked over my faults — will you be blind to them now, and hould out your hands once more to a poor Shaughraun?

OMNES. Hurroo! Hurroo! (*Till curtain.*)

MY PRETTY MAID

Where are you going, my pretty maid?
Where are you going, my pretty maid?
I'm going a-milking, sir, she said,
Sir, she said, Sir, she said,
I'm going a-milking, sir, she said.

Then what is your fortune, my pretty maid?
What is your fortune, my pretty maid?
My face is my fortune, sir, she said,
Sir, she said, Sir, she said,
My face is my fortune, sir, she said.

JUG OF PUNCH

If I were dead an' in my grave,
No other tombstone would I have
But I'd dig a grave both wide and deep,
With a jug of punch at my head and feet.
                    Ri tooral loo.

CONN, MY SON

Oh, then, Conn, my son, was a fine young man,
An' to every one cuish he had one shin;
Till he wint to the wars of a bloody day,
When a big cannon-ball whipped his own shins away,
An' my rickety a —

THE OOLAGHAUN

Male Voices —

Och, Oolaghaun! — och, Oolaghaun!
Make his bed both wide and deep!
Och, Oolaghaun! — och, Oolaghaun!
He's only gone to sleep!

Female Voices —

Why did ye die? — oh, why did ye die?
And lave us all alone to cry?

Together —

Why did ye die? — why did ye die?
Laving us to sigh, och hone!
Why did ye die? — why did ye die?
Oolaghaun! — oh, Oolaghaun!

ROBERT EMMET

CAST OF CHARACTERS

The play opened on 5 November 1884, at
McVicker's Theatre, Chicago

Robert Emmet   JOSEPH HAWORTH
Michael Dwyer   DION L. BOUCICAULT
Lord Kilwarden, *Chief Justice of the*
   King's Bench
Lord Norbury
Right Honorable John Philpot Curran
Captain Norman Claverhouse   DONALD ROBERTSON
Major Sirr   JOSEPH A. WILKES
Andy Devlin   DION G. BOUCICAULT
Michael Quigley   GUS REYNOLDS
Patrick Finerty
Father Donnelly
Brangan
Sarah Curran   HELEN LEIGH
Ann Devlin   MARY E. BARKER
Tiney Wolfe   NINA BOUCICAULT
Lady Katherine Yorke
English Officers and Soldiers, Irish Soldiers, Peasants and Citizens,
Link-boys and Footmen, a Drummer, Jury, Barristers, Jailers, etc.

SYNOPSIS OF SCENES

ACT ONE: SCENE ONE.   Rathfarnham, near Dublin. A Garden.
             SCENE TWO.   A street in Dublin.
             SCENE THREE.   A room in Dublin Castle.
ACT TWO: SCENE ONE.   The Cottage at Butterfield Lane.
             SCENE TWO.   A Gorge in the mountains near the
                            Scalp.
             SCENE THREE.   The Camp at the Scalp.
             SCENE FOUR.   A room in the house of Mrs Emmet.
             SCENE FIVE.   College Green and the Houses of
                            Parliament.
ACT THREE: SCENE ONE.   A room in the Vice-Regal Lodge,
                            Phoenix Park.
             SCENE TWO.   Ann Devlin's Cottage in Butterfield
                            Lane.
             SCENE THREE.   Glenmalure.
             SCENE FOUR.   The interior of Father Donnelly's — a
                            small Chapel.
             SCENE FIVE.   The yard outside Father Donnelly's
                            house.
ACT FOUR: SCENE ONE.   The Court House, Green Street.
             SCENE TWO.   A Prison.
             SCENE THREE.   The Bull Inn.
             TABLEAU —   Brangan's Wharf, Ring's End, near
                            Dublin.
             TABLEAU —   The yard of Kilmainham.

ACT ONE: SCENE ONE

Rathfarnham, near Dublin. A garden; night; on the R.H. is a house; the windows are lighted. A low wall across stage at back; a door in it L. of C. Shrubs R.H. up stage; spades, a scythe and garden tools R. against wall. Music.

Enter from the house, coming from the back, ANN DEVLIN; *she looks around with caution, then crosses to door on wall; listens; then recrosses to C. towards house; calls.*

ANN. Miss Sarah!
    (*Enter* SARAH CURRAN *from the house.*)
    Spake low.
SARAH. Is he there? (*Crosses to door L.C.*)
ANN. I don't know — rightly! I hear two voices whispering outside.
SARAH. He always brings some trusted follower with him to stand on guard during our meeting. It may be Dwyer, or Quigley.
ANN. No; it is a strange voice. (*Two knocks at door.*) Whist! that is not his signal. Go outside awhile until I see who is in it?
    (SARAH *runs back into the house;* ANN *opens the door. Music ceases. Enter* MAJOR SIRR; *his scarlet uniform is covered in a long cloak; his face is shaded by his hat.*)
ANN. What do you want?
SIRR. I want a word with your master.
ANN. He is engaged entertaining a party of friends at dinner.
SIRR. His friends must excuse him. I bring this summons from the Castle. (*Hands her a letter.*)
ANN (*taking it, reads superscriptions by the light from the hall*). 'To the Right Honorable Philpot Curran, on his majesty's service.'
SIRR. That business brooks no delay. See that it reaches him quickly.

334

(*Exit* ANN *into house.* SIRR *goes rapidly to door in wall.* QUIGLEY *and three men enter.*)

SIRR. You three fellows pass round to the porch of the house; don't show yourselves until you are called to act. (*Exeunt the three* OFFICERS *behind the shrubs and off R.U.E.*) You are certain the man we seek will present himself here tonight?

QUIGLEY. Never fear. Shure he's afther sendin' me ahead of himself to see the road is clear. He is hidin' now sumwhere widin' cast of my voice. He won't show up until he gets the offis from Miss Curran. Her maid, Ann Devlin raps three times agin that dure in the wall. He will answer wid one rap; and she opens it.

SIRR. And lets our bird into the trap? Return to your post outside.

QUIGLEY. More power, Major. (*Exit door in wall.*)
(*Enter* CURRAN *from the house, with the letter opened in his hand; he is in full court dress.*)

CURRAN. You are the bearer of this letter from the lord justices? Be good enough to precede me to them. I follow you at once. Tell their lordships I am at your heels. It is mighty provoking to be called away at such an hour.
(*Re-enter* ANN; *with his coat and hat.*)
Where is my daughter?

ANN. In her room, sir. (*He takes his hat and coat.*)

CURRAN. Explain to her the motive of my departure. She will see my guests cared for during my absence. (*Music. Exit into house, followed by* ANN.)

SIRR. Your daughter, Mr. Curran, will entertain a guest here tonight that I'll take care of! (*He disappears behind the shrubs C.*)
(*Re-enter* ANN *from house.*)

ANN (*looking round*). He is gone. (*She crosses to door, then knocks three times; a pause; one knock is heard; she opens it.*) Who is there?

QUIGLEY (*appearing*). Meself.

ANN. Quigley! Did you see a strange man lavin' this dure awhile ago?

QUIGLEY. I did. Shure I was houlding his horse for him while he was in here. Who was he?

ANN. A messenger from the castle!
(*Re-enter* SARAH.)

SARAH. Has he come?
(*Enter* ROBERT EMMET; *he wears a long blue coat.*)

335

ROBERT. Sarah!

SARAH. Robert! (*Embracing him.*)

ANN (*to* QUIGLEY). Stand aside.

(*Exit* QUIGLEY, *by door in wall. She locks the door after him.*)
I'll wait in the hall beyant, and watch over yez. I'm not aisy in
me mind tonight. (*Exit.*)

ROBERT. You tremble in my arms. You should fear nothing when
so sheltered! Or is it the chill night air? Let me protect my
treasure. (*Wraps his cloak around her.*) So! Its folds may retain
the sweet warmth of your form. Sit there — let me hear your
voice and look into your eyes. There are tears in them.

SARAH. They are for my father whom I deceive. They are for my
love, that I hide away as if it were a shame! During your long
absence in France, he constantly urged me to receive the
addresses of lovers to whom I could offer no objection,
excepting that there was another here in my heart; my old, old
playfellow to whom I had given my life long, long ago. You
came back at last, but in secret, concealing from everyone
your presence in Ireland. What is this enterprise in which you
are engaged?

ROBERT. It is one in which the fortunes and lives of others
associated with me are involved; all we possess is staked on an
event which will be assured within the next few days. Till then
be patient, dear one!

SARAH. Be it as you will! But I feel it is all so gloomy around us.
Oh, for the honest daylight when I can show the love of which
I am so proud; you have placed a crown of jewels on my head —
the emblem of a girl's nobility, but I may not wear it openly!

ROBERT. Oh, my love! what if we fail? What if I become broken
in fortune? a fugitive from my home? an exile from my
country?

SARAH. You have no fortune but my love; you cannot be bank-
rupt there; you have no home, but my heart; no country but
my arms; how can you be a fugitive or an exile?

(*Re-enter* ANN.)

ANN. Get him away quick for his life! Major Sirr with his
following are searching the house.

ROBERT (*rising*). Major Sirr! here!

ANN. 'Twas himself was in it a while ago! away wid ye!

(*The three men at back appear,* ANN *seizes the scythe and as
they try to intercept* ROBERT's *escape by the door in the
wall, she sweeps it round as if mowing at their legs.*)
Stand back! or I'll make twins of any one of ye.

(*They retreat.* SARAH *runs to the door and vainly tries to turn the key.*)

SARAH. It's rusted in the lock. I cannot turn it.

(*Enter* MAJOR SIRR, *R. at house, standing on step; he points a pistol at* ROBERT.)

SIRR. Robert Emmet. In the King's name I arrest you.

(EMMET *retreats to L.* SARAH *runs between* SIRR *and* EMMET, *and taking off the cloak holds it out so as to hide her lover.*)

SARAH. Unlock the door. I can't.

SIRR. Stand aside, girl!

(*As he advances, she advances to meet him. He tries to pass her, but she swiftly throws the cloak over him and the pistol, while* ROBERT *succeeds in escaping by the door;* SIRR *disengages his arms, and replaces the pistol in his belt.*)

The man you have aided to escape is the leader of a rebel movement that threatens this city with bloodshed and plunder. His confederates are watching his signal on the Wicklow Hills. The woods and bogs of Kildare are alive with them. You will have to answer for the blood that will flow from the streets of Dublin into the Liffey this night.

SARAH. Let there be oceans of it, rather than one drop of his.

(*Enter* NORMAN CLAVERHOUSE, *his sword is drawn.*)

CLAVERHOUSE. I was seeking for you, Miss Curran! Nae sooner your gude father had excused himself and left us, than a posse of black devils, savin' your respect, raided the hoose wi' whingers and pistols, searchin' everywhere. Even your ain rooms wor no sacred from their conseederations.

SIRR. My men have their warrant, Captain Claverhouse, for what they did.

CLAVERHOUSE. And I had mine, for dhrivin' them before me from the premises.

SIRR. I shall report your interference in this matter to the authorities at the Castle. (*Beckons to his men.*) We tracked a leader of the rebel movement to this house, to which he comes nightly, and in secret. We found him at the feet of that lady. By her assistance he escaped. But within ninety days he will be at the foot of the gallows. Good night.

ANN. Bad night to you, you prowlin' kite!

SIRR. Never fear, Ann Devlin. I'll get you in my clutches some day, and then I'll make it hot for you, my beauty!

(*Exeunt* OFFICERS *at door.*)

ANN. Never fear, Henry Sirr, the devil will get yer in his clutches

337

some day, and then he will make it hotter for you, my
dandy.

(*Exit* SIRR; *he carries* ROBERT's *cloak on his arm.* ANN
locks the door after him.)

SARAH. Leave us, Ann. (*Exit* ANN.)

CLAVERHOUSE. Miss Curran, I have made no disguise of my
feelings toward yourself; and your father encouraged me to
hope that, one day, I might persuade you to share my name;
for I have loved you verra-verra dearly!

SARAH. I — I know it.

CLAVERHOUSE. Was it true what that man said about you?

SARAH. Yes!

CLAVERHOUSE. You love this — other one?

SARAH. Ever since I knew how to love. I am sorry for you,
Norman. I tried very hard to care for you, as my father wished
me to do, but this other one returned — and then I knew I
had no heart to give you.

CLAVERHOUSE. You could na help it more than I can help loving
you. If I canno' reap the harvest of your life, I can assist in
bringing it home. I can ha' some share in your happiness. It seems
your lover that meets you here is implicated in this rebellion?

SARAH. He told me that he was engaged in some secret enterprise,
but until now I did not suspect its nature.

CLAVERHOUSE. Before tomorrow it will be known in Dublin that,
concealed in the house of the Right Honorable Philpot Curran,
his majesty's attorney general and member of the Privy Council,
the police discovered the rebel leader.

SARAH. My father is innocent. He had no knowledge, no
suspicion of his presence here. I —

CLAVERHOUSE. Will he protect his honour behind his daughter's
shame?

SARAH. What can I do? Oh, Norman! help me to shield him from
the consequence of my guilty folly!

CLAVERHOUSE. It is a cruel task you put upon me, Sarah. There is
no way but one. You maun gae to this lover tonight. You must
fly from your home. Seek him out.

SARAH. Go to him? — to Robert? — to Mr. Emmet?

CLAVERHOUSE. Aye, if that be his name. Bribe him wi' yerself
to abandon this cause. Take him away beyond the seas. Your
flight will clear your father from any suspeecion and will
explain the presence of Mr. Emmet in the house! 'Tis hard on
me to say the words; it is verra bitter, dear. Before this night is
past you must bear my rival's name.

SARAH. Oh, Norman, Norman! You deserve a better woman than I am. (*Calls.*) Ann, Ann — my hat and shawl! She will accompany and protect me.

CLAVERHOUSE. No; I will! I will never quit your side until you are Robert Emmet's wife.

(*Enter* ANN.)

CLAVERHOUSE. Where does he lodge?

ANN. In my father's cabin — Butterfield Lane. I'll meet you there, and bring with me what things she will need.

CLAVERHOUSE. Come!

ANN (*looking after them as they go out at garden door*). Every step she takes she treads upon his heart and he lets her do it. If Dwyer found I was fond of any other boy, he'd squeeze the life out o' my throat; and I'd love him all the betther for killin' me! I'd die happy.

ACT ONE: SCENE TWO

A street in Dublin. Enter QUIGLEY.

QUIGLEY (*calls*). Finerty — Pat. Finerty — Pat, ye divil, are ye
there?
    (*Enter* FINERTY.)
FINERTY. Is it yerself, Mike? Well, what luck?
QUIGLEY. Is he here? Has he come back?
FINERTY. Who?
QUIGLEY. Emmet.
FINERTY. Come back! D'ye mane to tell me he was not tuk?
QUIGLEY. No; bad luck to it! — he escaped.
FINERTY. Did he show fight?
QUIGLEY. No; but he showed two pair of heels. The thrap was all
right, and baited wid the girl. The Major's following — ten
blackguards, not including him nor meself — were in an' around
the house when I led him along fair and aisy into the middle of
them.
FINERTY. How did he escape from thim all?
QUIGLEY. Divil a know, I know! for, shure I could not shew in it.
I was outside in the lane, houlding the Major's horse, stooping
down wid my ear close agin the dure, when I heard Sirr's voice
calling on him to surrender. The dure flew open. I felt a fut
on me back, and before I could rise a cry, Emmet was in the
saddle, and out of sight.
FINERTY. Bad cess to the chance! Won't we lose the reward for
his capture — a hundred pounds — that the Major promised
should be paid to us tonight at the Castle?
QUIGLEY. Why not? We led thim to the bird; we gave thim a fair
shot; if they missed it we are not to blame. Whist! may I never
— but is not this himself?
    (*Enter* EMMET.)
ROBERT. Quigley, you saved my life! That horse you held ready

for me at the door was a godsend! Without it, the men stationed in the lane to intercept me would have made me prisoner. How did you escape?

QUIGLEY. While they were afther yer honour I made off, aisy enough. I rode straight to our depot at the Bull Inn where I left the animal in charge of Andy Devlin. (*Go to C.*)

(*Enter* ANDY.)

ANDY. More power, sir. I've got him safe in the stables. Your honour was wantin' a purty baste to carry himself to Wicklow Hills tonight where the boys are expectin' you.

ROBERT. We won't be there by midnight. We hold a council of war to decide on our plan of action. I have prepared them to submit to the staff the manifesto to the people, the list of our forces and place of action. Surely, I placed them in my breast. I cannot have lost — no, no! Where can I have placed them? If lost, and they should fall into the hands of — Ah! my cloak! They were in a breast pocket. I left it with Miss Curran. Run, Andy — quick to Rathfarnham — for your life; find your sister, Ann; get from her the cloak; bring it to Butterfield Lane, where you will find me.

ANDY. Will I take the Major's horse, sir?

ROBERT. No; the manner of my escape is known, and search is doubtless being made for the brute. He will be looked for and recognised.

ANDY. Awow! I left him wid Larry Fox and a pail of white paint. By this time the bast wud not know himself, for he's got three stockins and a bald face on him. Whoo, yer sowl! The Major will want another mount. I'll sell him this one tomorrow if yer honour's afraid to back him.

ROBERT. Be off, you imp, and be careful of the papers. (*Exit* ANDY.) This thoughtless act of mine might undo us all. He who undertakes the business of a people should have none of his own. Quigley — Finerty — you will be present tonight at the camp. The hours are pregnant with our cause. We cannot tell at what moment it may spring into life. (*Exit.*)

QUIGLEY. Pat, yer sowl! Our fortune is made! It is not one hundred pounds, but a thousand pounds, I am goin't to claim for this night's work.

FINERTY. A thousand pounds, Mike? What for?

QUIGLEY. For the list of our forces; for the plans of attack; for all the purtiklars of the whole business.

FINERTY. I see. You mane we should follow Andy Devlin and seize the papers on him?

341

QUIGLEY. No. The cloak was tuk away by Major Sirr. He has it now! But we never dhramed what a prize lies hid in the pocket of it. Tare alive, Pat! — is not a thousand too little to ax for all this? The lists, Pat! and all the names in Emmet's own handwritin' — ho, ho, big names! — men o' quality — that no one suspects. Put them down at ten pounds a head! — tottle them up like onions on a sthring. Then the plans!

FINERTY. It's little enough, indeed, to pay min like ourselves. for, afther all, when you think of it, sure it is the counthry itself that we have for sale.

QUIGLEY. Be jabers, Pat, it is not everybody that has got a counthry to sell! (*Exeunt.*)

ACT ONE: SCENE THREE

A room in Dublin Castle. LORD NORBURY *and* LORD KILWARDEN *seated at table, R.H., examining papers.* TINEY WOLFE *looks in at door.*

TINEY. May I come in?

KILWARDEN. Yes, if you will not stop very long.

NORBURY. I must overrule the objection. Stop as long as you please.

TINEY. Lord Norbury, you deserve a kiss for that.

NORBURY. Offering bribes to the Bench is an awful offence!

TINEY. You know, papa, we promised to call at the vice-regal lodge tonight. Shall you be detained here very long?

KILWARDEN. No, Tiney. We have some important business to transact with Mr. Curran, we expect at any moment.

NORBURY. I think, Kilwarden, you may leave this matter to me to settle. Your daughter is weary.

TINEY. You are very kind to consider me.

NORBURY. Who would fail to consider you? Had I so sweet and loving a child beside me I should be, perhaps, as good a man as your father is, my dear.

(*Enter* CURRAN.)

TINEY (*running to him*). Oh, Mr. Curran, I am so glad you have come! How is Sarah?

CURRAN. Complaining, Tiney. Complaining very badly, indeed.

TINEY. Oh, I am so sorry! What is her complaint?

CURRAN. That she sees so little of you.

TINEY. There is very little to see. Papa, dear, may I spend the evening tomorrow with Miss Curran?

KILWARDEN. Yes, dear; I'll lend you for a few hours.

TINEY. What will you charge for the loan?

KILWARDEN. A dozen big kisses which you will bring me back. Keep them fresh on your lips. There, run into the next room and amuse yourself while we despatch our business.

343

TINEY (*to* CURRAN *as she goes out*). Don't keep him very long. (*Exit.*)

CURRAN. The summons to attend your lordships found me at dinner with some friends. What has happened? Has a French expedition landed at Kerry? Has the British fleet broken into another mutiny?

KILWARDEN. The danger is much nearer home.

NORBURY. These depositions sworn this afternoon contain disclosures of an alarming condition of affairs in the adjoining counties of Wicklow and Kildare.

KILWARDEN. Dublin is threatened; two thousand men are now under arms, and are marching on the city.

CURRAN. Two thousand jackasses! I don't believe a word of it. These government spies are purveyors of mares' nests, and make a market of your fears! My lords, the revolutionary spirit of Ireland was broken in 'ninety-eight, and was buried three years ago, when the Act of Union swept our leading men cross the channel and into the British Parliament. It was a crafty measure for it left the body of the people without a head. I have just passed through the streets; the city is asleep and not dreaming of disturbance.

NORBURY. But these affidavits are very precise.

CURRAN. If the Government supports a host of spies, the rogues are bound to encourage your fears, and keep them alive! Whom do they pretend is at the head of this new insurrection?

KILWARDEN. Robert Emmet.

CURRAN. What? Robert? the son of my old friend, the doctor? Why, the boy is in France, and has been there for months past. Had he been in this country, mine is the first house he would have visited.

(*Enter* MAJOR SIRR.)

SIRR. He is here in Dublin. It is strange you should profess ignorance of his whereabouts, when he is a daily visitor at your house, where I found him in your daughter's company an hour ago.

CURRAN. You found him in my house?

SIRR. By virtue of a search warrant issued by the Privy Council! While you were entertaining your friends at dinner, she was entertaining her lover —

KILWARDEN. Silence, sir! You forget you are speaking to a father.

SIRR. When treason-felony is abroad, I forget everything but my duty.

344

CURRAN. What evidence do you bring to sustain this infamous charge?

SIRR. Come forward, Mr. Quigley. Step this way, Mr. Finerty. (*Enter* QUIGLEY, *followed by* FINERTY, *who carries* ROBERT's *cloak.*)

This man (*Points to* QUIGLEY) is associated with Emmet, and is his trusted follower.

QUIGLEY. 'Twas meself guided him to Mr. Curran's house awhile ago.

CURRAN. May I ask what office you hold besides that of traitor?

QUIGLEY. I'm colonel in the army of the Irish Republic.

KILWARDEN. Your face is familiar to me. Were you not on your trial for murder before me last year?

QUIGLEY. It was my brother, my lord, you hanged that time. It wasn't me.

CURRAN. And on no better evidence than the croak of this jailbird, you violated my house?

QUIGLEY. Never fear, if it is evidence you want, I hould a crop as fine as you ever handled. Here is Emmet's cloak that he left behind him in your garden, and in the pocket we find these papers. Wait now! (*He takes some packets of paper from the pockets of the cloak, and hands them to* SIRR.)

SIRR (*examining them*). Lists of the commanding officers and of the insurgent force in Kildare.

QUIGLEY. You'll find my name among the first on the list.

(SIRR *passes the paper to* NORBURY; *he and* KILWARDEN *examine it.*)

Here's another one. (SIRR *takes it.*)

SIRR. Plan of attack! Points of check. Lines of defence. This seems to be a well digested conspiracy to seize the city of Dublin. (*Passes the paper.*)

QUIGLEY. Divil a less! And it's short work we would make of you, Major, to begin with. You're the tit-bit our pikes are hungry for.

CURRAN. I must have some proof better than this to satisfy me that the son of my old friend and schoolmate, Dr. Emmet, is associated with these ruffians.

FINERTY. Maybe this bit o' writing will open your eyes. (*Hands letter to* CURRAN *who reads it silently.*)

(*Enter* TINEY *at back. She stops and listens.*)

CURRAN. My God! it is true!

QUIGLEY. Aha!

CURRAN. This letter is written by my unhappy child to Mr. Emmet, and it confirms all you have stated.

SIRR (*taking the letter from* CURRAN). It will form an interesting episode in the case — let us see what she says.

KILWARDEN (*putting his hand upon the paper*). Major Sirr, have you a daughter?

SIRR. I have.

KILWARDEN. So have I. (*He tears the paper.* TINEY *falls.*)

CURRAN. I ask your lordships to acquit me of all complicity in a knowledge of this business.

NORBURY. Be assured, we do so heartily.

KILWARDEN. We are convinced of your ignorance in the matter.

SIRR. 'Tis more than I am.

CURRAN. I am glad to have secured your evil estimation, sir; it entitles any gentleman to the respect of this community.

SIRR. I hold his majesty's commission.

CURRAN. So does the hangman! Good night, my lords! (*Exit.*)

KILWARDEN. There can be no doubt that we stand in presence of a formidable conspiracy.

NORBURY. The country is in danger.

QUIGLEY. And no lie in it.

NORBURY. What do these wretched men propose to do, to accomplish?

SIRR. They propose to seize the Castle of Dublin where a guard of seventeen men forms at present its sole defence; to carry off the lord-lieutenant to their camp on the mountains, there to hold the person of his excellency as a hostage and proclaim the Irish Republic.

QUIGLEY. One and indivisible.

NORBURY. What is to be done?

SIRR. These men hold offices of trust and command under Emmet — they are in our pay. The military must be called out promptly and secretly posted where their fire can sweep the streets of Dublin. Then Quigley and Finerty will give the people Emmet's signal to rise, and before he can arrive with his troops to control the mob, the regulars will make short work of the crowd.

KILWARDEN. You cannot proceed to use force until the people commit some breach of the peace.

QUIGLEY. Oho! be aisy. We'll get the pikes to work. Maybe I'd redden one o' them myself in the blood of some man — a big one — whose death would raise a howl.

KILWARDEN. This is horrible!

(TINEY *rises and listens.*)

NORBURY. Egad, Kilwarden, such means were successfully employed five years ago in '98.

SIRR. We must bring rebellion to a head.

QUIGLEY. And save your own?

FINERTY. Thrue for ye, Mike! — and we'd like to know the price of heads now.

QUIGLEY. Yes. What's to be our reward for the crop we bring?

SIRR. What do you claim?

QUIGLEY. That's the chat! We want a thousand pounds for Emmet's and fifty apiece for each other head we bring to the dock.

(TINEY *leans weeping with her face in her hands against the wall.*)

FINERTY. An' we'd like to see a little ready money down on account.

SIRR (*handing them a roll of notes*). Count that.

(FINERTY *and* QUIGLEY *eagerly bending over table. L.H. Counting money.*)

NORBURY. You expect the insurgents when they find the first outbreak is defeated will become discouraged? will desert and regain their homes?

SIRR. No! They will come here — ha! ha! 'Twill be a race among such men as those — (*Points to* FINERTY *and* QUIGLEY) who will get here first to betray their leaders.

QUIGLEY. Thirty-two — thirty-three! Divil a doubt about that. Thirty-five — hi! hi!

NORBURY (*commencing to write at table R.H.*). Lord Kilwarden is now on his road to the vice-regal lodge. He will submit to his excellency the measures you propose to precipitate the outbreak, by the help of our agents amongst the mob. I will draft your plan, Major, if you will repeat the particulars.

(MISS WOLFE *advances and stands beside* LORD KILWARDEN.)

SIRR (*turns and sees her*). Miss Wolfe!

KILWARDEN. Tiney!

QUIGLEY (*counting*). Fifty-eight, fifty-nine!

TINEY. Go on, don't mind me.

NORBURY. Affairs of state cannot be discussed before you.

TINEY. I see that you hesitate and look at each other as though the affairs of state were guilty things to which a father could not listen in the presence of his child. You dare not unfold your thoughts before her. Is it not so?

NORBURY. You are not old enough to judge —

TINEY. My father is, and he said it was horrible. You see, papa, I overheard what those men proposed. Forgive me if my heart comes to your side and pleads to stand by yours. You taught

347

the motherless little child how to be worthy of your name and of your race. She was nursed on your breast. Let her now give you back the teachings of your love. Have no share in this infamy. Set your honest face against it.

SIRR. Are we come to this? that the chief justice of Ireland cannot share our councils without an appeal to a schoolgirl.

TINEY. Nor can he preside on the bench over trials for conspiracy and murder planned here and executed by his compliance.

KILWARDEN. Lord Norbury, I will take charge of these papers. They will explain, if they do not justify, my resignation of the office I hold under the crown. Come, Tiney, let us go. (*He embraces her.*)

QUIGLEY (*counting money as* KILWARDEN *and* MISS WOLFE *go out*). Ninety-five, ninety-six. There's four pound short in this pile!

ACT-DROP FALLS.

ACT TWO: SCENE ONE

The cottage at Butterfield Lane. Enter ANN DEVLIN. *She carries a small valise; she looks around, advances, and feels for the table, on which she places the valise; then returns to the door.*

ANN. Come in, Miss.
   (*Enter* SARAH *and* NORMAN.)
   Wait till I fetch a light from the kitchen; maybe I'd find a sod o' turf alive in the fire there. (*Going out L.*) I must feel my way in the dark.

SARAH. So am I, Norman, feeling my way in the dark! — in doubt and in fear.

CLAVERHOUSE. There's no doubt between right and wrong — no fear where there is love.

SARAH. Can you not see the position in which I place him?

CLAVERHOUSE. I can. I wish I were in his place.
   (*Re-enter* ANN *with light.*)

ANN. I heard him moving overhead in his room. He is there. My brother Andy will soon be here wid the outside car, to take the masther to the mountains; for the camp is moved to the Scalp, and the boys are hungry for himself.
   (SARAH *sits at table.*)

CLAVERHOUSE. The Scalp! — Why, that pass is within sight of Dublin. Is rebellion so close to us?

ANN. Close! It looks up out of every cellar and down from every garret windy in the city. It runs in the gutters, and sweeps like the blast through the alleys and the lanes! You are breathing it — and you don't know it, nor feel it. Whist! I hear the masther comin'. Will I send for the priest, Miss, and bring him here?

SARAH. No! (*Rises quickly.*) Is it not enough that I present myself in so unmaidenly a manner? What will he take me for?

ANN. For betther or for worse! The sooner the betther; the later, the worse for you both. There's Father Donnelly lives at

349

Cabinteely, convaniant to the road from this to the Scalp. You can stop there an' wake him up. The business is short and sweet, and no delay. When it is over the masther must hurry to the boys in the mountains; he is expected there by midnight.

CLAVERHOUSE. By that time he must be on the seas. Oh, that I were at the bottom of them, while you and he were passing over me to a happy life!

ANN. He is here!

(*Enter* EMMET. *He is dressed in the Irish uniform.*)

ROBERT. Sarah — in this place! Who — what — brought you here?

CLAVERHOUSE. I did, Mr. Emmet. Permit me to present myself, that I may spare Miss Curran some embarrassment. I am Norman Claverhouse, Captain in His Majesty's Ninety-third Highlanders. I was a guest in Mr. Curran's house tonight, when Major Sirr arrived with a search warrant. (*Taking* SARAH's *hand.*) In the absence of our host — her father — I took the liberty of driving the Major and his posse from the place; and as her rejected lover I now bring her to the only man who can repair the injury this night's business may do to the name of a lady to whom we are equally devoted.

ROBERT. Are you aware, sir, to whom you have rendered this service?

CLAVERHOUSE. I have rendered this service to her who owns my life.

ROBERT. Do you know I am one whose name men whisper fearfully; an outlaw, whom to see and not to betray is a crime; a rebel, whom to serve is a capital offence?

CLAVERHOUSE. I only know that she loves you — that makes me at once your foe and your accomplice.

ROBERT. Martyrs have died in the flames who had not in their breasts so brave a heart; for they fell assured of paradise, while you suffer, renouncing your hopes of heaven. Let me feel your hand in mine; the other on my shoulder. So; I had rather be thus ennobled than feel the sword of a king there.

ANN (*aside*). Well! 'Tis mighty hard on women that one girl should have two such lovers, and waste one o' them like that.

SARAH. He brought me to your side; he bade me seek the refuge of your arms — it is all the home I have now. Hide me from myself, for I am ashamed of what I do.

ROBERT. We shall be married tonight; and if forthwith this gentleman will further extend his good offices, he will conduct you to my mother's house, where you will find the home I dare not enter.

CLAVERHOUSE. Why not?

ROBERT. Because I would not bring over it the cloud that now obscures my life! Because I would not make those I love the sharers of my fate!

CLAVERHOUSE. You must quit that life for her sake. Tonight after your marriage, you will leave Ireland and take her with you.

SARAH. Not for my sake, but for your mother's — for your own.

ROBERT. You ask me to abandon the cause into which my voice has drawn thousands of my fellow-countrymen; to desert them in the field on the brink of battle; to play the executioner, and leave them headless. Oh, it could be done so easily, for their trust in Robert Emmet is so blind! Bribed with your person, he can leave the fools in the fell-trap baited with his lies — to perish — as you know, sir, they will perish — like helpless dogs flung into the lion's den. Eternal scorn would point its finger at the deed! — and say the hand that Emmet gave to Curran's daughter was full of Ireland's blood; in the breast on which she rested was the heart of a renegade; and the name she shared was blasted with dishonour!

CLAVERHOUSE. You are so occupied with the peril in which your honour stands that you overlook hers. What matters it if her name be scathed with shame, if yours shall live unblemished? You say that you would not make those you love sharers of your fate; yet you would make her so! You would not bring the cloud that obscures your life over theirs, yet you would have her live in its shadow!

ROBERT. God, who knows my heart, have mercy on me, and direct me what to do!

SARAH (*at his feet*). And *you*, who know my heart, have mercy on *me!* — and on us both! Have mercy on my love, that now pleads for itself at your feet. Oh! I am helpless to persuade him; I ask him to spare his life that is my own — my own — all I have in this world.

ROBERT. Sir, have you no council to offer us?

CLAVERHOUSE. Yes; marry her! Follow your mad career; stop here, and I'll find myself within three months heir to your widow!

ANN (*aside*). O Michael Dwyer! If it wasn't for your ugly mug, that I'm so fond of, that fellow might make me a Scotchwoman any day that was plazin' to him. God bless him!

(*Enter* ANDY.)

ANDY. Where the masther?

351

ROBERT. Here!

ANN. What makes you so pale, dear?

ANDY. Bad news. I put the Major's horse into a car; for it's not between shafts they would be on the look for him. (*Pointing to* NORMAN.) Who's that?

ROBERT. Never mind him.

ANDY. 'Tis the coat on him that bothers me.

ANN. I'll go bail for what's behind it; go on, alanna!

ANDY. Divil a sowl was in your house, miss, when I got there; so I turned back. As I drove past Portobello Barracks, two men came out and hailed me, axed me to take them quick to Island Bridge. Be jabers! me heart stud still as they climbed outside the car, for one o' thim was Major Sorr himself — jauntin' behind his own horse.

ROBERT. You heard what they said?

ANDY. Maybe I didn't cock my ear! 'We've got him now,' ses he; 'he's pounded! The papers — the whole bag of insurgent thricks is in my hand. There's the list of their members; the names of their leaders; the plans of attack — all in Emmet's own writin', ses he, 'not to spake of his man and pestol,' ses he.

ANN. His what?

ANDY. 'Tis what he said — 'his man and pestol to the people.'

ROBERT. Manifesto!

ANDY. It's all the same to me!

ROBERT. But these papers were in the cloak I left with you.

SARAH. Sirr carried it away with him.

ROBERT. Betrayed! Betrayed!

ANDY. That's what the Major said. 'Tomorrow them papers will be published in the *Morning Journal,* and the news that Emmet has betrayed his followin' and sowld out o' the business. The Government has his own handwritin' to show for it. That news will put down the risin' quicker than all the horse, foot and artillery in the country could do it,' ses he.

CLAVERHOUSE. Fortune stands your friend. By this mischance your cause is lost.

ROBERT. Aye! Is it so! — so! — so! I'm trapped and caught! Now, by Saint Patrick, they shall find my foot upon their necks, choking the lie in their throats, before their black hearts have time to give it flight. Tomorrow, you said, they begin their work; tonight I shall begin mine. Before the sun rises on Dublin, a thousand men, now camped at the Scalp, shall descend upon the city and seize the Castle. Our drums will call the people to arms, and then at their head I'll meet this calumny.

SARAH. Robert, I beseech you —

ROBERT. It is too late, Sarah — too late! I have no choice but to vindicate my life; ask him.

CLAVERHOUSE. He is right.

ROBERT. Andy Devlin!

ANDY. That's me.

ROBERT. What men have we within call?

ANDY. Three, your honour, in the loft outside, and one howldin' the horse.

ROBERT. Give them the signal.

(ANDY *goes out to the door and whistles.*)

I must ask you, sir, to pledge your honour that what has passed here in your presence will be held sacred by you.

CLAVERHOUSE. When I leave this I shall make my way straight to the Castle, and report to his excellency every word of it.

ROBERT. I knew you would. (*Four men appear at the door.*) Reilly, you will stand guard with your men over this house until sunrise. Then, and not till then, you will liberate this gentleman. He is your prisoner for the night.

CLAVERHOUSE. What a release! I am obliged to you.

ROBERT. Ann Devlin, you will take Miss Curran to my mother's house in Stephen's Green; your brother Andy will drive you there. Farewell, my own one. I will bring you back a name you will be proud to wear (*He holds her in his arms*), or leave you a memory worthy of your love. Pray for me, Sarah! — It is not my will, but God's, that parts us now. Farewell! (*He embraces her. Exit.*)

SARAH (*falls on her knees as* ROBERT *leaves*). God bless and guard my love! (*Scene closes in.*)

ACT TWO: SCENE TWO

A gorge in the mountains near the Scalp. Enter QUIGLEY, *meeting*
BRANGAN; *both in uniform.*

QUIGLEY. Well, how are things workin' in the camp?

BRANGAN. Finely; the boys are getting wild as muzzled dogs!
There's no howldin' them.

QUIGLEY. The sight of Dublin lyin' asleep beyond there is mate
and dhrink to fellows starvin' for a fight! What news of Dwyer?

BRANGAN. He is lying still in the Devil's Glen, waitin' till he gets
the offer to join us wid four hundred Wexford men.

QUIGLEY. You must cross the hills tonight. Tell him that Emmet
has sold us all, body and bones, to the Castle. They are goin'
to make him a lord, an' rise him to a big place at coort — tell
him.

BRANGAN. Stop that — enough! When I get as far as that in the
lie, Dwyer will shut my mouth forever.

QUIGLEY. There's no lie in it; look at them sheets; they are fresh
and wet wid the ink from the Castle press. Rade them! (*He
hands him a small hand-bill.*) There's our secret plans, the roll-
call of our leading min, and the divil an' all, printed from papers
in Emmet's own handwritin', on show in Major Sirr's office.

BRANGAN. Have you seen them?

QUIGLEY. Sure, any one can see them. They will be cried for a
hapenny tomorrow at every corner in the city, from Ring's
End to Kilmainham. He has turned approver agin us.

BRANGAN. Tare alive! I did not think he would go do a thing like
that! — taking the very bread out of our mouths. He's as bad
as one of ourselves. The boys will go wild when they hear
this. O wurra! is it for this we have been drillin' and marchin'
and starvin' for weeks past! 'Tis mighty hard upon us, entirely
so it is!

QUIGLEY. Go amongst them; tell them so! Tell them the Bank

354

of Ireland must pay for it. It is full wid the poor man's money
— the rints he has paid to the landlords! Then there's the city
itself. Let us have a hack at it. Them Dublin tradesmen are
castle-fed pigs, rowlin' in goold.

BRANGAN. A bowld dash at them would fill our sacks, an' we
could be off to the hills and bogs before them redcoats could
fall in, or them dhragoons could saddle up.

QUIGLEY. That's the work! Go you among the men; scatter them
bills among them; I'll get a howlt of the officers. We will court-
martial Emmet — break him. What do we want, anyhow, wid a
general? Cock him up, and here's the end of it. Let aich county
folly its own leaders, and divil take the hindmost!

BRANGAN. I'm wid ye, Quigley. I was light porther for awhile
at Goggins', the jewellers, in Dame Street; I know the place in
the shop where a handful of diamonds is kept that would buy
a barony in Roscommon.

QUIGLEY. To work! Brangan — to work!

ACT TWO: SCENE THREE

The camp at the Scalp. Shed or ruined cabin R.H., which serves as headquarters; rude hovels are scattered over the hillside; watch-fires, around which figures are lying and pikes are piled; Dublin and the bay are seen below, in the distance; night; the city is sparkling with lights. FINERTY, DUGGAN, and MAHAFFEY are in this cabin; groups of men in green stuffs uniform are drinking, smoking, etc.; laughter. Chorus.

FINERTY. Ordher in the camp. How can the Council of War know what it is talking about if you blackguards don't howld your prate.

ALL. Thrue for ye, Pat. We'll be as quiet as oysthers. Three cheers for the Council of War.

MOTHER MAGAN. I wish there were less council and more war.
   (*Enter* QUIGLEY.)

QUIGLEY. You shall have your wishes. Your officers will debate wid open dures before you all. For why should we dale wid your lives, and never let on to you a haporth about the business?

ALL. He's right; thrue for ye. Hurroo!

QUIGLEY. I have come from Dublin where the people are lookin' out for ye. There's not a windy below there but howlds an impatient face, cursing your delay. Every ear is open for the thramp of your feet an' your cry 'to arrums!'

ALL. Hurroo for Dublin!

QUIGLEY. Aisy, boys. You'll be there soon enough; I'll go bail.
   (FINERTY *and the* OFFICERS *have brought out of the shed a barrel, on which they place the hatch door of the cabin, so as to form a table; two buckets, a basket, and a three-legged stool. The* OFFICERS *sit.*)

FINERTY. Colonel Quigley will take the chair. (*Offering him a stool with only one leg.*)

356

QUIGLEY. I'll wait till I take one in Dublin Castle.

ALL. Hurroo!

QUIGLEY. Ordher! Men of Kildare, your time has come! Boys of Wicklow, you have waited long enough! Dublin is waitin' for you like a bride, and widin two days from this she whill be in your arrums. You men from the County Meath will howld the Phoenix and the Lodge. James Hope, with eight hundred men from the County Down, is on his way from Drogheda, and will seize the Custom House. So much for the North. The Kildare boys will take the Castle.

ALL. We will! Down wid the red and up wid the green.

QUIGLEY. Finerty, wid a guard of honour, will bring the lord-lieutenant on an outside car, and lodge his excellency in our camp here. Wicklow boys, you will take the Bank of Ireland.

ALL. Hurroo!

MOTHER MAGAN. Begorra! Wicklow has the best of it.

QUIGLEY. Here is a list of the officers of the crown, the ministers, and all the big men. They will be on our hands. What's to be done wid them?

FINERTY. A few executions to begin wid might have a fine effect.

QUIGLEY. It would make our cause respectable.

MOTHER MAGAN. There's old Norbury! I'd like to see his mug in the dock.

QUIGLEY. And a jury of convicts drawn from Kilmainham in the box.

FINERTY. And before me on the bench.

ALL. Whoo! (*Tumult outside.*)

QUIGLEY. What's going on there?

MOTHER MAGAN. Maybe 'tis only a fight.

QUIGLEY. Can't they fight peaceably, without making a row?

(*Enter a crowd of men, with* BRANGAN; *some of the men have the bills in their hands.* BRANGAN *hands papers to the* OFFICERS *and to* QUIGLEY.)

BRANGAN. News from Dublin! Emmet has turned his green coat. It was lined with red all the while. He has sowld us.

ALL. Oo!

MOTHER MAGAN. Emmet a thraitor! (*Takes the papers from* BRANGAN.)

QUIGLEY. The proofs are plain enough.

MOTHER MAGAN. 'Tis a black lie, and you know it!

QUIGLEY. If you weren't a woman, I'd make ye put down them words on paper and ate them.

MOTHER MAGAN. Where did you get these bills?

BRANGAN. Where? — I — I did — I got them.

MOTHER MAGAN. You haven't a lie ready. See! they stick together; for the ink is wet. You got them at the printer's! What took you there? You knew what dirty scheme was at work in the Government office. Spake up. (*Seizing* BRANGAN.)

BRANGAN (*falling on his knees*). Oh! Oh! I know this grip.

MOTHER MAGAN. Would you whist. (*Aloud*) Is this all the proofs you have agin him?

QUIGLEY. If Robert Emmet is not a traitor, why is he not here? (EMMET *enters.*)

ROBERT. He is here!

MOTHER MAGAN. You may go now! (*Releases* BRANGAN, *who crawls away amazed.*)

(*All the men slowly retire to R., behind* QUIGLEY *and* FINERTY, *leaving* EMMET *alone with* MOTHER MAGAN, *L.H.*)

ROBERT. Why do you turn your faces from me? Speak, men!

MOTHER MAGAN. They have heard you have turned approver, to save your skin and fill your pockets.

ROBERT. Who accuses me?

FINERTY. That print.

ROBERT (*after looking at them*). I scorn to fight with lies. That they are so needs no words, for I am here. Quigley was with me when the thieves robbed me of those papers, and now they charge me with selling to them what they stole.

QUIGLEY. 'Tis all one how they got the information, we are betrayed. Now they are ready to meet and to crush us.

ROBERT. No, the documents they stole shall serve to deceive them; they shall fall into the trap they set for me. Tonight, before their troops can be moved, we shall swoop down upon Dublin.

QUIGLEY. Tonight?

ROBERT. Relying on this information, they will be unprepared.

QUIGLEY. What can we do with a handful of men?

ROBERT. With a handful of men Bonaparte put an end to the Reign of Terror and released France; with a handful of men Cortes conquered Mexico; with a corporal's guard Cromwell cleared the House of Commons, and founded the first English republic.

MOTHER MAGAN. Thrue fur ye; but they were men — not jailbirds, like Quigley and his gang of thieves.

QUIGLEY. Mother Magan, you will make me forget your sex.

ROBERT. What would these men have?

MOTHER MAGAN. They want six hours' free quarters in Dublin

for pillage and for plundher, then afther pikin' a few grandees, they would skip.

ROBERT. Let those amongst ye that are of this mind assemble round him yonder, so let me count how many honest men there be here who will stand by our cause and by their country.

(*The men go to the R.H., and stand behind* QUIGLEY, FINERTY, *and* BRANGAN.)

MOTHER MAGAN. There's only one honest man in the crowd, and, be jabers, that's a woman!

ROBERT (*after burying his face in his hands*). God forgive me for having done this thing! I have been self-deceived by my love for this helpless people — children of misery — by my blind devotion they have been brought to this infamous extremity. Let the penalty be mine alone; let no blood but mine be shed; accept my young life in expiation of my foolish faith. My friends — my countrymen! I go hence — to Dublin — alone, and in this uniform — the badge of treason; I carry with me that flag — the emblem of rebellion; I go with my life to redccm yours; to offer my hands to the chains, my head to the executioner! (*Some of the men cross to* EMMET's *side.*) There is yet time to retrieve your errors, and to make your submission. Put off those uniforms; bury them out of sight; and seek your homes quietly by unfrequented paths and by night!

ALL (*murmuring*). No! No! We'll stand by your honour to dcath.

(*Some more men join* EMMET's *side.*)

ROBERT. If you stand by me you must march as children of Erin, as united Irishmen, whose one hope is freedom; not as banditti, whose sole object is plunder. The green flag that led our countrymen at Fontenoy under Sarsfield has never been dishonoured, and it shall not be so under Robert Emmet, so help me God!

(*The rest of the men, uttering loud cries, join the crowd around him, some kneeling at his feet.*)

QUIGLEY. This is mighty fine, but it comes too late; two hundred biys from Kildare left for Dublin an hour ago. The divil himself could not stop them now.

MOTHER MAGAN. No, but Michael Dwyer could! His men, five hundred strong, the bodyguard of Emmet, are posted at the foot of this hill, wid orders to shut the road.

QUIGLEY. Michael Dwyer is at Glendalagh!

MOTHER MAGAN. You lie, Quigley! He is here. (*He removes his bonnet and wig.*)

ALL. Hurroo!

DWYER (*striding across to R.*). Now I am ready to ate the words Mother Magan spoke to you a while ago.

ROBERT. Hold, Dwyer! I'll have no fighting amongst you.

DWYER. Divil a fear o' that! Is there, Quigley? Give me your hand. (*He takes* QUIGLEY's *hand.*) By this and by that, by signs on your face that I never mistook yet, and by the pulse in our hearts that spake to one another in this grip, I know that I will die by your hand, or you will die by mine. (*Shakes his hand.*) Now, masther dear, I'm ready for your orders.

ROBERT. Lead three hundred of your men by Enniskery and Rathmines; enter the city on the south by Harcourt Street; your point is Stephen's Green; be there by two o'clock. Who commands under you?

DWYER. Phil Maguire; he is howldin' the Kildare boys below there.

QUIGLEY. Maguire! — the man is dumb.

DWYER. Thrue fur ye, so he can not turn informer. But he is mighty talkative wid his hands; don't get into any argument wid him.

ROBERT. Let Maguire unite the Kildare men with the rest of your Wexford boys, and sweep around, entering the city by James's Gate; rouse the liberties, and occupy Thomas Street by St. Patrick's.

QUIGLEY. The Kildare troops are under my command; they will not march without their officers.

DWYER. Oh, be aisy! You will be there at their head beside Maguire; he'll take care of you.

ROBERT. My men will march by Stellorgan and Brunswick Street; our point is College Green. Thus our forces, eleven hundred strong, penetrating the city on three sides, will meet at the Castle. Before sunrise Dublin will be ours; the citizens will awake to find Ireland a republic, and our people numbered among the nations of the world.

ALL. Hurroo! To Dublin!

ROBERT. Fall in! (*Repeat of the chorus, which the men fall into now; the scene closes in.*)

ACT TWO: SCENE FOUR

A room in the house of MRS EMMET. *Enter* CURRAN *and* LORD NORBURY, *preceded by a* SERVANT.

CURRAN. Be good enough to inform Miss Curran that her father is here and desires to see her. I believe she is in this house.
  (*Enter* ANN DEVLIN. *Exit* SERVANT.)

ANN. She is here, sir; sitting by the bedside of Mrs Emmet.

CURRAN. You were the companion of her flight.

ANN. No; she had a guard of honour all the way, and with him she left her home.

CURRAN. Your master, doubtless?

ANN. No; betther still. It was the lover you gave her — Captain Claverhouse.

NORBURY. My nephew! I can not believe it! Where is he?

ANN. I left him asleep by the fireside of Robert Emmet, where he is passing the night. Your honours look surprised to find young people have hearts, and hearts will have their own way. Two years ago you gave your daughter to young Emmet. Then you took her from him, to give her to young Claverhouse. You see she knew her own mind, if you didn't know yours, and that's the way of it.
  (*Enter* SARAH.)

CURRAN. Are you aware what you have done?

SARAH. Yes, father. I have become the bride of a rebel, and to rescue and protect your house from any suspicion I left it, when my presence there became a reproach.

NORBURY. My dear child, the man for whom you have made this useless sacrifice, betrayed by his own followers, is already doomed to an inevitable and ignominious death.

SARAH. He knows it, and will face it if it comes to that.

CURRAN. Is it my gentle Sarah, my daughter that speaks.

SARAH. No, father, it is the outlaw's wife; forgive me if I have

361

been true to myself. When your nephew, my lord, discovered how it was with me, he told me how I should vindicate my falling honour and my own heart; he stood by my side while I obeyed his counsel. Do not mistake my misfortune for my fault, and believe me, it was for your dear sake I was moved, not for my own.

ANN (*who has been looking from the window*). There is a carriage at the door.

NORBURY. It is mine; it brought us here.

ANN. There's a mighty big crowd gathering round it; I'll go see what they want. (*Exit.*)

NORBURY. The rogues want six months in Kilmainham, or a visit to Botany Bay.

SARAH. Be advised, my lord, and escape to your country house at Cloncilla. Emmet knows that Major Sirr has possession of the plans of the insurrection, and already he has changed them. (*Cries outside.*)

NORBURY (*running to the window*). The square below is full of the mob. What do they want?

SARAH. Hark! (*Cries of* 'NORBURY!' 'NORBURY!') Do you hear? They want you.
    (*Re-enter* ANN.)

ANN. Bar the door; make fast the shutters on the ground floor; let loose Master Robert's wolf hound and load the two blunderbusses in the hall.

CURRAN. What is the matter? What brings the people here?

ANN. All Dublin is awake tonight, and on foot. The air is full of growl and the rumbling of a storm. It wanted little to make it burst. They saw your liveries standing at this dure, and that invited the lightning. (*Blows heard below, and cries; smashing of glass.*)

CURRAN. They are attacking the house.

ANN. Divil a doubt of it!

NORBURY. What do they want?

ANN. Your life — no less.

CURRAN. Are they mad?

ANN. Aye! wid joy; for they say Emmet is entering Dublin from Ring's End and Rathmines, while Michael Dwyer, wid five hundred men, is at James's Gate.
    (*Enter* SERVANT, *who whispers to* ANN.)

NORBURY. Before help can arrive they will wreck the house, and we shall perish.

ANN. The girl says they have brought up a load of straw that they are pilin agin the dures and windies below; there's no fightin' agin fire.

SARAH. Leave me to defend you. (*She goes to the window; cries and shots; she advances on to the balcony, and raises her hand; silence.*) Men of Dublin — my name is Sarah Curran, and I am the bride of Robert Emmet.

ALL. Hurroo! Long life to ye! God bless ye both!

SARAH. This is my husband's house, his mother lies sick beside me; take that straw and lay it down carefully on the road, that her sleep may not be broken by the noises of the street. My father, John Philpot Curran, is here; he came in that carriage to see me; he will return home in it.

(*Cry. 'Three cheers for Curran!'*)

No! Be silent, and respect the rest of Emmet's mother. Good night to you all. Begone! (*She closes the window.*) You are safe, my lord. Ann and I will escort you by the back premises and the stable lane to Dawson Street, where we shall find a car. Meanwhile my father will enter your carriage in the presence of the crowd, and drive home. Come!

(*Exit* CURRAN, *preceded by a* SERVANT, *R.* ANN, SARAH *and* NORBURY *L.*)

ACT TWO: SCENE FIVE

Scene changes to College Green and the Houses of Parliament. Crowds of people; sellers of fruit, ballads, etc.; college lads; coal porters; a blind fiddler. Here's yer hot pitaties! Oysthers hot — hot! Cherries ripe, all ripe, a hapenny the stick! *Enter* ANDY.

ANDY. Here's the last new song, 'The night before Larry was stretched'; 'The Duke of York was a damned bad soldier.'

ALL. Ha! ha! ha!

ANDY (*sings*).
> 'The Duke of York was a damned bad soldier,
> From Dunkerque he ran away!'

Here comes Counsellor Flood and Hussey de Burgh. Three cheers, boys, for them that stood up for the people!
(*Enter two* GENTLEMEN.)

ALL. Long life to de Burgh. Hoo! Hurra!
(*The* GENTLEMEN *bow and pass out.*)

ANDY. Here's Sirr. Three groans for the Major — the drum major.
(*Enter* SIRR.)
I wish I had the drummin' of him.

ALL. Yah! oo!

ANDY (*sings*).
> Now Major Sirr
> He is a cur,
> And his kennel is the Castle, etc.

ALL. Ha! ha! ha!
(*Exit* SIRR.)

ANDY. A groan for the Castle hack.

ALL. Yah! (*Song* ANDY.)
(*Enter* QUIGLEY, FINERTY, *and* BRANGAN.)

QUIGLEY. We gave Maguire the slip in Patrick Street. How many of our boys followed you?

FINERTY. A score maybe. They are close by.

364

QUIGLEY. That's enough! (*He addresses the crowd.*) You, Brangan, go by Grafton Street and raise the cry 'To arms!' You, Finerty, by Dame Street; call on the people to turn out. Never fear; there's two regiments under arms, wid four pieces of artillery in the Castle yard, so look out for yourselves when you hear the rumbling of the guns. (*To the crowd.*) Min of Dublin, the hour has come! The boys from Wicklow, Wexford, and Kildare are amongst ye, well armed and ready to sthrike for Ireland! Down with the red flag, up wid the green!

ALL. Hurroo! hurroo!

(*An attack is made on the shops, which are broken open. The carriage of* LORD KILWARDEN, *in which* KILWARDEN *and* MISS WOLFE *are seen, is driven on, preceded by* LINK-BOYS *and running* FOOTMEN. *The crowd surround it.* KILWARDEN *is forced by them to descend.*)

KILWARDEN. My good friends, you do not know me. I am Kilwarden, chief justice of the King's bench.

QUIGLEY. Then you arc the man I want. (*Thrusts a pike into* KILWARDEN.) That's for my brother that you hung!

(TINEY *utters a cry and tries to intercept the blow. Enter* EMMET *and* DWYER.)

FINERTY. Let the cub go wid the wolf.

ANDY (*wrenching the pike from* FINERTY). Would you kill a girl?

ROBERT. Who has done this? (*Raising* TINEY, *who has fallen on her father's body.*)

DWYER (*seizing* FINERTY). I have him.

ROBERT. Tie him to the College rails, and let him be shot.

KILWARDEN (*raising himself*). No, let no one suffer death, excepting by due process of the law. Where is my child — my child?

TINEY. Oh, papa! my dear papa! (*He drops dead out of her arms;* ROBERT *holds her sobbing to his breast.*)

ROBERT. The coward who struck this good man planted his steel in the bosom of his country. Ireland was murdered by that blow!

ACT THREE: SCENE ONE

*A room in the vice-regal lodge, Phoenix Park. A large opening, C.
curtained; large lattice window at back, C.; the inner room is a
bedroom — toilet R., bed L.; in front room, door R.H. of opening;
door L.H.1E.; candles burning on toilet table; small lamp on table
next bed;* TINEY *in bed L.C.; music heard in distance;* LADY
KATHERINE YORKE *enters door R.H., creeps toward bed; she is
in ball dress.*

TINEY. I am not asleep, Katie.

LADY KATHERINE. You naughty girl; the doctor said that sleep
was the only medicine to restore your health.

TINEY. I have been listening to the music from the ballroom.
Come sit by me and tell me all about it; who were there? with
whom did you dance?

LADY KATHERINE (*sitting on bed*). Oh, if the Earl knew I steal in
here every night to keep you awake with my chatter.

TINEY. Tell your papa you are trying to make me forget mine. Oh,
Katie, you have brothers, sisters, mother, father — but he, my
darling, was all I had in the world.

LADY KATHERINE. Is there no one who could teach you to forget
him better than I can?

TINEY. What do you mean?

LADY KATHERINE. You speak as you sleep; I can hear you from my
bedroom, yonder. There is one name constantly on your lips.

TINEY. What name?

LADY KATHERINE. Let me whisper it — 'Robert.'

TINEY. I don't know anyone of that name.

LADY KATHERINE. Are you sure?

TINEY. Quite sure. (*After a pause*) — Oh, yes, I forgot.

LADY KATHERINE. Aha!

TINEY. Our under coachman! It was he that drove the carriage on
that horrid night.

366

LADY KATHERINE. A coachman! Oh, you cruel Tiney, to crush all my hopes of a secret romance. (*Goes to toilet and begins to take flowers from her hair.*) Oh! here is my bouquet! Let the flowers be your bed-fellows!

TINEY. How sweet they are! Here is sweetbriar, and here are violets. Oh, they bring the green fields and hedge rows to my bedside; who gave you this?

LADY KATHERINE. Our new under-secretary — Sir Barry Clinton.

TINEY. Is he handsome?

LADY KATHERINE. Very.

TINEY. How nice?

LADY KATHERINE. Very! and so clever! He has only been here a week, and he has already made his mark.

TINEY. On your heart, Katie?

LADY KATHERINE. Nonsense; papa says he will be a distinguished man.

TINEY. How often did he dance with you?

LADY KATHERINE. Well, he undertook to teach me the new German dance that is becoming quite the rage in London — it is called the waltz.

TINEY. Is it as a dancing master that he has made his mark?

LADY KATHERINE. No! it was while we were waltzing that Barry told me —

TINEY. It has come to 'Barry' already, has it? and he has only been here a week — oh! Katie!

LADY KATHERINE. Don't interrupt me.

TINEY. Go on; I'm shocked!

LADY KATHERINE. It seems that my Barry has succeeded in a great affair in which the police and Major Sirr have failed. Everybody believed that the dreadful young man Emmet had escaped to France. Barry has discovered that he has never left Dublin; he has been here all the while, concealed in a cottage in Butterfield Lane.

(TINEY *sits up in bed.*)

TINEY. Is — is he taken?

LADY KATHERINE. Not yet; they will arrest him tonight. What have you done with the hairpins? — oh, here they are! It seems that Barry was out fishing this morning at Dunleary; the boatman he employed, a fellow named Rafferty, tempted by the reward of eight hundred pounds offered for the capture of the rebel, told him where Mr. Emmet lay in hiding, and that his boat had been hired to take the fugitive across the Channel to France. Rather shabby of Mr. Rafferty, but it will make my

Barry's fortune. There — now I'll slip on my dressing-gown, and come back to bid you good night. (*Exit.*)

TINEY. Tonight! She said 'tonight he will be taken.' They will kill him, and I am helpless to save him. Oh, what can I do? He would have saved papa — he would have killed the man who murdered my darling — and I can do nothing! — (*Wrings her hands in despair*) — nothing! Oh, how tenderly he spoke to me. I felt the tears on my neck as he held me to his heart, and the eyes that shed them will be closed forever. His sweet face is ever present there — there — above mine. Oh, I know now whose name I spoke in my sleep.

(*Re-enter* LADY KATHERINE, *dressed in a wrapper.*)

LADY KATHERINE. There, I come to bid you good night. I will put out the lights. (*She extinguishes the candles. The moonlight falls through the window on the girl and over the bed.*) I declare, she is asleep already. Oh, what a weight off my conscience that is. Good night, sweet angel!

(*She takes the lamp, and draws the curtain so as to close in the recess, then goes out quietly, L.H. door; stage dark; after a pause, the face of* TINEY *appears between the curtains; she enters; she is dressed in a long peignoir; she tries to walk, but falls, kneeling near door R.H. in F.*)

TINEY. Oh, Merciful Father in Heaven, bear up my poor weak limbs! inspire my failing body with your will! grant me strength to reach him who saved my life! take it now, and let me die at his feet! (*She raises herself feebly, feels her way by the wall to the door — opens it — listens, and then creeps out. Scene changes.*)

ACT THREE: SCENE TWO

ANN DEVLIN's *cottage in Butterfield Lane;* ROBERT *seated at table C.;* ANN *asleep by fireside;* ANDY *lies across the door.*

ROBERT. Betrayed by knaves! deserted by cowards! tracked and hounded like a wild beast! It is the inexorable fate of all the saviours of the people! Oh, ye spirits! you immortal band of heroes who suffered for your faith! Bodyguard of Him who died for the human race! Accept into your ranks the humble life of one, who, loving his native land not wisely, but too well, followed in your footsteps upward to the Throne where sit the Eternal Trinity of Truth, Light, and Freedom! (*He rises.*) Men will call me visionary, a rash fool, and dupe. Ah! had those on whom Bonaparte relied failed him in the pinch! Had Washington misplaced his trust amongst traitors, these monarchs of men might have stood as I do now! An outcast! downfallen! the scoff of the world! The wood of which Fortune shapes a throne, is ready at need to build a gallows! (*Two knocks at door in F., followed by a whistle; then a third knock.*) It is the signal! (*He opens the door.*)
    (*Enter* DWYER, *who steps over* ANDY.)
DWYER. Is that the way he kapes watch over yur honour while I am away? Wait till I wake him up. (*Raises his whip.*)
ROBERT (*staying him*). Don't be hard on the boy. For three nights, while they hunted us from garret to cellar, he has had no rest. Let him sleep! What news?
DWYER. Wexford is ready and willing. Kildare, Carlow, Waterford and Kilkenny are waiting your word.
ROBERT (*sits at table*). Ay! So they told Lord Edward in '98! but what followed? — treachery in his camp — disconcerted plans — mutiny amongst the leaders — confusion — drunkenness and plunder amongst the men — havoc, panic, and despair. I will not give the signal for bloodshed!

369

DWYER. It is for your honour to say. (*He puts a shawl over* ANN.)

ROBERT. Why should you continue the fight?

DWYER. Maybe because it's all I am good for! Sure I'm only a dog at your heel, to watch for your bidding, and do it without axin' why.

ROBERT. My brave Dwyer, had I only five hundred men like yourself, I'd bid the world stand by to see our people made a nation! But our enterprise is beset with pitfalls — we are walking on a bog — the ground under our feet is rotten.

DWYER. Then save yourself. If you go on hanging 'round this place, you will lave your life here. (*Sits and lights his pipe.*)

ROBERT. I will leave Ireland tomorrow.

DWYER. Why not tonight? Joe Rafferty's hooker is lying in Dunleary — she will fly wid your honour to the French coast like a saygull.

ROBERT. Are you sure of Rafferty?

DWYER. Am I sure of my own sister's son?

ROBERT. This letter from Miss Curran appoints a meeting tonight at Father Donnelly's, at Glenmalure; he has consented to perform the ceremony of marriage between us — thence we go direct to France.

ANDY (*who has risen, and listens at the door*). Whist! there's a strange footfall in the lane! it stops at the gate!

(DWYER *puts down his pipe, brings out a pistol and a short iron bludgeon.*)

ANN (*waking*). Did your honour call me?

DWYER. Hould your prate.

ANDY. 'Tis mighty queer. I believe it is only a dog, for it has got no footsteps at all. (*Looks through keyhole.*) Hould your breath! It is here, close agin the dure.

DWYER. Throw it wide.

(ANDY *throws open the door.* TINEY *is leaning against the post.*)

ROBERT. Miss Wolfe! (*Runs to her and brings her down.*)

ANN. Here at this hour. She is perished with cold. We heard you were lying ill at the Lodge.

TINEY. So I was. 'Twas there, an hour ago, I learned that you were hiding here. They know it. They will come here tonight to arrest you.

ROBERT. Who could have betrayed us?

TINEY. A man named Rafferty, whose boat you are to take at Dunleary.

DWYER. Blood alive! My sisther's son — my own flesh.

ANN. Michael! For the Lord's sake, don't look so white.

DWYER. 'Tis Joe's winding sheet you see in my face.

ROBERT. And you rose from your bed to come here?

TINEY. Yes.

ANN. Not on foot? (*Kneels beside her.*)

TINEY. I dared not take a car. Look at my dress — I must look like a banshee. The carman would have driven me to Swift's hospital for the insane. (*She laughs.*)

ANN. Without shoes on your feet.

TINEY. It is so.

ANN. See how they bleed.

TINEY. I did not feel it. (*She faints.*)

ROBERT. She has fainted.

ANDY (*at door*). A crowd of men have stopped at the fut of the lane. One is on horseback.

DWYER (*blowing out the light*). If they are on the sarch, a light in the house at this hour will guide them. (*Goes to the door. Looks out.*) It is the Major.

ROBERT. Sirr?

(ANDY *runs to L.H. door. Looks out.*)

DWYER. Quick, sir; you have ten minutes before they can reach us.

ANDY. I see lights on this side. They are all around us.

ROBERT. Is there no escape?

ANN. Yes; the ould well by the shed outside. Hide yourselves in it. Down with yez, all three. There's not a fut of wather there. They will only find me here, and this poor sick child. Never mind us.

DWYER. She is right. Come, sir.

(*Exit* ROBERT *with* DWYER.)

ANN. Don't lave that coat there. (*Points to* ROBERT's *overcoat.*)

ANDY (*taking it up*). The Major will get his horse back afther all. Bad luck to the baste he'll tell on us, for he's stabled in the shed. Whoo! Wait a bit. (*Puts on the coat.*) I'll back him an' take a flier through the crowd o' them. I may as well be shot as hung. So here goes for which. (*Exit L.H. door.*)

ANN. Poor child. This night will kill her. (*Two blows on the door.*)

SIRR (*outside*). In the King's name open this door.

ANN (*turning*). In the devil's name — pull down the latch.

(*Enter* SIRR, *followed by* SERGEANT *and* SOLDIERS.)

SIRR. Who is the owner of this house?

ANN. I am, for want of a fetther.

371

SIRR. A man calling himself Ellis lodges here.

ANN. He does.

SIRR. Where is he?

ANN. There is his room — help yourself.

SIRR. Go search the place.

    (*Exit* SERGEANT *and two* SOLDIERS.)

I told you that some day you would fall into my hands, and here you are.

ANN. Here I am, sure enough.

SIRR. What girl is that? Stand aside! Miss Wolfe! What brings her here?

ANN. She brought a sportin' message that the hounds would meet here early in the mornin', and here you are.

    (*Re-enter* SERGEANT *and* SOLDIERS.)

SIRR. Not there — what is this — a letter in the handwriting of the man we want. The ink is still wet on the pen. He has been here within the last ten minutes. Will you tell us where your lodger is?

ANN. How would I know? It is no business of mine where he goes.

    (SIRR *goes up to the door.*)

SIRR. We'll sharpen your wits. Prepare a rope there. (*Speaks off at the door.*) Tilt back that car, with the shafts in the air. Haould it so, some of yez. That will sarve for an elegant gallows to suit this woman.

    (*She struggles with the* SOLDIERS *who would seize her; they present their bayonets so as to keep her prisoner against the wall.*)

Will you confess now? I'll give you two minutes.

ANN. You are not the priest. I have nothing to confess.

    (*They seize her.*)

You may murder me, you cowards, but not one word about him will you get out of Ann Devlin. Now do your worst.

TINEY (*recovering*). Ann! Where are you?

ANN. Good-bye, Miss.

TINEY. Release that woman! If you hurt a hair of her head, I will denounce the infamous plot you planned in Dublin Castle in my presence. It was by the hands of your accomplices my father fell. Assassin! Assassin!

    (*Cries outside; shots;* SIRR *runs to the door.*)

SIRR. My horse! Stop him! Cut him down! 'Tis Emmet. Shoot.

    (*Runs out followed by the* SOLDIERS, *who release* ANN; ANN *bars the door. Enter* EMMET *and* DWYER. TINEY *runs to* ROBERT. *Scene closes in.*)

ACT THREE: SCENE THREE

Glenmalure. Enter QUIGLEY.

QUIGLEY. Mind how you step across that single bit of road. This
way, Miss.
  (*Enter* SARAH.)
SARAH. Are we near to Father Donnelly's?
QUIGLEY. You may see his chapel there beyant.
SARAH. You are sure Mr. Emmet received my letter?
QUIGLEY. Never fear, Miss.
SARAH. Then I will ask you to leave me here, and return to the
car at the foot of the hill where we shall join you.
QUIGLEY. More power, Miss. (*Exit.*)
SARAH. There was no way but this to save him. (*Exit.*)
  (QUIGLEY *returns.*)
QUIGLEY. There she goes straight into the thrap!
  (*Enter* SIRR.)
He! he! There will be a gay weddin' tonight at Father
Donnelly's!
SIRR. Go to the Enniskerry road. See the men are posted there,
so as to close his escape that way. I'll take with me twenty
rank and file to surround the house.
QUIGLEY (*going R.*). More power! be jabers we'll put the net
securely over him this time. Whist! look here! d'ye see them
two shadows creepin' down the side o' the hill?
SIRR. They are cattle, maybe!
QUIGLEY. Cattle on two legs, Major! they are makin' straight for
the priest's house.
SIRR. They must be two of our fellows that got astray.
QUIGLEY. Divil a man you had that could foot the hillside like
them two. Look now! the big one is in the moonlight! 'Tis
Michael Dwyer! and his follower is Andy Devlin! Whoo! yer
sowl! we'll bag the whole covey!

373

SIRR. Hark! I hear the hoofs of a horse!

QUIGLEY. And so does Dwyer! Ye see — he stops to listen!

SIRR. Yonder comes a man riding a piebald!

QUIGLEY. 'Tis your own baste, Major! and Emmet himself is across him! 'Tis yourself is in luck, sir, this night.

SIRR. You are right; the two fellows have joined the horseman, and they are going together towards the house.

(CLAVERHOUSE, *outside, sings verse of Bonnie Dundee.*)

QUIGLEY. What is that!

SIRR. The officer in command of the detachment sent to assist me in this capture. Confound the fool, he will betray our presence.

QUIGLEY. And scare the game.

(*Enter* CLAVERHOUSE.)

SIRR. Do you always sing, sir, when you are in sight of danger?

CLAVERHOUSE. No; sometimes I smoke.

SIRR. You are betraying our presence to the foe we are in pursuit of.

CLAVERHOUSE. British troops always betray their presence. D'ye want us to skulk?

SIRR. Captain Claverhouse, you see those three men yonder, standing before that house?

CLAVERHOUSE. I see two men and a half.

SIRR. Then you see Robert Emmet and Michael Dwyer.

QUIGLEY. And the half is Andy Devlin; but he's a half that can tackle a whole one as big as yourself.

SIRR. You see your duty before you? it is to place your men so as to surround and command those premises, and to make prisoners of all we find there. Are you prepared, sir, to perform that duty?

CLAVERHOUSE. Needs must, sir, when the devil drives.

SIRR. Do you mean that for a joke, or an insult?

CLAVERHOUSE. Both; and I hope you mean to resent it. This is a convenient spot, and there's no time like the present. Are you agreeable?

SIRR. Duty before pleasure, captain. After we have lodged our prisoners in Kilmainham, I'll take a walk with you in the Phaynix, if you are so minded.

CLAVERHOUSE (*aside as he goes out*). How can I warn him of his danger? (*Exit L.*)

SIRR. Follow me! (*Exit R.*)

QUIGLEY (*looks around*). There will be hot work when they try to tackle Dwyer. Wh'ere will I find a safe hidin' place convenient to see it all? There's a clump of bushes that looks well out of harm's way. (*Goes R.; recoils.*) It is movin'! 'tare an 'ouns! there's somebody inside! maybe he's got his gun fixed on me! (*Creeps off L.H.*)

(*Enter* FINERTY *very pale.*)

FINERTY. Stop!

QUIGLEY. Don't shoot!

FINERTY. 'Tis meself, Finerty.

QUIGLEY. I thought it was one of Dwyer's men; what brings you here?

FINERTY. I'm nearly dead. I dare not show in the streets of Dublin. I'd be killed. The people say I sould the life of Emmet. So I was hidin' here when Dwyer's men caught sight of me, and have been huntin' me like a rat. I believe I know every hole in these hills.

QUIGLEY. Are Dwyer's men about here?

FINERTY. An hour ago they were here as thick as flies, but they vanished over the hill towards Dernamuck.

QUIGLEY. They were scared by the redcoats; but now himself is here, there will be wigs on the green before sunrise. Pat, this is no place for us. I've got the car below here. I'll take ye back to Dublin where you will get safe lodgin' in Kilmainham until we get the reward, and then we'll show Ireland our heels.

FINERTY. The sooner the betther. (*Going*) After we pocket our pay, I'll go to America and take some other name.

QUIGLEY. Be jabers, Pat, but that will be mighty hard on the man whose name you take. (*Exeunt.*)

ACT THREE: SCENE FOUR

The interior of FATHER DONNELLY's — *a small chapel is seen L.H. through an arch in the wall, facing audience; a large bay-window R.H.; door R.H.; fireplace L.H.; candles are lighted in the altar in chapel; door L.H.3E. at entrance to chapel.*

SARAH (*at bay-window*). I thought I heard the sound of a horse in the road.

FATHER DONNELLY. You are listening with your heart.

SARAH. Oh, father! I can hear nothing else! Fear and hope possess me, that my being feels like one great pulse! Now, do you hear! my ears do not deceive me!

(*Enter* ROBERT.)

Thank Heaven!

ROBERT. Do so, with all your heart on which I come to rest! for mine is well nigh sped! I have none for further struggle! I have slighted your love for a wanton infatuation! My other love has betrayed and deserted me; I come to you for forgiveness, for comfort, and for peace!

(*Enter* DWYER.)

DWYER. Get to work, your reverence! there's something wrong! for I told Maguire to meet me at Stony Creek beyant, but the hillside was as bare as a bog — not a sign of one of my people to the fore.

(*Exit* FATHER DONNELLY.)

SARAH. What do you fear?

DWYER. There's somebody in the mountains tonight besides ourselves and the grouse; as I came over Glenmalure I did not hear a cock crow, nor a plover cry.

(*Enter* ANDY *with gun.*)

ANDY. I found your gun in furze bush as you said, and this beside it. (*Shows a pike broken in two pieces.*)

ROBERT. What is it?

DWYER. A letter to me from Phil Maguire. Did you mind how them pieces lay?

ANDY. I did.

DWYER. Which way did pike end point?

ANDY. To Tallaght.

DWYER. There are redcoats there, and in power o' them, or Phil would not have shown his heels. How did the shaft lay?

ANDY. Pointing to Dernamuck.

DWYER. He has gone there to join two hundred men in the Glen of Emall. How will I let on to him that I am here?

ANDY. I lighted the furze bush before I left.

DWYER. Andy, me bouchal, asthure ye were — you are worth your weight in one-pound notes. Bar the dure!

(ANDY *looks out before closing the door.*)

How did you get here, Miss?

SARAH. On an outside car.

DWYER. Who drove ye?

SARAH. Quigley.

DWYER. Ah! Did he know your business here, and that his honour was to meet you?

SARAH. Yes.

DWYER. We are trapped! You guided the redcoats! You little knew you had their escort behind you all the way from Dublin.

ROBERT. I cannot believe Quigley capable of such dastardly treason. (*A shot is fired outside.*)

ANDY. Ah! (*Pulls to the door.*) Quick, Mike! help me to pull down the bar!

(DWYER *runs up and bars the door.*)

DWYER (*aside to him*). Were you hit?

ANDY. It is nothing.

DWYER (*to* ROBERT). Do you believe it now?

(*Re-enter* FATHER DONNELLY *in his vestments.*)

Get into the chapel, your reverence, and take the lady; the walls are thick — you'll be snug then! Oh! if we can only howld out for an hour!

ROBERT. We cannot hold it for a quarter. They will soon break in the door.

DWYER. Not while I stand here. (*Three shots.*) Andy, blow out the light there! it guides their fire!

(ANDY *blows out the light;* ROBERT *draws* SARAH *into the chapel.*)

377

DWYER. Now, Andy, we'll take a hand in the game! Let us see how it lies — there's a crack in them shutters!

(ANDY *and* DWYER *enter the bay-window behind the curtains. The scene changes.*)

ACT THREE: SCENE FIVE

The R.H. flat revolves and comes down oblique, enclosing L.H. side of stage, showing a yard enclosed by a low stone wall; the R.H. flat serves as exterior of house with porch; the wall is lined with SOLDIERS; SIRR *amongst them. Enter* CLAVERHOUSE.

CLAVERHOUSE. Stop firing! Who gave the order?

SIRR. I did.

CLAVERHOUSE. Mind your business, and don't presume to take my command. (*To* DRUMMER *beside him*) Roll!

   (DRUMMER *gives a sharp roll on drum.*)

   Father Donnelly — we are under orders to search your house, where we have information Mr. Emmet is concealed.

SARAH. 'Tis Norman!

CLAVERHOUSE. We call on you in the King's name to open your doors that we may do our duty! if you refuse, we must employ force! and if resisted, our directions are to destroy your house and chapel and bring you prisoners to Dublin!

   (*The door opens:* FATHER DONNELLY *appears in it, dressed in his vestments.*)

FATHER DONNELLY. Strangers came to my door and claimed my ministry; I led them to the foot of the altar. God forbids I should violate that sanctuary as you would have me do! You will do your duty to your Master, as I shall do mine to Him whose commission I bear. (*He retires and closes the door.*)

SIRR. Now, captain, as we have no time to lose, pour a couple of volleys into the rat-trap, and set fire to the stable beyant — that will fetch them out.

CLAVERHOUSE. There is a lady there.

SIRR. We do not regard the sex of a viper when we crush it — so with rebels.

DWYER. Oh, Phil Maguire! why arn't you widin call?

ANDY. Maybe he is, but is waitin' for your ordhers.

ROBERT. Sarah — I cannot sacrifice this noble old man. I cannot wreck his house and consign him to prison. I will surrender.

SARAH. No! no! death here, with us together! (*Clings to him.*)

ANDY (*aside to* DWYER). Michael, listen hither, my arm is broke; that first shot did it. 'Tis no good. If we are tuk, it is a dog's death by the rope on the next tree.

DWYER. That's it.

ANDY. Stand by me, while I show you o' thrick to draw their fire; and when they have emptied their guns, make a dash over the wall and through their line; gain the hills, and before they are through wid ourselves, you will be back wid Maguire and his men.

DWYER. What are you going to do?

ANDY. Lave me alone. Kiss me, Mike, for Ann. Lend me your gun — be ready now for the rush! (*He throws open the door — entering the yard.*) Hurrah! Ireland forever! (*He fires.*) Come on, boys! (*A volley is fired at him; he staggers forward crying.*) Now, Mike, now! (*Falls*) tare alive! off wid ye, before they can load again!

DWYER. Andy! Andy me boy! what have you done?

SIRR. Down with him! 'Tis Michael Dwyer!

ROBERT (*entering*). Hold! I surrender!

ANDY. No! no! — no surrender! I hear the thramp of the Wexford boys! (*Whistles from behind every rock, and up the valley appear crowds of insurgents.* DWYER *and* ROBERT *raise* ANDY.) Ha! they are comin'!

(*Enter* SARAH *and* FATHER DONNELLY.)

Ha! ha! ha! — the redcoats fell into the trap! I laid for them! I emptied their barrels, and the masther is safe! Sure, it is not for me you are crying, miss? God bless you, I'm good for nothing. Don't waste a prayer over me, your riverence; I'm not worth it. I ax your pardon for dyin' like this, and thrubblin' you all. Kiss me, Mike! I believe I — am goin' now! 'Tis asier than I thought! (*Dies.*)

TABLEAU

ACT FOUR: SCENE ONE

The court house, Green Street; the trial of EMMET; NORBURY *on the bench;* JURY; BARRISTERS; OFFICERS; PUBLIC.

NORBURY. Prisoner at the bar! You have heard the evidence brought against you by the crown. You have been found guilty of a treasonable conspiracy to betray your country into the power of our common foe, the French. With this infamous object you provoke an insurrection, and became an accomplice in the most brutal murder of Lord Kilwarden, chief justice of the King's bench. To these and diverse other capital charges you have offered no defence. It is needless for me to impress on a man of your high attainments and position the baseness and infamy of such crimes. What have you now to say why judgment of death and execution should not be awarded against you?

ROBERT (*after a pause*). My lord; why judgment and execution should not be passed upon me, I have nothing to say. If I were condemned to suffer death only, I should bow in silence to my fate. A man dies — but his memory lives. Your sentence that delivers my body to the executioner shall not deliver my soul to the contempt of generations to come. You charge me with being the emissary of France. It is false! I would accept from France, for my country, the same assistance in our struggle for independence that Franklin obtained for America. But were the French, or any other foreign nation to come here as invaders, I would meet them on the shore, and if compelled to retire before superior discipline, I would dispute every inch of Irish soil, every blade of grass; and my last entrenchment should be my grave! I did not seek to free Ireland from the tyranny of one foreign power — Great Britain — to deliver her unto the bonds of another. Had I done so, I would have earned the execration of the country which gave me birth, and to which I would have given freedom.

NORBURY. Mr. Emmet, you must confine yourself to showing cause why judgment should not pass upon you; instead of doing so, you are broaching treason the most abominable.

ROBERT. I am showing cause, my lord, why the judgment of the world should not condemn me to a more shameful ignominy than the scaffold; why the calumnies you have uttered should not rest upon my name. If I stand at the bar of this court and am forbidden to vindicate my motives, what a farce is your justice! If I stand at this bar before you, and dare not vindicate my character, how dare you assail it? Does the sentence of death condemn my tongue to silence, when it would defend that immortal part of me which must survive; and is the only thing — God help me! — I can leave to those I honour and love, and to the people for whose sake I am proud to suffer? You have charged me with the murder of Lord Kilwarden; I would he were sitting there to judge me now, to sweeten death as he deplored the sentence he was bound by law to pronounce. If I call on God to witness that I had no share in that foul deed — it is because I have no other witness to testify in my defence.

(TINEY *rises, crosses over to the dock and gives him her hand.*)

My sweet child, do you absolve me? — would I had died in your father's place!

NORBURY. He who lets loose the storm is responsible for the havoc in its path.

ROBERT. My enterprise failed; had it been otherwise, your lordship might have occupied my place here at this moment, and I, yours!

NORBURY. Have you done, sir?

ROBERT. You are impatient for the sacrifice, my lord! — bear with me awhile, I have but few more words to say, and these, not to you — but to my people. See! For your sake I am parting with all that is dear to me in this life — family — friends — but most of all with her — (SARAH *rises with a cry*) — the woman I have loved. (*She goes to him.*) My love — Oh! My love! It was not thus I had thought to have requited your affection! (*He kisses her.*) Farewell! (CURRAN *receives her as she faints.*) Farewell! I pass away into the grave. I ask of the world only one favour at my departure. Let no man write my epitaph, for as no man who knows my motives dares now to vindicate them, let not prejudice or ignorance asperse them; let my tomb be uninscribed until other men and other times can do justice to my character! When my country shall take her place amongst the nations of the earth — then — and not till then, let my epitaph be written! I have done. (*Murmurs in the court.*)

THE CRIER. Silence in the court — while his lordship the judge passes sentence of death upon the prisoner at the bar.

(*As* NORBURY *assumes the black cap, the scene closes in.*)

ACT FOUR: SCENE TWO

A prison. Enter FINERTY *— followed by* QUIGLEY.

QUIGLEY. It is done at last. He is condemned.

FINERTY. When is he to die?

QUIGLEY. Tomorrow mornin'.

FINERTY. That's a short day.

QUIGLEY. Long enough for Dwyer and his boys to pull down Newgate, to get him out.

FINERTY. It will be a hard nut to crack.

QUIGLEY. And they will find it a blind one. They will draw it blank, for Emmet will lodge here tonight.

FINERTY. Here? in Kilmainham?

QUIGLEY. The police say there's not a turnkey in Newgate that is to be trusted. They would throw open the prison doors to the people.

FINERTY. Are you sure of the jailors here? One of them gave me the offer awhile ago. He is one of Dwyer's men — the place is full of them.

QUIGLEY. Kilmainham will be held tonight by a company of redcoats; meanwhile, a special warden has been appointed to watch the prisoner and sleep with him in his cell.

FINERTY. I hope they have picked a sure man?

QUIGLEY. They have. One I recommended. Yourself.

FINERTY. Me?

QUIGLEY. That's to be your duty this night.

FINERTY. But sure I can't stay here. The vessel that was to take you and me across the says to America will sail at daybreak.

QUIGLEY. You axed the Government to put you in here for protection. You could only be admitted as a prisoner, and a warrant for your release must be sent from the Castle before they can let you out. Be aisy; I'll take care of you.

FINERTY. And the money — the reward — it is due.

QUIGLEY. And will be paid tonight.

FINERTY. To you?

QUIGLEY. To me! Who else?

FINERTY. Where will it be paid? Will Sirr bring it here?

QUIGLEY. No; he will meet me at Brangan's wharf at Ring's End.

FINERTY. Furninst the spot where the ship lies moored and ready to sail! Quigley, you wouldn't go back on me, and run off wid my share of the reward?

QUIGLEY. Pat, I'm sorry for you; but the polis have found out that you tuk a hand in the killin' of Crawford.

FINERTY. You were there, and helped.

QUIGLEY. Then they say you were the man that murthered Kilwarden.

FINERTY. 'Twas yourself!

QUIGLEY. They dare not let you go.

FINERTY. Not let me out? Do you main they are going to keep me here a prisoner?

QUIGLEY. Until the next batch is transported to the penal settlement in Botany Bay. You are in for life, Pat.

FINERTY. Quigley, you are jokin'.

QUIGLEY. 'Tis a sorry joke. I brought the ordher from the Castle, and left it at the gate as I came in.

FINERTY. The ordher to kape me here? I won't believe it.

QUIGLEY. You see that dure? I am goin' out of it, just try to lave this place along wid me, and you *will* believe it, maybe; good bye, Pat. (*Exit.*)

(*As* FINERTY *follows him, a* JAILOR *appears and stops him.*)

FINERTY. It is true! Oh, the villain! the — the traitor! and to think while I am caged here, he will be sailin' away wid my money in his pocket, and a grin on his mug. Oh! no! no! not so fast misther Quigley. Aha! two can play at your game. (*To the* JAILOR.) Come here! 'twas you gave me the offis awhile ago; give me your hand. You know this Wexford grip? I am one of yourselves — mind me now. I'll give you a paper; it is for Michael Dwyer, and must reach him, say widin an hour. Lend me your back to write it. (*He takes a pencil and note-book from his pocket and writes.*) 'Quigley will meet Major Sirr tonight at Brangan's wharf, Ring's End — there to receive the price of Robert Emmet's head. Patrick Finerty.' You have heard, and you know what's in it; don't delay a minute. (*Gives him the note.*)

(*Exit* JAILOR, *closing door, locking it.*)

Ha! ha! so, I have set the dog to watch the rathole.

385

(*Enter* CLAVERHOUSE.)

CLAVERHOUSE. Are you the warden charged with the care of Mr. Emmet?

FINERTY. So I am tould.

CLAVERHOUSE. I am the officer in command of the men detailed to protect the jail.

FINERTY. I know your honour well.

CLAVERHOUSE. They are preparing the cell in which he will pass the night — you can keep watch in the corridor.

FINERTY. Thrue for you, sir! The less he sees of me the betther for us both.

> (*As* FINERTY *goes to the door, he suddenly retires and conceals himself behind it as* ROBERT, *accompanied by two* TURNKEYS, *enters. He is manacled.*)

CLAVERHOUSE. Remove those chains. If these walls are not responsible for the prisoner's safeguard I will be so.

> (*They remove the chains.*)

See! They have cut into his wrists; they bleed.

ROBERT. It is nothing!

> (FINERTY *escapes. The* TURNKEY *retires.*)

Are you on duty here?

CLAVERHOUSE. Yes.

ROBERT. So am I. We are prisoners both! You to watch and to guard; I to await my release. Yours is the more painful office.

CLAVERHOUSE. I bring you a visitor. Will you see him?

ROBERT. Whom?

CLAVERHOUSE. Mr. Curran.

ROBERT. Ah! With all my heart! (NORMAN *goes to the door.*) For it owes him a debt.

> (*Enter* CURRAN.)

Oh, sir! I know I have done you a very severe injury — greater than I can atone for with my life. Let my love for your daughter plead for me. Do not turn away. Do not let a man with the coldness of death upon him feel any other coldness.

CURRAN. Robert, my poor boy, I would hide my weakness from you. God forbid I should turn away from the son of my old friend — the child who has played about my knees!

CLAVERHOUSE. We have no time for bletherin'. Why don't you tell the lad what has been done for his sake.

CURRAN. Miss Wolfe and my daughter have been with the lord-lieutenant pleading for a commutation of your sentence.

I urged my own claim on the Government for many and valuable services. His excellency was much moved by their prayers, and, at last, in consideration of your youth and your distraction, he yielded so far as to receive your petition to the crown for its mercy, to be forwarded to London. (*Hands* ROBERT *a paper.*)

CLAVERHOUSE. I have seen my uncle, Norbury. He will back the prayer.

CURRAN. Meanwhile execution will be stayed.

ROBERT (*reading to himself*). 'To the King's Most Excellent Majesty. The humble petition of Robert Emmet, a prisoner lying under sentence of death.' (*Reads the rest in silence.*) Oh, sir! This is a beggar's petition for life! for life at any price. What shall I say? What answer can I make to those angels of love and pity. I see their pleading faces, their sweet eyes blinded with tears, lifted to mine. I see the sweet, childish mouth of Tiney trembling with her tender supplication! Yet between my kisses I would say I cannot crawl to the foot of the throne and sue for pardon. My country is my accomplice! Shall I indict her by confessing my penitence? Ah, sir, you may call me mad. It may be so. Call me rash. The fool of vain hopes. Tell his excellency I am sensible of his goodness, but I cannot accept a few dishonourable years as the price of my life to come.

CURRAN. You refuse the royal clemency?

ROBERT. No! I will accept so much of it as his majesty may grant to one so poor as I am. I ask to face the death of a soldier. Let me stand before a platoon of brave fellows, and wearing the uniform of my country, let me fall like a man, and not die by the rope like a dog.

CLAVERHOUSE. Thankee, sir; thankee! I'm proud o' ye! 'Tis a shame to waste a mon like yersel'.

CURRAN. Must I take back this answer to his excellency?

(*Enter a* TURNKEY *who speaks with* NORMAN *at back.*)

ROBERT. I have staked my life, and have lost the game. It is a debt of honour, and as such must be paid within twenty-four hours. (*Smiling, as he offers* CURRAN *his hand.*) You see, sir, it takes all I have in the world to meet the claim.

CURRAN. Give me some ground to plead upon. Will you not promise to forsake the cause that has betrayed you?

ROBERT. Ask me to forsake your daughter, and be foresworn to my love. Bear with me, sir — and let me live out my life — what is left of it is full of her. Her dear image is before me. I have no other care — no other thought — this is the eve of my wedding night. I lie down in my grave to dream of her until I wake to meet my bride at the altar of heaven. Tell her I wait her there.

CLAVERHOUSE. Your cell is ready.

CURRAN. Farewell, Robert, my son.

ROBERT. God bless you, sir; for that word — farewell! (*Exeunt* ROBERT *with* TURNKEY. *R.* CURRAN *and* NORMAN *L.*)

ACT FOUR: SCENE THREE

The Bull Inn, a low class public house of the period. It occupies
a cellar, approached by a short flight of steps, R.H. in F., door
leading to street. Doors R. and L. Secret door, L.H. in F. Tables
R. and L., at which men are drinking, smoking clay pipes, and two
are playing at cards. Enter by secret door, DWYER.

DWYER. Boys! attention! There is brave work to be done this
night; listen to this! (*Reads paper.*) 'At eleven o'clock Quigley
will be at Brangan's wharf, Ring's End, to receive from Major
Sirr the reward agreed wid the Government as the price of
Robert Emmet's head. Signed Patrick Finerty.' What d'ye say
should be this black traitor's reward?

ALL. Death!

DWYER. That's enough. Lave the payment of the debt to me.
(*Enter* ANN DEVLIN.)

ANN. Dwyer, are you there?

DWYER. Is it yourself, Ann? Did you see the Major?

ANN. Yes, and I followed your bidding. But oh, Mike, 'tis a
terrible thing you axed me to do.

DWYER. What did he say?

ANN. He is close behind me, wid a guard of soldiers at his heels.

ALL. Redcoats! comin' here? (*Tumult.*)

DWYER. Order! fall in! If there's any one of you dares not thrust
his life in the hands of Michael Dwyer let him fall out! The
dure is open to him; the road is clear. This woman wid a man's
heart in her breast, is worth a boatload of your cowardly
carcasses. Hark! I hear the thramp of the soldiers; they are
comin' here to this place! There's time to escape by that dure
to the house in Marshalsea Lane that backs on this; you can
save your dirty skins that way! Be off still! Be quick! When
a man has no heart left, and he loses his head, he takes to his
legs.

ANN. Don't be so hard upon them, Mike. They mane to stand by you.

ALL. Ay! Ay! never fear!

DWYER. Go back to your pipes then, and to your games! and lave me alone to play mine!

(*The* MEN *resume their places at the tables. A* SERGEANT *and* SOLDIERS *appear at the door; they enter. Enter* MAJOR SIRR.)

SIRR. This is the Bull Inn? (*To* ANN.) Beware, woman, how you trifle with us. You have laid information that this place is a depot of concealed arms, and the resort of rebels.

ANN. Yes.

SIRR. The Bull Inn, though poor, bears a good name.

ANN. The pikes and guns are stored in the house in Marshalsea Lane that backs on this. There's a secret passage between the two. D'ye see that row of pegs? Pull the third one. (*Points back to the secret panel.*) Pull it down.

(*A* SERGEANT *approaches the row of pegs, and pulls it down; the secret door opens.*)

SIRR. Sergeant, take your file of men in there and report what you find!

(*Exit* SERGEANT *with all the* SOLDIERS *but two that remain on guard.*)

So far, good! Now you promise to deliver into my hands the person of a leader of the insurrection, for whose capture the Government has already offered a reward of five hundred pounds; there are only three rebels worth that sum. I am here by your agreement to put the head of this man in my hands — to whom do you refer? Where is he?

ANN. Where is he? (*She struggles with her emotion.*) No! no! I — I can't do it — Oh Mike! it is more than my heart can bare.

SIRR. You said 'Mike' — you cannot mean Michael Dwyer?

DWYER. That's what she does mane! and I am he! (*Advances and faces* SIRR.)

SIRR. You — Michael Dwyer?

DWYER. Himself.

SIRR. If you are he, we met at Vinegue Hill when I put a bullet in your throat.

DWYER. I believe the compliment was returned at Bally Ellis, when I put a pike in your ribs.

SIRR. We are quits. (*Offers his hand.*)

DWYER (*taking it*). Not until you get me where Robert Emmet is now!

(*Re-enter the* SERGEANT *with two* MEN.)

SIRR. Lads, have you found the arms?

SERGEANT. We have, sir; the place is full of them.

SIRR. And this woman has betrayed you?

DWYER. This woman is my wife that was to be, and she obeyed me; I wanted to sell my life, she made the bargain. Have you the money there?

SIRR. Here it is. (*Offers it to* ANN.)

ANN (*repelling it*). No! no!

DWYER. Give it to me. (*He receives the money from* SIRR.) There, boys, divide that between yez. 'Tis what the Castle says Michael Dwyer is worth. They came here wid me to rescue Emmet. Those are keys to every gate in Kilmainham. You seventy redcoats there wouldn't be a mouthful amongst two thousand undher my command. The turnkeys are united Irishmen. There are eight hundred prisoners, like wild bastes, behind your bars, hungry for liberty and your death.

SIRR. Then why did you not attempt this release?

DWYER. Captain Claverhouse ordhered the irons off him and shared wid him his own quarters in the prison, taking only his word not to escape, and Emmet will kape it. That's why we failed. These arms are no good now. I give them up and sell my life on condition no other shall be taken. (*Sits on a keg.*)

SIRR. And if I refuse your terms?

DWYER. You won't do that.

SIRR. Why not — you are in my power.

DWYER. I'll show you why not! I am setting on a hundred weight of gunpowder. (*He strikes in the bung of the cask; the powder flows out.*) Patsey, lend me your pipe.

(*The* SOLDIERS *make a move for the steps.*)

SIRR. No, stop.

DWYER. We are not afraid of death, and this way will save law costs.

SIRR. I accept your terms — the men can go.

DWYER. You give your word not one of them will come to harm?

SIRR. Will you rely on it?

DWYER. Yes. I know a man when I've fought wid him! You will kape your word. Go home boys, paceable, and tell the rest outside there's nothin' more to be done — this time. Good-bye, God bliss you.

(*Exeunt the* MEN.)

SIRR. Sergeant, march your men back to the Castle. You can leave me here.

(DWYER *leans over* ANN, *who has been seated L. crying.*)

SIRR. Michael Dwyer, here are two passes to America by the vessel that lies off the north wall and sails tomorrow at daybreak. Take Ann Devlin with you. You are free.

ANN. Oh, Major, do you main it? Mike, d'ye hear what he says?

DWYER. I do, Ann, but I want more than that, or nothing. Read that paper.

(SIRR *reads it apart, handed to him by* DWYER.)

SIRR. It is true — we meet there in an hour.

DWYER. The money will be paid in gold?

SIRR. Gold and silver.

DWYER. 'Twill be quite a weight.

SIRR. Yes, I'll take it on a car.

DWYER. I'll dhrive yer honour. 'Twill be quite convanient for me and Ann to get aboard the ship, and I've a trifle to pay Quigley before I go. So when your business is done you can lave me wid him.

SIRR. I understand. Bring the car to the Castle yard at once, I will be there to meet you. (*Exit.*)

ANN. Michael, what are you going to do to Quigley?

DWYER. As sure as God made us both, one of us will go to render his life account up there tonight. Come. (*Scene closes in.*)

392

ACT FOUR: TABLEAU

Brangan's wharf, Ring's End, near Dublin; a rude shed; a flight of steps, L.H.; a door, L.C. in flat, looking out on the river; a boat appears at door; QUIGLEY *looks. around — strikes a light, and lights lamp on table, L.C.; chair and keg.*

QUIGLEY. St. Patrick's is after strikin' eleven. It is time for the Major to come. This boat will save me to get aboard the ship! There she lies! 'Tis time I got away out o' this country. That's too hot to howld me. Whist! I heard the wheels of a car! Ay! it stops! (*Goes to door L.C.*) It is mighty dark; there comes a lanthorn! 'Tis himself! (*Retires to R., and closes door in flat.*)

    (*Enter* SIRR *with lantern, followed by* DWYER *carrying bag.* DWYER *has a huge carman's coat; a beard conceals his face.*)

I thought you would come alone.

SIRR. And carry half a hundred weight of coin? Lave the bag there, my man, and go mind your horse.

    (*Exit* DWYER *with lantern.*)

Now, sir, count out your money.

    (QUIGLEY *seizes the bag.*)

QUIGLEY (*counting*). He! he! oh, but there's nothing in life so sweet as that sound of coin. (*As he counts.*) Your honour promised me two free passages for myself and Finerty to New York.

SIRR. You will get them when you are done your count there, never fear.

QUIGLEY. I knew you would be as good as your word, sir. There's three hundred — how they shine! (*Opens his vest, takes from his waist a belt;* MAJOR SIRR *rises and after walking up and down, exit L.;* QUIGLEY *continues.*)

QUIGLEY. There's two hundred more! Ho! ho! I'm in luck! (*He puts the money into the belt.*)

(*Enter* DWYER, *without his beard or coat; he takes the seat recently occupied by* MAJOR SIRR.)

QUIGLEY. Fifty — seventy — eighty — a hundred — six hundred — and I see there's two hundred more! (*He sweeps it all into the belt, and buckles it around his waist.*) There's no knowin' what kind of a crew I will find aboard that ship; and if they knew what cargo I had in my hold, it is a poor chance I'd have to land it. So (*Buttons his coat*), 'tis a heavy load; but it gives a lightness to my heart. Now for the passes, and good-bye, Major!

(DWYER *advances his hand as he takes* QUIGLEY'*s hand,* QUIGLEY *looks up; their faces meet; the candle between.*)

Mother o' mercy! It is a ghost!

DWYER. I tould you Quigley that some day I would die by your hand, or you would die by mine; that day has come.

QUIGLEY. Would you murdher me, and rob me afther?

DWYER. It would be no murdher to kill a rat! It is not your money I want, it is your life! Keep the price of blood! There are the passes, and there (*Throws two knives on the table before* QUIGLEY) choose one of these — they are alike!

(QUIGLEY *takes the knives and examines them by the candle; suddenly he blows the candle out, and springs on* DWYER, *who, leaping to one side, avoids him.*)

Egorra! I forgot the blackguard I was dalin' wid! (*As he dodges around the table, he meets the chair in which he had been seated; he seizes it, and holds* QUIGLEY *at bay; he calls.*) Ann — Ann avourneen! Come!

(ANN *appears at door L.H. with lantern.*)

ANN. What's the matter?

DWYER. All right — stand there and give us a light!

ANN. Kill him, Mike! kill him! (*Holds the light above her head.*)

DWYER. Never fear!

ANN. Will I help you?

DWYER. No; I'll be equal to the dirty work. Come on, Quigley! Are ye afeerd of an unarmed man? Don't be bashful! why a rat would make a better fight. (*As* QUIGLEY *makes a rush at him, he claps the chair over his head, which appears through the legs and rails, while his arms are pinioned to the back legs and side rails.*) The rat is in the trap! (*He pins him against the wall; holding him then with one hand, he seizes his throat by the other.*) D'ye remember the grip?

QUIGLEY. Mer — mercy!

DWYER. I don't hear what you are saying! Spake up, man!

(QUIGLEY *drops the knives.*)

That's right, be aisy now; you are goin' into the Liffey, where the price of blood will take you to the bottom. So, he's gone to where he will meet Masther Robert tomorrow — to where I must answer one day for what I have done tonight. Now you can help me, Ann, to poison the tide.

(*She opens the door at back; he throws* QUIGLEY *out; they get into the boat and disappear; the shed is drawn off; the river appears; they are in the boat; a vessel with lights burning is seen about a quarter of a mile away.*)

END OF TABLEAU

ACT FOUR: LAST TABLEAU

The yard of Kilmainham. Muffled drums are heard. Enter
SERGEANT *with a file of* MEN, *followed by* NORMAN
CLAVERHOUSE *and* EMMET.

ROBERT. So! this is the place! and this is my last day. Look! the
sun never lighted a brighter one! Do not be cast down, my
friend. If I had fallen in the strife of battle, it would not have
been a more glorious ending. I sought no other. You promised
me to see my mother this morning, and bring to me her
blessing. Have you seen her?

CLAVERHOUSE. No, Robert, for you will receive your blessing
from herself.

ROBERT. She is coming to see me?

CLAVERHOUSE. No; you are going to see her.

ROBERT. She — she is dead?

CLAVERHOUSE. She died last night.

ROBERT. My sentence killed her! God forgive me! Well, I go to
seek her pardon! (*A bell tolls; a black flag on the flag-post is
seen to rise half-mast high over the prison.*) Is that the signal?
Ay, I see it is. (*Takes off his coat and cravat.*) Sergeant, accept
this watch; let it remind you of this hour. (*Takes out his purse.*)
You brave fellows will accept these few pieces — they are
useless to me now. (*Gives purse to* SERGEANT.) Let me be
buried in my uniform, and with this portrait, that has lain for
years upon my heart; tell her it was pressed to my lips when I
blessed her name with my last breath; tell her to be happy. (*Bell
tolls;* NORMAN *falls in his arms weeping.*) Come, come, do not
let your tears unman me. Men! you have your duty to perform
— do it bravely, as I have done mine! This death is a boon, not
a penalty! It is an honour to fall before you! and I receive your
salute over my grave! I am ready!

SERGEANT. Right wheel, march!

(*The file of* MEN *wheel round and exeunt R. The* SERGEANT *re-enters and stands R.* ROBERT *embraces* NORMAN *tenderly.*)

ROBERT. This for Sarah, and this for Tiney. (*Kisses him twice farewell. He goes up L.C. to the wall of the prison; stands a moment as if in prayer, then pressing the medallion to his lips, he extends his left arm in which he holds his cravat.*) God bless my country! (*He drops the cravat; a volley is heard; he falls on his knees, his hand on his heart; the shots strike the wall, and show where they have scarred the masonry. Small clouds of dust fall to the ground. The black flag is raised. Bell tolls. Stage dark.* NORMAN *stands with his head averted. The wall behind* EMMET *slowly opens. A vista of pale blue clouds appears. The figure of Ireland clothed in palest green and with a coronet of shamrocks in her hair descends slowly; and bending forward when she reaches the spot behind* EMMET, *she kneels. Two* CHILDREN *at her feet, R. and L., draw slowly back the body of* EMMET *until his head lies looking up into her face.*)

TABLEAU

THE END

A SELECTED CHECKLIST

compiled by Frances-Jane French

Introductory Note
As many of Boucicault's published plays were originally published in various undated acting editions, this Bibliographical Checklist includes dates of first stage productions — which in the case of the published plays frequently coincided with their initial publication. Only first editions, English and American, are listed below.

1. Plays

A Legend of the Devil's Dyke — Produced: Brighton, 1838.
Published: (J. Dicks), London, [c. 1898] — [Dick's Standard Plays, No. 1, 043].

London Assurance — Produced: London, 1841.
Published: (J. Andrews), London, 1841.
The full original text, adapted for the modern stage and edited by Ronald Eyre with introduction by Peter Thomson, (Methuen & Co. Ltd.), London, 1971 — [Methuen's Theatre Classics].

An Irish Heiress — Produced: London, 1842.
[Also entitled: *West End*].
Published: (J. Andrews), London, 1842.
(William V. Spencer), Boston, [?1857] — [Spencer's Boston Theatre, No. 210].

A Lover by Proxy — Produced: London, 1842.
Published: (Webster & Co.); (Sherwood, Gilbert and Piper); (William Strange), London, 1842 — [Webster's Acting National Drama, No. 102].
(Samuel French & Son), New York, [?1856] — [French's Minor Drama — The Acting Edition, No. 246].

Alma Mater or *A Cure for Coquettes* — Produced: London, 1842.
Published: (Webster & Co.); (Sherwood, Gilbert & Piper); (William Strange), London, [1842] — [Webster's Acting National Drama, No. 105]; [On cover: edited by B. Webster].
An edition, entitled: *A Cure for Coquettes* or *Alma Mater*, (Happy Hours Co.), New York, [187?] — [The Acting Drama, No. 88].

The Old Guard — Produced: London, 1843. [Revised version of *Napoleon's Old Guard*].
[Originally Produced: Brentford, 1838 as: *Napoleon's Old Guard*].

Published: (J. Douglas), New York, 184? — [The Minor Drama, No. 29].

Used Up — Produced: London, 1844.

[Written in collaboration with Charles James Mathews. An adaptation of: *L'homme blasé*, by Augustin-Théodore de Lauzanne de Vaux Roussel, and Félix Auguste Duvert, (Paris), 1843].

Published: (National Acting Drama Office), London, ?1848, [Vol. 15] — [with an engraving by Mr. Brewer].

[Charles James Mathew's Edition] headed: from the French of L'Homme Blasé: (Samuel French, Publisher), New York, 185? — [The Minor Drama, No. 10].

Old Heads and Young Hearts — Produced: London, 1844.

Published: (The National Acting Drama Office), London, [etc.] ? 1845 — [Webster's Acting National Drama, No. 130] — [Illus. with an engraving by Mr. Brewer].

(William Taylor & Co.), New York, 1845 — [Modern Standard Drama, No. 62].

Peg Woffington or *The State Secret* — Produced: London, 1845.

Published: (John Dicks), London, ?1907 — [Dick's Standard Plays, No. 1,064].

The School for Scheming — Produced: London, 1847.

[Revised version, entitled: *Love and Money* — Produced: London, 1847].

Published: (National Acting Drama Office), London, ?1847 — [Webster's Acting National Drama, No. 140] — [Dedicated to The Duke of Beaufort by Dion de P. Bourcicault].

(H. Roorbach), New York, [185?] — [played at Wallack's Theatre under the title: *Love and Money* a comedy by Dion de P. Boucicault.

A Romance in the Life of Sextus the Fifth, entitled The Broken Vow — Produced: London, 1851.

[Adaptation of *L'Abbaye de Castro* by Prosper Goubaux & Gustave Lemoine, (Paris), 1840. Written in conjunction with John Vipon Bridgeman].

Published: [under title] *The Broken Vow: A Romance in the Life of Sextus the Fifth*, (Hailes Lacy), London, 1851.

Later revised and re-entitled: *The Pope of Rome* — Produced: New York, 1858.

?Adaptation of *Bel Dominic* (Samuel French), New York, [?1858] — [French's Standard Drama, No. 227].

Love in a Maze — Produced: London, 1851.

Published: (Hailes Lacy), London, 1851.

The Queen of Spades or *The Gambler's Secret* — Produced: London, 1851.

[Also produced as: *The Dame of Spades*. Adaptation from the French comic opera, entitled: *La Dame de Pique*, by Augustin-Eugène Scribe, (Paris), 1851 — with Music by Henri Laurent].

Published: (Atkinson [*sic*] Thomas Hailes Lacy), London, 1856 — [Lacy's Acting Edition, No. 356 — edited by T.H. Lacy].

Pauline — Produced: London, 1851.

[Adaptation of *Pauline or Buried Alive* — A Tale of Normandy, (a novel) by Alexander Dumas, (The Elder), published in Murray's Colonial and Home Library, (London), 1849].

Published: (Samuel French), New York, [c. 1861]. (J.K. Chapman & Co. London, 1851), (T.H. Lacy), London, [c. 1851] — [Lacy's Acting Edition, No. 61].

The Corsican Brothers or *The Vendetta* or *The Fatal Duel* — Produced: London, 1852.

[Based on *Les Frères Corses*, (a novel) by Alexander Dumas, (The Elder), and dramatized by Eugène Grange & Xavier Aymon de Montépin; produced: Paris, 1850].

Published: (J.K. Chapman & Co.), London, 1852.

(J. Reddington), Hoxton Oldtown, USA. [c. 1852]. [Reddington's Juvenile Drama].

[NB. (Thomas Hailes Lacy), London, 1852 — Lacy's Acting Edition Vol. 6, is not Dion Boucicault's play, but a straight translation from the French].

The Prima Donna — Produced: London, 1852.

Published: (Samuel French), London; (Samuel French & Son), New York, [?1852].

(T.H. Lacy), London, 1852 — [Lacy's Acting Edition of Plays, No. 106].

The Vampire — Produced: London, 1852.

[Adaptation of *Le Vampire*, by Carmouche, A. de Jouffroy & Charles Nodier. Published: (Paris), 1820; later shortened and re-entitled: *The Phantom or The Prodigal* — Produced: Philadelphia, 1856].

Published: (Samuel French), New York, ?1856 — [French's Standard Drama, No. 165].

Andy Blake or *The Irish Diamond* — Produced: Boston, 1854.

[Adaptation of *Le Gamin de Paris, ou l'Enfant de Genevière*, by Fanny Claudet Richomme, (Mme. Prosper), Paris, 1837. The play later re-entitled: *The Dublin Boy* or *The Irish Boy* — Produced: London, 1862, under title: *The Dublin Boy*]. Published: (Samuel French), New York, 1856 — [French's Standard Drama, No. 266].

Faust and Marguerite — Produced: London, 1854.

[Translated from the French work of the same title by Michel Carré, (Paris), 1849, by Thomas William Robertson. English version attributed variously to Dion Boucicault and to Thomas William Robertson. Dion Boucicault subsequently claimed the work publicly in *The Era Almanack*].

Published: (T.H. Lacy), London, [1850] — [Lacy's Acting Edition of Plays, No. 213].

(Samuel French), New York, [185?] — [French's Standard Drama, No. 279].

Louis XI [King of France] — Produced: London, 1855.

[Adaptation of a French play of the same title, by Casimir Jean François Delavigne, (Paris), 1832].

Privately printed: (John K. Chapman), London, (c. 1855).

The Life of an Actress — Produced: Cincinnati, Ohio, 1855.

[Also entitled: *Grimaldi* or *Scenes in the Life of an Actress*]. Produced: New Orleans, 1855, as *Grimaldi*.

[Also entitled: *Violet or Scenes from the Life of an Actress*].

[Adaptation of *La Vie d'une Comédienne*, by Anicet Bourgeois and Théodore Barrière, (Paris), 1854].

Published: [as *A Life of an Actress*], (Samuel French), New York, 1856 — [French's Standard Drama, No. 159] — [On cover: Bourcicault's (*sic*) Dramatic Works].

(John Dicks), London, 1886 — [Dick's Standard Plays, No. 440].

The Poor of New York — Produced: New York, 1857.

[Produced in various cities in America and England under various titles, among these: *The Poor of Liverpool* — Liverpool, 1864; *The Streets of Liverpool*; *The Streets of London* — New York, 1857; *The Poor of the London Street* — London, 1866; *The Streets of Dublin*; *The Streets of Philadelphia*; *The Money Panic of '57* — Appropriate minor adaptations being made for the various cities involved].

[The play itself, an adaptation of: *Les Pauvres de Paris*, by Eugène Nus & Édouard Brisebarre, with music by M. Artus, (Paris), 1856. Published: (Samuel French), New York, 1857: as *The Streets of New York* in [French's Standard Drama — The Acting Edition, No. 189].

402

Published as: *The Streets of London*, (John Dicks), London, ?[1883] — [Dicks Standard Plays, No. 381].

Jessie Brown, or The Relief of Lucknow — Produced: New York, 1858.

[Based on an episode in the Indian Mutiny].

Published: (T.H. Lacy), London, [1858] — [Lacy's Acting Edition, Vol. V, No. 10].

(Samuel French), New York, 1858.

The Octoroon or Life in Louisiana — Produced: New York, 1859.

[Based on Thomas Mayne Reid's novel, entitled: *The Quadroon or A Lover's Adventures in Louisianna*, (3 vols.), (London), 1856 — later re-entitled: *Love's Vengeance*, which was itself adapted from *The Creole or Love's Fetters*, by Shirley Brooks.

Published: (Samuel French), New York, [?1859] — [French's Acting Edition, No. 962].

(T.H. Lacy), London, [?1861] — [Lacy's Acting Edition, No. 963].

The Colleen Bawn, [The Fair Haired Girl] *or The Brides of Garryowen* —

Produced: New York, 1860.

[Founded on Gerald Griffin's novel, entitled: *The Collegians*, (Saunders & Otley), London, 1829, (3 vols.)].

Published: (T.H. Lacy), London, [186?] — [Lacy's Acting Edition, No. 932] — [entirely new music, including an overture, composed and arranged by Thomas Baker].

(T.H. French), [*sic*], New York, [186?] — [French's Standard Drama, The Acting Edition, No. 366].

The Lily of Killarney, [Grand Opera] libretto by John Oxenford and Dion Boucicault, with music composed by Sir Julius Benedict. Produced: London, 1862.

Published: (Chappell & Co.), London, 1862 — [Complete opera consists of overture and 22 songs, which are also published separately; also published separately, 24 books of piano arrangements].

(Boosey & Co.), London & New York, [187?] — [Edited by J. Pittman — the opera entitled: *The Lily of Killarney* is a musical version of the drama of *The Colleen Bawn*] — [The Royal Edition Operas, No. 272].

Arrah-na-Pogue, [Arrah of the Kiss] *or the Wicklow Wedding* —

Produced: Dublin, 1864.

(Dramatic Publishing Co.), Chicago, [c. 1865] — [Sergel's Acting Drama, No. 365].

Shaun the Post, [Romantic Opera] — [A musical adaptation of *Arrah-na-Pogue*, libretto and lyrics by R.J. Hughes, with music by 'Dermot MacMurrough'] — [Harold R. White], (Piggot & Co. Ltd.), Dublin, [1924] — [words only].

Rip Van Winkle or The Sleep of Twenty Years — Produced: London, 1865.

[Dramatisation of Washington Irving's tale, by Joseph Jefferson & Dion Boucicault].

Published: (Samuel French), New York, [c. 1866] — [The Acting Editon, No. 174].

(S.N. Morang & Co. Ltd.), Toronto, 1899 — [with introduction by Joseph Jepherson [*sic*]].

The Long Strike — Produced: London, 1866.

[Based on two stories by Elizabeth Cleghorn Gaskell, entitled: 'Mary Barton' — a tale of Manchester life, (2 vols.), London, 1848, and 'Lizzie Leigh' — a domestic tale, New York, 1850].

Published: (T.H. French), New York, [?1866], London, [1871] — [French's Standard Drama, No. 360].

After Dark: A Tale of London Life — Produced: London, 1868.

[Authorised adaptation of a French play, entitled: *Les Bohemiens de Paris*, by Eugène Grange & Adolphe d'Ennery].

Published: (De Witt's Publishing House), New York, [?1868] — [De Witt's Acting Plays, No. 364].

Formosa ('The Most Beautiful') or *The Railroad to Ruin* — Produced: London, 1869.

Published: (Dramatic Publishing Co.), Chicago, [?1869] — [Sergel's Acting Drama].

The Rapparee or The Treaty of Limerick — Produced: London, 1870.

Published: ?[R.M. De Witt], New York, [?1882] — [De Witt's Acting Plays].

Jezebel or The Dead Reckoning — Produced: London, 1870.

[First two of the three acts, based on *Le Pendu*, by Auguste Anicet-Bourgeois and Auguste Michel Benoit Gauichot Masson, (Paris), 1854].

Published: ?(De Witt's Publishing House), New York, [?1870] — [De Witt's Acting Plays].

Night and Morning — Produced: Manchester, 1871.

[Revised as: *Kerry or Night and Morning*. Adaptation of French play entitled: *La Joie Fait Peur*, by Delphine (Gay) de Girandin, (Paris), 1854].

Published: (Dramatic Publishing Co.), Chicago, [c. 1871] — [Sergel's Acting Drama, No. 370].

Babil and Bijou or The Lost Regalia — Produced: London, 1872.

[A Grand Fairy Spectacular Opera — Written in Conjuction with James Robinson Planché].

Produced: [in revised form, with new lyrics by Frank W. Smith, with music composed and arranged by Georges Jacobi] : ?London, 1882.

Published: (J. Miles & Co.), London, 1882.

Daddy O'Dowd or Turn About is Fair Play — Produced: New York, 1873.

[Adaptation of *Les Crochets du Père Martin*, by Eugène Cromon & Eugène Grange, (Paris), 1858, by John Oxenford and Dion Boucicault].

Published: (Samuel French), New York, 1875 — [French's Standard Drama].

Play later revised and re-entitled: *The O'Dowd or Life in Galway*. Published: (Samuel French), London, [?1906] — [French's Acting Edition of Plays, Vol. 156].

[The play was later re-revised and re-entitled: *Guil-a-man or Life in Galway*].

[Play also entitled: *The O'Dowd or The Golden Fetters*].

Led Astray — Produced: New York, 1873.

[Adaptation of a play by Octave Feuillet, entitled: *La Tentation*, (Paris), 1860].

Published: (Samuel French & Son), New York, [c. 1873] — [French's Standard Drama, No. 372].

The Shaughraun — Produced: New York, 1874.

Published: (Samuel French), London; (Samuel French & Son), New York, [1875] — [French's Acting Edition of Plays, No. 1834].

Forbidden Fruit — Produced: New York, 1878.

[Adaptation of: *Le Procès Vandradieux* and of *Les Dominos Roses*].

Privately printed 1876: [For Private Use, by the Metropolitan Printing Co.; Not Published or Sold].

Printed in: *Forbidden Fruit and Other Plays*, edited by Allardyce Nicoll and F. Theodore Cloak, (Princeton Un. Press), Princeton, New Jersey, 1940.

Robert Emmet — Produced: Greenwich, England, 1884.

Published: (Samuel French), New York, [nd] — [Standard Acting Drama, No. 295] — [Frank Marshall was originally commissioned to write the play specially for Sir Henry Irving, who bore a strong physical resemblance to Emmet. But Irving was informed by H.M.G. that the play would be regarded as *persona non grata* in London, due to agrarian unrest in Ireland, so the production was abandoned. Later Marshall's unfinished MSS was handed to Dion Boucicault by Irving, DB rewrote and completed the play. DB's play was first performed in Chicago on the night of Cleveland's election as President of the USA. This event overshadowed the play, which Boucicault did not subsequently revive].

The Jilt — Produced: San Francisco, 1885.
Published: (Samuel French Ltd.), London; (Samuel French), New York, 1904 — [French's Acting Edition, No. 2266].

2. Prose
Foul Play, [Novel], by Charles Reade and Dion Boucicault, (Bradbury, Evans & Co.), London, 1868.
The Fireside Story of Ireland, (M.H. Gill & Son), Dublin, ?[1881].
The Story of Ireland, (James Osgood & Co.), Boston, 1881 — [*The Story of Ireland* is the American title for *The Fireside Story of Ireland*].
The Art of Writing, with introduction by Otis Skinner with notes by Brander Matthews, (Dramatic Museum of Columbia Un.), New York, 1926 — (Publications of the Dramatic Museum of Columbia Un. — 5th Series: Papers on Acting I).
The Art of Acting: a discussion by Constant Coquelin, Henry Irving and Dion Boucicault, (Dramatic Museum of Columbia Un.), New York, 1926.

3. Contributions to Periodicals
'MacCready in Mobile', *The Era Almanack*, (London), 1868, Vol. 1, p. 86, and 1876, Vol. 8, pp. 85-86.
'Golden Words', *The Era Almanack*, (London), 1876.
'The Decline of the Drama', *North American Review*, (New York), Sept. 1877, Vol. CXXV, pp. 235-245.
'The Art of Dramatic Composition', *North American Review*, (New York), Jan.-Feb. 1878, Vol. CXXVI, pp. 40-52.
'Rejected Plots', *The Era Almanack*, London, 1883.
'Opera', *North American Review*, (New York), Apr. 1887, Vol. CVLIV, pp. 340-348.
'Parnell and The Times', *North American Review*, (New York), June, 1887, Vol. CXLIV, pp. 648-649.
'The Decline and Fall of the Press', *North American Review*, (New York), July, 1887, Vol. CXLV, pp. 32-39.
'Coquelin-Irving', *North American Review*, (New York), Aug. 1887, Vol. CXLV, pp. 158-161.

'My Pupils', *North American Review*, (New York), Oct. 1888, Vol. CXLII, pp. 435-440.

'Coquelin and Hading', *North American Review*, (New York), Nov. 1888, Vol. CXLVII, pp. 581-583.

'Shakespeare's Influence on the Drama', *North American Review*, Dec. 1888, Vol. CXLVII, pp. 681-685.

'Mutilations of Shakespeare — The Poet Interviews', *North American Review*, (New York), Feb. 1889, Vol. CXLVIII, pp. 266-268.

'At the Goethe Society', *North American Review*, (New York), Mar. 1889, Vol. CXLVIII, pp. 335-343.

'The Debut of a Dramatist', *North American Review*, (New York), Apr. 1889, Vol. CXLVIII, pp. 454-463.

'Early Days of a Dramatist', *North American Review*, (New York), May 1889, Vol. CXLVIII, pp. 584-593.

'Leaves from a Dramatist's Diary', *North American Review*, (New York), Aug. 1889, Vol. CXLIX, pp. 228-236.

'Theatre Halls and Audiences', *North American Review*, (New York), Oct. 1889, Vol. CXLIX, pp. 429-436.

'The Future American Drama', *The Arena*, (Boston), (Vol. II [No. 6],) Nov. 1890, pp. 641-652 — [Published posthumously].

4. Biographies

The Career of Dion Boucicault, by Townsend Walsh, (The Dunlap Soc.), New York, 1915.

Dion Boucicault, by Robert Hogan, (Twayne), New York, 1969 — [Twayne's United States Author Series, No. 163].

Dion Boucicault, the Shaughraun, by Sven Erie Molin and Robin Goodefellowe, (George Spelvin's Theatre Books, II), 1979.

Dion Boucicault, by Richard Fawkes, (Quartet Books), London, Melbourne & New York, 1979.

© *Frances-Jane French*
June, 1986

SELECTED PLAYS
LENNOX ROBINSON

Chosen and Introduced by Christopher Murray

SELECTED PLAYS
DENIS JOHNSTON

Chosen and Introduced by Joseph Ronsley

SELECTED PLAYS
LADY GREGORY

Chosen and Introduced by Mary FitzGerald

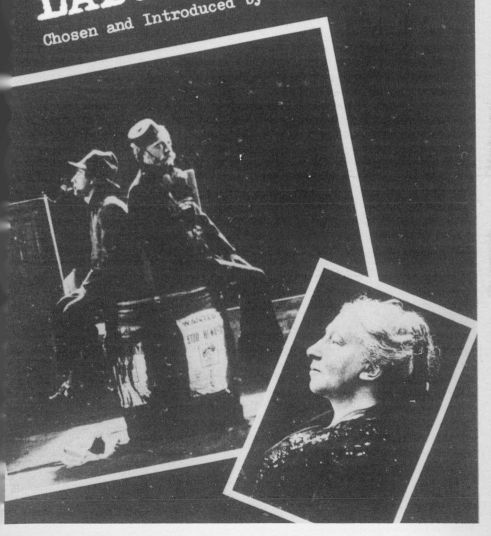

Irish Drama Selections 5

SELECTED PLAYS
ST. JOHN ERVINE

Chosen and Introduced by John Cronin

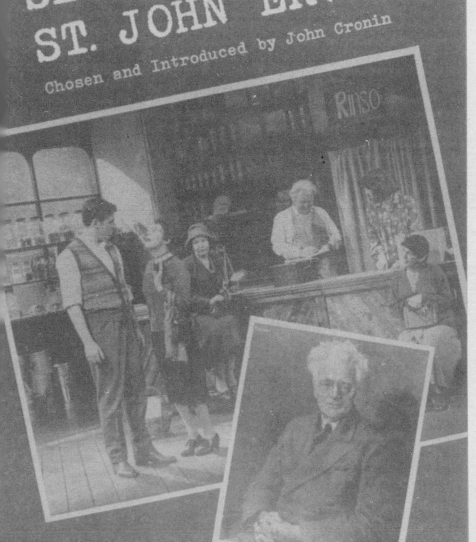